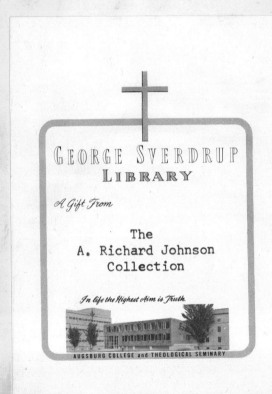

ENGLISH APPRENTICESHIP
AND CHILD LABOUR

ENGLISH APPRENTICE-SHIP & CHILD LABOUR

A HISTORY

BY

O. JOCELYN DUNLOP

WITH A SUPPLEMENTARY SECTION ON THE
MODERN PROBLEM OF JUVENILE LABOUR

BY

O. JOCELYN DUNLOP

AND

RICHARD D. DENMAN, M.P.

FORMERLY CHAIRMAN OF THE LONDON
JUVENILE ADVISORY COMMITTEE

T. FISHER UNWIN

LONDON: ADELPHI TERRACE

LEIPSIC: INSELSTRASSE 20

1912

To

ONE WHO HAS TRAINED MANY APPRENTICES,

LILIAN KNOWLES, Litt.D.

PREFATORY NOTE

I WISH to take this opportunity of expressing my indebtedness to Mr. and Mrs. Sidney Webb for their suggestion of this subject ; to Girton College for the award of the Cairnes Scholarship ; to the London School of Economics for the opportunities for research provided by it ; to the Municipal Authorities of Bath, Bristol, Norwich, Cambridge, Oxford, Hertford, and Great Yarmouth, and to Lord Methuen and Mr. J. C. Tingey for the facilities they gave me for consulting manuscripts belonging to them or under their charge ; to Miss Hermia Durham and Mr. Cyril Jackson for information and advice ; and to the Secretaries of various Trade Unions who most kindly spared time to answer my inquiries. But especially do I wish to express my gratitude to Dr. Lilian Knowles, Reader in Economic History in the University of London, for her generous help and encouragement.

Information relative to apprenticeship is to be gathered chiefly from the records of cities, gilds, companies, and courts of law. A certain number of such records, probably a large number, still lie little honoured and often unread ; and though it is unlikely that anything fundamentally new with regard to apprenticeship would now be discovered, since the system was common to the whole of England, those interested in the subject would still find a considerable amount of information on local matters and minor points. The records of the more important cities and gilds have already been very largely

transcribed in histories of those corporations. Full use has
been made of such transcripts here, references being given
with the short title of the book at the foot of each page.
The full title of works referred to will be found in the
bibliography.

O. J. D.

August, 1911.

CONTENTS

CONTENTS 13

INTRODUCTION

THE story of juvenile labour is one of peculiar interest and importance, yet it has been strangely ignored, save in its later phases during the last fifty or a hundred years, with the result that it is not uncommon to come across the belief that children were not regularly employed until the beginning of the last century, when factory work began. This, however, is far from the truth. In Mediæval England children were employed as freely and at as early an age as ever they have been under the factory system. Indeed, their labour has throughout English history been so integral a factor in the country's economic development that they may be said to have contributed largely to the attainment of our position as a world-wide power to-day.

In itself, therefore, the subject is worthy of study.

From another point of view, moreover, a knowledge of the conditions under which children have been employed in the past is of especial value at the present time. It is a commonplace of social study that one of the most pressing questions of our own time is the misuse and mis-direction of juvenile labour. Numbers of children and young people are drawn each year into occupations which have little or no prospect of permanence and no educative value either for citizenship or for adult work. Consequently, when they are no longer able to support themselves upon juvenile wages, they are turned adrift, and younger workers are taken in their place. They must make a fresh start in life, and whereas when they first sought work they were easily able to obtain a situation because they were cheap, they have now lost this valuable quality, and as a rule possess nothing to take its place, no special skill, no experience beyond their outgrown job, nor the discipline given by sound training. It is now admitted that this method of employing young people, though it may be profitable for the given trade, is not necessarily profitable for the nation. If the boys and girls who are dismissed from purely juvenile work cannot be absorbed into some other occupation, but instead drift into the ranks of the unemployed, the assumption is that the country is paying too heavily for the extra profits of the manufacturer. Yet though this is recognised, it is hard to decide from which direction the problem can best be attacked. Questions at once arise as to whether certain classes of work should be prohibited, whether training should be compulsory, and, if so, whether the State or the employer should bear the expense of that training. No doubt at the present time the conditions of the problem are widely different from what they were in the past. It is nevertheless impossible to study the earlier stages of this question without being struck by the constant recurrence of aspects which are fundamentally similar, and without recognising how much present-day solutions are capable of being modelled on previous experience.

An interesting feature of the history of juvenile labour is the varying degree of emphasis laid on the obligation of the master to the child or young person whom he employed. We shall have to trace the growth, in early mediæval times, of a strong bond between the master and the youth, who worked under his personal supervision in the workshop, and lived in his house as a member of his family. The close personal bond between the young people and their employers kept constantly before the notice of the latter their responsibility for the rising generation and the workmen of the future. It was a twofold responsibility: the master was answerable for the health and moral development of the lad while in his employment, and for his service to the State and career as an adult, since this service and his career depended on his physical, moral, and technical training as a boy. When, with the growth of capitalism and the expansion of trade in the eighteenth century, large businesses developed, the bond became looser. Close personal supervision was less practical when work was concentrated in large factories, while the ascendancy of the doctrines of *laissez faire* relieved masters who failed to accept their responsibilities from the pressure of public opinion. The workman gradually became the "hand," and his employer not so much ignored as was hardly conscious of any obligation towards him save that of paying wages. Neither the sense of responsibility for the immediate welfare of the youth nor for his future career survived these changes in industrial conditions and economic theory. The result was the terrible over-working of young people in the factories and workshops of the early nineteenth century. The abuses were so acute that they worked their own cure. There was an awakening of the national conscience, the fruits of which are to be seen in the factory and labour laws of that period, which reaffirmed the responsibility of the employer for the physical and immediate welfare of his juvenile employees. But no attempt was made to reconstruct that sense of responsibility for the young people's future which had existed in earlier times. The history of juvenile labour will show how far keener this sense was in the fourteenth century than in the nineteenth, and if the old methods of enforcing employers to observe their obligations are no longer applicable, the principles which underlie them are as true to-day as they were then.

The conflict between the interests of the individual and of Society in regard to the employment of children as cheap labour is a second aspect which is illumined by past history. It is, of course, the business of the manufacturer to pursue the cheapest methods of production. In itself this is a sound principle. Its application gives rise to this difficulty, that what is to the interest of the individual may not be to the interest of the nation or of the class most concerned in production. Juvenile labour is a form of cheap labour, and as such it has been constantly used, sometimes wisely, sometimes unwisely, as a means of reducing working expenses. On the whole the tendency has been for employers to succumb to the temptation of apparent economy and, whenever they have not been coerced by some external

authority, to employ an excessive amount of juvenile labour.
If we turn to mediæval times we find that the value of child
labour as cheap labour was even then recognised, and that
many master craftsmen sought to employ an undue number
of young people, all of whom would not be required in the
trade, and whose thorough training was more than one man
could accomplish.   In those days, however, the Trade
Associations, the Gilds, were strong enough to exert the
necessary external authority to prevent the exploitation of
child labour.   There is no need to assume that the craftsmen
who were members of these gilds realised the ultimate and
national lack of economy in an excessive employment of
children.   What they did certainly understand was its
danger to themselves : they recognised that if large numbers
of young people were employed and trained there would be
keener competition in the labour market and less security of
work for established workmen and their sons.   Organised
into their gilds, they were able to enforce rules limiting the
number of young people who might be employed.   But
whenever their pressure was relaxed the individual tended at
once to pursue what he considered his own interest regardless
of whether or no it advanced the common good.   It was, in
fact, only by organisation, persistent effort, and compulsory
limitation that the regulation which contemporaries considered just and necessary could be maintained.   From this
point of view the story is suggestive of the constant vigilance
which Society must exercise if it would see that the future
generation of workers is not sacrificed to the industrial greed
of the moment.

Yet another problem with which Society has had to deal
afresh at each stage of its industrial history is that of
training its work-people.   The Middle Ages solved this
problem by apprenticeship, a great system of technical
training evolved by the craftsmen of the thirteenth century,
maintained by their successors for two centuries and longer,
and adopted by Elizabeth as the English system, and so
handed on to succeeding generations for two and a half
centuries more.   At the present day the question of training

is especially acute because in this, as in other matters, the State's appreciation of social needs has lagged behind industrial development, and the lack of organised systems of preparation for adult occupation is widely felt.

It is when considered in these its wider aspects that the real significance of the history of juvenile labour is revealed. It then becomes apparent that its story has a practical interest and is not a mere antiquarian study, although the narrating of it involves a detailed account of what is now largely an effete institution, namely, apprenticeship. The chief interest centres around this system, and even its outworn features must be dealt with fully, because almost all children engaged in trades, manufactures, and commerce were, from mediæval times until the nineteenth century, compelled to work as apprentices, and the story of apprenticeship is therefore their story.

A brief summary of its history will perhaps assist the reader to appreciate the relationship of the parts to the whole.

Child labour had been an integral part of the industrial system from mediæval times, and probably as large a proportion of children were then employed as in the worst days of the factories. They appear to have been engaged in all forms of labour, however arduous, and there is no doubt that they worked for long hours and at an early age. Unfortunately our information is incomplete and in some cases altogether lacking. For example, although children were engaged in field work in the Middle Ages, as we can gather from incidental references, no records were kept of their labour. This is true, too, of their employment in trades and handicrafts prior to the thirteenth century. But towards the close of that century records become more fruitful. There are then clear indications of the customary employment of children and of the development of apprenticeship, a system of training for the industrial child, in which boys and girls were taught a trade in return for their services. The essential features of that system were the contract of service and instruction for a definite term of years, usually seven ; the active supervision by the local community of the operations of that contract ; the withdrawal of the youth from his own home and the influence of his parents throughout the term of training, during which the master stood to him *in loco parentis*. Its effects, more especially in its later developments, were not only that generally speaking all children who entered industrial forms of work were virtually certain of after employment and a permanent career, but also that regulation was introduced over the whole area of industrial juvenile labour. The apprenticeship system gave little opportunity for the sweating master, great or small ; and though there were individual cases of ill-treatment, the juvenile worker on the whole received a fair return for his labour, while the nation was not burdened with the human wastage of workshop and mill.

Used at first by individuals as a convenient device for training their assistants, apprenticeship was later adopted by the gilds and in time was made compulsory by them within the area over which they held sway. The system had obtained a firm hold by the fifteenth century, and in the sixteenth it was given a national stamp by Elizabeth's Statute, becoming thenceforth the universal and compulsory system of technical training for the industrial classes. As the Government had insufficient machinery of its own for enforcing the Statute, it was obliged to depend upon the gilds for the greater part of its administration. One result of the continued influence of the gilds was that all tendencies on the part of individuals to use children as cheap labour was still kept in check. Further, since the apprenticeship law suited their interests, they were the readier to give it their support. Gild rules supplemented the law, and gild officers exercised a general supervision over the daily life of the apprentice, both in the workshop and in his master's house, where he was lodged. England thus had an efficient system of technical training, and during those centuries when opinion was probably hardest towards youth and when there was least idea that child labour might be harmful, the conditions of employment were even minutely regulated.

This regulation must have had considerable influence in mitigating or preventing the ill-effects of children's work upon the national health ; in fact, apprenticeship had an eugenic value.

Its advantages, however, were limited in extent, for even in the best days of the system it was only children connected with our trades and manufactures who benefited by it, while in the latter half of the seventeenth century the large but still limited number of those whose labour was regulated began to decline, the gilds being unable now to enforce apprenticeship with their old vigour. Men who were not members of any gild denied the right of the companies to monopolise trade, and put their views very stoutly into practice. The dispute was fought out upon numerous petty points, but the underlying principle was in all cases identical. For a century the struggle was continued, and all through that time the gilds and companies lost in prestige, authority, and wealth in proportion as the "free traders" set them at defiance, and as they incurred heavy legal expenses in suppressing, or failing to suppress, these intruders. With the collapse of the gilds, which had been the chief administrators of the apprenticeship system, the conditions of children's employment underwent a change. It was not so well-ordered as it had been, for now that apprenticeship was less uniformly enforced, there was more scope for odd job work and more opportunity for the exploitation and misuse of juvenile labour. The gilds made desperate efforts to limit the number of apprentices, but they could not check the replacement of adults by children and young persons. Not all their rules could avail against the increasing feeling in favour of the freedom of the individual and the hostility, steadily accumulating, towards gild privileges. Their influence dwindled, and with them disappeared systematic technical training and the regulation of child labour.

The inevitable dissolution of apprenticeship took place in the chief industries of the country at the beginning of the eighteenth century, and by its close the seven years' training as enjoined by the Act was no longer enforced ; speaking generally, it was maintained only where the trade was carried on in the old way under gild control. The freedom of the individual to pursue his own interest was championed now by the economists, and became part of our political and industrial creed. *Laissez faire*, it was held, was necessary to commercial supremacy and industrial prosperity.

To the child this freedom of the employer was far from advantageous. It is only too common to find that the labour of young children was being recklessly exploited by employers, not only, let it be remembered, in factories and big workshops, but even more by the small and struggling man of the back streets. It was not the master-manufacturer but the spirit of the age which was to blame for the over-working of children and the indifference as to what became of them afterwards. The employment of children in factories by concentrating abuses brought them the sooner before the notice of the public. Even while the misuse of child labour was at its worst, namely, in the early nineteenth century, the movement for reform began.

The reorganisation of the industrial world upon modern lines not only brought about the breakdown of the regulation of juvenile labour, but in various ways actually changed the character of that labour. Hitherto it had been subsidiary to adult labour, but with the introduction of machinery it became independent; children worked not as assistants to master craftsmen but as principal, tending a machine. Further, they were now wage-earners on their own account, whereas the apprentice of former days, in his character of a learner, received no wages. As principals, too, children were systematically employed in a class of work which appears in a distinguishable form in the nineteenth century. This comprised all those branches of message and odd job work which are demanded by modern society. Both this work and machine-minding were of so simple a nature that they were hardly worth adult wages, and yet they were indispensable. In the nineteenth century, therefore, the demand for juvenile labour increased, while the occupations of child and young person were more various in number and in quality. He appears now in large numbers as an important element in the industrial scheme as wage-earner, as independent workman, as machine-minder, and as the ubiquitous message, errand, or van boy, and odd jobs lad. These changes and struggles took place in connection with industrial labour, the fortunes of the agricultural child were strangely unmomentous. Children were seldom apprenticed to husbandry, and there is therefore no story to relate of the regulation of their labour, the collapse of that control, and their transformation into wage-earners. Thus the interest of the development of juvenile labour centres around the industrial child. His is a story the greater part of which unravels itself through the daily and humdrum events of small tradesmen, to whom, as to the tradesmen of to-day, it would be absurd to ascribe a full recognition of the economic problems involved in the questions of the regulation of juvenile labour, its exploitation, its relations to adult labour, and the changes it was undergoing. But it is for us, reading the history of township and gild and individual merchant, to bear in mind through the confusion of detail the wider issues.

ENGLISH APPRENTICESHIP AND CHILD LABOUR UNTIL MODERN TIMES

English Apprenticeship and Child Labour

CHAPTER I

CHILD LABOUR IN MEDIÆVAL TIMES AND THE ORIGIN OF APPRENTICESHIP

FAR from its being a phase of modern industry, as we are sometimes inclined to believe, child labour existed in the earliest times. It is, of course, natural to suppose that children would have helped their parents in their work, whatever it might be; this was their most obvious and easy method of learning an occupation and making a start in life, and there was no compulsory education to draw them away from fields and workshop. But quite distinct from this casual labour of children in their homes is their regular employment both in agriculture and trades. The child, in fact, had a recognised place in the labour market long before the days of factories and the nineteenth century.

In the eleventh and twelfth centuries, when the peasantry were for the greater part unfree men, holding their small farms upon condition of personal service, the labour of their children was often definitely contracted for in the agreements between overlord and villein;[1] and in the industrial world boys played their independent part, working not necessarily with fathers and relations, but with stranger masters.

Unfortunately there is very little information as to the conditions of children's employment in agriculture, which must have absorbed by far the largest proportion of working-

---

[1] Ashley, Econ. Hist. and Theory, p. 9.

27

class children. In the Middle Ages there was but a small industrial population; in 1066 there were only eighty boroughs in England,[1] and until the end of the fourteenth century there was practically no foreign trade in manufactured goods. Handicrafts and manufactures were centred in towns, some of which, though they succeeded in affording the necessary protection to craftsmen, were no larger than our villages to-day. Such information as we possess relates, therefore, to a minority, though an interesting minority, the children engaged in trades in towns. It is drawn mainly from the papers of the gilds, which began early to make and preserve their records. These gilds were associations of men who often, in the first place, had united for religious purposes, but between whom ultimately the bond was their common occupation. Almost all the trades and manufactures of England were under gild control, so that the children engaged in handicrafts who were not within the cognisance of the gilds and their recorders must have been few in number. The gildsmen made regulations for the conduct of their trade, and by combining themselves into a body their members were able not only to win rights and privileges from king and overlord, but to push their business in neighbouring towns, and exact for themselves justice and consideration. These associations were in their origin voluntary, and it was quite possible for one or other group of craftsmen in some town to refrain from forming themselves into a gild, or for a town not to possess any gild at all. But whenever they were formed they did in time make membership compulsory. No one would be allowed to practise a trade within a town where a gild existed before he had been made a member ; he would be obliged, probably, to pay for admittance, and he would have to work in accordance with the gild rules. Very early in their history the gilds began to supervise the instruction of those young workmen who were employed by their members, and who would themselves claim admittance when old enough. These prospective members were either children working with their parents or apprentices bound to master

[1] Mentioned in Domesday Book. *Cf.* Ashley, *op. cit.*, pp. 68, 114.

craftsmen, who taught and maintained them in return for their services. This assumption of control by the gilds was prompted by several motives. By regulating the work of children the gilds could protect their members from the competition of cheaper labour; while, secondly, but quite as important, their supervision ensured that the rising generation of workmen was thoroughly taught, and consequently was likely to maintain the gild's reputation for sound work, by which alone, and not, as now, by low prices, goods could command a market. Later on, when the gilds had grown in wealth and reputation, and industry had become more remunerative, gild membership, or, as it was called, the freedom, was greatly coveted, and the gilds, by governing apprentices and by making training compulsory, were able to keep down the number of workmen, and so reserve the trade of the town to members and to members' sons, and protect them from serious competition. For similar reasons the towns either gave willing support to the gilds or themselves supervised apprentices. Thus apprenticeship was gradually adopted, and by 1450 was practised by most gilds and towns. The result was that the England of the fifteenth century possessed a definite system of technical training, a fact which is remarkable indeed when we remember how modern is the modern movement for technical instruction. From that time onwards children and young persons engaged in trades and manufactures were, as a general rule, working as apprentices. The early history of child labour in the industrial world is, therefore, the history of apprenticeship.

The term apprenticeship is first mentioned in England in the thirteenth century; one of the earliest references appears in an ordinance of the London Lorimers in 1261, fixing the term of service at seven years, and forbidding one master to entice away another's apprentice from him.[1] Possibly the discovery of fresh records may give us information of an

---

[1] Munimenta Gildhallæ Londoniensis, vol. ii. Part I., ed. Riley.
Liber Cus., pp. 78, 536. The word is first found in an endorsement of a writ, 20 Ed. I., "De attornatis et apprenticis." This may be a later addition. Lambert, Two Thousand Years, p. 195.

earlier date ; meanwhile we may safely say that by the close of the thirteenth century apprenticeship was practised by most of the London gilds, for in 1300 there is an act of the Common Council of the City which deals with the enrolment of apprentices. The matter-of-course manner in which apprenticeship is mentioned presupposes that it was a common feature of economic life, and that it must have been in use for some length of time. Further, it shows that apprentices were so frequently employed by Londoners that legislation concerning them was necessary. This was in 1300. Some two and a half centuries later the apprenticeship system, which had hitherto been merely voluntary and local, and had rested only upon gild authority, was transformed into a national institution. The Statute of Artificers, passed in 1562, made apprenticeship a necessary prelude for all who wished to engage in a craft or a trade. Technical training, in fact, became compulsory.

It is difficult to give a precise account of the development of apprenticeship from its origin down to 1562, for though we have a considerable amount of information, the records of no one locality or trade are so complete as to give a view of the whole system, and our knowledge is gathered from a rule of one gild, the court minutes of another, and the accounts, let us say, of a third. Sometimes the reference to one or other detail is intelligible only because similar phrases appear, with their explanations, in the records of a much later period. It is, however, possible to trace the course along which apprenticeship developed.

Early apprenticeship was merely a local custom, voluntarily adopted, and varying in character according to the needs and idiosyncrasies of town or gild. The custom of London served as a standard for provincial craft gilds and towns ; but though there was thus a certain amount of uniformity, there were many local variations even as late as 1562. Yet though apprenticeship was adopted locally and voluntarily, it developed throughout the country upon certain main lines.

The most important feature in its development is its

gradual evolution from an insignificant private custom into a public institution. Apprenticeship was originally a private arrangement; the engagement of apprentices was left to the discretion of the individual, while the conditions of service were a matter of agreement between father and master. Gradually, however, it became a public or quasi-public affair, falling under the control of the municipal authority or of the gild. Throughout the early years of apprenticeship we see this transformation in progress, a transformation in connection with which two points are especially noticeable. On the one hand, the change appears in London about a century earlier than in the country; on the other, the degree to which public bodies supervised apprenticeship increased as the centuries advanced, so that whilst in the thirteenth century it was little more than recognised by the gilds, there were, by 1562, minute rules for the regulation, or, as the old rules word it, the "ordering" of apprentices. A second feature of early apprenticeship is the manner in which, for various reasons, it steadily gained in popularity, and was more and more generally employed. Thus, though it was at first but one way, and that not the most important way, of entering a gild or obtaining the freedom of a borough, it gradually took a more prominent place, and by 1562 was the most usual method of gaining the freedom, whether of town or gild. Lastly, we shall have to notice a phase in apprenticeship which was more or less general in the fifteenth century. By that time the gildsmen had become jealous of their privileges, and in their hands apprenticeship became a powerful weapon for enforcing and preserving the industrial monopoly of the gilds.

With these main features to guide us through the maze of detail, we must now turn to the records of local customs, and attempt to trace the history of apprenticeship until 1562.

The years 1250 to 1450 form, roughly speaking, the period which saw the gradual adoption of apprenticeship. We have seen that one of the earliest references to apprenticeship in England is a bye-law of the Lorimers in 1261, and that in

1300 the City Corporation was making regulations for apprentices. Most of the London gilds seem to have adopted apprenticeship by 1400, for rules regulating it are common at this date. Some are concerned with the enrolment of the boys' names, others with the length of service, or the fees to be charged, the number of apprentices that each man might employ, or the qualifications either of master or apprentice. Amongst these numerous and varying rules we can trace the rise of a London custom, which was so well defined by 1350 that reference could be made to it as to a known and recognised system. The Braelers in 1355,[1] and the Masons [2] in the following year, passed bye-laws enforcing a minimum term of seven years, " according to the usages of the City." In the provinces, Bristol, then second in importance to London, is one of the first towns to make enactments for apprentices. There is a rule of 1344 recognising the right of apprentices who had served their term to the freedom of the city.[3] In Lincoln rules were made even earlier ; [4] but not many of the provincial towns or gilds made regulations, so far as we know, until the fifteenth century.[5] This may have been merely because there was less trade, and regulation was therefore unnecessary ; but it seems more likely that apprenticeship was not adopted as early in the country as in London.

Throughout this early period apprenticeship was being gradually brought under public control, that, namely, of the gilds and towns. The truth of the matter is that as it became more and more customary for their members to take apprentices, the gilds were obliged to step in and to make rules for their employment. Originally the gilds had countenanced apprenticeship, but it had been no more than a private arrangement between the adult and the young worker, as we can tell from the gild rules, very few of which

[1] Riley, Mems., 277.
[2] Ibid., 280.
[3] Bickley, Little Red Book, 36.
[4] Toulmin Smith, English Gilds, 183.   Tailors' Rules, 1328.
[5] E.g., rules were made in York in 1415; Northampton in 1430 ; Exeter in 1450, and in numerous other towns which were then centres of industry.

are, prior to 1300, concerned with apprenticeship, though a large number were made for the regulation of trade; it is, indeed, exceptional to find a town or craft before 1300 regarding the supervision of apprentices as within its province. But this attitude of passive acceptance disappeared before the general adoption of apprenticeship. The gilds were then compelled to undertake the work of supervision. The earliest rules have for their object the preservation of fair play between members, brethren being forbidden to entice away each other's apprentices.[1] The next step taken by the gilds was to regulate the binding of apprentices. They realised that such regulation was necessary if they wished to safeguard themselves from the intrusion of ignorant workmen, claiming admittance upon the pretence of having served apprenticeship. The plan they adopted was the enrolment of the names of all apprentices in a book kept by the gild or town clerk. This was enforced in London from 1300,[2] and in the country somewhat later. The apprentice had to be bound by indentures, which were inspected by the officers of the gild or town, and his name and the date of binding were then recorded.[3] In the fifteenth century this "ordering" of apprentices was more strictly enforced; in many places the indentures had to be enrolled within a limited period after their sealing, and definite days were instituted upon which apprentices should be brought by their masters before the

---

[1] Welch, Pewterers, p. 4. Rules, 1348. "Also that none of the crafte grete ne smale purloine othirs alowes."

Toulmin Smith, *op. cit.*, 183. Lincoln Tailors, 1328; p. 333, Exeter Cordwainers; p. 336, Exeter Bakers.

Northampton Records, Markham, i. 228, Liber Cus., 1450.

Cf. Toulmin Smith, Brentano's Introduction, cxxxi.

[2] Calendar Letter Book C, 78.

[3] One of the earliest rules for enrolment is that of the Fishmongers in 1279, ordering that no apprentice was to work "after Sunday" until he and his master had been to the Gildhall and had there enrolled the bond (Liber Albus, Riley, p. 331).

Heath, Grocers, 55. Rules, 1348.

Letter Book E, f. cxlix, Plumbers, 1365.

Black, Leathersellers, 21. Rules, 1398.

Prideaux, Goldsmiths, 9. Rules, 1370, 1385.

3

court of the gild, and presented to the masters and wardens.[1]
Fees were charged by the gilds for these entries, and
ordinances were made fixing the charges both for apprentices
and for admitting them, when they had served their time, as
free brethren of the craft gild.[2]   Rules were also made as to
the length of time which an apprentice must serve before he
might work as free master.   No doubt the gilds feared that
discredit would be brought upon them if a youth were
allowed to work on his own account before he had thoroughly
learnt his trade.   Moreover, it was the business of the crafts
to preserve fair and equal conditions for all, and this was best
achieved by enforcing uniform regulations.   Ricarte, in his
Calendar of the Mayor of Bristol, says that the custom of
London was seven years[3]—that is to say, seven years was the
minimum term, according to the bye-laws of the City.   Craft
gilds could, of course, impose a longer term if they so pleased ;
we know that the Goldsmiths insisted upon ten years.[4]

[1] Nicholl, Ironmongers, 121.   Rules, 1498.   Must bind within a year.

Bacon Annals of Ipswich, 40.   Mins., March 24, 1477.   Indenture to be
enrolled within "a yere and a day or suche shall not be of force to obtain theire
freedome."   Cf. Toulmin Smith, op. cit., p. 316, Exeter Tailors.

Black, op. cit., 40.   Rules, 1482.

Surtees, Merch, Adven., 2.   Rules, 20 Ed. IV.

Mercers, Charter, p. 83.   Presentment must be made within a month.
Cf. Benham, Red Book, Colchester 29.   Weavers' and Fullers' Rules.

Welch, Pewterers, 109.   Rules, 1522.

Bickley, Little Red Book, ii. 123.   Weavers' Rules, 1490.

Arber, Stationers, i. pp. 37 seq., 182 seq.

[2] Prideaux, op. cit., i. p. 11.   Rules, 1370.

Ibid., pp. 1–3.   Crt. Mins., 1336–53.   Enroll. of names and fees of 2s. each.

Toulmin Smith, op. cit., 183.   Lincoln Tailors' Rules, 1328.   Fee, 2s.

Clode, Merch. Tailors, 517.   Accounts, 1453-70.   Fee, 3s. 4d. each
apprentice.

Ibid., 522.   Accounts, 1545-57.   Apprentice fee, 2s. 6d.   Freemen,
usually 3s. 4d.

Surtees, Merch. Adven., Newcastle, 2.   Rules, 1481, Apprentices, 20d.

Noake, Worcester, p. 29.   Cordwainers' apprentices, 2s. 6d.   Freemen,
3s. 4d.

Lambert, Two Thousand Years, p. 238.   Tailors' Rules, 1550.   Fee, 6d.

Benham, Red Book, Colchester, 29.   Apprentice fee, 4d., 1523.

Heath, Grocers, 49.   Rules, 1345.   Freemen, £2.

[3] Ricarte, Calendar, Camden Society, p. 102, c. 1479.

[4] Prideaux, op. cit., i. p. 9.   Rules, 1370.

Seven years, however, both in London and in the country, seems to have been the most usual term,[1] though in Colchester, as late as the reign of Henry VIII., there is a town ordinance whereby it is ordained " by the assent of the Bayles of the Aldermen, and by assent and graunt of the Comune Councell of the toune, that no man take none apprentice of the said crafts of wefyng, ne of fullynge, nor of none other craft within the ffraunchise of this toune, lesse that the terme ef v yere." [2]

From 1450 there are records which point to still further supervision by the gild and town authorities. In some places rules were made regulating the private relations of master and apprentice ; others supervise the dress of apprentices ; elsewhere the gilds are supplanting or supporting the master in his control of the apprentice out of work hours. The Ironmongers made a bye-law as to the dress and appearance of apprentices, whose hair, it was expressly stated, must not be suffered to grow so long.[3] At Colchester the innkeepers were forbidden to allow any apprentice to enter their houses on Sundays,[4] while the corporation of Carlisle forbade apprentices to go out after ten o'clock at night, unless upon their masters' business.[5] Account and court books also

[1] MSS. Norwich Court Book, 1540–49, p. 126.
Surtees, Newcastle Merch. Adven., p. 2. Rules, 20 Ed. IV. Ibid., p. 6.
Letter Book E, f. cxlix, London Plumbers, 1365.
Letter Book G, f. xli, Masons, 1356.
Toulmin Smith, *op. cit.*, 390, Worcester.
Cox, Northampton Records, ii. 280. Butchers' Rules, 1558.
Cotton, Elizabethan Gild, 16. Rules, 1561.
Riley's Mems., 216 ; Girdlers, 1344.
Noake, *op. cit.*, p. 28. Cordwainers, c. 1505.
Lambert, *op. cit*, 205, Weavers, 1490. Ibid., p. 225, Brewers' Rules.
Bickley, *op. cit.*, ii. 142, Fullers, 1415.
Ibid., p. 138, Barbers, 1418.
Ibid., p. 163, Hoopers, 1439.
Cf. Ashley, Econ. History, p. 86.
[2] Benham, Red Book, p. 25.
[3] Nicholl, Ironmongers, p. 121. Rules, 1498.
Cf. Surtees, Merch. Adven., Newcastle, p. 20. Rules, 1554.
[4] Benham, Red Book, p. 23. Rules, 1549.
[5] Ferguson, Carlisle Records, p. 69. Dormont Book, 1561. Ibid., p. 137.
Smiths' Rules, 1562.

bear testimony to supervision of the gilds. The Merchant Tailors fined a master five shillings for unlawfully beating his apprentice,[1] while another master was fined ten shillings for clothing his boy ill, "to the great disgrace of the mistery." [2] In the next century this supervision of the domestic life of apprentices is much more pronounced, but slight and casual as it may have been in the fifteenth century, it yet marks clearly the great growth of official supervision since 1300.

It must not be imagined that because many regulations were made for apprenticeship, it was the only method of entering a trade. So far as we can gather, it was not necessary for a journeyman to be apprenticed,[3] though in the fifteenth century the rule against employing any but apprenticed men was growing stricter. There is no doubt that men who were not content to remain journeymen had to become free of the local gild before they could set up as free masters, working on their own account. Still, a man could become free in other ways than by apprenticeship. From early days he had been allowed to prove himself, before qualified judges, to be a sufficient workman, a method which we find lasting on into the days of apprenticeship. In 1348 the Pewterers of London ordered that no person was to meddle with the trade before he was admitted by apprenticeship, or otherwise a lawful workman, known and tried.[4] It appears from an ordinance of the Fullers in 1363 that any skilful workman was allowed by them to work at fulling, but if he were declared by the masters of the mystery to be incompetent, he had either to become an

---

[1] Clode, *op. cit.*, p. 510.

[2] Ibid., p. 521.
   Cf. Prideaux, *op. cit.*, i. pp. 17, 30, Accounts. See also p. 17, Entries, 1411.

[3] *Cf.* Ashley, Econ. Hist., i. (1901), p. 89.

[4] Welch, *op. cit.*, p. 3.
   Cf. Clode, Merch. Tailors, p. 513. Rules, 1371.
   Riley, Mems., Letter Book F, f. clv.
   Toulmin Smith, *op. cit.*, p. 313. At Exeter every "full craftsman worth 20l." was to belong to the craft.

apprentice and learn his business, or else leave the trade altogether.[1] The Northampton Fullers also allowed both methods of admittance. " eu'y ffuller," ran their rule, " which has nott bien Apprentice to the same crafte in the toun of Norht by the terme of iiij yere at the leste trewly served and ffullfilled that shall sett vp crafte and occupie housholde in the same toun may be proved be the Maisters of the same crafte suffycyaunte and able to occupie and kepe charge and rewle of mennes good affore the maire for the tyme beyng And to paie to the sustinaunce of the seide lightes. vjs. viijd. And to the seid Maire as Comen tresoure for the toun vjs. viijd. at his comyng in and begynnyng."[2] Men who had served apprenticeship had also to be vouched for as sufficient and able, but paid only twenty pence to the gild and town. At Hull the Glovers admitted " able " men at the close of the fifteenth century,[3] and at Bristol the Dyers had a similar practice.[4] The Northampton tailors, like the Fullers of that town, recognised the two methods of qualification for the freedom, and in 1444 appointed two entrance fees, the one for strangers, who were admitted upon payment of 3s. 4d., and the other a fee of twenty pence, to be paid by every other person trained in the manner of an apprentice.[5] This bye-law was re-enacted as late as 1537, showing that the custom of admitting all the skilled workers of a trade to a gild, whether they were apprenticed or not, existed until quite late, possibly even until Elizabeth's day. Entrance to the gilds could also be conferred as a privilege or purchased

[1] No stranger of the mistery coming to the City to be allowed to keep house or shop unless he be examined to see if he is able and sufficient. If so, he shall appear before the Mayor and Aldermen to be made free by the masters of the mistery and none other. No one to receive a workman until he be approved by the masters and the amount that he ought to take for a day's wage be fixed. If he be declared unfit, that he be ousted from the mistery unless he be willing to become an apprentice (Calendar of Letter Books of the City, LetterBook G, ed. R. Sharpe, p. 159). [2] Northampton Records, Markham, i. p. 292.

[3] Lambert, *op. cit.*, 217. Ordins. 9, 1499. [4] Little Red Book, ii. p. 172.

[5] Markham, Northampton Records, i. p. 281, Liber Cus.

Dr. Cunningham considers such men would have been apprenticed in some other town.

at the discretion of the brethren,[1] while the eldest of the sons born to a man after he had become a free master succeeded his father in the trade by right of patrimony.[2] As old, probably, as this right was the acquisition of freemanship by the marriage with the daughter or widow of a freeman. " Also it is ordeyned and establisshed by Auctorite aforsaid," runs the rule of the Bristol Merchant Adventurers, " that evy psone Burgeis of the said Toun that hath obteyned or shall obteyn his libtie of the same Toun by redempcion or by mariage of any Widowe or Doughter late of any Burgeis of Bristowe afforsaid and will be oon of the said feliship of marchaunts shall make fyne therfor with the said maister and wardeyns as they shall reasonably agre bitwen theym." [3]

Apprenticeship was nevertheless gaining upon these older methods, partly no doubt because it was a convenient manner of training the young workman, and also in part because preference was always given in the Middle Ages to anything that was systematic and could be done by rule. Traces of this growing dominance of apprenticeship are to be seen in the Leathersellers' rule of 1398, enacting that from henceforth " no one shall set any man child or woman to work in the same trade, if such person be not first bound apprentice, and enrolled in the trade ; their wives and children only excepted." [4] Similar rules are found elsewhere, while the custom of admitting "sufficient" workmen dropped out of use.[5]

---

[1] Prideaux, Goldsmiths, pp. xiv, 12.   Seventeen strangers pay for admission.
Northampton Records, ii., Cox, p. 311.
Riley, Mems., 217. Girdlers' Rule, 1344. " Also that no strange man shall be permitted to work in the trade if he will not be an apprentice or buy his freedom."
Toulmin Smith, *op. cit.*, 390, Worcester.   Rules, 1466.
Surtees, Newcastle Adven., ii. 184.   Rules, 1514.
Lambert, *op. cit.*, Hull Tailors.   Rules, 1550, ix.
[2] Cox, *op. cit.*, Butchers' Rules, 1558.   Toulmin Smith, *op. cit.*, p. 390.
Cotton, Elizabethan Gild, pp. 8, 16, 173.
[3] Latimer, *op. cit.*, p. 33.
[4] Black, Leathersellers, p. 21.
[5] Fox, Merch. Tailors, p. 46.   Rules, 1560.
Bickley, Little Red Book, ii. p. 156.   Barbers' Rules, 1439.   No one to employ a servant in covenant unless he had been apprenticed "by dede" seven years complete.

There were two somewhat more complex reasons for the predominance of apprenticeship at the close of the fifteenth century. In the first place, service as an apprentice entitled a man to the municipal freedom, which was well worth attaining, since it conferred a certain degree of social status, and free citizens shared in whatever privileges were held by charter or custom. More important still, it was only freemen who could, unshackled, trade within the town.[1] Non-freemen were aliens, and could engage in industrial pursuits only under various restraints.[2] They had frequently to pay extra dues, and were allowed to trade only at certain times and places, as in market on market days; or again, as at Bristol,[3] they might only sell and buy from freemen and not

Noake, *op. cit.*, p. 28. Cordwainers' Rules, 1504.

Ibid., p. 38. Tailors and Drapers, 1551.

Lambert, *op. cit.*, 205. Hull Weavers' Rules, 1490. Ibid., Brewers, 4 & 5 My. 8. Dr. Cunningham has suggested (at a meeting of the Royal Historical Society) January 19, 1911, that apprenticeship was supported by City corporations, and was so favoured by the gildsmen, who, it must be remembered, were burgesses, largely because it was of great value in civic government. There can be no doubt that its value in this respect was fully realised by the freemen of the larger boroughs—for instance, London and Norwich. There is an interesting rule of the Weavers' at Bristol which reveals their appreciation of the order and regularity of life which apprenticeship involved. See p. 69, note.

[1] Bickley, *op. cit.*, p. 135. No one to poll or shave unless a free burgess and member of the Barbers' gild. But every family servant may poll and shave his master and the sons and daughters of the house.

Markham, Northampton, i. p. 239. Rules, 1430. Every carpenter coming to the town to work by the day or by the piece, must pay 12d. to the craft, if he stay beyond four weeks. If he be a master and stay longer than a year, he must be admitted to the liberty of the town according to custom and usage.

Prideaux, Goldsmiths, i. p. 14.

Toulmin Smith, *op. cit.*, p. 355. Non-freemen may not have a booth within Winchester. Ibid., p. 333, Exeter Cordwainers.

Williams, Barber Surgeons of Norwich, p. 8. Rules, 1561.

Clode, Merch. Tailors, p. 211. Rules for " foreyns straungers and fforeyns denizens," 1507.

Norwich Records, Hudson and Tingey, p. 178. Custumal, cap. 36.

[2] Toulmin Smith, pp. 179, 336, 349, 383, 390. Rules of Winchester, Worcester, Exeter.

25 H. VIII. c. 19. No stranger allowed to practise the trade of pewterer.

Cf. Cunningham, *op. cit.* (1890), pp. 350, 351, 387.

[3] Bickley, Little Red Book, ii. p. 49. Fee for the freedom of the city is £10. Those who wish to trade or exercise their craft within the town,

from one another. The municipal freedom, like the freedom of the gilds, was hereditary, and a man could become free by right of patrimony.[1] He could also become a burgess by gift, purchase, marriage,[2] or by serving as an apprentice to a freeman.[3] If a man was not so fortunate as to be the eldest son of a freeman, his best course was to serve an apprenticeship, since he could thus become, by right, free of his craft and free of the town. Otherwise he would have to purchase both the gild and the municipal freedom, and the right to do so might, of course, be denied him, while the fees were either higher or were unfixed, so that the applicant was at the mercy of the officers.

There was a second reason why apprenticeship gained upon the older methods of obtaining admittance to gild and trade. In the fifteenth century the craftsmen, who had by this time become jealously exclusive, discovered that the enforcement of a narrow system of apprenticeship was as simple a way as any of preventing competition, and apprenticeship accordingly became increasingly popular with them. At the close of the fifteenth century a great number of the gilds framed bye-laws, the tendency of which was to favour present members and their sons, and to make it harder for outsiders to enter the gild, either because they had to pay higher fees or because admittance was strictly limited to those who had been apprenticed, adult strangers being thus

---

and have not the means or will not pay the said sum of £10, in order to be enfranchised, may be received as portmen and pay fine to the Commonalty according to the discretion of the Mayor."

    Bickley, Little Red Book, ii. pp. 4, 26, 182, 96. Rules of various trades.
    Cox, Northampton Records, ii. p. 293. Shoemakers' Rules, 1561.
[1] Ibid., p. 280. Rules, 1558.
    Latimer, Bristol Merch. Adven., p. 32. Rules, 1500.
[2] Ferguson, Carlisle Records, p. 59. Dormont Book, 1561.
    Bickley, op. cit., p. 62.
    Cox, op. cit., p. 315. Fees reduced for men marrying widows.
[3] Toulmin Smith, op. cit., p. 390. Worcester Rules, 1466.
    Calendar Letter Book H, f. cxxxi, 1366.
    Turner, Oxford Records, p. 205. Rules, 1551.
    Bickley, op. cit., pp. 36, 49.
    Ricarte's Calendar, p. 102.

barred out ; or, again, because apprentices had to serve longer terms, or comply with various qualifications before they were permitted to become bound ; and, lastly, the gilds would accept only a certain number of apprentices. These rules undoubtedly served to obstruct the entry of new members, and indicate a jealously exclusive spirit on the part of their makers.[1] No doubt there was some excuse for the narrower policy now adopted. During the reign of Edward III. there was a great advance in commerce and industry, and, thanks to this economic development, the industrial classes began both to have the means and the inclination to sink money in business.[2] Having done so, they were naturally anxious that their investments should not be imperilled by over-competition. It was equally natural that a number of new men, attracted by the greater lucrativeness of trade, should desire to enter industrial occupations. These newcomers either sought admission to the craft gilds, or, more greatly daring, worked secretly in "chambers."[3] Very possibly this pressure of outsiders upon the gilds was increased by the immigration to the towns of that part of the population which had been thrown out of employment by the enclosure of tillage into sheep farms, a change which was taking place just at this time.[4] There seems to be little doubt that there really was reason to fear that the gilds would be over-stocked with workmen. Complaints were made by some of the gilds that their members were unable to gain a living. The Pewterers declared that their apprentices could not find work when they came out of their time, and "the nowmber of the said crafte is soo encreased that oon of theym is not able honestlye to lyve by a nother.

[1] *Cf.* Cunningham, *op. cit.*, pp. 397, 455, 452.
Unwin, Industrial Organisation, pp. 48, 55.
[2] *Cf.* Toulmin Smith, *op. cit.*, pp. cxxxvii, cl, and Cunningham, *op. cit.*, 338.
[3] Clode, Merch. Tailors, p. 211. "Th'acte for Chambre-holders." Ordinance against persons who "keep chambres secretly in aleys and upon steyers and houses in corners, and cutte and make almaner of garments, and they same persons be nother free of the citee nor of the said felishp of Merchant Taillours."
Cf. Unwin, *op. cit.*, pp. 47, 55.
[4] Cunningham, *op. cit.*, 339.

And soom that haue bene apprentice and spent thevr tymes
of apprentyshode at thende of their termes haue been compelled for theyr lyvinge to vse other occupacyons bothe
within the cytie and without to theyr greate losse hurte
sorrowe and hyndraunce.   And also a Slaunder of the saide
crafte." [1]   The Leathersellers have a similar complaint to
make. [2]   This was a state of affairs which it was the avowed
business of the gilds to avert, and their officers would be
supported by public opinion for refusing to admit new
members if there was not employment enough for all.   There
was a fear, too, that if these unapprenticed men were permitted to work, goods of a lower standard would be put upon
the market, and the gild would lose its reputation and its
customers.   At Bristol the Dyers complained that many
who had no knowledge of dyeing had practised the trade.
The cloth had been badly dressed and worked owing to
their ignorance, "to the great injury of the owners and
scandal of all the craft aforesaid, and to the drapery of the
said town." [3]   The Dyers therefore ordered that no one, not
even an apprentice, should be admitted unless he were
proved to be " able." [4]   This was a severe rule, but it may
have been justifiable under the circumstances. [5] Possibly class
jealousy was also responsible to some extent for the increasing spirit of monopoly ; at any rate, the adoption of the
narrower policy by the gilds coincides with that emphasising
of class distinctions between merchant, liveryman, and artisan
which took place in the reign of Edward III. [6]   At this date
it is almost impossible to say which of these various causes
played the greatest part in provoking the spirit of exclusive-
ness, but one point seems to be quite clear, it was by means
of apprenticeship that the gilds enforced their monopoly.

---

[1] Welch, Pewterers, pp. 111.   Rules, 1522.
[2] Black, Leathersellers, pp. 34, 39, 40.   Docuts., 1467, 1482.
   Cf. 1 R. III. c. 9.
[3] Bickley, Little Red Book, ii. 82.   Rules, 1407.
[4] Ibid., ibid.   Rule 84.
[5] Cf. MSS. Norwich, Ordinances of Worsted Weavers.   Rule as to age, 1511.
   Musicians Co., p. 11.   Rules, 1518, 1555.
[6] Cf. Cunningham, English Industry, i. (1890), p. 341.

In the first place, a more general adoption of apprenticeship served to keep out the adult stranger. The gilds made it extremely hard for a craftsman to enter the trade by any other method than apprenticeship. Sometimes they raised the sum for which the freedom could be bought,[1] or discouraged redemptioners by placing them at a disadvantage to other workers, as at Newcastle, where the Adventurers forbade them to take apprentices or to ship wool and skins.[2] The custom of admitting workmen upon proof of skill was, apparently, discountenanced. It is still to be found, but it is exceptional.

Having made apprenticeship almost the one path to free mastership, the gilds reduced the number which could pass along it by insisting that the apprentice should possess certain qualifications. Unfree birth was in some gilds erected into an insurmountable barrier, brethren being prohibited from taking villeins' sons as apprentices.[3] A property qualification was insisted upon by statute ; Henry IV. passed an Act forbidding any person who was unable to dispend twenty shillings by the year to apprentice his children to a trade.[4] Indirectly, the craft gilds, by their fees, ensured that a new member should be of some circumstance.[5] Another statutory qualification, which was made in the interests of agriculture, was that children who had "used husbandry" until the age of twelve years might not leave it for an industrial occupation,[6] but whether or no this was enforced,

---

[1] Toulmin Smith, *op. cit.*, p. 316, Exeter, c. 1460.
  Clode, Mems. Merch. Tailors, p. 522.   Account Bk. iv.   Fees, 8s. to 20s.
  Cox, Northampton Records, ii. p. 311.
  Surtees, Newcastle Adventurers, ii. p. 184.   Fee, £3 6s. 6d.
[2] Cox, *op. cit.*, p. 10.   Rules, 1520.
[3] Ashley, Econ. Hist., i. p. 88.
  Wadmore, Skinners, p. 29.   Rules, 1486.
  Jupp, Carpenters, p. 351.
  Mercers, pp. 86, 87.   Rules, 1504.
  Welch, Pewterers, p. 109.   Rules, 1522.
[4] 7 H. IV c. 17.   This was repealed for London by 8 H. VI c. 11, and for Yarmouth and Lynn woollen trades by 9 & 15 H. VIII c. 3.
[5] *E.g.*, Clode, Mems. Merchant Tailors, p. 209.   Rules, 1507. A free master must be worth ten marks.
[6] 12 R. II. c. 5.

it is hard to say. Other disqualifications were bastardy, [1] and deformity,[2] while an even more common barrier was alien birth [3], a term which was held to include not merely foreigners such as Frenchmen and Scots, but the rebels of Ireland,[4] and even the men of a neighbouring district.[5] Towards the close of this period, in Henry VIII's reign, an Act was passed forbidding strangers born out of the King's obeisance to take any but English subjects as apprentices.[6] Some years later Pewterers, even though native born, were forbidden by statute to take alien apprentices.[7]

In some gilds still stricter rules were instituted, as in the Goldsmiths' Company, in which masters were not allowed to take as apprentices boys whose fathers were not in the trade,[8] nor those lads who had been in other employments. John Mabban, a master goldsmith, wished to bind his two brothers, but was not allowed to do so, since one had begged his bread and the other had been a miller and then a cobbler.[9] Age served as another means of restriction; the Newcastle Adventurers would not accept any apprentice under sixteen years, and the Ironmongers and the Norwich Weavers forbade

---

[1] Surtees, Newcastle Merch. Adven., i. p. 15. Rules, 1513. "No bastard shalbe free with this Feloship though he have served and bene vii yer apprentyce."

[2] Black, Leathersellers, p. 34. Rules, 1467. Apprentices to be presented to see if they were " of clenly feture and not deformed in his visage, nor in noe other parts or limbs of his body." *Cf.* Wadmore, Skinners, p. 24. Mercers, pp. 86, 87. Rules, 1504.

[3] Welch, Pewterers, p. 109. Rules, 1522.

Lambert, Two Thousand Years, p. 216, Hull Glovers. Rules, 1499.

Norwich MSS., Case X., Shelf B., Worsted Weavers, 1511. "No man of the said craft take noo Skotte Frenchman or other alien born out of the realm as apprentice."

Docs. relating to Town Close Estate, Norwich, p. 65. Assembly Book, 1535.

[4] Bickley, Little Red Book, ii. p. 163, Bristol Hoopers, 1439. Apprentices to be "no rebel of Irlonde nor alyene but of the Englyschyre and liege man to the Kyng."

[5] Surtees Society, Newcastle Adventurers, p. 27. No boys to be taken apprentice from "Tyndall or Reddisdall." Rules, 1554.

[6] 14 and 15 H. VIII. c. 2.

[7] 25 H. VIII. c. 19.

[8] Prideaux, Goldsmiths, p. 8. Crt. Mins., 1370.

[9] Ibid., p. 17. Crt. Mins., 1411.

the binding of boys under fourteen.[1]   One or two companies
insisted upon severe educational tests. The Goldsmiths refused
apprentices who could not read,[2] while the Leathersellers
ordered that all boys were to be examined to see if they were
expert and cunning.[3]

An even surer method of limiting the number of brethren
was to limit the number of apprentices which any one
gildsman might employ. Bye-laws are frequent in the
fifteenth century forbidding a master to have more than two,
three, or four apprentices at a time.[4]   The Exeter tailors did
not allow more than one apprentice and three journeymen
without special leave.[5]   The Musicians[6] and the Newcastle
Adventurers[7] forbade more than one apprentice at a time.
At Norwich members within the city were given an advantage over those in the country, and were allowed four
apprentices to the countryman's two.[8]   The plea, of course,
was that townsmen had heavier financial burdens to bear,
and some of the other rules may have been made because the
trade was really over-stocked with workmen.[9]   The Pewterers
had an even narrower rule made in favour of the inner circle

[1]   Surtees Society, Merch. Adven., p. 10.   Rules, 1555.
   Nicholl, Ironmongers, p. 121.   Rules, 1498.
   Norwich MSS., Case X., Shelf B.   Rules, 1511.
   Mercers, p. 80.   Rules, 1504.
[2]   Prideaux, op. cit., p. 26.   Court Mins., 1478.   Fine for taking an apprentice
who could not read or write.   Ibid., p. 27.   Entries, 1483.
[3]   Black, op. cit., p. 126.   Rules, 1517.
[4]   Cf Ashley, Econ. Hist., 1901, i. p. 90.
   Black, Leathersellers, p. 34.   Rules, 1467.
   Lambert, Two Thousand Years, p. 206.   Rules, 1490, Weavers.
   Mercers, p. 87.   Rules, 1504.
[5]   Toulmin Smith, op. cit., p. 315, c. 1465.
[6]   Musicians Co., p. 11.   Rules, 1518.   "To the intent that the apprentice
may thus better be applied lerned or sette at work."
[7]   Surtees Society, Newcastle Adventurers, pp. 9, 10.   Rules, 1520, 1548.
[8]   MSS. Norwich, Case X., Shelf B.   Worsted Weavers' Rules, 1511.
[9]   There is an early rule of the Fishmongers in 1279, when the monopolistic
spirit was not yet acute.   No fishmonger was allowed more than two or three
apprentices at a time, "and that as he is of ability to support them" (Riley,
Liber Albus, p. 330).   This may have been passed to prevent members underselling each other by employing cheap labour.   There seems to be no other
as early rule on the subject.

in the craft gild, the Liverymen, who were the wealthier brethren. They were allowed two apprentices, but members out of the "clothing" were allowed only one.[1] More generous was the Newcastle Adventurers' policy of permitting a man to take a new apprentice a year or two before the term of his old apprentice had expired, so that he might not be left with no helper except a raw boy.[2] Yet one more variation in the rule is to be found in the Skinner's bye-laws : an old Master might take four apprentices in seven years ; a Warden, three ; and an ordinary Master two in seven years.[3] These rules for the limitation of apprentices were very generally adopted, for they served not only to keep down the number of master craftsmen, but also protected adult workmen from the competition of juvenile labour. At this early date workmen were for the most part their own masters and employers, and there was therefore no question that they might be, as at the present day, dismissed by a large employer and replaced by children. But child labour was nevertheless a menace ; indirectly, it could replace them, for a master craftsman of their own standing might, by employing an excessive number of children, turn out his goods at a lower cost, and thus gain command of the market, while his fellows were left out of work. The strict regulation of juvenile labour was, therefore, undertaken by adult workmen as a means of self-protection.

There was another method by which the gilds checked the number of new members at the outset ; this was by raising the fee for apprentices. It had been about 2s., but at the end of the fifteenth century and the beginning of the sixteenth fees varied from 2s. 6d. to £2.[4] The fees for

---

[1] Welch, Pewterers, p. 111.

[2] Surtees, *op. cit.*, p. 10. Rules, 1548.

[3] Wadmore, Skinners, p. 29. Rules, 1486.
Cf. Musicians, p. 11.
Welch, Pewterers, p. 238. Crt. Mins., Sept. 21, 1520.
Surtees, *op. cit.*, p. 9. Rules, 1520.

[4] *E.g.*, Mercers, p. 86. Rules, 1504. Fee, 20s.
Surtees, Newcastle, Merch. Adven., p. 15. Rules, 1555. Fee, 22s. 6d.
Wadmore, Skinners, p. 29. Rules, 1486. Fee, 20s.

the freedom were also raised from 3s. 4d. to as much as 20s. and more, while "benevolences" and breakfasts were frequently insisted upon in those gilds in which the old fee was nominally retained.[1]

Another obstacle to membership which we find in some localities was the insistence upon more than seven years' service. The Newcastle Adventurers frankly state that by reason of only seven or eight years' service "the number of this Felowship is so augmented, and dayly doith increas, that if spedie remedie in this case were not provided it would be the utter distruction of this hole Felowship," and therefore they introduced a ten years' service.[2] The Goldsmiths also instituted a ten years' term, but granted special privileges to those born in the trade ; apprentices who were related to their masters need not serve so long.[3] In 1498 the Ironmongers adopted this longer period : " No person," it was ordered," shall take noon apprentice excepte he have sewertie and bonde for him in Cli sterling that he may, and yf he may not he shall take a bond of Cs at least ; and shall take noon apprentice under the age of xiiij years and for no lesse term than x years except it be his first apprentice taken for necessitie, and for him he shal ax licence of the wardeyns." [4]

Lastly, some masters went to the root of the matter, and

[1] Clode, Mems. Merchant Tailors, p. 517. Account Book, ii. 1453. Fees vary.
Turner, Oxford Records, p. 107. Council forbade crafts to take more than 20s.
Surtees Society, Merch. Adven., Newcastle, p. 15. Fee 11s.
Cox, Northampton Records, ii. p. 280. Butcher's fee, 10s.
Lambert, *op. cit.*, p. 225. Brewer's Rule, 4 and 5 Mary.
Cf. Ashley, *op. cit.*, p. 90.
Unwin, Industrial Organisation, p. 48.
Aber, Stationers, i. p. 33. Mins., 1555. " Item receyd of John Aldaye for his breakfaste and his benervolence to the hall vj iij." Numerous similar entries, *cf.* p. 34. Croke pays 3s. 4d. for his breakfast and " of his benevolence " 2s.
Toulmin Smith, *op. cit.*, pp. cii, 316. Exeter Tailors had to give a silver spoon to the craft and a breakfast to the brethren when they became freemen.

[2] Surtees, Newc. Merc. Adven., p. 10. Rules, 1555.
[3] Prideaux, *op. cit.*, p. 9. Entries, 1370.
[4] Nicholl, Ironmongers, p. 121. Rules, 1498.
Cf. Mercers, p. 85. Rules, 1504.

obliged their apprentices to swear that they would not set up for themselves upon the expiration of their terms.[1]

Nearly every one of these rules is, separately, more or less excusable when judged by the economic theories of their age. But when the gilds adopted at one and the same time a narrower policy, raised their fees, and made restrictive rules on every side, there can be little doubt that a spirit of monopoly was at work. Indeed, it was recognised by the Government, and was considered sufficiently injurious to demand legislative action. Henry VIII. passed an Act making it illegal for masters to demand any oath from their apprentices.[2]   An earlier Act dealt with the exactions levied on apprentices.[3]   The preamble states that divers wardens and fellowships have made acts after their own sinister minds and pleasure that every apprentice shall pay at his first entry in their common hall a fee varying from 3s. 4d. to 40s. " to the great hurt of the Kinges true subjects putting their children to be Prentices." The legal fee was fixed at 2s. 6d. for entrance, and 3s. 4d. for the freedom. This Act was, presumably, of little effect, for a few years later the levying of heavy fines had again to be forbidden.[4]   An attempt was made as early as 1437 to curb the oppressive legislation of the gilds by requiring them to submit any new ordinances to the justices of the peace.[5]   In 1503 a similar statute forbade the gilds to enforce their bye-laws, new or old, unless they had been approved by the Chancellor or the Justices of Assize.[6]

The ease with which the gilds could divert apprenticeship from its proper use as a method of training, and employ it as an instrument of monopoly, undoubtedly detracted from its general value. Some, at any rate, and possibly many children must have been prevented from entering the work suited to them by the refusal of the gilds to receive them as apprentices. There is, however, another side to the case. It is but to give an inadequate idea of their value to say of the

[1] 28 H. VIII. c. 5, Preamble.   [2] 28 H. VIII. c. 5.
[3] 22 H. VIII. c. 4.   [4] 28 H. VIII. c. 5.
[5] 15 H. VI. c. 6.   [6] 19 H. VII. c. 7.

gilds that without the protection which they afforded our industries would less readily have taken root ; while the trade between even neighbouring towns, still more international trade, would have been far slower in developing if our merchants had not been supported by the strength and prestige of their gilds, which won them consideration and an open door for their goods. For the apprenticeship system which the gilds evolved, it may be said that though by the fifteenth century it tended to be undemocratic and narrow, it supplied a sound industrial training and, for those who undertook it, a sure start in life. The wastage and misdirection of labour, the groping about for a suitable entry into business, which are the attendant evils of a freer industrial system, were reduced to the lowest limit by apprenticeship, irksome though it may have been to many.

CHAPTER II

TECHNICAL TRAINING IN 1550

FROM the various records of towns and gilds a very fair idea can be gained of the industrial conditions of child labour about 1550.

By that time apprenticeship had become the most usual method of entering a trade, and the life of the average working-class child in the towns is the life of an apprentice.

It has been seen that in earlier days any "sufficient" workman could gain admittance to a gild, while it was customary to admit the eldest son of a freeman or the husband of his widow or daughter. But in the sixteenth century skill was no longer regarded as a qualification for admittance, and though patrimony was a right looked upon with favour by the crafts, some of which actually reduced the entrance fees for sons,[1] apprenticeship was the general rule, and admittance by grant, redemption, marriage, or patrimony, though permitted, was exceptional.

If, then, a father wished his son to learn a trade other than his own, which he could teach him unbound, he had to find some master willing to take the lad apprentice. No doubt he would try to select as master a craftsman for whom he had a respect and liking, but there were many points other than personal feelings to be considered in the choice, for nearly all the gilds had strict rules as to who might and who might not take an apprentice. If the father bound his boy to a man not qualified to be a master, the craft gild could refuse to sanction the agreement; or if by chance the laches were

[1] Wadmore, Skinners, p. 30. Rules, 1577. Son pays no fee.
Northampton Records, Cox, ii. 280. Butchers' Rules.

not discovered until later, the freedom of the gild might be refused the lad when he had served his term.

From the earliest days one qualification had been held to be indispensable, the master must be a freeman of his gild.[1] Indirectly, this meant also that he must be a freeman of the town or city, for the gilds would not receive as members men who were not freemen of the town.[2]

Other conditions appear in later bye-laws, though possibly they were customary at as early a date. Two of the more common rules are that a master must be a householder or propertied person, dwelling within the town,[3] and secondly, that he must be of English birth.[4] Additional rules were adopted by individual gilds : one or two ordered that a man

[1] Riley, Mems., p. 216.   Girdlers' Rules.

Letter Book, f. 88.   Cutlers' Rules.

Ibid., f. 147.   Hatters, 1347.

Letter Book G, f. 32.   Braelers' Rules.

Letter Book E, f. 120.

Prideaux, Goldsmiths, p. 9.   Court Mins., 1370.

[2] See p. 39.

Liber Albus, trans. Riley, p. 237.

Riley, Mems., p. 247.   Shearmen's Rules.   No one of the trade to receive an apprentice unless he had been a freeman of the City for seven years.

Ibid., p. 179.   Taficers' Rules, 1331.   "Also . . . they have ordained that no man shall keep any manner of handwerke of the said trade, if he be not free of the City : and that if any such shall be found, it shall be forfeited to the said Chamber, . . . and that no man of the said trade, other than a free-man, shall take an apprentice in such trade," except by leave of the Mayor and Aldermen.

[3] MSS. Norwich Court Mins., 1540–49, p. 44.

Norwich Records, Tingey, p. 105.   Rules, 1415.

Black, Leathersellers, p. 34.   Chamberholders forbidden to take apprentices.

Turner, Oxford Records, p. 208.   Rules, 1551.   Apprentices serving with masters outside the town to be adjudged foreigners.

Mercers, p. 79.   Rules, 1504.   Master must be worth of his own goods or have a stock worth £100 at least.

Clode, Mems. Merch. Tailors, p. 209.   Master must be worth x.marks.

[4] 25 H. VIII. c. 19.

21 H. VIII. c. 16.

14 & 15 H. VIII. c. 3.

Bickley, Little Red Book, p. 117.   Complaints to the mayor of Bristol that cordwainers have employed strangers, not born under the king's power.

Permission to take an apprentice might be granted if the master paid higher fee.   Two Dutchmen were allowed to take apprentices by the Goldsmiths, and paid 13s. 4d. each.   Prideaux, Goldsmiths, p. 12.   Entries, 1374.

who wished to take an apprentice should prove himself able
to teach, employ, and maintain him.[1]   The Pewterers elected
certain freemen " to wey Indifferently the state of the whole
companye who is able to maynteyn and kepe prentice and
who is not." [2]   At Carlisle there was a rule that the master
must be a married man ; [3] at Coventry he must be quit of his
dues to the gild.[4]

The master, in his turn, would make sure that the boy
offered to him as an apprentice had a right to serve, for there
were many qualifications for an apprentice as well as for a
master.   These have been already considered at length,[5] and
we have seen that by 1560 it was usual to insist upon certain
qualifications, whether of birth, class, age, property, education,
or sound physique, or of several of them.   At Norwich we
find a stipulation which appears frequently in later years,
that no married man was to be taken as an apprentice.[6]
Statutory conditions were a property qualification and, in
certain cases, native birth.[7] The Common Council of London
to some extent supported the gild rules as to age by insisting
that apprentices should be at least twenty-four years of age
when they came out of their apprenticeship.   The Act states
that "forasmuche as greate pouertie, penuyre and lacke of
lyvynge hathe of late years followith . . . and one of chiefest
occasions thereof as it is thought . . . is by reason of the over
hastie marriages and over sone setting up of householdes of
and by the youth and young folkes of the said citie, which
hath comonly used, and yet do, to marry themselves as sone

---

[1] Wadmore, Skinners, p. 30.   Rules, 1486.
   Black, *op cit.*, p. 123.   Rules, 1501.
   Surtees, Newc. Merch. Adven., i. p. 9.   Rules, 1520.
   Lambert, Two Thousand Years, p. 136, Hull minstrels, 1561.
   Letter Book G, f. xxxii.   Braelers, 1355.
[2] Welch, Pewterers, p. 200.   Court Mins., 1558.
[3] Ferguson, Carlisle Records, p. 149.   Court Mins., 1558.
   Cf. Surtees, Merch. Adven., i. p. 10.   Master must have been married one
year.
[4] Fretton, Fullers Gild, p. 27.   Rules, c. 1507.
[5] See Chapter I.
[6] MSS. Norwich, Case X., Shelf B.
[7] See p. 44.

as ever they come oute of theyer apprenticehode, be thaye
never so young and unskilful, yea, and often tymes many
of them so poore that they scantily have of their proper
goodeyes wherewith to buye theire marriage apparel . . .
and forasmuch as the chiefest occasion of the sayde inconvenience is, as it is very evydent, by reson that dyvers and
sundry apprentices, as well of the sayd artificers as also
of other citizens of the said citie, are commonly bounde for
so fewe years that there termes of apprenticiallitie expireth
and endeth oversone, and that thei are thereupon incon-
tinently made fre of the said citie . . . for remedy, stay and
reformation whereof it is ordained . . . that no manner of
persons . . . shall be by any manner of wayes or means
made free of the sayde citie . . . untill suche time as he and
they shall severally attayne to the age of 24 Years." [1]

In his selection of an apprentice there was no occasion for
a master, at this time, to keep a windward eye on the fee
which the father would be able to pay for his son's instruction. Premiums did not come into vogue until the seventeenth century, though possibly members of one or two of
the wealthier merchant companies had already begun to
demand them, for there is a rule of the Newcastle Adventurers, made in 1555, imposing a fine of £10 on any master
who took money or other goods with his apprentice by way
of covenant.[2]

If the master agreed to take the boy the indentures
would be drawn up and signed. There is a strong simi-
larity between the indentures employed in the different
gilds and companies even at this early date, when printed
forms were unknown. All state the names of the contracting
parties, the date, and the term of service ; the various conditions as to the instruction of the lad and his conduct
towards his master are then given, the words often being
arranged in a rhythmic form.[3] Every gild seems to have

---

[1] Arber, Stationers, i. p. xli, Sept. 27, 1556.
[2] Surtees, Merch. Adven., i. p. 11.
[3] See Appendix.
   Cf. Cunningham, Growth of English Industry and Commerce, i. (1910), p. 349.
   Transcript of an indenture of 1480. MS. at Trinity College, Cambridge.

insisted upon some minimum term for which a lad must serve. By 1569 the rule was, with few exceptions, seven years at least. This had been the common practice of London since 1300, and had been adopted in many other towns at the close of the fifteenth century. A shorter minimum term is seldom found at this date. Colchester, where it was only five years as late as Henry VIII.'s reign, had fallen into line by 1560.[1] A longer term was, as a rule, left to the discretion of the master and the parents, though a few companies insisted upon eight and even ten years. The desire of one or other of the parties contracting, or the rule that an apprentice must be twenty-four before he came out of his time, are probably accountable for long terms in companies where no exceptional rule existed; for instance, for such variations as are found in the records of the Stationers' Company, where the terms vary from seven to twelve years.[2]

Within a certain period of taking a lad, sometimes a year and a day, sometimes a month, the master had to present the boy and his indentures before the Master and Wardens assembled in court.[3] If the indentures were in order, and there was no objection to either master or apprentice, the lad's name and the date of his binding were entered in the company's books, and either the master or the lad paid the enrolment fee and any other court dues.[4] If all went

---

[1] Benham, Red Book, p. 29.

[2] Arber, Transcript Stationers' Records, i. p. 68 *seq.* *E.g.*—

Year, July 22, 1561–July 24, 1562.			Year 1562–1563.		
23 apprentices bound for		7 years.	7 apprentices bound for		7 years.
16	,, ,,	8 ,,	6	,, ,,	8 ,,
7	,, ,,	9 ,,	3	,, ,,	9 ,,
14	,, ,,	10 ,,	6	,, ,,	10 ,,
3	,, ,,	11 ,,	2	,, ,,	12 ,,
1	,, ,,	12 ,,	1	,, ,,	13 ,,
2	,, ,,	13 ,,			
1	,, ,,	16 ,,			

[3] See p. 34.

[4] The master seems generally to have paid, but at Carlisle the Smiths' rule was that the apprentice should pay if he could; if not, then the master should pay it for him (Ferguson, Carlisle, p. 135. Rules, 1562). There were often fees to the clerk and beadle. *Cf.* Welch, Pewterers, p. 197, Mercers' Charter, p. 86.

well the lad did not appear in court again until, at the end of his service, he came to take up his freedom. Meanwhile, he lived in his master's house learning his trade.

There are few records at this time of the private life of the apprentice. Indentures show that he invariably lived with his master, and in return for his service received instruction, bed, board, and clothing. We are accustomed to think of apprenticeship merely as a method by which a lad is taught his trade, but until comparatively lately the constant personal relations between master and boy were one of the most important features of apprenticeship, and it was an integral part of the system that the lad should live in his master's house and be entirely under his control. The apprentice received no wages,[1] his labour being supposed to be adequately requited by the return made him in kind. In his indentures he had to promise good conduct and civility, and abstention from games such as dice and cards, and the "haunting" of taverns. At the close of this period a certain number of towns and gilds enforced by their rules and penalties the customary promises which the apprentice made when bound. Although no wages were given, the boy sometimes received small sums of pocket-money, or a small lump sum, clothes or tools, at the end of his term, to help him make his start in life. There is an interesting indenture at Norwich, dated 1543, by which a boy is bound for eight years to a dornix weaver. He is to be found in board, lodging, and all other things necessary, and his master is "to pay to his saint yerely during vij of the first yere 9^{d} and the eight and last yere 5/-," while he is to have 6s. 8d. in money and two suits of apparel at the end of his term.[2] Such conditions, however, do not seem to have been so general at this time as they were in the seventeenth and eighteenth centuries; at any rate, there are few recorded instances of their payment.

The apprentice, however young, probably worked the same

---

[1] *E.g.*, Mercers, p. 86.
[2] MSS. Norwich, Press E, Case X.
     Cf. Cox, Northampton Records, ii. p. 323.

hours as did his master, but night-work was forbidden by the mediæval gilds,[1] and there were so many saints' days that a lad had frequent half-holidays. An idea of the working day can be gained from a rule of the Leathersellers, setting forth that work shall not begin before six in the morning nor continue after six o'clock at night, while on Saturdays, vigils, and festivals work was to cease at three o'clock.[2]

Apprentices were not allowed to trade on their own account,[3] though possibly the merchant companies made an exception to this rule; the Newcastle Adventurers, at any rate, allowed apprentices to trade after five years' service, and with a stock limited to the value of five marks.[4]

The gilds did not altogether lose sight of the apprentice during his period of service, for each had its two appointed Searchers, whose business it was to search out and condemn bad work, and report upon any unfair dealings on the part of the brethren.[5] These officers, in making their rounds, inci-

---

[1] Night-work was forbidden, not out of consideration for the health of the workers, but because, owing partly to the poor lighting, it was conducive to bad work. There was also a danger that fraudulent work would be done in hours when there was no fear of the Searchers' inspection.

Cf. Cunningham, English Industry, i. (1390), p. 314, and Ashley, i. p. 91.

Black, Leathersellers, p. 21. Rules, 1398.

Prideaux, Goldsmiths, i. p. 10.

[2] Black, *op. cit.*, p. 40. Rules, 1482.

Cf. Riley, Mems., p. 219, Cutlers' Rules; p. 278, Braelers; p. 307, Weavers; p. 217, Girdlers.

Fox, Merch. Tailors, Bristol, p. 68.

Arber, Stationers, i. pp. 124, 182. Accounts, 1559, 1561. Fines for keeping shops open on Sundays.

Coventry Leet Book, Part III., transcrd. M. D. Harris, p. 673.

Cappers' Rule, 1520. Every journeyman of the craft shall, from Michaelmas to Easter, "cum to ther worke at syx of the Cloke in the mornyng and worke vntyll vij of the Clok at nyght, and from Ester to Michelmas to cum at v of the Clok and work till vij at nyght."

[3] Fretton, Fullers of Coventry, p. 30. Rules, 1507.

Musicians Co., p. 11. Rules, 1518.

[4] Surtees, Merch. Adven., i. p. 6. Rules, 1515.

[5] Bickley, Little Red Book, ii. pp. 114, 93.

The Bristol Fullers, in 1406, order their Searchers to make the round twice a week. Ibid., ii. p. 77.

Prideaux, Goldsmiths, i. p. 10. Search twice a quarter.

Cf. Cunningham, *op. cit.*, i. (1890), 314.

dentally saw to it that the boy was properly cared for and taught; while if there were any serious cause of complaint, whether of ill conduct on the part of the boy or of unfair treatment by the master, the injured party could appeal to the court of the craft.[1]   The municipal authorities also exercised supervision; at Norwich the Mayor held his court once a week, and dealt, amongst other matters, with all pleas of apprentices.[2]   Masters were allowed to correct their own apprentices, and indeed were expected to do so; they would only appeal to external authority if the boy proved incorrigible.   The gilds, however, intervened if the master abused his powers.   The wardens of the Merchant Tailors " comytted Thomas Palmer to pryson for that he hath broke Henry Bourefelde his apprentice hede without any juste cause." [3]

The services of an apprentice were a piece of property which a man had a right to dispose of, and masters occasionally sold some years of an apprentice's service to another freeman.[4]   Ricarte of Bristol, in his Calendar, which was compiled in 1479, describes the custom of London.   " Et fait assavoire qe chescun eiant tiel apprentice, poet vender et deviser son dit apprentice a qi qil voudra de mesme part aux comme son chatel." [5]   This custom of sale or turnover, as it was called, was open to abuse in the days when the number of apprentices which any one master might take was strictly limited.   Men who did not want apprentices could take their legitimate number of boys, and then turn them over for a sum of money to some master who wanted more apprentices

---

[1] Clode, Merch. Tailors, pp. 519, 521, 531.
    Toulmin Smith, English Gilds, p. 322.

[2] Tingey, Norwich Records, p. 101.

[3] Clode, *op. cit.*, p. 531.

[4] Apparently, in those days masters sometimes sold to their apprentices a portion of their term, or freed them from a portion of their obligations.   There is a rule of the Goldsmiths, " If any apprentice buys his term or part thereof, or if his master pardons him his term or releases him, he shall not hold shop during his term, nor be enfranchised, nor do work in private places, but be bound freeman of the mystery, unless by assent of the Wardens and with a voluntary contribution " (Prideaux, p. 7.   Rules, 1368).
    Cf. Sharpe, Calendar of Wills, p. 231.

[5] Ricarte's Calendar, p. 163.

than the bye-laws allowed him.   The gilds were therefore
obliged to make rules restricting turnover.   Any master
wishing to transfer his apprentice had to obtain the sanction
of his gild and pay a part of the sum received to the use of
the brethren.[1]   From the account books of the Merchant
Tailors we see that a master was fined for selling his
apprentice without leave, and also that sales were lucrative
transactions.   There is an entry in the accounts of 1547,
"From Harry Whytehorne, for the third part of the gain he
had of the sale of his apprentice 8/10."[2]   Harry therefore
pocketed 17s. 8d.—a considerable sum in those days.

If a master died before the expiration of his contract, or if
he became bankrupt, or in any way unable to employ his
apprentice, the latter either served out his time with the
widow or heirs, or was "turned over" to a suitable master
for the remainder of his time.   Such a transference was
supervised by the gild, and a small sum was charged for
entering the change in the books.[3]

At the end of the term of service the master and apprentice again came before the court of the gild, and the master,
according to his promise in the indenture, "took up" the
freedom for his apprentice.[4]   The fees, though fixed by

[1] Wadmore, Skinners, p. 163.

Prideaux, Goldsmiths, p. 14.   Rules, 1384.   "No one shall sell to an apprentice the remainder of his term or to any other person of any other trade, but only
to a freeman of the same trade and of the same city, and that the seller shall pay
half of what he receives to the alms, and shall give no quittance till the apprentice
has sworn before the Wardens to keep the ordinances, on pain of 100/-"

[2] Clode, op. cit., pp. 519, 525.

[3] Arber, Stationers, i. p. 98.   Court Mins.   Boy set over.
Cotton, Elizabethan Gild, p. 17.   Rules, 1561.

[4] In London the master had to make his apprentice free without any charge to
the latter.   See Nicholl, Ironmongers, 114.   Rules, 1498.

Letter Book E, f. cxliv.

The Leathersellers order apprentices to take up their freedoms within a year
after their terms have expired.   Otherwise they should not be given employment
(Black, op. cit., p. 41).   The fear, of course, was that men would learn the trade and
practise it, without paying their dues to the company.

Surtees, Merch. Adven., i. p. 2.   Rules, 20 Ed. IV.   Fees for apprenticing,
20d.; for freedom, 5s.

Toulmin Smith, p. 316.   Exeter Tailors' Rules, 1460.

statute at 2s. 6d. for enrolment and 3s. 4d. for the freedom, were frequently much higher, and the gifts, benevolences, and dinners which were often exacted considerably increased the expenses. The fees paid, the young man's name was entered on the roll of freemen. His next duty was to go to the town hall on the following court day and take up his municipal freedom, without which he could not work as a free crafts-man.[1] It appears that he then could, if he had the means, set up for himself as a master; otherwise, he would work as a journeyman until he had earned the wherewithal to buy tools and material and take his little shop or booth.[2] These were the typical features in the career of an apprentice, whether bound in London or in the provinces; but it must always be remembered that no account of apprenticeship can be true in every detail of all towns and gilds alike since, as even the rules quoted here will show, there were many varia-tions in all the minor matters connected with apprenticeship.

[1] Benham, Red Book (Colchester), p. 24. Ibid., p. 29.
Turner, Oxford Records, p. 206. Council Rules, 1551.
See Chapter I.

[2] In a discussion following a paper read by me to the Royal Historical Society, the question was raised as to whether an apprentice was not obliged to serve as a journeyman upon completing his apprenticeship, before he was allowed to set up as a free master. This is a view which is sometimes held. Such a period of service is not imposed by the gilds, according to their rules, until a later date, and then only very exceptionally. The rules of the gilds are explicit, and their omission to mention any such journeyman year appears to me to be explainable only by the fact that no such service was enforced.

CHAPTER III

THE PART PLAYED BY APPRENTICESHIP IN DOMESTIC POLITICS

EARLY in 1562 the Statute of Artificers was passed, and in November of the same year it came into force.[1] Although many of the details of Elizabethan apprenticeship as we know it from 1562 to 1814 are based upon custom and usage, this Act is the foundation as well as the starting-point of the national system of apprenticeship. Hitherto it had been a gild custom voluntarily adopted; the Act transformed it into a national institution by imposing a compulsory servitude of seven years at least upon all who henceforth wished to enter any industrial calling, and by adopting for the whole country the custom of London, local variations being thus, generally speaking, superseded by one universal practice.

As a whole, the Act is long and somewhat confusing, since it deals with a variety of subjects—the hiring of artisans and labourers, assessment of wages, the wandering of rogues and vagabonds, and other matters of which apprenticeship is but one. It is, in fact, a code intended to meet the economic and social needs of the time.

Two reasons are given in the preamble for drawing up the Act; one, the need of a readjustment of the standard of wages; the other, the necessity of codifying the numerous laws on the employment of servants and apprentices. Many of these were out of date, while others were contradictory, and the need for reform and the better regulation of industry had for some time been felt, as is clear from the experimental

[1] 5 Eliz. c. 4.

legislation and the proposed legislative remedies of the decade preceding Elizabeth's attempt. Acts for journeymen had been passed in 1550 and 1552,[1] while Bills for the regulation of apprentices and artificers had been passed or proposed in 1550, 1552, and 1559.[2]

It is natural that in an Act which purports to be a codification there should be little that is new. The various clauses are for the most part based on earlier statutes; even the remarkable prohibition against unapprenticed people earning their livelihood by means of a trade, a clause which introduced a new order of things, was not, as we shall see, altogether an innovation. But there was any amount of modification and adaptation, and it is here that the statesmanship of Elizabeth and her advisers reveals itself. From a medley of old statutes, ineffectually trying to cope with the problems of the day, they sifted what was useful, and digested it into two great general Acts—the Statute of Artificers and the Poor Law of 1601. These Acts comprise within themselves the Elizabethan remedies for the social and economic troubles of the time, the decay of towns, the social unrest, with which went the instability of the rural population, the increase of pauperism and unemployment, and the diminution, actual or feared, of industrial skill. Apprenticeship, which is dealt with in both Acts, was one of the means they employed to remedy these evils. No doubt the chief reason for making apprenticeship compulsory was the desire to promote English arts and industries by maintaining a high standard of skill amongst our workmen. But there is equally no doubt that apprenticeship was an integral part of the new system for the relief of the poor, and that in addition it was used by the

---

[1] Commons Jals., vol. i. p. 15 : Jan. 21, 1550, Bill for Journeymen.
Ibid., p. 18.   Feb. 20, 1552.
[2] Ibid., p. 15.   Jan. 21 and 22.   Bills for Apprentices.
Ibid., p. 22.   April 11, 1552.   Bill touching journeymen and prentices.
Ibid., p. 60.   April 21, 1559.   Bill for taking and having of prentices and journeymen.
   Cf. Ibid., p. 18.   Feb. 20.   Bill for divers Handicraftsmen to dwell in towns
P. 25.   March 15.   Bill for artificers to dwell in cities and towns corporate.
March 17.   Bill for apprentices to be taken at Bristol as London or Norwich.
P. 48.   Feb. 11, 1558.   Bill for apprentices to be taken in divers towns.

Government as a means both to maintain the rural population and to resuscitate the waning prosperity of corporate towns. It may perhaps be thought that this is to claim too much for Tudor statesmanship. But any study of the work of Burleigh and his Queen shows their extraordinary ability for grasping things as a whole. Further, it is possible to analyse the motives of the Statute and, as it were, to watch the workings of the framers' minds by reading it in close connection with the Acts upon which it is based, and with its complementary Act, the poor law of 1601.

Before dealing with these Acts in detail, one general word is necessary as to the contemporary political theories which prompted the legislation of Elizabeth and her immediate predecessors. By the beginning of the sixteenth century the importance of money as the sinews of war had been realised. "The King cannot have treasure when his subjects have none," was a truth which the Crown had learnt by experience, and statesmen accordingly sought by every means in their power "to increase the funds" from which contributions could be drawn.[1] The promotion of national prosperity, whether by foreign treaties or by detailed legis- lation, was regarded as the duty of any conscientious Government, and it was a matter of no consequence if, in achieving it, the interests of private persons were injured.

This desire to increase "funds" naturally led statesmen to foster commerce and the arts and crafts. In the opinion of the sixteenth century a wide market was best secured, not by underselling our rivals, but by producing goods of a higher standard than theirs. To promote skill and check the production of bad work were thus the immediate con- cern of any Government.

For the same reason, namely, the promotion of national strength, the Crown set itself to curb the social unrest due to the economic changes of the fifteenth and sixteenth centuries. It was firmly believed that the duty of the agricultural labourer both to God and to the nation was to

---

[1] See Cunningham, Growth of English Industry, ii. (1903), pp. 1–3.

Hales, Discourse of the Commonwealth, p. 35, quoted by Cunningham.

remain on the soil and so keep up the strength of the military class, and do his duty in that state of life not, it should be noticed, to which he should be called, but in which he actually found himself. This religious objection to change is foreign to the twentieth century, but it had a very real practical influence in Elizabeth's day. In addition to these two reasons social stability was desired because it was thought to be conducive to wealth, whereas a population in a state of ebb and flow was regarded as productive of pauperism and unemployment.

Lastly, it was on account of this same desire to increase "funds" that the Government sought to encourage corporate towns, the nurseries of the arts and crafts, and the best units for revenue purposes.

Recognition of the political importance of industrial prosperity led succeeding rulers to pass numerous statutes to prevent bad work. Five distinct methods were devised to preserve and promote industrial skill. Specialisation was insisted upon ; for instance, shoemakers, tanners, curriers, and cordwainers were each forbidden to practise the trade of the others,[1] and brewers were prohibited from using the coopers' trade of barrel-making,[2] the presumption being that a man would be inefficient in any but his own trade.[3] The second method was a direct attempt to ensure the work being up to standard by defining either the processes which were to be employed,[4] or the exact length, breadth, and weight of the goods produced. Acts on these lines were passed for the pewter trade, and for calendaring, dyeing and weaving, and coopering.[5] A new method was tried by Henry VII. in 1494. A law was passed for Norwich, forbidding any one to become a worsted weaver unless he had

---

[1] 2 H. VI. c. 7 (1423); 1 H. VII. c. 5 (1485); 19 H. VII. c. 19; 24 H. VIII. c. 1 (1532).

[2] 23 H. VIII. c. 4.

[3] 2 H. VI. c. 7 ; 19 H. VII. c. 6.

[4] 5 H. VIII. c. 4 (1513); 24 H. VIII. c. 2 (dyers); 23 H. VIII. c. 4 (coopers).

[5] 19 H. VII. c. 6 (weight of pewter ; 5 H. VIII. c. 2 (length of cloth); 3 & 4 Ed. VI. c. 2.

been apprenticed for seven years or had received permission from the mayor.[1] This method was extended in 1513 to calendaring;[2] in 1522 seven years' apprenticeship was made compulsory for worsted weavers in Yarmouth and Lynn,[3] and in 1555 for all weavers except those of Yorkshire, Cumberland, Northumberland, and Westmoreland.[4] A fourth device for preventing bad work was the use of marks, which was made legally necessary in the pewter,[5] woollen,[6] and coopering[7] trades. The fifth and last method was that of granting powers of search to masters and wardens of craft gilds within cities and boroughs,[8] and to officers of the Crown in villages and hamlets.[9]

Each one of these Acts may have made some improvement in the trades with which they were respectively concerned, but they did not aim so high as a general remedy. It was this which Elizabeth and her advisers attempted to provide. From amongst the various statutory measures which were then in use they chose out one which had hitherto been legally enforced only in the woollen trade, compulsory apprenticeship of seven years, and extended it to all industries. The system of marks was of doubtful value. Search by gilds could be successful only in towns where the trade was strong, while the method of ensuring good work by defining the processes to be employed was open to objection, since it involved the passing of separate and detailed Acts for practically every trade—Acts which, when passed, were easy to evade. Compulsory apprenticeship was a less cumbersome method, and had one great advantage, it could be applied universally to all trades and in all places. Thus it promised greater equity as well as a greater degree of success. In making their choice Elizabeth and her Privy Council were, no doubt, influenced by the fact that some form or other of apprenticeship was already practised in

[1] 11 H. VII. c. 11.   [2] 5 H. VIII. c. 4.
[3] 14 & 15 H. VIII. c. 4.   [4] 2 & 3 Ph. & M. c. 11.
[5] 19 H. VII. c. 6.   [6] 5 H. VIII. c. 2.
[7] 23 H. VIII. c. 4.
[8] 3 H. VIII. c. 10 (1511); 23 H. VIII. c. 4; 24 H. VIII. c. 1.
[9] 3 & 4 Ed. VI. c. 2 (1549).

a large number of trades and towns, and was believed by
master craftsmen to be of real value in maintaining a high
standard of skill. Their adoption of compulsory apprenticeship meant, therefore, an extension, not a change of custom ;
it involved no upheaval in the social system. Moreover,
it was in accordance with the opinion of freemen of towns
and gilds, whose support promised it at the very outset some
measure of success as a solution of the problem.

It was natural enough that, if apprenticeship was to be
supported by the Government at all, it should have been
the London custom that was adopted, since from the first, it
had been copied by provincial towns, and thus approxi-
mated nearer to a national system than the custom of any
other locality. The Act states that any one who henceforth
wished to practise a trade should be apprenticed to it for
seven years at least, "after the custom and order of the city
of London."[1] The chief features of the London system were
binding by indenture, the due recording of the agreement,
a minimum term of seven years on the indoor system, and the
close personal relation of master and apprentice, inseparable
from which was the master's entire control of the boy. These
now became the chief characteristics of the national system.[2]
Two of the lesser features of the London system were mentioned at length : the apprentice must not come out of his
time before he had reached the age of twenty-four,[3] while
only householders might take apprentices.[4] The mention of
these two points in clauses which are concerned with the promotion of industry is a reminder of the wide policy which
prompted the statute, for the one was a part of the Elizabethan
policy of poor relief, while the other was connected with the
attempt to restore the prosperity of towns.

The decay of towns was so serious in Henry VII.'s reign that
he had been obliged to exempt several of them from a part
of their assessment.[5] He and his successors endeavoured to
resuscitate the towns by curbing the monopolistic spirit of their

[1] 5 Eliz. c. 4, f. 26.
[2] Ibid., f. 26.
[3] Ibid., f. 26.
[4] Ibid., f. 26, f. 28.
[5] Cunningham, *op. cit.*, i. p. 402.

gilds,[1] and by giving them special advantages over country districts, either by reserving the use of certain trades to townsmen,[2] or by forbidding countrymen to engage in any form of retail business except at times of fairs.[3] Some improvement was probably effected by these various statutes, but no complete cure, for the evil was still felt in the middle of the sixteenth century. Apprenticeship was the remedy that Elizabeth applied. Ratepayers, the pillars of municipal society, were given an advantage over lodgers within the town, as well as over country workmen. In the towns only householders might employ cheap labour, or in other words might take apprentices,[4] while the lucrative field of trade and commerce was practically closed to the sons of husbandmen ; only the sons of townsmen might be apprenticed to craftsmen within the towns.[5] A special clause reserved the wealthiest trades, such as that of merchant and goldsmith, to the sons of propertied persons.[6] A similar restriction was applied to the woollen trade, the chief manufacture of the country.[7] Crafts such as that of the wheelwright, smith, and thatcher, which were practised in the country rather than in the town, were exempted from these regulations, and so, too, were fulling and pottery-making, which had necessarily to be practised in those localities which could best supply the materials used in the trade.[8]

It has been suggested that the Statute of Artificers marks the victory of the privileged freemen of the towns over those non-free intruders who had competed with municipal craftsmen while they did not pay equal dues. However that may be, the statute certainly made an attempt to safeguard muni-

---

[1] 15 H. VI. c. 6 (1436) ; 19 H. VII. c. 7.

[2] The Worcestershire weaving towns were decaying owing to the competition of neighbouring villages, and these now were forbidden to weave (25 H. VIII. c. 18, 1534). Similar Acts were passed for the rope trade at Bridport (21 H. VIII. c. 10), and coverlet making at York (34 & 35 H. VII. c. 10), and the weaving industry throughout the country ; an Act of Philip and Mary forbade men to engage in it outside corporate towns (2 & 3 Philip & Mary, c. 12), though by a later Act a few places were exempted (1 Eliz. c. 14). *Cf.* Cunningham, *op. cit.* ii. p. 26.

[3] 1 & 2 Ph. and M. c. 7.   [4] 5 Eliz. c. 4, f. 26, f. 28.

[5] Ibid.   [6] Ibid., f. 27.   [7] Ibid., f. 32.   [8] Ibid., f. 30.

cipal interests. It favoured corporate towns rather than the country districts. Dr. Cunningham has pointed out that "the clothiers, who had established themselves in rural districts, were not forced back into the towns, but there does not seem to have been a continued drain from urban centres. The raising of the standard of rural training, together with the change by which burgesses were permitted to draw on a lower social grade than heretofore for apprentices, seems to have checked the trend of the artisan class from corporate towns to market towns and rural districts." [1] That the Act really did succeed in restoring the prosperity of the towns is indicated by the fact that complaints of decay cease from Elizabeth's time.[2]

It would be a mistake to suppose that these clauses were prompted solely by a wish to restore municipal prosperity. Then, as now, motives were mixed. The mediæval idea of fairness, which plays so large a part in the bye-laws of the gilds, appears over and over again in the statutes of the time, and is certainly not absent from the Act of 1562. The assessment of wages was obviously an effort to attain the goal of a fair day's wage for a fair day's work, and the limitation of one trade, and no more, to each craftsman is less obviously, but no less certainly, prompted, in part at any rate, by the feeling of what is right and fair. Further, the old policy of keeping up the military strength of the nation by encouraging tillage and an agricultural population finds a place in the Act. Agriculture was encouraged by giving to landlords special facilities for obtaining labour. Apprentices to husbandry might be taken by householders with half a ploughland in tillage,[3] and compulsory service could be exacted from all artificers and labourers during harvest,[4] while writs of capias could be issued by justices and bailiffs against apprentices and servants deserting their masters.[5] The exodus of the rural population from the land was checked by this same clause, and by the clause ordering that a servant should not leave one place of service for another without first

[1] *Op cit.*, ii. 32.
[2] Cunningham, *op cit.*, ii. 32.
[3] 5 Eliz. c. 4, f. 25.
[4] Ibid., f. 22.
[5] Ibid., f. 47.

obtaining a testimonial setting forth the particulars of his departure.[1] Possibly this desire to maintain an agricultural population is partly accountable for those clauses which placed the sons of countrymen at a disadvantage to town lads with regard to entering a trade.[2]

When we come to the question of how far apprenticeship was a part of the Elizabethan system of poor relief, the cross-motives underlying the Act become an even greater source of difficulty. It seems, however, that though apprenticeship was adopted primarily in the interests of trade and manufactures, it was regarded by the Government with additional favour as a partial solution of the problem of pauperism.

The relief of the poor was, when the Statute of Artificers was passed, one of the most pressing questions of the day, and the increase of vagabondage and idleness the evil most widely deplored and condemned. It is only natural to suppose that in framing the Act the Government should have had these difficulties in mind, and this assumption is borne out by those clauses which deal with the employment of labourers and artisans. Powers were given to justices of the peace to compel unemployed persons, under certain conditions, to work at husbandry upon the request of any person using the same, or at a craft which the unemployed person in question had used for three years.[3] Thus wilful idleness was checked. Obstacles were placed in the road of those who wished to roam ; long, instead of short, hirings were insisted upon for the general rule,[4] and regulations were made for change of service.[5] The employee had to give due notice of his departure, and might not travel in search of fresh employment without a testimonial stating the cause.[6] These clauses are based upon the Acts of

[1] 5 Eliz. f. 10, f. 11. [2] See p. 66.

[3] 5 Eliz. c. 4, f. 35, f. 4, f. 7.

[4] Ibid., f. 3. Annual hirings for a large number of trades.

[5] Ibid., f. 5, f. 6. Three months' warning necessary on both sides.

[6] Ibid., f. 8 and f. 9. Penalties for non-observance.

Ibid., f. 10.

F. 5. Cause of dismissal to be determined by the justices.

F. 11. Testimonial must be shown on application for fresh situation.

F. 47. Justices empowered to issue writs of capias against servants or apprentices in agriculture deserting their masters.

Richard II., Henry VI., and Edward VI., which respectively obliged servants to obtain testimonials if they wished to travel from one place to another, to give six months' warning to their masters, and to engage themselves by the year and not by the day.[1]

Various motives had prompted the passing of these statutes—for instance, the maintenance of the agricultural population and military strength of the country, or, again, the preservation of that stationary order of society which it was the ambition of mediæval Governments to maintain : they were not aimed solely against vagrancy. We cannot therefore claim that the clauses in the Act of 1562 which were based upon these earlier statutes were entirely concerned with the prevention of poverty. The probability is that here, too, motives were mixed. Which was the chief does not, as far as we are concerned, much matter ; it is sufficient to notice that similar legislation had been passed in earlier reigns to remedy, amongst others, the evils of vagrancy and pauperism which in Elizabeth's reign were even more acute. A noteworthy fact is that, amongst those clauses of the Act definitely dealing with apprenticeship, it was laid down that an apprentice must be twenty-four years of age before he came out of his servitude. It will be remembered that a like rule was enacted by the Common Council of London in 1556, by which no one might be made free of the City until he was twenty-four years old, a rule which incidentally prevented a man below that age from setting up as a free master. This rule was passed owing to the alarming increase of poverty, one of the chief

---

[1] 12 R. II. c. 3 (1388) ; 23 H. VI. c. 13 (1444) ; 3 & 4 Ed. VI. c. 22 (1549).

The gilds recognised the value of apprenticeship as a means of keeping the youths of the district from idleness and pauperism. The following rule is illustrative : "Item That for-as-much the poverty within the City daily increaseth and the number great of idle young boys born within the City which wander and range abroad and about the City for want of Masters, and are not placed into service to some trade or occupation whereby to get their living and keep them out of idleness. It is therefore now provided and established that no Weaver or Craftholder of the Company shall from henceforth take any apprentice into his service but such as are born within the City and liberties thereof. . . ." (Fox and Taylor, Weavers of Bristol, p. 51, 1562.)

reasons of which was believed to be "the over hastie marriages and over sone setting up of householdes of and by the young folk of the said citie." [1]

The connection between the Elizabethan systems of poor relief and apprenticeship becomes increasingly plain when we turn to the poor laws. By an Act of Henry VIII. vagrant children between the ages of five and fourteen were to be bound apprentice.[2]   Edward VI. developed this policy ; sons of vagrants might be apprenticed until twenty-four, daughters until twenty ; punishment for rebellion was slavery.[3]   There was therefore by 1562 a well-established political tradition that apprenticeship was a remedy for vagrancy, and that the possession of a skilled trade would keep a man from poverty and vagabondage.   The Statute of Artificers gave to justices of the peace and officers of towns the power to bind any unemployed person under twenty-one years of age as an apprentice to a trade or to husbandry, provided his services were demanded by a householder possessing at least half a ploughland in tillage.[4]   By a later statute the poor law of 1601,[5] justices of the peace were given the further power of apprenticing the children, not merely of paupers and vagrants, but of parents "ouer burthened with children," [6] poor persons who, in the opinion of the Bench, were unable to support their children, so that there was a fear that either the parents or their offspring might come upon the poor rates.   The full significance of apprenticeship as a part of Elizabethan poor relief is self-evident when the Acts are thus read together.

These were the various political beliefs and needs which prompted the Statute of Artificers, and dictated the form which it finally took ; they influenced Elizabeth and her advisers, and were responsible for those details and exceptions in the Act which, upon its first reading, appear somewhat incomprehensible.   It is not to be

---

[1] Arber, Transcript Stationers' Records, i. p. xli.
[2] 27 H. VIII. c. 25.   [3] 1 Ed. VI. c. 3.
[4] 5 Eliz. c. 4, f. 35, 36.   [5] 43 Eliz. c. 2 (1601).
[6] Dalton, Country Justice (1619), p. 85.

whole trade, not at one branch only. The Government, in fact, to all intents and purposes supervised the contract between the employer and the least protected of his employees, the child. It is a degree of supervision which was not ventured upon by the reformers of the nineteenth century, nor even by those who, in the opening years of the twentieth, were most keenly alive to the evils of uncontrolled juvenile labour.

At first, however, there was a danger that it would be little more than a paper system ; for though the Act made apprenticeship compulsory, and defined the conditions under which it was to be served, it made no provision for the enforcement of those clauses. Machinery was devised for that part of the Act which dealt with wages ; the justices of the peace in every district were ordered to meet twice a year, at definite seasons, to assess the wages of the various grades of labourers, due consideration being given to the prices of necessaries in their localities. But no mention is made as to how the Act as a whole was to be enforced, and the question naturally arises, Were the apprenticeship clauses of the statute enforced at all ? The Tudor monarchy relied very largely upon common informers for the administration of the law. These men received as a rule half the fines of those they prosecuted, and they were therefore inclined to be hawk-eyed for law-breakers. But regular administration of the Act was not within their power, and there seems little doubt that the Act was not strictly observed nor well enforced. Complaints were made that it was ignored, and even that it was wilfully broken.[1] One writer declares that " manie of her [Elizabeth's] subjects haue so farre ronne into the daunger of the saide statute by the penalties therin con- teyned That if thextremitie therof shoulde be lade upon theym it woulde prove to theire utter undoinge." [2] This period of ineffectiveness and consequent complaint continued for about twenty years. That the statute should at once

---

[1] S. P. D., El. 88, 11.
 Lansd. MSS., 114, 5.
 Ibid., 38, 14 (1583).
[2] Ibid., 114, 5.

have provided a remedy for industrial grievances could hardly have been expected, but considerable criticism was aroused by its prolonged ineffectiveness.   This was attributed to the omission of any administrative machinery, more especially to no provision having been made for the registration of apprentices, and in 1574 a petition was presented to the Queen proposing that the signatories should be appointed by letters patent for thirty-one years, to keep "on Recorde all such thinges as are appoynted to be done by the statute made in A° v^{to} of her Maties reigne touchinge byndinge and servinge of apprentices (the saide statute havinge appoynted an office but no officer)." [1] Complaint is made of this same defect in another paper. The Act made void any apprenticeship which was not served after the custom of London, and according to the London custom, an apprentice must be bound by indenture, and the effect of the indentures enrolled, and at the end of his term " due certificate shalbe made howe the appntice hathe served his apprenticeship.   All which things together with making the appntice free, are entred and kepte on recorde by officers thereto appointed."   But since no provision was made for registration, the majority of journeymen and apprentices had no means of attesting their services ; indentures alone proved little, for " manie are bounde that never serve," while to certify his service by witnesses would be a heavy charge to the apprentice. A certificate based on records would avoid these difficulties, and the writer suggests the appointment of an officer to keep those records and enrolments without which the clauses of the Act referring to apprentices, journeymen, and the setting up of masters were of little effect.[2]   In 1606 there is a similar complaint : no one has been appointed to keep the register, and masters do not know to whom they should go, while men " dare not " teach their apprentices the full trade, because they know the indentures will not constrain the lads to serve according to contract.   Further, the apprentice who has truly fulfilled his obligations " cannot travel to get his

[1] Lansd. MSS., 114, 5.   [2] Lansd. MSS., 114, 3.

living freely but many times is troubled by informers because
he cannot produce proof of where he hath served." [1]   This
want of administrative machinery not only encouraged
masters and apprentices to disregard the law, but also
handicapped the justices in their duty of enforcing it.
Municipal officers and justices of the peace were supposed
to make an annual inquiry into offences against the Act ;
but this duty, it was said, was omitted by the justices everywhere, " and the rather because there is no clarcke or register
appointed to attend uppon them to wryte and keepe suche
things on recorde " as should be necessary.   The justices
were said to be loth to enter into inquisitions, for it was " an
unprofitable thing to inquire how an apprentice was bound
and served and not to make a record of how he proved it." [2]
The renewal in 1626 of the proposal to appoint an officer [3]
shows that even sixty years after the passing of the Act there
was still cause for complaint.

Nevertheless, before this date, the Act was being fairly
regularly enforced by means of the gilds, the justices of the
peace, and the municipal authorities.

In the second half of Elizabeth's reign there was a marked
outburst of activity amongst the gilds, or as they were now
often called, the companies.[4]   A large number of them applied
for a renewal of their charters, and passed or re-enacted bye-
laws.[5] It is worth suggesting that the action of the companies
may have been caused by their discovery that the statute was
not a panacea for industrial grievances, and that they must
trust to their own exertions if a remedy were to be found. However that may be, there can be no doubt that the gilds were
definitely encouraged by the Crown.   It was a matter of
common opinion that the simplest method of ensuring the
observance of the Statute was to insist upon the enrolment of

[1] S. P. D., J. I., xxiv. 72.   [2] Lansd. MSS., cxiv. 3.
[3] S. P. D., Ch. I. xliv. 29.
[4] These later gilds and companies may in some or in many cases have differed
from the earlier gilds. The important point for us is that they were associations of craftsmen, able to regulate their trade and to enforce rules on
apprenticeship and other matters.
[5] Cf. Cunningham, English Industry, ii. p. 35.

apprentices.   Unless apprentices are bound by indenture, and
the indentures enrolled, it is impossible to bring the orders
provided by law into due observance, says one writer.   But
the taking and keeping of such a record would be a great
occasion to bring and preserve such good order among
artificers as will avoid all inconveniences before remembered,
and that none shall unlawfully enter or introduce others into
those occupations that they were not brought up in.[1]   This
registration, which was so necessary, but for which no provision was made in the Statute, was exactly the work which the
gilds could undertake, and the Government consequently gave
them its support.   From 1570 onwards the granting of
charters and the confirmation of bye-laws progressed apace.
These rules for the registration of apprentices are identical
with those earlier ordinances which we have already considered
at length.   They order the enrolment of the apprentice's name
upon the books of the company, either within a certain date
after he was bound, or in some cases before he began to work
at all.[2]   To prevent all fraud, the boy had to be presented
with his indentures to the Master and Wardens in the company's court.   Typical of these rules is a bye-law of the
Merchant Tailors: " Also it is ordeyned that no freeman of
this fellowshipp shall take into his service any apprentice to be
bound unto him to serve him after the manner of an apprentice,
but that he doe first present the same apprentice before the
Maister and Wardens for the tyme being at their Comon Hall
to th'intent that they by theire examynation may understand

[1] S. P. D., Eliz. xciii. 26.
[2] *E.g.*, MSS. Hertford, v. p. 55, Constitutions, Jan. 18, 1638.
  Overall, Clockmakers, p. 33.   Rules, 1632.   Presentation within a month.
  Stevenson, Nottingham, iv. p. 186.   Rules, 1578.
  Leader, Sheffield Cutlers, ii. p. 9.   Rules, 1625.
  Ferguson, Kendal, p. 93.   Rules, 1575.
  Ibid., p. 138.   Rules, 1587.   Within two court days.
  Ibid., p. 176.   Clothiers and Shearmen.   Ibid., p. 180.   Mercers, &c.
  Cox, Northampton, p. 277.   Rules for various trades, 1574.
  Ferguson, Carlisle, p. 94.
  Guilding, Reading Records, i. p. 452.   Rules, 1599.
  Goldney, Chippenham, p. 5.   Rules, 1597.
  MSS. Norwich, Mercers' Book, ii., Case X., Shelf B.
  V. C. H., Worcestershire, ii. p. 291.   Weavers.

that he be of free Birth and not challenged for a Bondman and borne under the Kinges obeyance, or made Denizen upon the payne of 40s. over and above the somme of presenting of everie suche apprentice." [1] Masters who broke these rules were fined, while the apprenticeship of boys who served unbound and unenrolled was null and void.[2]

In addition to the work of registration the gilds were of value in enforcing the Act because their bye-laws reiterated the national law. In the constitutions of the gilds two rules are invariably to be found : no apprentice was to be taken for less than seven years,[3] and no one was to work at a trade save apprentices and those who had been apprenticed for seven years at least,[4] with the exception of sons working with their fathers and those who had been specially licensed by the Wardens. Wherever, therefore, a gild existed, no one could

[1] Clode, Mems. Merch. Tailors, p. 208. Rules, 1613.
 Cf. Welch, Pewterers, i. p. 239. Rules, 1564.
 Leader, *op. cit.*, ii. p. 3. Rules, 1590.
 Rep. on MSS. Miscel., vol. i. p. 75. Wilts Weavers' Rules, 1603.
 Musicians Co., p. 61. Rules, 1606.
[2] The fines evidently varied :—
 Jan. 28, 1577. John Alde, for keeping apprentice unrepresented, ij vj.
 Feb., 1578. John Oswald fined for keeping two young men in work unpresented, ijs.
 June, 1597. John Wyndet took two apprentices, bound them by indenture, and enrolled them without presenting them, xls.
 Arber, Stationers, iii. f. 404, 405 ; ii. f. 396.
[3] MSS. Norwich, Mercers' Book, ii. Rule, 14 1623.
 Lambert, Two Thousand Years, p. 207. Weavers' Rules, 1564.
 Ibid., p. 278. Bricklayers' Rules.
 Latimer, Merch. Adven., Bristol, p. 76. Rules, 1618.
 Overall, Clockmakers, p. 43. Rules, 1632.
 Burton, Kidderminster, p. 76. Charter, 1640.
[4] Ferguson, Kendal, p. 140. Boke of Recorde, Mercers, Drapers, 1587.
 Ibid., p. 144. Glovers, 1588, p. 149. Tanners, 1592, p. 176. Clothiers, 1619.
 Noake, Worcestershire, p. 21. Weavers' Rules.
 V. C. H., Worcestershire, ii. p. 190.
 Needlemakers, p. 23. Charter, 1664.
 Leader, Sheffield Cutlers, ii. p. 3. Rules, 1590. P. 8, Rules, 1624.
 Lambert, *op. cit.*, p. 286. Coopers, 1598.
 Ibid., pp. 219, 254, 279.
 Arber, Stationers, iv. p. 531.
 Fox, Merch. Tailors, Bristol, p. 85, Rules.

work at that trade contrary to statute law, without simul-
taneously infringing gild rules and running the risk of
punishment by the gild for such infraction. Gild rules touched
the artificer at every stage in his career, and it was not easy
for the illegal workman to escape discovery for any length of
time. The youth who had not served his apprenticeship
would at once be questioned if he attempted to set up his
workshop or become free of the gild. In some places the rule
was peculiarly strict; at Bristol the apprentice of the Merchant
Adventurers had to show his indenture made in due form
according to the custom of the city, and a letter from his
master, if not present, to testify to his true service.[1] The
London Pewterers would not license any man to set up or
open shop until he had appeared before the Master and
Wardens in company with the master with whom he had
served as apprentice, and his master had reported upon his
behaviour, and had stated " what substance he is and what
workeman he is."[2] Nor was it only master craftsmen who
would be questioned as to training ; no journeyman might be
employed unless he had been admitted a brother of the gild,
or had special permission, and he could not gain that admittance unless he had duly served his term.[3] In Wiltshire,
a man who sought employment as a journeyman weaver was
obliged to bring a certificate of his seven years' service, or else
his master had to testify to it.[4] The Bristol Tailors had a
similar rule.[5] In Bath the Merchant Tailors refused to allow

[1] Latimer, Merch. Adven., p. 77. Rules, 1618.
   Cf. MSS. Norwich. Mercers' Book, ii., 1623.
   Fox, Merch. Tailors, p. 85. Rule, 1640.
   Lambert, op. cit., p. 218. Rules, 1598.
[2] Welch, Pewterers, i. p. 243. Rules, 1564.
[3] Overall, Clockmakers, p. 23. Rules, 1632.
   Ferguson, Carlisle, p. 181. Shoemakers' Rules, 1598. No journeyman to be em-
ployed until he showed his indentures and brought testimony to his apprenticeship.
   Ferguson, Kendal, p. 176.
   Leader, Sheffield Cutlers, ii. p. 3. Rules, 1590. Prospective workman
must bring his indenture and sign the ordinances.
[4] Rep. MSS. Miscel., vol. i. (1901), p. 75. Wilts Quarter Sessions. Weavers
Rules, 1603.
[5] Fox, Merch. Tailors, p. 82. Rules, 1640.

strangers to work unless they brought proof of their service. " No stranger or foreigner at any time hereafter shall openly set up use or exercise the Craft or Mistery of Taylor within the said City of Bath. Except he be first allowed to be a good workman by the Masters of the said Company for the time being or by the greater part of the said Company, and shall also first be made free of the said City of Bath as all times heretofore used and except he shall likewise make good proof unto the Masters of the said Company for the time being that he hath served and been brought up as an apprentice in the said craft or Mistery of a Taylor by the space of seven years as above."[1]   The assumption is that even where it is not so stated a man would have to show his indenture of apprenticeship and freeman's certificate before he would be allowed to work, at any rate, in a place where he was not known.   If an illegal workman escaped detection in the earlier stages of his career, he would run the hazard of the law yet again if he attempted to open a shop, for none but those who were freemen and fully qualified were allowed to set up or keep shops.[2]   He would find himself further handicapped in his competition with lawful workmen by being unable to employ cheap labour ; for the gilds had a rule that none but those who had served their apprenticeships and were free masters might take apprentices,[3] and if any unqualified man attempted to do

---

[1] Shickle, Merch. Tailors, p. 50. Rules, 1629.

Cf. Leader, Sheffield Cutlers, ii. p. 3. Rules, 1590. Apprentice, before he sets up for himself, shall bring his indenture to the jury and set his hand to the acts and ordinances.

[2] Leader, *op. cit.*, p. 3. Rules, 1590.

Lambert, *op. cit.*, p. 218. Glovers' Rule, 1598. Ibid., p. 265. Goldsmiths, &c., 1598.

MSS. Norwich. Mercers' Book, ii., 1623.

Davies, Southampton, p. 135. Rules, *cf.* p. 171.

Overall, Clockmakers, p. 31. Rules, 1632. Ibid., p. 36. Master and Wardens may shut up the shop of any person who takes an apprentice or works not having served seven years.

Ibid., pp. 144, 141, 180. Rules of Shearmen and Mercers.

[3] Leader, *op, cit.*, ii. p. 2.

Lambert, *op. cit.*, p. 219. Glovers' Rules. Ibid., p. 254. Joiners, 1598. Ibid., p. 287. Coopers, p. 279. Bricklayers' Rules.

Clothworkers' Rules and Orders, p. 150. Ordins., 50, 1639.

so, his right to exercise this privilege would be called in question when he went to the court to enrol the boy, or when, omitting to do so, he was summoned by the Wardens.

The gilds also provided inspectors. It was their general rule to have officers named searchers, whose duty it was to make periodical search for offenders against the ordinances. The chief object of these inquisitions was to prevent bad work, but inquiries were also made into a man's right to work or to take apprentices.[1]   The gilds were thus doubly useful :

Norwich MSS.   Mercers' Book, ii. Bye-laws, 1623.

" 8. The headman and wardens shall not give lysense to anyone to kepe open any shopp, howse, chamber, cellar or rometh therein to exercise his trade before he shall have proved that he have served or been brought up as an apprentice unto the said trade or some other merchandizinge trade by the space of seven years and ys a freeman."

Arber, Stationers, iv. p. 531.

Rep. on MSS. Miscel., vol. i. p. 75.   Rules for woollen trade, 1603.

Ferguson, Kendal, pp. 137, 141.

Fox, *op. cit.*, p. 62.   " No Covenaunt seruant journeyman or apprentice shall holde or keepe a servant or apprentise under him openly or prively untill he be infraunchised in maner and forme abouesaid."

Merch. Tailors' Rule, 21 Eliz.

[1] The following extracts from the Norwich Court Books will give some idea of the work of the searchers :—

MS. Mercers' Book, ii., Aug. 19.   If Wardens of the several trades do not make due search from time to time for apprentices bound by indenture and presented to the Masters of the Grand Company respectively, each defaulting Warden shall pay 20s. a fault.   If they do not enforce the fines, they shall be fined themselves.

MS. Court Book, xv.   Nov. 19, 1615.   " Coblers apprentices Willm Wakefield apprentice his name ys Edmond Porter and Gregory Harryson, Henry Salter his apprentice named Thomas Sely, Nicholas Kylletts apprentice his name ys Robt Kyllett but he sayth he ys retained by ye yeare."   This entry points to an inquiry into cobblers' apprentices.

Ibid., ibid., July 12, 1615.   Twelve worsted weavers are sworn, and present a man for making cloth half a nail narrower than the regulation breadth.   Eight dornix weavers are sworn, and present four men for making too short or narrow pieces.   Such entries occur with almost unfailing regularity in the minutes of each court day.

Dec. 7, 1615.   Six cordwainers sworn, " who fynde a payer of lynd Slippers of Thomas Semers made of horse leather contrary to the Statute and prise them ij."   There are four other cases, and again on Dec. 13. *Cf.* 1615, Aug. 30, Jan. 15, Feb. 11 and 18, March 6.   Sometimes resistance was made.   " John Longe Dornixweau beinge psented by the wardens of the

they did the work of registration of apprentices, and they enforced a seven years' apprenticeship.

The gilds were well supported by the municipal authorities. Far from there being jealousy between the towns and companies, they seem to have worked excellently together. The towns supported the gilds by making apprenticeship the usual qualification for the franchise, by promoting or aiding in sessions of inquiry, and by freely affirming gild rules. At Salisbury the Common Council would not grant the municipal freedom to any one without the knowledge of the company to which he belonged. No apprentice might be made free unless he was admitted to one of the companies in the city and, as a freeman, was presented by the Wardens to the Common Council.[1] At Warwick[2] and Reading[3] the mayor and head burgesses held sessions to inquire into apprenticeship. It was the general rule for masters to enrol their

---

dornix weauers for not suffering them to search in his house for defective ware contrary to an order in their booke." Court Book, 15, July 8, 1615.

Every gild had its searchers.

Clode, Mems. Merchant Taylors, p. 210. Rule 8, 1613 : "As well for weights, measures yardes and Ells as for non presenting of apprentices, non enrolling of them and of keeping of fforeyns contrary to the Lawes and use of the said city."

Overall, Clockmakers, p. 34. Rules, 1632. Ordin. for Search.

Jupp, Carpenters, pp. 135–154.

Ferguson, Carlisle, p. 178. Shoemakers' Rule. Two new searchers to be appointed every quarter-day.

Glass-sellers, p. 122.

Clothworkers, p. 149. Rule 28, 1639.

Needlemakers, p. 29.

Lambert, *op. cit.*, Glovers' Rules, p. 218 ; Tailors, 239 ; Joiners, p. 253 ; Coopers, p. 287 ; Cordwainers, p. 316.

[1] Benson, Old and New Sarum. Charter, 1613.

[2] Book of John Fisher, ed. Kemp, p. 157. Nov. 9, 1586. Session held to inquire into apprentices. " Item if any person dwelling in this borough which in the said fiveth yere of o^r said sovreign lady the quene did not then exercise & use his mystery & occupation nor sithens hath bene brought up and servid as Apprentice therin by the space of seven yeres at the least, have sett upp & used the said occupacion or mistery within this borough, or if any such have set any person not then a workman or sithens brought up in the same occupacion seven yeres togither ye shall, &c." All apprentices to be presented and their indentures compared with the town records.

[3] Guilding, Reading Records, i. p. 446, &c.

apprentices' names on the town books, so that there should be some record of service if later the lads wished to take up their municipal freedom. In towns, therefore, where no, or only a few, trades were organised into gilds, the municipal authorities did a useful national service by enrolling apprentices. The work of the gilds was further supplemented by the towns, whose rule was that none but freemen might work at a craft or engage in trade within the town, and this freedom could be obtained only by patrimony, purchase, or apprenticeship for seven years within the town.[1]

Although the Wardens made periodical search for offenders, informers were encouraged,[2] and occasional inquisitions were made by company or town, men evidently did break these rules and escaped discovery, for we find instances in the court books of illegalities, some of which date back long before the complaint was lodged.[3] Nevertheless, the companies and towns enforced the Act upon the nation to a degree which would have been impossible without them. They had the necessary organisation both for the work of registration and for the enforcement of *bona-fide* apprenticeship. Their officers, the Masters, Wardens, Clerks, and Beadles, could supervise enrolment; and the gilds in particular had a system of search which could at least check

---

[1] *E.g.*, Norwich MSS., Court Book, xv., June 23, 1620. "An Action of debt ys ordered to be brought against Willm Bolter for usinge his trade not being free. And Mr. ffidell ys appointed to be Attorney therein and Edward Yonge & Roger Wilyreffe are ordered to be talked wthall for his manner of tradinge."

Ibid., Aug. 30. Order to sue Robert Brett in an action for debt for using the trade, not being free.

[2] Latimer, *op. cit.*, p. 79. Rules, 1618. Lawful for any brother to inform the Master, Wardens, and Treasurer of offences, mentioning time, place, and all the circumstances, which information the clerk shall register in a book to be kept secretly and only shown to the Master and Wardens.

[3] *E.g.*, Stevenson, Nottingham, iv. p. 50, Dec. 3, 1578. Man presented at the Guildhall for trading as an ironmonger without having served apprenticeship for seven years. Has done so for eleven months.

Atkinson, North Riding Quarter Sessions, ii. p. 23, Helmesley, June 8, 1613. A carpenter presented for entertaining a person as his apprentice for six years and "never had Indentures."

Prideaux, Goldsmiths, i. p. 114, 1610. Man fined for keeping apprentice two years unpresented.

infringements of the Act. Evasion of the statute, even though it was not impossible, was rendered unprofitable. The master who was not himself qualified was liable to have his stock seized or his shop closed, and he could not have an apprentice to aid him in his work. The apprentice who had not served legally was, according to the bye-laws, debarred from the freedom of his company and his town, and was consequently unable to set up openly as a master or to work as a journeyman. The Crown could not have supplied nor controlled the machinery which the gilds had ready to hand.

There was one obvious drawback in leaving the administration of the statute to authorities which were narrowly local. In the country, and in villages and small towns where the gilds were weak or non-existent, or where there was no corporation, there seems to have been considerable disregard of the Act. Prosecutions were made by the justices of the peace and quarter sessions, but evasion must have been far easier than in a town, where there was less chance of secrecy, and where the body of tradesmen were jealously on the watch for competitors. But with the accession of James I. this laxness began to be remedied. The Stuarts delighted in the details of government which Elizabeth had delegated to quasi-private bodies and petty officials, and one result of the greater part played by the central authority in the minor matters of local government was the increased activity of the justices of the peace and quarter sessions. We find entries of prosecutions of masters who were practising trades to which they had never been bound, or who were employing boys nominally as apprentices, but unbound by indenture.[1]

---

[1] Rep. on MSS. Miscel., i. p. 71. Wilts Hilary Sessions, 1602. Presentments for keeping journeymen and apprentices and looms by unqualified persons.

Atkinson, *op. cit.*, i. p. 69. Thirske Sessions, Apr. 14, 1607. Wm Watson of Sheriff Hutton presented for exercising the mystery of a tailor, not having served any master as apprentice.

Ibid., ii. p. 231. 1620. A Pickering tailor presented " for that being no Apprentice he useth the said trade of tailor."

Ibid., i. p. 111. 1608 ; p. 198. 1610. Presentments.

Stevenson, Nottingham, iv. p. 325. Extracts from presentments at quarter

Lads who left their masters in order to work on their own account were forced to serve their seven years or more.[1] In the North Riding, where complaint has been made "as well by masters as servants of sundry abuses committed against the Statute of Labourers and Apprentices, and of the neglect in keeping the Sessions appointed by yt law," the justices of the peace were ordered to keep special sessions twice a year, to inquire into defaults against the Act.[2]

The Statute of Artificers seems to have been best administered during the personal government of Charles I. A cessation of complaints, coupled with a greater number of prosecutions at quarter sessions,[3] indicates that Charles was successful in arousing the justices into activity sufficient to cope with the lawbreakers. The credit for this better administration of the Act must not, however, be entirely attributed to the justices, for it seems that the towns and companies were also more strenuous during those same years of personal government. In the year 1634, for instance, there are numerous entries in the Norwich records of the punishment of apprentices, and the prosecution of unfree men who practised trades.[4] Even more significant are some other entries which are not connected with any infraction of the apprenticeship law. These are the notes of presentments of craftsmen by the overseers of the gilds on account of their bad or deceitful work.[5] Such indictments show that the gilds'

---

sessions, 1614. "We present John Krystyon for yousing the trad of hatmaking and was neuer prentyse to it 10s."

Stevenson, Nottingham, v. p. 103. Presentments, 1695. A labourer presented for using the trade of a shoesmith, not apprenticed.

[1] Humpherus, Watermen, i. p. 215. Rules, 1626. Every apprentice for a month's absence obliged to serve a year.

[2] Atkinson, op. cit., i. p. 204. Topcliffe Sessions, 1610.

[3] Hardy, Herts Quarter Sessions, pp. 59, 65, 102. Indictments.

Stevenson, Nottingham, v. p. 136. Information against three unlawful wheelwrights, 1629.

Willis Bund, Worcestershire Quarter Sessions, p. 554.

MSS. Norwich, Book ix. May 25, 1631.

[4] MSS. Norwich Court, Book xx. Apprentices punished, pp. 5, 6, 8, 13, 25, 37, 47, 48.

Ibid. Presentments for using trades not free, pp. 6, 14, 48.

[5] Ibid., pp. 7, 10, 12, 17, 23, 25, 45, 46, 51, 54, 56, 59.

officers were on the alert, and we know that if they made their
rounds in search of bad work, they would at the same time
have prevented illegalities connected with apprenticeship.
With regard to the details of this gild activity there is little
worthy of note, as the measures taken to enforce the Act or
the companies' bye-laws are similar to those hitherto employed.   Men were prosecuted for practising trades to which
they had not served apprenticeship, or, again, for dismissing
apprentices without the permission of the company.[1]   Irregu-
larities of all sorts were punished by fines.   The only change
to be noticed in the work of companies at this time is in the
method of registration of apprentices.   In Charles's reign the
records are on the whole more detailed and more regularly
inscribed.   It is common to find in the books of towns and
companies during this period, not merely an entry of the
apprentice's name, age, master, and length of service, but
information as to the social position and the home of his
parents, whether his father is dead or alive, and whether the
lad is to receive any pocket-money, or is to have a double suit
of apparel or merely a pair of shoes at the end of his time.[2]
The unlawful departure of apprentices was registered, so that
if later on they attempted to obtain work in the neighbour-

---

[1] *E.g.*, Leader, Sheffield Cutlers, i. p. 55. 1632. "Geo. Sykes of Whitten-
ton for putting away an apprentice without the consent of ye Co. 5. o."
" Geo. Pye for keeping an apprentice unbound above three months 3. 4."
    Ibid., ii. p. 127.
    Clode, Mems. Merchant Taylors, p. 549, Court Mins., June 20, 1630.
    " 20/ annually allowed to the Wardens of the Clothworkers Company to be
given to such as they shall employ to discover and give information of the abuses
committed by divers working clothworkers, in neglecting the due observation of
the Saboth Daie, and in taking and keeping more apprentices than they ought to
doe.   And where before the Company did allow 30/ towards a friendly meeting
or dinner upon the searches with the Wardens of the Clothworkers and others accompanying them in these searches fower tymes in the year, ordired that from henceforth there be 40/ allowed towards the charge of every such Dynner."
    MSS. Norwich, Mercers' Book, ii.   Warden fined 20s. if they omitted to
make due search.   Aug. 9, 1623.
    [2] MSS. Hertford, xxvii., Enrolts. 1630–41.
    MSS. Bristol, Enrolts., 1626–40.
    MSS. Oxford, Hanaster Books to 1647.
    Brit. Mus. MS., 33,353.
    See p. 170.

hood, their omission to serve the full time would more surely
be discovered.[1]   This change may be a minor matter, but
it is perhaps significant of the greater care to enforce the
Act.

Yet though it is possible that under the stronger government of Charles I. the gild and municipal authorities were more
active, and that the system of search was more regularly enforced,[2] it must be left as a matter for conjecture until more evidence is available. It is at least clear that the more systematic
enrolment of apprentices during this period of personal government would have made it easier to enforce the statute ; and
this, together with the greater activity of the justices, and the
continued activity of the gilds and towns, naturally prompts
the belief that during the personal government of Charles I.
the Act was more thoroughly enforced than it had hitherto
been.   This view is confirmed by the comparative freedom
from complaint.

In one respect the Act undoubtedly failed. It did not
prevent the system of apprenticeship from being used by the
gilds as a bulwark of their monopoly.   Indeed, the probability
is that, far from being checked, the narrow policy of the gilds
was indirectly encouraged by the statute. We have seen
that in earlier times gild rule had been marred by a jealous
spirit which revealed itself in an unwillingness to admit new
members, and in such bye-laws as those limiting the number
of apprentices, or enforcing prohibitive fees. Burleigh no
doubt hoped to check this evil by introducing a uniform
system ; it is noticeable that masters were left free to take as
many apprentices as they pleased ; and that though apprenticeship was made legally necessary, the conditions under
which it had to be served were such as could be complied
with by almost any one.   But however clearly he may have

---

[1] Overall, Clockmakers, p. 32. Rules, 1632.

Arber, Stationers, iv. p. 525. Decree of Star Chamber, July 11, 1637. I.
apprentice runs away, may not take second until first is crossed off the books.

[2] The duties of Searchers are at this time more regularly defined.

Overall, Clockmakers, p. 15. Charter, 1631. Searchers to seize goods made
by men who have not served full time. Ibid., Rules, 1632. Shops of such persons
to be closed.

recognised the evil, any attempts to remedy it were rendered nugatory by the dependence of the Government upon the gilds for the enforcement of the Statute. That lack of administrative machinery, which, as we have seen, was the weakness of the Act, made the gilds the masters of the situation. Naturally enough, they did not enforce the law in any way which, however indirectly, would have been to their disadvantage. This is well illustrated by the survival of the right of patrimony which had existed in the companies from early times, and was a cherished privilege since it gave to members and their sons an advantage over those outsiders who wished to gain admittance. According to the Statute of Artificers, the only means by which a man could enter a trade was by serving as an indentured apprentice to a qualified master. But the companies ignored the law in the interests of this customary right. Notwithstanding the Act, men who had not been regularly apprenticed, but had been taught merely by their fathers, claimed and received admittance into the gilds, and no objection was made to their working as masters or ordinary workmen. Indeed, the custom of patrimony was everywhere preserved, and in the ordinances of the gilds it is ranked with apprenticeship as entitling a man to the freedom of his company.[1]

[1] Cotton, English Gild, p. 16, c. 1560. Rules, p. 60, 1594. Every son of a freeman may claim by patrimony.

Cox, Northampton, 288. Fullers' Rules, 1585.

Surtees, Merch. Adven., Newcastle, p. 72. 1573.

Sellers, Eastland Co., York, pp. 4, 5. Oath of those made free by patrimony.

Overall, Clockmakers, p. 33. Rules, 1632.

Latimer, Merch. Adven., Bristol, p. 63. Rules, 1605. From the Bristol records we learn the qualifications necessary for admittance by patrimony. "All persons Clayming the Freedome of this companie by Patrimonie shall bee born meere Englishe, that is to saie, within the Kings maiesties Dominions, or made a Denizen by Acte of parliament, and bee the sonne of a brother of this Socitie, lawfully and orderly admitted." Ibid., p. 76. Rules, 1618.

Leader, Sheffield Cutlers, ii. p. 4. Rules, 1590. Ibid., p. 8. No person to take an apprentice unless he has been seven years apprenticed, or so long instructed by his father, as to be a sufficient workman.

Lambert, Two Thousand Years, p. 174. Patrimony not allowed in the Merchant Gild of St. George until about 1677.

Surtees, Hostmen, p. 24. Only free burgesses, and men free of the trade by patrimony or service, to be admitted.

This was against the letter and spirit of the Act, but the assistance of the gilds was too valuable for the Government to care to pursue an over strict policy, or to refuse to sanction bye-laws which the gilds considered necessary to their welfare. Another result of the lack of administrative machinery, and the consequent dependence on the gilds, was that they were able to enforce rules the object of which was the preservation of their respective monopolies. For instance, although longer periods were often served, the law required no more than seven years' apprenticeship. But several companies actually insisted upon a minimum service of eight or nine years before they would allow an apprentice to take up his freedom.[1]   Again, although the Act left masters at

Add. MS., 18,913, Merch. Adven. of England : " No person of what degree or state soever, shalbe admitted into the freedome of this ffellowshippe of merchants adventurers of England, except he bee rightly Intituled thereunto by patrimony or by serving with a free brother by indenture orderly made."

The gilds continued to make their rules for entry by purchase.   It would be interesting to trace the antecedents of these " redemptioners."

They may have been men who had legally served their apprenticeship in some other town, but who, having left the place of their service, and coming in as strangers, were obliged to purchase the right to practise their crafts in their new home.   Or were they now, as they appear to have been sometimes in the old days, men who had not served apprenticeship, and could not obtain the gild freedom in the usual way?   If so, admittance by redemption would be another instance of the divergence of gild custom from the principles of the Statute.

Add. MSS., 18,913, Merch. Adven.   Redemption fee £200 at least.   1608.

Cox, Northampton, p. 288.   Fullers' Constns., 1585.   Any man of the country desiring to be received into the town and made free of the company, shall at his entrance make to the whole company of fullers and shearmen a dinner at his own cost, and pay the company 13s. 4d.

Ferguson, Kendal, p. 176. July, 19 1619.   Clothiers and Shearmen, Rule for admittance.   By apprenticeship ; or freemen of the borough who have paid a composition.

Ibid., p. 181, c. 1619.   Mercers, Grocers, and Drapers forbade admission by composition.

Fox, Bristol Merchant Tailors, p. 19.   1649.   Complaint that the company had been unduly enlarged by taking in strangers by way of redemption.

Fretton, Hist. of Fullers, p. 29, Coventry.   1636.   Election of a love-brother. Extra entrance fee £1.

Leader, Hallamshire, ii. p. 3.   Rule 11, 1590.   Composition fee £5.

Sharpe, Shipwrights, p. 25.   Ordins., 1620.

Sellers, op. cit., pp. 4, 5.

[1] Add. MSS., 18,913.   Merch. Adven., 1608.   Eight years at least.

liberty to employ as many apprentices as their work demanded, the gilds were rigorous in limiting the number. Rules forbidding members to have more than one, two, or three apprentices are almost invariably to be found in ordinances which at this time were everywhere being enacted or confirmed. Such limitations, which differed with localities and trades, had been made by many gilds in the fifteenth century. Now, as then, the alleged reason for passing these rules was that without them the trade would be over supplied with workmen, and that want and poverty would ensue.[1]

Cotton, *op. cit.*, p. 172. Court Mins., 1578. Eight years.

Cox, *op. cit.*, p. 277. Regulations for various trades, 1574.

Sellers, *op. cit.*, p. 17. Eight years. 1617.

Welch, Pewterers, i. p. 290. Rules, 1582. Nine years.

Lambert, *op. cit.*, p. 174. Hull Merchant Gild insisted upon eight years until 1649.

[1] Add. MSS. (Brit. Mus.), 33,852, p. 64. York Bakers, one only, 1577.

Add. MSS. (Brit. Mus.), 18,913, p. 29. Merch. Adven., one only.

MSS. Norwich, Court Book, 1583. March 6 (from Mr. Tingey's copy).

" This daye Mr. Maiour caused a presentment of wursted weuers to be entred as followeth

"Itm in the yere of our Lord God 1582 the xix daie of September, a serche was made by the viij wardeins belongyng to the mistery of wursted weuers Item we fynde that thear bee certeyn offenders wch hath more apprentices by the ordynaunces and lawes provided then they ought to haue as is confessed by the journeymen and apprentices.

" Walter Marcell hath vij apprentices as the apprentices confesse.

" Edmund Allen hath vij apprentices by their own confession and the journeymen lykewise " Six others have five each, and one has six. The number allowed is four.

Arber, Stationers, ii. p. 881. " The Peticons of the poore men of this Companie for their Relief.

" j That they may haue woorke

" 2 That no woorke be put to forens or strangers

" 3 That they maie be well and trulie paide for their woork

" 4 That the printers and others of this companie maie not be suffered to haue excessive nomber of apprentices to the hindraunce of poore fremen of this mystery.

" 5 That the Ffrenchmen and straungers beinge Denizens maie not haue excessive nomber of apprentices

" yt is Aunswered on the parte of the master wardens and assistants . . . that the peticon is reasonable but the complainte is too uncertaine and generall and therefore yt is ordered that suche brother of this companie as shall herein finde himself greeved shall exhibite his complainte . . . against the person

There may well have been some truth in this, but there can
be little doubt that both the older rules, and their more
general adoption in the sixteenth century, were to a
considerable extent due to the jealousy of established
workmen towards newcomers.

There is yet another indication of narrowness and monopoly
in the gilds. Many of them appear to have demanded
higher fees for the admittance of new members than was
allowed by the law. The question of fees and the comparative value of money payments at different periods is always
a difficult one, and is especially so during the Tudor
monarchy, when the value of money was rapidly changing.
It is rash, therefore, to make any very definite statement as

---

offendinge in having moe Apprentices then by the orders of the cumpanie he
oughte to haue . . .

"5 Yt is answered that such strangers haue noe Apprentices bounde to them
but haue apprentices of other men appointed to serue with them to learne their
arte."

Arber, *op. cit.*, iv. p. 535. Decree of Star Chamber, 1637.

Burkitt, Curriers, p. 11. More apprentices allowed on account of the
plague. 1593.

Cox, *op. cit.*, 324. Three allowed, 1619.

Ferguson, Carlisle, p. 148. Tailors, c. 1558. None to take a second until
first has served five years, without leave. Fine, 20s. Ibid., p. 173. Shoemakers, 1595.

Fox, Merchant Tailors, Bristol, p. 62.

Lambert, Two Thousand Years, p. 287. Coopers, 1598. Ibid., p. 278,
Bricklayers, 1599.

Leader, Sheffield Cutlers, ii. p. 8. Rules, 1624. One apprentice besides
own son or sons. After five years another apprentice may be taken.

Musicians, p. 62. Rules, 1606.

MSS. Norwich, Mercers' Book, ii. Rule 16, 1623. Two only.

Overall, Clockmakers, p. 29. Rules, 1632.

Report MSS. Commission, Miscel., vol. i. (1901), p. 75. Wilts Weavers,
1603.

Sharpe, Shipwrights, p. 23. Rules, 1620. Three allowed.

Surtees, Merch. Adven., Newcastle, p. 11. None for a time, then one.
1575.

S. P. D., Eliz. cxc. 48.

Sellers, Eastland Company, p. 16. Rules, 1617.

Welch, Pewterers, ii. p. 44. Court Mins., 1603. Man who is lame is
allowed an extra apprentice. 1653. Man who has more work than he can do
is allowed an extra apprentice on payment of £10 to company.

to the degree to which the gilds were raising their fees. It may be that in some cases where the fee was raised the amount charged was more nominally, but no more comparatively than the old fee. There seems reason to believe, however, that some companies were charging unduly high fees. Some of their ordinances are suspiciously evasive. They circumvented the law, which fixed the enrolment fee at 2s. 6d. and freeman's fee at 3s. 4d., by obliging the aspirant to the freedom to provide a dinner to the company, or, of his kindness, to undertake some work of repair, or make a gift.[1] We may safely assume that this charity was an enforced virtue. Other companies left to their Masters and Wardens the task of deciding for what sum a man should be admitted. The Oxford Mercers passed a rule providing that a man must, upon admittance, " pay a reasonable sum of money as the Master and Wardens shall think good and also 10/ to poor allms folk of the same felship and give the felship a dinner or compound for the same."[2] This was a dangerously vague rule, and certainly gave scope for unfairness and oppression.

From these rules as to fees, and from those dealing with the length of service, number of apprentices, and methods

---

[1] Clode, Merchant Tailors, p. 54, 1623, apprentice's fee raised to £1, in 1625 to £1 5s.

Sellers, Eastland Company, p. 40. Rule 39, 1617. Fee 10s. to the company.

Ferguson, Carlisle, p. 95. Merch. Gld. Bk., i. Rule 6, 1624, fee 6s. 8d.

Latimer, Merch. Adven., p. 63. Min. Bk., Dec. 31, 1605. Shall pay " only 6s. 8d."

MSS. Norwich, Mercers' Book, ii. Fee for apprentices not freeborn sons of citizens, 13s. 4d.

Cox, Northampton, p. 288. Fullers, 1585. Man must provide a sufficient dinner and pay 6s. 8d.

MSS., 10,407, Brit. Mus. York Silkweavers, November 5, 1611. Fee 3s. 4d. brotherhood money, and 6s. 8d. to the charges of the company.

MSS. 33,853, Brit. Mus. York Bakers. Fee 20s., besides all other accustomed charges.

Clode, *op. cit.*, p. 546. Crt. Mins., March 2, 1611. John Horsley gave a gilt spoon, weighing 1½ oz., "as a token of his love and thankfulness for the said freedome."

Cf. Ferguson, Kendal, p. 118. Boke off Recorde, September 17, 1579.

[2] MSS. Oxford, Mercers' Book, c. 1572.

of admittance, it is obvious that one result of relying upon the gilds for the enforcement of the Act was to give them an opportunity to pursue their own interests, and, consequently, that there was a perpetuation of a considerable number of local variations in place of that national uniformity which it was the object of the Act to introduce.

Numerous rules on all matters connected with the domestic life of apprentices were made during this period. It is, however, unnecessary to consider them in detail, for they are practically identical with the earlier ordinances, which have already been described. The Statute did not make, nor was it intended to make, any change in the daily life of apprentices. The common round went on as before, and it is not, therefore, the domestic side of the picture which is of interest, but rather all those questions which are concerned with the administration of the Act. The want of administrative machinery is the crux of the matter. It led to the early ineffectiveness of the Act, and the Government's dependence on the gilds, a dependence which, as we have seen, gave an opportunity to the companies to establish their monopolies, one result of which was that the Elizabethan apprenticeship system was not the apprenticeship system of the Statute of Artificers, but of the Statute as interpreted by the gilds. This is a difference the significance of which will be obvious if we remember that the limitation of the number of apprentices, patrimony, and premiums, all of which are vital parts of the apprenticeship system, are not mentioned in the Statute of Artificers. The chief point of interest for us is how gild monopoly affected juvenile employment. There can be little doubt that if the Government had itself been able to administer the Statute more children would have benefited by the State regulation of labour, for the gild limitation of numbers must have closed the door of training and protection in the face of many, who would be obliged to occupy themselves, therefore, in unregulated fields of work. Still, it has to be admitted that it was just because their narrow apprenticeship rules were openly or tacitly sanctioned, that the companies were willing to champion apprenticeship, even to the extent of bearing the chief brunt in legal proceedings against unlawful workmen. From the child's point of view this vigilance was important, for it meant that he did not serve his seven years only to find himself thrown aside, forestalled by men who had not undergone the burden of training. On the contrary, his after career was practically secure. Thus the narrow policy of the gilds was not without its value.

CHAPTER V

CHILDREN IN UNSKILLED LABOUR

IN any branch of English industrial history, and in an account of apprenticeship especially, much must necessarily be said of the gildsmen, their organisation of trade, and their bye-laws, which are concerned almost entirely with adult skilled labour and the training of skilled craftsmen for the future. Indeed, if we read no further than the gild records, the impression given would be one of a male working world, so well ordered as to be spared the miseries of our own, peopled by skilled men, most of them their own masters, working harmoniously together, without competition, each sure of his job; and with them working the boys and youths who were to succeed them, all duly bound as apprentices, so that they were sure of care in their youth, and of a training which would enable them to command a livelihood when launched in life. But, as a matter of fact, the workshop and the market were never the monopoly of the male adult. Poverty sometimes, shortage of labour perhaps, or natural ability for business, must have driven or called women from their homes, for they took a large share in the skilled trades, and even in rougher manual labour. Children, too, were employed, not merely to learn their trades as apprentices, but unapprenticed also, for directly commercial reasons, because their labour was available and was cheap. Further, many of the problems of the labour market, which are sometimes thought to be of modern date, existed even in the best days of apprenticeship and gild control. There was misuse of unprotected labour—that, namely, of women and children; there was a tale of unskilled men attached to most trades;

competition and unemployment were not unknown; [1] and there was frequent ill-adjustment of the supply of labour to the needs of particular trades. These difficulties were kept in check, it is true, by the minute regulations of the gilds and the Statute of Artificers ; both compulsory training and the craft rules tended to limit the number of workmen, and thereby prevented over-crowding in the skilled trades ; both, too, secured to the young workers generally fair treatment and thorough instruction. Yet even in the handicrafts conditions were not perfect either for adult or juvenile labour. Complaints of unemployment suggest that not all those who underwent the burden of seven years' apprenticeship were sure of commanding a living ; some of the men engaged in skilled trades were unskilled, and some of the children who worked were not apprenticed, while even master craftsmen worked under what to-day would be considered bad conditions. And, after all, compulsory apprenticeship and gild control were limited to the skilled trades. Outside the sphere of the Statute of Artificers and the gilds there was a vast array of low skilled and unskilled labourers who had to take their chance of unemployment and competition, while the children who worked with them could look to no authority to supervise their welfare. These children received no systematic training, such as was afforded by apprenticeship, but passed haphazard through the difficult years of youth into the working world. It is most important to remember their existence, for they probably formed a very large proportion of our juvenile workers. Their number can be only dimly conjectured by noting the various forms of unskilled labour and the apparent preponderance of low-grade workmen over finished craftsmen.

It is sometimes thought that under the apprenticeship system the proportion of skilled to unskilled workmen was greater than at present, but it is doubtful whether this was ever the case. Unfortunately there is no census at this early

---

[1] As is shown by complaints of comparatively wealthy gilds. See also 1 R. III. c. 9, in which the misery and poverty of many artificers is complained of.

date, and there is a further difficulty in estimating the number
of skilled workmen owing to the fact that men engaged in
labourers' work, or in what would now be mere manual
labour, were sometimes organised into gilds. There was a
Woodmongers' Gild in London,[1] and at Norwich carters and
porters were included in the Grocers' Gild.[2] It may, however, be said with certainty that until the rapid development
of our manufactures in the late eighteenth century, a large
part of the population were engaged in the various low-
skilled branches of labour required by husbandry, then the
chief occupation of the nation. In addition to the mass of
agricultural labourers, there was in the skilled trades a certain
amount of unapprenticed low-grade labour. The plumber
and mason, and artificers in similar occupations, frequently
had their "mates," who helped them, and did the unskilled
jobs in the trade. They had official recognition in the
assessments of wages. In a Wiltshire assessment it was
ordered that every labourer who attended to serve a carpenter, freemason, roughmason, bricklayer, plumber, glasier,
carver, joiner, millwright, wheelwright, or plasterer, was to
have not above threepence daily, or sixpence if the engagement did not include meat and drink.[3] Such men may, of
course, have served their apprenticeship, and have been unable to pay the fees for free mastership, but it is significant
that the word "labourer" is used. In the printing trade the
order stood that only skilled men or apprentices were to be
employed, "save onely in the pulling off knots of mettle
hangeing at the end of letters when they are first cast, in
which work it shall be lawfull for every Master Founder to
imploy one boy onely that is not, nor hath been bound to
the trade of Founding letters."[4] Unskilled labour was per-

---

[1] Some Memorials of the Controversie with the Woodmongers, 669, f. 20.
Brit. Museum.

[2] MS. Mercers' Book, ii., Norwich. When in 1622 all Norwich trades were
divided into twelve great companies, the Grocers included rafemen, reed-sellers,
reeders, carters, and porters. Rules by Town Council for the Crafts, Aug. 17,
20 J. I. See Norwich Records, ii. p. 383.

[3] Rep. on MSS., vol. i., 1901, p. 165 (1603).

[4] Arber, Transcript Stationers' Records, iv. p. 535. Decree of Star Chamber,
July 11, 1637. Clause 30.

mitted in the silk manufacture. By an Act of Charles II. men, women, and children, if native subjects, though not apprentices, might be employed to turn the mill, tie threads, and double and wind silk, "as formerly."[1] It seems to have been generally accepted that if a trade could be shown to require unskilled labour, the company connected with it could license its use, notwithstanding the Statute. At the close of the seventeenth century the Sheffield Cutlers gave temporary permission to their members to employ any common labourer to assist them in grinding and hammering, "it being judged impossible otherwise for them to make scythes so cheap as they were made in other places."[2] The calico printers were therefore suggesting no innovation when, in 1777, they petitioned Parliament for a Bill to legalise the employment of labourers, since "the trade does not require that all the Men they employ should be brought up to it, common Labourers are sufficient; for there is a part of the Trade that good Workmen will not do."[3] There is no information as to the sources from which these labourers were drawn; in some cases they may have been men who had begun but never finished their apprenticeship, or who had served an apprenticeship to some trade but could not find the capital nor an opening to set up in it. These men would have to reckon as unskilled if they were driven to seek employment in a trade to which they had not served. Or they may have been husbandmen who were attracted into industry by hopes of better conditions. At any rate, the unskilled men in or connected with trades would have picked up their business casually. Such men, added to the number of labourers in agriculture, probably outnumbered the fully trained craftsmen.

Children entering these classes of work did so as a rule without any special training. Apprenticeship in agriculture was permitted by the Statute of Artificers, but it was not made compulsory, and was, apparently, seldom practised, for

[1] 13 & 14 Ch. II. c. 15.
[2] Leader, Sheffield Cutlers, i. p. 62, c. 1680.
[3] Coms. Jals., vol. 36, p. 194; cf. p. 504.

any indentures which exist are those of parish apprentices ; we hear nothing of the binding of ordinary children to agriculture. The fact that a large number of juvenile workers did not come within the scope of the Act goes some way to confute the idea which occasionally obtains, that during the days of apprenticeship young people worked solely in order to learn their trade, and under good conditions, and that the abuses of child labour, the employment of very young children at an early age, simply as a means of reducing working expenses, came in with the factory system. There is no doubt that, long before the days of factory labour, children were employed in agriculture and in all forms of trade as cheap labour ; they began to work at a very early age ; they worked long hours ; and a large number were so engaged, proportionately as many, probably, as in the factories. In the best trades and companies children were not taken as apprentices until the age of twelve or fourteen at the least, ages at which they may begin full-time work to-day. But indentures and enrolments show that in many trades they were taken as apprentices when under ten years old, even when those trades were organised into gilds. In the fields they began to work when fully as young ; the Act of 1389 forbids the apprenticeship to trades of boys and girls who had worked till twelve years old at agriculture.[1] At a later date casual mention of the early age at which children worked is frequently made by contemporary writers. It was said that in the blanket trade at Witney there were threescore blanketers employing one hundred and fifty looms, and " near 3,000 poor people, from children of eight years old to decrepit old age." [2] Arthur Young, writing in 1768, declared that in the weaving trade girls worked at fifteen or sixteen years old at spinning, and from seven or eight years old at rolling quills.[3] In Worcestershire children of seven years old were working at nail-making at the close of the eighteenth century,[4] and there is no reason to suppose that the condi-

[1] 12 R. II. c. 5 and 7 H. IV. c. 17.
[2] Plot, Natural History of Oxfordshire (1677).
[3] Six Weeks' Tour in the Southern Counties, p. 67, cf. p. 59.
[4] Nash, Hist. of Worcestershire (1799), ii., correc. and add., p. 57.

tions of work, including the employment of children, were in any way different at that date from what they had been a century earlier, since the Industrial Revolution had not touched the nail trade. In the Worcestershire needle trade children were apprenticed at seven years old, according to Nash, who wrote about 1799,[1] thirty years before machinery had begun to change the conditions of work in the trade.[2] Even when, by the rules of the gild, apprentices might not be taken before fourteen years old, it is probable that craftsmen could employ their own families at an earlier age, for it was a long-established custom to allow a man to employ his wife and children unapprenticed.[3] As to the hours of work, there were no special regulations for children, so that we may suppose that they worked as long as it was convenient to their elders to employ them, presumably during the adult working day, which was governed, roughly speaking, by the hours of daylight. There seems little doubt that over-work and work of an injurious nature were endured by children long before their work in factories. The following extract from the papers of the Sheffield Scissorsmiths, who were amongst the better class of workmen, shows what the young people sometimes had to suffer. " To all Xtian people &c Whereas great mischeifes and inconveniences have heretofore and dailie doe arise and accrue . . . by some of the professo^{rs} of the s^d trade or occupacon, who for hieres sake doe work both themselves, their apprentices, and servants most unreasonablie, both in respect of tyme and hard labour, whereby many of them become lame and in a little tyme whollie disenabled to follow their callings . . . neither we nor any of vs, nor any of our apprentices shall . . . duringe the terme of two whole yeares next ensuing . . . doe any manner of worke whatsoever belonginge to ye s^d trade before ye hower of six of the clocke in the morning, nor after the hower of eight of the clocke in the evening."[4] They must indeed have been

---

[1] Nash, *op. cit.*, ii. p. 404 n.
[2] Victoria County History, Worcestershire ii. p. 274.
[3] See p. 148.
[4] Leader, Sheffield Cutlers, i. p. 64. 1680.

working "unreasonablie" if a possible fourteen hours' day was considered as a reform.

The chances of after employment for juvenile workers in agriculture and in the skilled trades seem to have been fairly equal. The records of the poor law authorities show that husbandmen suffered at times from unemployment; and throughout the days of national apprenticeship there are complaints, sometimes in one trade, sometimes in another, that experienced craftsmen had not enough work to support them. The low skilled and casual labour which fringed the skilled trades probably suffered most from irregularity and lack of employment. But there was no great army of unemployed, and it may be supposed that the rising generation found a place, without great difficulty, in the ranks of adult labour.

No definite figures can be given for the number of children employed in the various trades and in agriculture. The enrolment books of some towns are preserved, and from them can be gathered the number of apprentices in those places, but there is no record as to the number of apprentices in the country as a whole. Nor, if there were, would it show the total amount of juvenile labour, since young people worked unapprenticed at agriculture, and, as we have seen, under certain conditions in trades. Sometimes a later writer gives a rough estimate of the number of children employed in some branch of work in a certain locality. It was said that there were 3,000 apprentices in the weaving and clothing trade in Worcestershire in 1575.[1] In Kidderminster alone in 1667 there were said to be 115 apprentices to 157 master weavers.[2] In 1772, 250 looms were being used in the Kidderminster carpet trade, and each loom was reported to have one weaver and one draw-boy.[3] Such estimates are, however, really of less value than the general fact that it was more natural than not that children should work. There was no compulsory school attendance to prevent their doing so; there was no

[1] V. C. H. Worcestershire, ii. p. 292.
[2] Burton, Kidderminster, p. 180.
[3] Nash, op. cit., ii. p. 42.

feeling that work was bad for them: the labour and poor laws of Elizabeth's time are imbued with the idea that children could and should work, while philanthropists of the late eighteenth century regarded it as a matter for congratulation when the inmates of a charitable home or school could maintain themselves as soon as they could crawl. Indeed, all the evidence is in favour of the belief that by far the greater number of children of the working classes began to work, not as independent wage-earners, perhaps, but as assistants, at an early age. Though they worked at home or in small shops, under conditions which were pleasanter, and possibly morally better, if quite as insanitary, the probability is that the number employed was proportionately as large as the number employed in the worst days of the factories, and that they began to work when fully as young. It is at any rate quite certain that the employment of large numbers of children at an early age was no innovation when, at the beginning of the nineteenth century, Owen and Peel took up the cause of the children and startled the nation with their revelations.

CHAPTER VI

THE EFFECTS OF THE CIVIL WAR ON APPRENTICESHIP

THE fortunes of apprenticeship during the Civil War but add
to the evidence that in this time of internal commotion the
industrial life of the country was paralysed. When corporate
towns were invested first by one side and then by the other,
when money was scarce, and to be wealthy was to court
assessment if not plunder, no development of trade could be
expected. This natural assumption is fully borne out by
those records which directly or indirectly relate to apprenticeship. They show that not only capital but workmen also
were diverted from the workshop to the army, and, secondly,
that the Statute of Artificers, upon which, after all, the whole
industrial system of the country rested, was very indifferently
observed. That trade and the crafts suffered seriously is
proved by the decrease in the number of journeymen and
apprentices enrolled. Young men who formerly would have
been engaged in some trade now joined the army, or if they
did not do so were at any rate disinclined to risk setting up
in business. Of this the records of Sheffield offer a startling
proof: there, until the outbreak of the war, men had been
taking up the freedom of the Cutlers' Company at the rate of
fifty or sixty a year; in 1642 three freemen were admitted;
in 1643 the number was twelve.[1] There is a corresponding
decrease in the number of apprentices enrolled at Oxford;
from sixty to eighty or ninety apprentices had been taken
annually during the personal government of Charles I.; [2] in
1644, the number fell to forty-eight, and in the next year only

[1] Leader, Hallamshire Cutlers, p. 41.
[2] Oxford MSS., Hanaster Books in Town Hall.

forty-four were admitted. At Bristol there was a similar falling off in numbers, there being in the years 1643, 1644, and 1645 about one hundred fewer enrolments a year than the average number in preceding years.[1] The records of Norwich[2] and Sheffield[3] tell a like story. It may be suggested in passing that this reduction in the number of enrolments, marked as it is, does not show the full extent of the disorganisation. Where the enrolments are detailed, as at Bristol and Oxford, in which cities mention was regularly made of the parents' professions, we find that in a far greater number of cases than usual the fathers are entered as dead.[4] Thus there seems reason to suppose that even of the fewer boys apprenticed some were bound for motives other than industrial. Preoccupied guardians and anxious mothers naturally accepted the one form of training and education which was open to the mass of the middle class, and apprenticed the lads whom the war had left fatherless, mainly in order to keep them under proper control.

Not only was the supply of labour reduced by the entrance into industry of fewer lads and men than usual, but many of those who were already bound left their masters' service to enlist.[5] From all accounts, the latter received no redress for this desertion, and indeed the leaders on both sides seem to have encouraged apprentices to leave their various employments. In 1643 Mr. Sergeant Wilde and Mr. Nichols were appointed by the House of Commons to prepare an ordinance granting an indemnity to such watermen as entered the service of the Parliament, and promising that apprentices

---

[1] Bristol MSS., Enrolt. Bks., 1626–1640.

[2] Norwich MSS., Enrolt. Bk., 1625–1640. From 30 to 80 was the ordinary number of apprentices. 1643, 21 were bound ; 1648–1650, 19 a year.

[3] Leader, *op. cit.*, p. 41. 1638, 38 apprentices enrolled ; 1641, 49 ; 1642, 7 ; 1643, 11 ; 1648, 9.

[4] Bristol MSS., Enrolts., 1645. Number of enrolts. examined, 49 ; number of fathers dead, 26.

Oxford MSS., Enrolts., 1647, 36 yeomen's sons apprenticed, 17 of the fathers are dead.

[5] S. P. D., Ch. I., ccecliii., 33 & 43.

Rep. on MSS., i. p. 114.

Surtees, Merch. Adven., Newcastle, p. 141. Mins., July 2, 1646.

who enlisted, even without their masters' permission, should be regarded as serving their time, and allowed to work on their own account with no more delay than if they had served an unbroken apprenticeship. It was said that "whereas, in times of common danger and necessity, the interest of private persons ought to give way to the public, it is ordered and decreed by the Lords and Commons in Parliament that such apprentices unto watermen plying and rowing upon the river of Thames, as have been or shall be listed to serve as soldiers for the defence of the Protestant religion and liberty of the kingdom, his Majesty's regal person, the Parliament, and the City of London, under the command of Sir William Waller, their sureties and such as stand engaged for them, shall be secured against their masters their executors and administrators, from all loss and inconveniency by forfeiture of bonds, covenants, and enfranchisements, or otherwise ; and that after this public service ended, the master of such apprentices shall be commanded and required to receive them again into their service, without imposing any punishment, loss or prejudice for their absence in the defence of the Commonwealth."[1]   If lads were to be encouraged to quit their masters, it was clearly not to the latter's interest to take apprentices according to the Statute, and this is one reason for believing that the Act was not observed.   The inability of masters to exact due service, or to maintain orderly behaviour amongst the boys,[2] must have been a distinct discouragement to them to comply with the Act.

Nor was one man likely to serve his seven years and to observe all those clauses of the Act which related to the qualifications of apprentices, when his neighbour broke them with impunity. Before the war it was the minute supervision of towns and gilds, and constant watchfulness on the part of the Privy Council and justices, which alone had ensured any conformity with the law. Now that the country was in a state of civil commotion, this paternal control could

[1] Humpherus, Watermen, i. p. 246. Mins., Sept. 12, 1643.
[2] There is a good deal of complaint of rioting among apprentices during the war. S. P. D., Ch. I., cccliii. 96 ; cccliv. 33 & 43. S. P. D., 1650, 61.

be no longer exercised, and illegal trading, which had caused complaint and annoyance even during the personal government of Charles I., now increased apace.[1] Probably the wrongdoers escaped the natural hostility of gildsmen in the confusion of the time, while the Privy Council and justices were practically non-existent. At any rate, the system of search broke down. The writer of an interesting pamphlet on the woollen trade declares that it had fallen into disuse not only in market towns and in the country, but also in corporate towns.[2] In a similar complaint a few years later, it is said that " in Villages and out of Corporations there are no such officers [searchers] established, because nobody takes upon him to present fit persons (qualified to these Services) to the Justices of the Peace, who are by the Law appointed to administer the oath nor are any such Persons forward to seek Imployment because the Sallary is very small and the work lies scattered and despised and will not acquite his paines and charge who shall undertake the same." [3]

These and other complaints concern themselves mainly with the disrepute into which the trade had fallen owing to lack of supervision, and the " deceipts " which had sprung up within it to the nation's discredit. But if the system of search failed upon one side, it would certainly have also failed to regulate the binding of apprentices and their proper instruction. Indeed, in the " Golden Fleece " it is expressly stated that "the want of instruction and teaching in clothing is the principall cause that the Manufactures of wooll are so abusively and deceptiously made ; and teaching is thus wanting because there is no regular or legall course followed, either for time or form in working; there is not any of the relations to clothing which doth observe this rule of appren-

---

[1] Clode, Mems. Merchant Tailors. Appeal of poor working tailors against free traders. 1649.

Jupp, Carpenters, p, 309. Petition, 1653.

Rep. MSS., vol. i. (1901), p. 114.

[2] W. S., Golden Fleece (1656), p. 91. Quoted by Cunningham, *op. cit.*, ii. p. 311.

[3] Essay for Recovery of Trade (1661), p. 7., *cf.* S. P. D., 1651, xvi. 139.

Burton, Kidderminster, p. 175. Ordins., 1650, 14.

ticeship notwithstanding it is enjoyed in very strict and penall manner by the Statute Lawes." [1]

The woollen trade was perhaps one into which illegalities could most easily creep, because it was diffused throughout the countryside, but even trades concentrated in towns, under the control of gilds, did not escape disorganisation. So powerful a company as the Merchant Adventurers of Newcastle could not enforce their authority. They allowed their bye-laws to be set aside, "considering the distracted times," [2] and the company could not keep its accustomed courts [3] at which all business was conducted, whether the enrolling of apprentices, or inquiring into their qualifications and punishing offenders. The worst period was whilst the Scotch army was in occupation of the city ; and though there was a revival of the old duties when Newcastle was evacuated, both here and elsewhere it required some years of quiet government before the old order could be re-introduced.

[1] W. S., Golden Fleece, pp. 72, 73.
[2] Surtees, Merch. Adven., p. 139.   Mins., Feb. 19, 1646.
[3] Ibid., p. 130.   Oct. 15, 1641.

CHAPTER VII

THAT collapse of the apprenticeship system which first became noticeable about 1645 was temporary only. It had been occasioned not by any widespread aversion to the principles of the Statute of Artificers, but by the utter impossibility of enforcing its provisions in a time of civil commotion. This being so, no objection was made by the Governments of the Commonwealth and the Restoration to the resumption by the gilds of their old activities, the chief of which was now, as heretofore, the enforcement of apprenticeship. Opposition to restrictions on a man's industrial freedom was undoubtedly growing, but it was not yet organised nor universal. There was still a very general belief that if the industry of the country were to prosper, it must be controlled, and consequently public opinion still supported the Elizabethan system of apprenticeship, which made for efficiency and order in trade, and was the basis of the strength of the gilds, those unpaid police of the industrial world.

During the Commonwealth and the early years of the Restoration the history of apprenticeship was one of a struggle for recovery. The disorganisation of the central government and of municipal life during the Civil War had made it easy for men to practise trades to which they had never been bound. Naturally enough, younger men felt little respect for an Act which they saw openly violated, and the gilds, on resuming their activities, had a heavy task in re-enforcing its observance, a task which in all probability was increased on the final cessation of war by the discharge of soldiers, many of whom aspired to industry.[1]

The companies were driven to act, not merely because the law was broken, and their privileges infringed, but also because there was a very real distress among the industrial population owing to the overstocking of various trades. For example, the Ancient Weavers of Westbury complain, that whereas by the former good laws of their trade, no one could exercise the same until he had served an apprenticeship for seven years, and attained the age of twenty-four, now in these disordered times, many apprentices having forsaken parents and masters under colour of following the wars, the wars being ended, refuse to serve out their time, but before they are eighteen or twenty years old betake themselves to marriage or the gaining of a loom's work for themselves, whereby the ancient weavers are often without work.[2]

The Merchant Tailors of London complained in 1649 that their trade was overrun with foreign workmen and free traders, who worked sometimes under nominal apprenticeships and sometimes without any qualification, at lower wages, to their prejudice.[3] It was said that "foreigners" were kept as household servants though really employed as tailors. The working tailors begged that no one should be employed until he had shown his papers of freemanship to his employer. They urged, also, that the informers appointed by the Company should be called to account as so little good

---

[1] An apprentice, having been for some years from his master, is ordered to bring a certificate from "some commission officer's hand" in the army stating that he had been in the State's service. Otherwise not to receive his freedom. Surtees, Merch. Adven., Newcastle, p. 191. Mins., March 3, 1658; ibid., p. 141, Mins., July 2, 1646; ibid., p. 206, April 15, 1663.

Apprentice who has served under Monk given permission to find a new master and finish his term.

North Riding Quarter Sessions, vol. v. p. 119.

"The tyme Percivall Trewhitt, a shoemaker served as a soldier in the Parliament's service to be allowed him in the time of his apprenticeship, as if he had continued with his master."

[2] Report MSS., vol. i., Miscel., p. 114.

[3] Clode, Mems. Merch. Taylors, p. 24.

appeared to result to the trade from their employment.[1]
Prosecutions were undertaken by the company, and the
Common Council of the City was called upon to expel all
foreign tailors from the houses of citizens.   Apparently there
was little improvement, for two years later the complaints
were renewed.   The company revived the committee for
prosecutions which had been appointed in 1649, though the
Master told the petitioners " that in regard so little fruit hath
arisen, notwithstanding the expence of about 100l. in prosecution of suites against fforeyners tailors, and in charge of the
Committee sitting, the Company hath very little or no
encouragement to continue the said Committee." [2]

In the Goldsmiths' Company matters were almost as
bad.   In April, 1653, the Wardens and some of the committee were instructed to advise with the Recorder and
other counsel concerning the suppression of strangers ; [3]
in October a petition was presented to the Court of
Assistants complaining of the encroachment of alien
strangers who worked privately, and who, it was said,
were so numerous that they had taken upon them, " under
the pretence of religion, a liberty of conscience to petition
the Parliament for a toleration of free trade, to the
general ruin of the freemen of London."   At the request
of the petitioners several men were appointed to expel
the aliens,[4] the company paying expenses.[5]   There are
similar complaints from other trades.[6]   The gilds sought
to remedy these various grievances by enforcing the legal
method of entry into trade, a seven years' apprenticeship.

[1] Clode, Mems. Merch. Taylors, p. 26.
[2] Ibid., p. 27.
[3] Prideaux, Goldsmiths, ii. 35.
[4] Ibid., p. 46.
[5] Ibid., p. 56.
[6] Burton, Kidderminster, p. 175.   Rule 14, 1650.
Surtees, Newcastle Advens., p. 162.   Trade not sufficient to support the
great number.   Mins., July 21, 1650.
Prideaux, Goldsmiths, ii. 29.   Mins., July 28, 1653.
Jupp, Carpenters, p. 309.   Petitn., 1653.
Overall, Clockmakers, p. 63.   Petitn., 1656.   Ibid., p. 151.
Ferguson, Carlisle, p. 104.   Merch. Gild, Rule 23, 1656.

They re-enacted their bye-laws as to the admittance of members and the registration of apprentices,[1] and careful inquiries seem to have been made by their officers into the antecedents of claimants for admission.[2]

Under Charles II. a very large number of gilds, or companies, as they were now more commonly called, passed or re-enacted bye-laws dealing with apprenticeship. Men were forbidden to trade or to work as journeymen unless they had served seven years as apprentices.[3] "And likewise," ran the rule of the Hull Weavers, "that noe Person exercising the Trade of a Weaver not having served Seaven years as an Apprentice to the said Art or Occupation, and not free Burgesses as aforesaid, and free of their company, shall keep any Shopp or sett up Loom, or work in his own or another man's Loom, or any other work about the said Trade within this town, or the Liberty's thereof, upon Pain of Tenn Pounds, to be paid for every week he soe offends, and so after rate for more or lesse time." [4]

The rule that only members of the company might

[1] Burton, Kidderminster, p. 175. Weavers' Rules, 1650.
Ibid., p. 174. Smiths, tailors, shoemakers, Rule 5.
Ferguson, Carlisle, p. 99. Merch. Gild, 1656.
Holmes, Pontefract, p. 368. Butchers' Rules, 1652.
Sellers, Eastland Company, p. 77. Court Mins., Feb. 27, 1655.
Ferguson, Kendal, p. 185, Pewterers. Ibid., p. 196, Weavers.

[2] See p. 111, note 2.
Surtees, Merch. Adven., p. 137.

[3] Ferguson, Kendal, p. 194. Joiners' Rules, 28 Ch. II. Ibid., pp. 188, 197.
Rules, Pewterers, and Weavers.
Lambert, Two Thousand Years, p. 343. Hull Shipwrights' Rules, 1682.
Ibid., p. 363. Surgeons', Perukemakers' Rules, 1714.
Arber, Stationers, i. pp. 5, 167.
Williams, Norwich Barbers, pp. 8, 9. Rules, 1684.
MSS. Norwich. Mercers' Rules, 1688.
Needlemakers, p. 23. Charter, 1664.
Holmes, Pontefract, p. 368. Butchers' Rules, 1652.
Watermen, Constns. of the Company, 1708, p. 22.
Scott, Wheelwrights, p. 13. Charter, 1670.
Rochester, p. 35, Appen. Rules, 1673.
One or two companies insisted upon more than seven years' service, while longer terms were sometimes voluntarily served. See pp. 139, 166.

[4] Lambert, op. cit., p. 210. Rules, 1673.

use the trade was of course re-enacted, and the enrolment of indentures within a reasonable period, and the payment of fees to the court for the same, were insisted upon now as ever.[1] Now, too, as formerly, men had to take up the freedom of the town before they could practise their trades.[2]

The question is, of course, how far these rules were enforced. The court books of the gilds show that attempts were made to punish offenders against these bye-laws,[3]

[1] Brit. Mus., Add. MS., 27,462. Sandwich enrolts., 1661.

Surtees, Hostmen, p. 87. Indentures of apprentices to be publicly read in court, 1646. Ibid., p. 163. Mins., April 27, 1655.

Lambert, *op. cit.*, 244. Tailors' Rules, 1680.

Ibid., p. 296. Coopers, 1681.

Ibid., p. 346. Shipwrights, 1682.

Surtees, Merch. Adven., i. p. 163. Mins., 1650. Apprentices on trial.

Cf. transcripts of rules, &c., all of this period.

Ferguson, Carlisle, pp. 101, 128, 212.

Ferguson, Kendal, p. 204.

Clode, Mems. Merch. Taylors, p. 240.

Glass sellers, p. 124.

Holmes, Pontefract, p. 372.

Scott, Wheelwrights, pp. 58, 59.

Williams, Barber Surgeons, Norwich, 1684.

Rochester, p. 63, App.

Toulmin Smith, p. 209.

Dowling, Poulterers, p. 36.

Nottingham, Stevenson and Baker, v. p. 387.

Watermen, Constns. of the Company, pp. 22, 26.

[2] Lambert, *op cit.*, p. 244. Rule 5, 1680.

Ibid., 34, Shipwrights. Rule 4, 1682.

Ibid., 361, Barber Surgeons. Rule 5, 1714.

Ibid., 210, Weavers. Rule 4.

Holmes, Pontefract, p. 368, Bk. of Entries, Butchers, 1652.

Surtees, Merch. Adven., p. 182, Oct. 13, 1654.

[3] Addit. MSS., 27,462, Sandwich Clothworkers. Aug. 6, 1655, men fined. June 4, 1656. Complaints laid.

Surtees, Hostmen, p. 153. Mins., 1692. Apprentice has done no service to his master. Freedom refused him unless he becomes new bound.

Ibid., p. 160. Mins., Feb. 14, 1702 ; Apr. 14, 1703 ; Nov. 18, 1702.

Ibid., p. 164. Mins., 1704. Master has not a visible colliery, therefore apprentice not to be bound.

Surtees, Merch. Adven., p. 199. Mins., 1660. Ibid., p. 248, Mins., 1711. Man has served only three years and has kept a tavern. The freedom is refused him.

Ibid., ibid. Mins., June 6, 1711. Complaint of an apprentice who, though he has two years to serve, has been married and kept open shop.

while the work of the gilds on other sides, such as the regulation of turnovers and the supervision of the private relations of master and apprentice, suggests that the officers were no longer inactive.

It is probable, however, that the gilds were not really strong enough to enforce their rules. For one thing, their system of search was less vigorous now, so that offenders could not have been brought to book as in the days of the early Stuarts. Moreover, they had no longer the active support of the Crown. Charles II. confirmed numbers of charters, but in all probability he did so mainly because the confirmation of a charter had a financial value. Certainly he did nothing further to help the gilds, though his policy being one of non-interference, he did not stand in their way, but left them free to do what they could. The officers of the Crown, the quarter session judges, and the justices of the peace enforced the Statute of Artificers in the course of their work. But there was no longer a powerful Privy Council to institute those commissions of inquiry which we know had been necessary in the old days in order to keep the justices up to the mark. In short, the gilds were countenanced by the magistrates, but they received little active assistance. Typical of this is the issue of warrants by the Essex magistrates requiring the Wardens of the Coggeshall Weavers and the constables of the town to prosecute all intruders into the trade and offenders against the orders.[1]

While the gilds now had less support from the central Government, there is no doubt that the task of enforcing apprenticeship was harder than it had ever been before owing to the increasing numbers of those who set up in trade without having been bound. The companies had suffered in earlier days from the intrusion of unqualified workmen, but, save in the exceptional years of the war, they had been able to cope more or less successfully with the law-breakers. From 1660 onwards the gilds slowly but perceptibly began to lose ground in the fight. The nature and condition of the struggle had changed. In the old days the

[1] Beaumont, Hist. of Coggeshall, p. 190, 1664.

minute supervision which they exercised, and the enforcement of the Statute of Artificers, were regarded as indispensable to the well-being of the industrial life of the country. The Crown therefore actively supported the gilds, so too did the municipalities, while public opinion throughout the country was on their side. Consequently illegal workmen practised their trades secretly, and at risk of immediate prosecution. In the Restoration period the belief in the value of minute regulation of trade was declining. Dr. Cunningham has pointed out that the Government "abandoned the attempt to exercise an effective supervision over the quality of goods," and that "maintenance of quality, as well as the terms of prices, were henceforth left to be determined by the action of skilled wholesale buyers."[1] There was now open criticism of the older methods, which were still the methods of the gilds and the Statute of Artificers. Nothing illustrates the change better than the fact that illegal workmen complained of the companies as much as the latter did of them, and that freedom of trade was championed publicly by pamphleteers and writers.[2] Open, too, was the practical defiance of the law. Irregular workmen no longer hid away "in chambres," but kept open shop. They held that they were entitled to earn their living as best they could. Mr. Ogle, of Newcastle, who was forbidden by the Merchant Adventurers to sell figs, answered in a manner typical of their spirit, that "if he could make profit he would not onely sell figgs but sugar allso, and that after the figgs he had were sold he would order to London for twenty barralls more."[3]

The stronghold of illegal tradesmen lay in the rural districts, but they ventured into every town and trade, as is

[1] Growth of English Industry, ii. (1903), p. 203.
[2] Discourse of Motives for Enlargement and Freedom of Trade (1645), pp. 4, 44.
Propositions for Improving Manufactures, Agriculture, and Commerce (1763), p. 16.
Some Memorials of the Controversie with the Woodmongers, Brit. Mus., 669, f. 20, 1657.
[3] Surtees, Merch. Adven., p. 248. Mins., May 15, 1713.

apparent from the complaints of gildsmen and the minutes of their courts, as well as from the minutes of quarter, petty, and borough sessions.[1]

This struggle between the gilds and unapprenticed persons is similar to the conflict between the merchant companies and non-members, the "interlopers," who, disregarding the special privileges of the chartered companies, traded on their own account with foreign countries. The difficulties of the

[1] MSS. in charge of Town Clerk, Hertford.

"Present of Jury at ye Generall Sessions of the Peace for the Burrough. 11 Jan., 1675

"Wee p^resent John Holder of the said Burrough for ffollowing the trade of a Carpenter for a month last past not beeing ffree

"Wee p^resent Richard Broadbarke of the said Burrough for following the Trade of a Grocer for one month last past and not serving seven years of a Apprentiship

"We p^resent Beniamen Butt for following the trade of a Barber within this Burrough before his seven yeares of apprentiship is expired."

See also Addit. MSS., 6694, Brit. Mus., f. 96. Case of Mercers' Co., Derby, 1709.

MSS. Norwich, Munit. Room, Case X., Shelf B, Grocers' Bye-laws, 1688, 1698.

Surtees, vol. 93, Merch. Adven., p. 238. Mins., Sept. 20, 1693. P. 241, ibid. Mins., July 24, 1701. P. 248, ibid. Mins., July 10, 1705. P. 248, ibid. Mins., June 6, 1711.

Jupp, Carpenters, p. 278, Nov. 5, 1666.

Hamilton, Devon Quarter Sessions, p. 164.

Ballard, Chronicles of Woodstock, p. 29. May 2, 1704.

Cf. above, note 1, p. 111.

Hardy, Herts Quarter Session Records.

P. 109. Man presented for using the Dyers' trade, not having served an apprenticeship, 1655. Cf. pp. 119, 122, 125, 133, 155, 167; presentments of men for using trades illegally, 1657–1664. One had worked as a brewer for a year before he was prosecuted (155). Another, a yeoman, had worked as a grocer for eleven months.

P. 171. Information against a husbandmen for using the trade of a barber, 1665.

Other prosecutions, pp. 171, 183, 194, 202, 227 (1665–1672). Thornton, of Hitchen, worked for two years as a grocer before he was prosecuted, p. 183, 1666.

Ibid., vol. i. Indictments, pp. 235, 252, 254, 278, 294, 329, 373.

Ibid., vol. ii. pp. 2, 38, 56. Indictments of 1669, 1700 (labourer using the art of a clockmaker), 1707, 1721, respectively.

Cf. Coms. Jals., vol. xv,, p. 632. Petition of Master, Wardens, and assistants of the Company of Free Fishermen of the Thames. Many persons are using fishery not free of the company. Pray for Act to force fishermen to bind their apprentices, 1708.

merchant companies, however, began earlier : the Merchant Adventurers were first seriously troubled by the interlopers about 1610,[1] though the struggle was long continued, and came to a climax in 1643 and again in 1662.[2] The first African Company failed in 1618 owing to the successful competition of free traders ;[3] and the East India Company, though it had never altogether escaped their molestations, especially suffered in the Restoration period.[4] In the eighteenth century the conflict was at its height in the Turkey Company.[5] Thus the interloper was a foe to be reckoned with in foreign trade some time before he was a serious annoyance at home. In the end he won, both in commerce and industry, though in both he had a hard fight for it, and his victory was due not merely to his own efforts, but to the change in public opinion as to the respective merits of economic freedom and of regulation by means of privileged bodies. The resemblance between the "interlopers" in external and internal trade is perhaps most apparent in the struggle between shopkeepers and itinerant tradesmen. At the close of the seventeenth century there was a fierce outcry against pedlars and hawkers, or those who, on the plea of possessing hawkers' licences, ousted the lawful workman from his trade. The Grocers of Norwich complain that " many persons goe barely about wandering in the Streets and Markett place of this City with Grocery wares and small wares in theire hands and doe otherwhiles offer and putt the same to sale by Retaile in Basketts and Poakes and such like and sell theire wares

---

[1] Cunningham, Growth of English Industry, ii. p. 229.

[2] Ibid., p, 231.

[3] Ibid., pp. 272, 273.

[4] Ibid., p. 264.

Harl. MSS., 4139, f. 125. Case of E. Ind. Co. v. Sandys.

Cf. Coms. Jals., ix. p. 376. Coventry men v. E. Ind. Co.

[5] Propositions for Improving the Manufactures, Agriculture, and Commerce of Great Britain, 1763, p. 16.

Cunningham, op. cit., p. 253.

Cf. Coms. Jals., x. p. 456. Disputes with the Hamburg Co., 1695.

Ibid., xi. Disputes with the African Co., pp. 475, 525 (1695), pp. 616–617, 639 (1696).

disorderly upon Stalls, Trussells, Boards, Bulkes, and upon the ground to the great hindrance of Shopkeepers and Grocers that be freemen of this City."[1]   The London Glass-sellers petitioned for the suppression of pedlars. They pointed out that their trade, "they dealing in Commodities yt take up a great deale of Roome, oblidge them to hire great houses & sitt at great Rents," and that the competition of men who hawked their goods from door to door was palpably unfair.   It was said in 1691 that the chapmen had grown "so presumpteous as to cry and proffer both glasses and Earthing ware before the very dores and Shops of these that are legall sellers."[2]

As time went on and the feeling against economic restraints and monopolies increased, the gilds found it harder than ever to enforce the apprenticeship law and their own bye-rules.   Indeed, in the late seventeenth and early eighteenth centuries they seem to have found it sometimes well-nigh impossible.   It is noteworthy that the fines to which those who broke the rules were liable were often remitted, or were only nominally imposed, no attempt being made to

---

[1] MSS. Norwich, Munit. Room, Case X., Shelf B.

[2] Sloane MSS., 857, 80 (c. 1688).   Petition of the Glass-sellers.

Ibid., Case of the Glass sellers, c. 1691.

Cf. 816, m. 12 (12), Brit. Mus.   Further Reasons for Suppressing all Pedlars and Hawkers.   "It gives opportunity to such roving, unsettled and rapacious persons, some to abstain from settled work, and others to evade or wholly to neglect any Homes of their own; and instead of being at all useful to the Publick, they greatly discourage and disable those that are, and that have a right to Trade, by serving apprenticeships, to the utter ruine of their Families, and the desolation of the towns where they dwell, as is but too visible in many places."

Strype's Stow, 6th edition, 1755, ii. p. 560: "When I was treating of Tradesmen, I had forgot to mention the Nusances of the Town, the itinerant Pedlars, who deal in Toys and hard Ware, and those who pretend to sell foreign Silks, Linen, India Handkerchiefs, and other prohibited Goods: these we meet with at every Coffeehouse and Corner of Streets, and they visit also every private House."

Commons Jals., ix. pp. 328, 335, 336, 371.   Complaints, 1675.

Ibid., x. p. 736.   Petition of Poulterers, 1692.

Ibid., xxi. p. 447.   Petitions from Westminster, Halifax, Leeds, Preston, Skipton, Oxford, Shrewsbury, Tiverton, Bedford, Plymouth, Gloucester, &c., 1729.

collect them.[1] Public sympathy was with the offenders, and the probability is that they were often not informed against or presented for trial. The proceedings of the Hertfordshire Quarter Sessions are given with valuable fulness in the minutes, and we find that many a time a year or more could elapse before an illegal workman could be brought to book.[2] Further, the expenses of legal proceedings were heavy, and financial considerations hampered companies and corporations in their fight against the intruders.[3]   At Nottingham, the Common Council order "that a convenient number of persons in every ward shall be appointed to get what contributions they can for that purpose," namely, the suppression of all foreigners, and of all burgesses who had not served seven years.[4] The London Wheelwrights levied a special contribution towards legal expenses in 1676[5]; and in 1705 we find the Carlisle Shoemakers ordering that all who work at the trade, whether free masters or no, should "contribute proportionally to the charges of the suits begun or to be begun."[6]   But clearly the expense of a prosecution could not

[1] Leader, Sheffield Cutlers, ii. p. 17.

Ibid., i. p. 69. In 1685, freemen were supposed to be of three years' standing before they took apprentices. There are few inflictions of the fine for breaking the rule.

Brit. Mus. Addit. MSS., 27,462. Sandwich Mercers' Co. constantly sends for offenders who generally do not come. Much taken up with arranging collations, c. 1655.

Monk, Witney, p. 73.

[2] Hardy, Herts Quarter Sessions, p. 167. Man presented after using baker's trade for eleven months (1664).

Ibid., p. 183. Two men had illegally used trade of grocer at Hitchen for two years (1666).

Ibid., p. 202. Illegal brewer practised his trade for eleven months (1668).

[3] Brit. Mus., Add. MSS., 6694, f. 96, Case of Derby Mercers, 1709.

Welch, Pewterers, ii. p. 169. Mins., 1697.

Ballard, Woodstock, p. 29. 1704.

[4] Stevenson, Nottingham, v. p. 397. Mins. Com. Council, April 13, 1698.

[5] Scott, Wheelwrights, p. 55. Nov. 9, 1676.

[6] Ferguson, Carlisle, p. 188. Jan. 25, 1705.

Mar. 31, 1706. Two men to be elected to receive complaints; Jan. 24, 1793, agree to prosecute all persons not brothers of the gild "who shall make or presume to make any new shoes or boots or to translate old ones."

Cf. Leader, Hallamshire Cutlers, p. 63. 1698. "To Mr. Banks for suit charges occasioned by Jo. Thornley and Brounel, and Bailiff fees, £01 09 01."

always be afforded, and when this was so, the companies either had to leave the lawbreaker in unmerited peace or let him compound for admittance into the company, or pay an annual fee for the right to work. The Merchant Adventurers had considerable trouble with illegal traders at Newcastle.[1] Officers were appointed to seize the goods of such persons,[2] but the offenders did not readily submit. It was not only that they used annoyingly abusive language,[3] but they also took legal action against the company, which involved it in further expense. In 1676 the company agreed " that any Action or Suit att law commenced or hereafter shall be commenced against the Wardens " for certain seizures, " the expense thereof shall be paid by the Merchants' Company."[4] In June, 1726, a committee had been appointed to consider the whole question. There were said to be 114 persons who traded illegally in the town. The Committee reported that " knowing by experience that inditements are tedious and expensive this Committee does therefore humbly desire that the said offenders may be punished by a weekly assessment laid on them for the use and benefit of the poor." [5]

There is at this time an increasing amount of admittance by redemption, and it is worth suggesting that this was not due only and always to a greed of gain, but that, in some cases at any rate, the companies admitted redemptioners because they had not the money nor the power to undertake legal proceedings against them.

There was another reason why gilds and companies allowed unapprenticed persons to work either unmolested, or upon the payment of a small sum. Legal opinion was in the seventeenth century gradually becoming adverse to the Statute of Artificers. This hostility was based upon the dogma that liberty of trade was a natural and common law right, and the legal profession was always opposed to any law which was in restraint of " natural right." The courts could not alter the letter of the law, but they did very

---

[1] Surtees, Newcastle Adventurers, p. 138, Minutes.
[2] Ibid., pp. 31, 78, Rules ; pp. 139, 140, 144, 149, Minutes.
[3] Ibid., p. 254.   [4] Ibid., p. 253.   [5] Ibid., p. 253.

effectually change it in spirit and practice, by interpreting it as narrowly as possible.   As early as 1669 it was decided in a case brought before the King's Bench that the using of a trade in a country village was not within the Statute.[1]   In other words, apprenticeship was adjudged to be compulsory for townsmen only, and any one at all might practise a trade, or set up as large a business as he pleased, so long as he did not dwell within a town.   This decision did not prevent prosecutions from being undertaken against unapprenticed tradesmen in the villages ; suits were still brought against them, and penalties imposed.   But there was always the danger now that if an appeal were carried to the high courts, the decision would not necessarily be given against the law-breaker.   In yet another way the decisions of the courts aimed a blow at compulsory apprenticeship.   By the Statute of Artificers a man was legally qualified to use a trade only if he had been apprenticed to it for seven years.   The gilds had been allowed to admit members by redemption and patrimony, the rights of membership, of course, including the right to trade.   Now, by the verdict of the courts, the obligation of apprenticeship was set aside for those who had used a trade for seven years.   In 1698 it was decided that a boy who had served as an apprentice beyond the sea, but who had never been bound, was to be regarded as a lawful workman in his trade.[2]   In 1708 the verdict given in a similar case made it sufficient to follow a trade for seven years, without binding, or any pretence of apprenticeship, " this being a hard law." [3]   Apparently, if a man was presented as an illegal workman during the seven years, he would not be entitled to use his trade, but if he could successfully evade the law during the necessary period, he would be reckoned for ever after as a lawful workman.[4]

[1] I am much indebted to Mr. P. C. Hayman for kindly veryifying my legal references.

Modern Reports (1700), p. 26.   Rex v. Turnith.

[2] Salkeld's Reps., p. 67 (1698).

[3] Const. Laws Relating to the Poor, p. 589.   Reg. v. Maddox.

[4] Ibid., p. 590.   Waller v. Holton, 33 Geo. II.   Cf. Chitty, Law of Apprenticeship, p. 128.   Man served six years as apprentice and one as journeyman, and was said to be entitled to use the trade.

Men who, in the opinion of the courts, were entitled to practise a trade through having used it for seven years, are sometimes spoken of as holding that right by "apprenticeship by custom." This is a misleading term, for no apprenticeship was necessary; indeed, it seems to have made no difference whether a man worked at his trade as an acknowledged learner, or for part or the whole time as a master or wage-earning journeyman.

These decisions must have rendered the gilds more chary of attacking illegal workmen, for if the pressure of their own officers proved insufficient in forcing wrongdoers to conform to gild rules, the case would have to be taken before the justices of the peace or quarter sessions, from whom appeal might be made to the higher courts. And the higher courts were as likely as not to find for the defendants. The gilds realised that the loss of the case to them meant not only heavy expenses,[1] but a loss of prestige in face of which it was hard to enforce their authority. They were alive to the fact that the trend of legal opinion was against them, and they preferred to avoid defeat. The Newcastle Adventurers took counsel's advice as to the advisability of enforcing their bye-laws on the transfer and trading of apprentices.[2] At Kendal, Thomas Dalton, the Recorder in 1685 added a note to the bye-laws to the effect that "these laws and Constitutions although they are never so good and firm in law (quod plane dubito) yet I would not advise the Weavers to be too strict and severe with their elder brothers the Shearmen. Nor the Butchers with their younger Brothers coming out of the country for these remaining Bylaws meet with no favour in Westminster Hall and your own Moothall

---

(3 Keble 400) Lord Kenyon decided that a man who had served as clerk and porter to ironfounder for fifteen years, was entitled to his freedom, though he did not know how to make the commodity.

[1] Brit. Mus. Addit. MSS., 6694, f. 96, 1709.   Derby Mercers.

Clode, Mems. Merch. Tailors, p. 27.

[2] Surtees, Merch. Adven., p. 167.

Cf. Welch, Pewterers. ii. p. 171. Dec. 14, 1698–1699. "Spent . . . with severall members to consult how to obstruct M$_r$ Sandys from taking apprentice a ffrench youth naturalised 2l. 2s. od."

is altogether improper since no man is admitted to be judex in propria causa."[1]

The observance of the rule of apprenticeship suffered also through the declining zeal of the towns in administering it. In Elizabethan and early Stuart days the municipal authorities had themselves enforced it, and had refused to admit unapprenticed men as freemen save in certain exceptional cases. In the later seventeenth and early eighteenth centuries the attitude of the towns towards apprenticeship underwent a change. The records of the time show that there was a growing tendency to admit men to the freedom for a money payment, and this increasing admittance of redemptioners adversely affected the observance of apprenticeship. The extent to which this practice had developed is illustrated by the dispute between the Corporation of Hertford and some of the poorer citizens. In 1698 Joseph Tayler, a freeman, complained that the Mayor and Aldermen "have of late years taken upon themselves to grant and have as this Deponent hath been informed and Verily believes granted by divers Coppys or Instruments under the seal of the said Corporation to Several Persons inhabiting in places remote from the said Corporation and Parishes thereof the Libertie and priviledge of being Freemen."[2] This complaint apparently had no effect, for a few years later a petition signed by a number of freemen was presented to the Mayor. "Wee doe request and desire yo[u] that yo[u] make noemore Straingers freemen by redempcon o[r] that have not served out their times by Indentures duly. The nonobservance wherof hath and still doth impoverish the trade of that Towne. And greater detrim[t] may follow, for that therby our poore are much increased, our Right and privileges greatly obstructed, our Comons eaten up and

[1] Ferguson, Kendal, p. 206.

Cf. Ballard, Woodstock, p. 29. Dec. 16, 1723. Corporation agreed, "that advice be taken whether making ourselves a Company will keep out all traders that are not free of such Company, and if it is the opinion of Counsel that it will be effectual that proper methods be taken to procure such Charter at the Corp[n] charge."

[2] MSS. Hertford, xxv. p. 35. July 29, 1698.

distroyed by them whoe have noe Right, all which mischiefes
have falne upon us by reason those Orders and Constitucons
our forefathers have sett us have not beine followed and
pursued by yo", wch by yor oaths yo" are bound to mainteyn,
now in hopes yo" willnot denye us this our reasonable
request wch will be abundantly satisfactory to us and oblige
us yor truly loving neighbours and ffriends."[1] But the
prayer of the loving neighbours was all in vain ; in 1698 the
names of twenty-six persons are entered as " traders made
free that never were inhabitants in ye Borrough nor served
ther apprenticeships to freemen yt were Inhabitants." [2]
Another entry, about 1705 gives the names of twenty-six
more unqualified men.[3] In 1708 there is a list of twenty-
five.[4]

Greed of gain may have prompted the towns to admit
these redemptioners. The political sense of the country was
increasing during the seventeenth century, and as the desire
for the parliamentary vote increased the municipal freedom,
by which it could be gained, also rose in value. Boroughs
had therefore a tempting source of revenue open to them in
the sale of their freedoms.[5] But it is worth suggesting that
the real reason why the towns no longer enforced apprenticeship was because it had ceased to be of any great advantage
to themselves. It had been of use to the towns, because
they had made a general rule that no one should be granted
the municipal freedom unless he had been apprenticed to a

[1] MSS. Hertford, xxv. p. 37.   Undated.   Between entries 1698 and 1699.

[2] Ibid., p. 38.   Undated.   c. 1698.

[3] Ibid., p. 47.

[4] Ibid., p. 49.   May 4, 1708.

[5] In the notorious elections of 1773 at Northampton, the admittances were
doubled. In 1726 to 1727 the number of freemen admitted was 209. In 1733-1734
it was 452 (Northampton Records, Cox, ii. p. 317). Redemption fees varied in
different places and at different dates. It seems that each case might be considered on its merits, and the fee would then be placed as high as the claimant
for admission could bear.

Add. MSS., 27,462. Peter van de Brooker admitted, and paid, according to
the vote of the company, 50s. Aug. 6, 1666.

Holmes, Pontefract, p. 368, Booke of Entries, Butchers' Rules. Man must
pay 40s. to his company and 20s. to the Mayor for the borough franchise, and
make a dinner to the whole company.

freeman of the town, and had served actually within the town the freedom of which he was claiming. It is obvious that such a rule must limit the number of those who might share the municipal privileges, amongst which was the right to trade freely; in other words, it gave townsmen a close monopoly of their trade.[1] So long, therefore, as this rule could be enforced, they naturally enough favoured apprenticeship. In the late seventeenth century, however, the old bye-laws met with less unquestioning obedience from the general public, while legal opinion was definitely forming against them. Finally, in the case of Winton *v.* Wilks, it was decided that the custom was bad that no one should exercise a trade in a town except persons free of the Gilda Mercatoria there.[2] By common law, it was held, every man had liberty to trade, and there could be no restraint without

[1] Guilding, Reading Records, iii. p. 183. Feb. 11, 1645. " Francis Ward, glasier, apprentice in London, being a forreyner was forbidden to use his trade any longer in Reading."

Stevenson and Baker, Nottingham, v. p. 397. April 13, 1698. " Ordered that specyall care shalbee taken to prosecute and suppresse all forrainers from and for vseing any Trade within the said Towne, and alsoe all others who shall vse any Trade in the said towne vnto which they haue not served as an Apprentice within the said Towne, tho' he, or they be a Burges or Freeman of the said Towne."

Fox, Bristol Tailors, p. 21. Rules, 1662.

Lambert, *op. cit.*, p. 210. Rules, Weavers.

Rochester, p. 70, App. Rules, 1689.

Ferguson, Carlisle, p. 225. Glovers' Rules, 1780, repeat order of 1696.

Holmes, Pontefract, p. 372. Rules, 1664. No man dwelling within the borough who has not served as apprentice seven years in the borough may set up a trade unless he pays extra fees.

[2] *Cf.* Hobart's Reps., 5th edition, 1724, p. 210.

Norris *v.* Stapps, Pasch., 14 Jac., Rot. 907. This is an earlier case, interesting because it presages the future hostility of the law. Norris and Truffle, guardians, and the fellowship of the Weavers of Newbury brought an action of debt of 5 points against Stapps. They declared that Elizabeth had given them letters patent to the effect that none should practise weaving in that town unless first admitted a gild member, and that none should practise weaving unless he had been an apprentice in the said town for five years according to 19 Henry VII. The guardians showed that the defendant had used the art; had not been apprenticed; nor used the same art there five years before the ordinance; nor was admitted, &c. The defendant pleaded " nihil debet." Court found for plaintiffs, and yet judgment was given against them by reason of gross faults in declaration.

a consideration, because trade was a great benefit to the public. All persons were at liberty to live in Winchester, and therefore they could not be restrained from using a lawful means of living.[1] When the municipal authorities could no longer reserve the privileges of trade to native-born townsmen, apprenticeship, which had been the chief means employed for preserving their monopoly, was of little further interest to them. They could not overrule the ancient custom of admittance to the freedom by right of apprenticeship, and indeed they probably had no desire to do so, but it was hardly to be expected that they would go out of their way to enforce the Statute of Artificers.

It is open to question whether much of the revolt against apprenticeship in the late seventeenth and early eighteenth centuries was not really opposition to gild monopoly. When judged dispassionately, apprenticeship was still favourably regarded as an excellent means of training, even though it was no longer considered necessary to the prosperity of our industries. But the gilds rendered it unpopular; they preserved their privileges largely through its medium, thus causing a confusion between monopoly and apprenticeship, and, for their own purposes, they enforced rules which had nothing to do with the Elizabethan system. No doubt, they had always done so, but there is reason to believe that during this period they adopted a more exclusive policy, and were attempting to reserve their privileges to those who were already freemen, and to freemen's sons. There are various indications of this more jealous spirit. Outsiders were acceptable only when they paid heavily for admission, while some companies raised their fees even for members.[2] Others

---

[1] Salkeld, i. p. 203. Mayor of Winton v. Wilks. Tried by Chief Justice Holt, Easter Term, 1705.

[2] Or, what was the same thing, aspirants to the freedom were obliged to make gifts, or give dinners or breakfasts.

Holmes, Pontefract, p. 368, Bk. of Entries, 1852, Butchers. 3s. 4d. to the company and give a breakfast. Sons pay 3s. 4d. only. Ibid., p. 372. Wrights and Bowers. Breakfast and 2s.

Add. MSS., 27,462, Sandwich. Aug. 1, 1664. Man having served seven years to a member of the company, pays 3s. 4d. and gave 5s. towards the dinner.

introduced a new method of limiting numbers; in addition
to the old rules forbidding a man to take more than two or
three apprentices, certain gilds now insisted upon his having
traded as a free master for a definite period before he might
have a lad bound to him; the period varied in different companies.[1] Long terms, which had proved an effective check
on numbers in earlier days, were going out of fashion, and it
was hard to reimpose them; but some gildsmen adopted
the plan of obliging their apprentices to serve on after their
apprenticeship, as covenant servants or hireman, before they
were allowed to work as masters.[1] At Bristol it is quite
usual to find in the enrolments of indentures at the middle
of the seventeenth century, that the apprentice, besides
promising good and faithful service during his term, further
pledged himself to serve on for a certain period, sometimes
only a month, sometimes a year, for a wage it is true, but a
small one.[2]

Dowling, Poulterers, p. 40. Rules, 1692, 25. Fee, 2s. 6d. and a silver
spoon worth 13s. 4d.

Ferguson, Carlisle, p. 101. Merch. Gild, 1656. Sons admitted by patrimony
pay 3s. 4d. Apprentices, 6s. 8d.

Clode, Mems. Merch. Taylors, p. 240. Rules, 1661. Apprentices to be
admitted to the freedom with fee of 20s., 13s. 4d., 10s., and 6s. 8d., according
to their class.

Needlemakers, p. 31. Rules, 1664. 10s. to company.

Scott, Wheelwrights, p. 15. Rules, 1670. Fee, 13s. 4d. Some men gave
more, "for kindness." Feb. 9, 1681. "This day John Norriss who served
7 yeares with Mr. William Cradock and his widow, wass now made free and
paid 13s. 0d. admittance and promised to be as kind as others," p. 57.

[1] Such rules occasionally appear earlier, *e.g.*, Humpherus, Watermen, i. 214.
Rules, 1626, 9.

At a later date:

Burton, Kidderminster, p. 175. Weavers. Rule 14, 1650. Must have
traded one year.

Ferguson, Carlisle, 102. Merch. Gild, 1656, 16. Six months necessary.

Needlemakers, 31. Rules, 1664. Three years.

Scott, Wheelwrights, 58. Mins., July 5, 1683. Five years.

Humpherus, *op. cit.*, i. 284. Rules, 1662, 2. Five years and nine months.

Surtees, Hostmen, 133. Rules, 1669. Three years.

Lambert, Two Thousand Years, p. 346. Shipwrights, 1682, 15. Six months.

Leader, Sheffield Cutlers, i. p. 69. 1785. Three years customary.

[2] Bristol MSS. Enrolment Book, 1640-1658.

July 29, 1649, boy bound eight years and two months covenant; 5s. at the end.

It may be worth while to call attention to the fact that
a large proportion of cases brought before quarter sessions
were those against men dwelling in villages within easy
reach of a corporate town.   It seems as though the narrow
policy of the gilds at this time had an effect similar to that
occasioned by their oppressive policy at the close of the
fourteenth century.   Then workmen left the towns and set
up for themselves in the country, outside the sphere of gild
supervision, rather than submit to burdensome regulations.[1]
Migration from the towns in the eighteenth century may not
have been general, but some there certainly was.   Non-
freemen tailors who had been prosecuted by the Merchant
Tailors of Bath set up in surrounding villages, some in
Walcot and Bathwick, and even more in Lyncombe and
Widcombe.[2]   They came secretly into the city to take their
measurements and orders.   The clothes, when finished, were
smuggled into Bath, either at night, or by some person not
a tailor, by a woman under her cloak, or in a washerwoman's
basket.   Occasionally, these pirate tailors were discovered
and punished, but though they worked at some risk, they
apparently considered that immunity from oppressive rules
and fees was recompense enough.

We may fairly surmise that in other parts of the country
also there was migration from the towns, for everywhere
village tradesmen were prospering at the expense of workmen in adjacent towns.[3]   At any rate, it is only their pros-

April 27, 1654. Francis Robins, seven years and a covenant year ; 50s. at end.

Cf. May 16, 17, 22, 29, and June 1, 7, 1654. Wages vary from 20s. to 50s.

Cf. Thorold Rogers, Agriculture and Prices, iv. p. 98. In an indenture of
1451, the apprentice promises to serve one year as journeyman at 20s.

A similar practice had been in vogue at Carlisle. There the rule had been
that apprentices must be taken for seven years at least and the eighth year as
hiremen. But the compulsory hireman year was dropping out of use from 1662.
Ferguson, *op. cit.*, p. 146 ; p. 153, Tailors' rules ; p. 127, Weavers'.

[1] Cunningham, *op. cit.*, i. (1890), p. 395.

[2] Shickle, Merchant Tailors, p. 23, c. 1714 and onwards.

[3] To what extent there was a migration from the towns or growth of village
trade at their expense, can be discovered only by a minute study of individual
villages. Miss Maud Davies, who made such a study of the village of Corsley,
Wilts, found there was immigration of well-to-do townsmen to Corsley in the
reign of George I., and that from 1727 to 1760 this movement continued.

perity which can account for the number of prosecutions undertaken against them. Of course, this increase of trade in the villages may have been due to the settlement there of men who, in former times, would have paid for the municipal freedom and set up within the city, and who now, out of love for their pockets and their freedom, checked their movement townwards at some village on the outskirts. In other words, we have to consider not merely a possible migration from the towns, but also a cessation of the flow of fresh labour to them from the country. But whichever played the chief part, the result was the same: the towns suffered owing to the conservative spirit of their gildsmen.

Nevertheless the monopolistic policy of the gilds must not be exaggerated. No doubt their regulations and their claims to special privileges were regarded as oppressive by a large part of the population, but there is something to be said on the side of the gilds. The truth was, the Statute of Artificers, and the regulation of trade by petty agents, were definitely out of date, and had the gilds adopted the most generous of policies they would still have been increasingly unpopular. As it was, they were blind to the signs of the times, and knowing that, legally, they had not a bad case, they struggled to maintain their rights. It may be suggested that often enough the stricter rules which they adopted were not wholly due to a more jealous spirit, but were part of their honest attempt to carry on their duties in the face of new opposition and new difficulties. There was at the close of the seventeenth century a definite increase in the amount of colourable or false apprenticeship. Men frequently had lads bound to themselves, not because they had sufficient work upon which to employ them, nor because the trade required more hands, but because they intended to transfer them at a profit to some other master. From a record of the Newcastle Adventurers we can gather that now, as hitherto, such a transfer, or turnover, was a profitable transaction ; so much so, indeed, as to be a means of support to poor

Weaving was started, and other trades grew up to provide for the manufacturing population. (Life in an English Village, p. 34.)

brethren.   For instance, Oswald Mitford, being "an ancient
member and necessitous," was allowed to take an apprentice,
to set him over to a trading brother.[1]   Masters to whom the
lads were turned over might be in the same company, or in an
utterly different trade, and they took these apprentices and
were willing to pay a considerable price for them, because
they had already the maximum number of apprentices
allowed by their gilds.   Rules as to the limitation of apprentices could thus be evaded, which was a matter for congratulation to the individual master, but their gilds found that all
their attempts to ensure the fair employment of journeymen
and to prevent over-crowding were being rendered useless.
The Clockmakers complained that " for some years past there
hath been some restraint upon the Members of the Company
as to the time when they might first bind an apprentice, and
when a second, and so successively, and by reason thereof
divers Members have by secret shifts and undue means pro-
cured apprentices to be bound to other companies, and to be
turned over or committed to themselves contrary to the Company's Ordinances in that behalf, whereby this Company hath
been, is and will be much damaged, and a great increase made
of Artists or Clockmakers and Workers in the Art, which are
or will be freemen of these other companies to which they are
bound."[2]   The Cutlers of Sheffield complain that members
were taking apprentices with the intention of transferring
them "for love of a little present money."[3]   The gilds
attempted to check this abuse of turnover by stricter rules,
insisting upon the payment of a fee or fine to the company when any such transfer was made, or by forbidding
turnovers, without permission from the Warden.[4]   The New-

---

[1] Surtees, vol. 93, p. 198.   July 22, 1659.
    See Chapter II. p. 58.
[2] Overall, Clockmakers (p. 153) Co.'s Jrnl., Sept. 29, 1684.
[3] Leader, Sheffield Cutlers, i. p. 67 (1711).
[4] Dowling, Poulterers, p. 38.   Rule 23, 1692.   Fee, 2s. to company, 2s. to
clerk and beadle.
    Leader, op. cit., ii. p. 17.   1711.   Fee of £3., i. p. 67.
    Watermen, Constns. of, 1708, p. 24.   Rule 12.
    Lambert, Two Thousand Years, p. 281.   Bricklayers, 2, 1665.

castle Hostmen were driven to act by the discovery that one man had three turnovers in his employment, a fact which brought it home to them that, "there being noe restraint against takeing turnovers, . . . it gave great Incouragement to many frauds and ill practices in the Company."[1] The Clockmakers were so troubled by colourable bindings that they decided that prosecutions should be undertaken against all persons who bound their apprentices to other companies.[2]

Since turnover apprentices were not necessarily transferred to men in the same company, they did not by any means always learn the craft to which they had been bound. But there was no doubt they did actual work, for there would not otherwise have been any traffic in them. There was another class of apprentices whose binding was only colourable, but in their case work was more or less of a pretence. These young men had either wished to gain the freedom of one of the large companies because it was in itself a privilege and a dignity,[3] or, and these probably were the majority, they were bound to trades which they had no intention of learning, because apprenticeship entitled them to the municipal freedom, which in its turn gave them the parliamentary franchise. At Pontefract the Grocers were obliged to make a rule forbidding the Warden to make an apprentice free unless his master or mistress could vouch for his faithful service during seven years.[4]   In 1669 a petition was sent to the Warden of

Lambert, Two Thousand Years, p. 347.   Shipwrights, 18.   1682.
Ibid., 211.   Weavers, Rule 10, 1673.   Turnover forbidden.
Ferguson, Carlisle, p. 128.   Weavers' Ordinances, 1679.
"That no brother shall take an apprentice with intent to sell him again or make advantage thereof, or put him away under colour or pretence whereof the trade may be damnified upon pain of 20/."
Scott, Wheelwrights, p. 59.   No freeman to take a turnover without permission, 1683.
Toulmin Smith, English Guilds, p. 209.   Worcester Joiners' and Carpenters' Rules, 1793.   Penalty of £5 for taking an apprentice to sell him again.

[1] Surtees, Hostmen, p. 165.   March 16, 1703-1704.
[2] Overall, Clockmakers (p. 153) Company's Jnl., Jan. 16, 1681.
[3] Latimer, Merch. Advens., Bristol, p. 224.   Freedom to trade taken up by son of Sir John Hawkins, 1720.
[4] Pontefract, p. 379.   Ordins., 14, 1700.

the Hostmen's Company by several of the brethren pray-
ing that the freedom might be refused to various pretended
apprentices.   Attention having been thus drawn to the
matter, inquiries were made, and the Warden ordered that
the names of five apprentices should be expunged from
the books, unless cause were shown to the contrary on the
next court day.[1]   These were abuses of apprenticeship
which the gilds had every right to attack.

A second difficulty which at this time was presented to the
gilds was that of the overcrowding of the labour market.
Forced willy-nilly to admit, or tacitly license, workmen who
had never served apprenticeship, the gilds feared, rightly
or wrongly, lest there should not be work enough for all.
In earlier days they had attempted to protect their members
against unemployment by limiting the number of apprentices
which any one master might employ at a time, and in some
cases by insisting upon more than seven years' service.   Now,
in the face of this undesirable increase in the number of workmen, the gilds and companies set to work to invent new
methods of self-protection.   The old laws were continued,[2]
but in addition other methods were adopted.   The higher fees,
and the rule that masters must have been freemen for a
certain number of years before employing apprentices, may
perhaps be attributed in part to this attempt to prevent

---

[1] Surtees, Hostmen, p. 133.

[2] Needlemakers, p. 32.   Bye-laws, 1664.

Glass-sellers, p. 121.   Rules, 1664.

Case and proposals of the free journeymen printers in and about London,
1666.

Overall, Clockmakers, p. 153.   Nov. 6, 1676.

Welch, Pewterers, ii.   P. 152 : Court Mins., 1675.   April 8, committee
appointed ; May 20, rules recommended ; June 22, rules accepted.

Ferguson, Carlisle, p. 105.   Merch. Gld. Bk., ii., June 30, 1682.

Lambert, *op. cit.*, 313.   Hull Cobblers, 1680.

Ibid., 293.   Coopers, 12, 1681.

Ibid., 346.   Shipwrights' Rules, 15, 1682.

Dowling, Poulterers, p. 46.   Rule 34, 1692.

Norwich MSS., Case X., Shelf B.   Grocers' Rules, 9, 1688.

Ferguson, Kendal, p. 203.   Butchers, 34 Ch. II.

Ibid., p. 193.   Joiners Ch. II. (undated).

Ibid., p. 198.   Weavers, 34 Ch. II.

unemployment.   Some companies went further, and levied a
fine upon a master when he took an apprentice, even when he
had not exceeded the number allowed him by the ordinances
of the company.[1]   It is doubtful whether the gilds were always
strong enough to enforce these rules.   This last bye-law, at any
rate, seems to have been a dead letter in Sheffield, where the
fine was £5, but appears not to have been paid.   There are,
at all events, no entries of its payment in the books.[2]

How far there was actual reason to fear unemployment it
is difficult to say.   It is quite possible that there really was
some distress, and it may have been that the attempt to
keep down numbers was a policy forced upon the governors
of the gilds by the rank and file of their members.   It was
certainly not rich men's greed, but poor men's fears for their
employment, which prompted the efforts made from time to
time to check the admission of new members for money payments or by special privileges, practices which were favoured
by the governing class.   It was not to their interest to
promote rules such as that passed by the Eastland Company
in 1655, to the effect that " noe stranger be admitted into the
Societie by redemtion, but such as are rightly qualified and
produce a certificate thereof under ye hands of ye Depute
and ten brethren resident in the place of his abode or next
adjacent thereunto."[3]   The Kendal Pewterers had a rule forbidding the Warden to make any man free for any composition unless he had served seven years.[4]   In 1671 a rule was
passed by the Kidderminster Weavers on behalf of poor
journeymen.   Henceforth any weaver employing two apprentices must likewise employ two journeymen.[5]   Such a rule is

---

[1] Ferguson, Carlisle, p. 129, Weavers, 1685 ; ibid., p. 194, Shoemakers, 1780 ;
cf. ibid., 253, Butchers' Rule, £5, 1740 ; p. 261, £20, 1806.

[2] Leader, Sheffield Cutlers, i. pp. 69, 70.

[3] Sellers, Eastland Co., p. 77.   Crt. Bk., 1655.

[4] Ferguson, Kendal, p. 188.   Rules, 13 Ch. II. ; ibid., p. 204, Butchers
forbid admission by redemption.

Cf. Rochester, p. 70.   App. Rules, 1689.

Ferguson, Carlisle, pp. 99, 139.   Rules, 1656, 1691.

Surtees, Merch. Adven., p. 18.   1697.

[5] Burton, Kidderminster, p. 176.

Cf. Lambert, op. cit., 246.   Tailors, 1680.

suggestive of discontent and unemployment amongst the workmen, but not of cupidity nor any specially monopolistic spirit on the part of the ruler. There are, too, a few instances of the prohibition of patrimony; sons were not to be admitted unless they had served as apprentices.[1] This rule points to an honest effort on the part of its framers to keep down numbers, and is alien to the policy of reserving privileges to members and to members' sons.

The significant feature in the history of child labour during the period 1650 to 1720 is undoubtedly the increasing disregard for the Statute of Artificers, because this non-observance, though not yet by any means universal, is the first step in the breakdown of the apprenticeship system, in which was involved not merely juvenile training, but the regulation and protection of industrial child labour. There is, therefore, a really dramatic and national interest in the petty disputes between the gilds and those unqualified workmen who set the privileged bodies at defiance, and illegally practised their trades. As we have seen, the gilds were now almost alone in their efforts to enforce apprentice-ship; the Government no longer took a prominent part in the administration of the Act; the law courts were definitely opposed to it; and the municipal authorities were becoming indifferent to apprenticeship, as they found themselves unable to use it to their own advantage. The fate of child labour was consequently more dependent upon the fortunes of the gilds than it had hitherto been, and their struggles to maintain their power, though prompted often by narrow motives, have yet a national aspect. They were fighting for their own rights, it is true, but general issues were at stake: the difficult economic question was involved of how far employers should be free to reduce their expenses by replacing adult by juvenile labour; the protection of the child in his contract with his master now hung in the

---

[1] Needlemakers, p. 39. Rules, 1664. Men not to teach their sons unless they are bound.

Williams, Norwich Barber Surgeons. Rules, 1684. Masters must bind their sons, who will be counted as one of the apprentices allowed them.

balance. These questions were really answered at the close of this period. Apprenticeship was clearly losing ground, the more so, perhaps, because it was advocated almost entirely by the gilds, and apprenticeship and monopoly were thus confused in men's minds. Already, then, the conditions of child labour had entered upon a period of transition, and the regulation and protection afforded by apprenticeship were giving way to the greater freedom of the employer to utilise child labour as he chose, a freedom which is by no means synonymous with the freedom of the juvenile worker. It would be a mistake to suppose that the ultimate importance of the changes which were now in progress were recognised by contemporaries. The wider point of view can be gained only from a distance, and from the men of the seventeenth century it was concealed by the little events of every day. The punishment of lawbreakers, and even their victories, were but side-issues to the gildsmen, who carried on apprenticeship as before, and in whose opinions it was as important as ever. The changes which really impressed them were the increase in the amount of premiums, or the alterations in the fashions of dress and behaviour of their apprentices, with whom they quarrelled over the wearing of wigs. They carried on their routine work of binding boys and training them as busily as ever, but to give an account of it would be mere repetition. It is sufficient to say that, though changes were certainly in process, apprenticeship was still the national training ground for the army of industrial workers, and was still the greatest system of training and education for the working-class boy which this country has ever possessed.

CHAPTER VIII

THE SUPPLY OF INDUSTRIAL LABOUR

THE industrial labour market depended for its fresh supplies of labour almost entirely upon one source, the boys who at about fourteen years old joined the ranks of industry as apprentices. A certain number of girls were employed in our crafts and manufactures, and in spite of the vigilance of the gilds, some unapprenticed adults did slip in to the strict preserves of the skilled trades. But their combined numbers were insignificant as compared to that of the male apprentices.

The age at which boys enlisted in the industrial army was not quite uniform. In some companies there were definite rules as to the earliest or latest age at which they might be taken. In Carlisle no one was allowed to take an apprentice under fourteen years old;[1] the age of binding amongst the Newcastle Adventurers was sixteen,[2] while the London Watermen were forbidden by the Lord Mayor and Corporation to take any but young men of eighteen as apprentices,[3] the idea being that less responsible lads would endanger the lives of the public. In companies where such rules existed some sort of evidence had probably to be produced before the court would have consented to enrol the boy. At Newcastle, the Merchant Adventurers ordered, in 1645, that no indentures were to be enrolled until " there be a testimoniall produced from the minister of the parish where he [the apprentice] was borne, or two sufficient men there,

[1] Ferguson, Carlisle, p. 101, Merch. Gld. Bk., ii. 1656.
[2] Surtees, Newcastle Adven., p. 14.
   Cf. Surtees, Hostmen, p. 178. Fourteen years old 1708, raised to 15 in 1716.
[3] Humpherus, Watermen, i. p. 396. Rules, 1694.

that the party is sixteen yeares of age who is to be bound." [1]

In 1673 the company was obliged to alter this rule, which had proved useless because many apprentices were not baptized in a church, and there was therefore no record of their names on the register. A certificate from a justice of the peace was now substituted for the clergyman's testimonial; henceforth, no indenture was to be enrolled unless parents or friends took an oath before a magistrate as to the place, parish, county, and time where and when the apprentice was born, and the same was testified under the hand and seal of the justice. If during his term it were proved to be false the time the apprentice had served was of no effect. [2] Where there are no rules, we can gather incidentally, from indentures and enrolments, that fourteen was a very usual age at which to bind apprentices. But rules forbidding the apprenticeship of married men suggest that others than mere boys were sometimes apprenticed [3]; while boys under fourteen were undoubtedly taken ; in Sheffield the minimum age for cutlers' apprentices was twelve years. [4]

There were other qualifications besides that of age. For the most part they were the same qualifications as had been deemed necessary before the days of national apprenticeship, and, as was the case before 1562, they varied in different places or in different gilds. The most general requirements were those of native birth [5] and bachelorhood; [6] in some cases,

---

[1] Surtees, Merch. Adven., p. 13.

[2] Ibid., p. 14. Rules, 1673.

Ibid., p. 257. Oct. 29, 1735. Mr. Leighton has neither certificate of age nor estate of his apprentice, therefore he promised in court that he would not employ the boy.

Cf. Surtees, Hostmen, p. 178. Dec. 8, 1708. " It's ordered that for the future none be taken nor bound apprentices without Contract or oath of their being att least fourteen years of age before they are bound apprentices."

[3] See note 6.

[4] Leader, i. p. 46. In 1748 age was raised to 12.

[5] See Chapter II.

Dowling, Poulterers, p. 35. Rules, 1692.

Holme, Pontefract, p. 373. Rules, 1664, vi.

Prideaux, Goldsmiths, i. p. 105. Precept from the Lord Mayor commanding the wardens in the Queen's behalf to cause diligent search to be had that thence-

none but the sons of townsmen might be apprenticed.[1]   In others, we find that lads from certain districts were disqualified : boys from "beneth Blackford"[2] might not be apprenticed in Carlisle, nor those "beyond Irdin,"[3] districts in the fells and near Scotland.   The Newcastle Adventurers would not allow their members to take apprentices from Tyndale and Riddesdale until 1676, when the prohibition was removed, those parts of the country being admittedly "more civilised than formerly."[4]

Certain companies had rules peculiar to themselves.   The Musicians' Company in 1606 required an apprentice to be free-born, clean and whole of limb, a rule unusual at this date.[5]   In Kendal, children who could not read or write might not be bound apprentice[6]; and at Newcastle the Adventurers refused apprentices "not known to be well

forth no members of the company take any apprentice other than the child of an Englishman born within the Queen's dominions.

Ferguson, Carlisle, p. 184. Shoemakers' Rules, 1595.

Dumville Smythe, Girdlers, p. 133. Rules, c. 1600.

Clode, Mems. Merch. Tailors, p. 217. Rule 20, 1613.

Surtees, Hostmen, p. 153. 1696.

[6] Surtees, Merch. Adven., p. 28. Rules, 1575. No apprentice to marry before the expiraton of his term. Ibid., p. 194. Mins., Feb. 9, 1659.

John Bell, apprentice to Mr. William Rea, set over by order of court to Miss Susanna Blaxistone, left his mistress 4 months ago, married, having not then served 4 years and 8 months, was crossed off the books.

Cf. p. 139 (1646).

Surtees, Hostmen, p. 100. Apr. 27, 1655. Indentures of William Heath, apprentice, read, and prayed to be inrolled, but the court was informed he was a married man before he was bound apprentice, and therefore wholly rejected the same. *Cf.* pp. 153, 154, 192.

Latimer, Merch. Adven. (Bristol), p. 77. Rules, 1618.

Lambert, Two Thousand Years, p. 281. Bricklayers', &c., Rules, 1665. No person of the company shall take any married man as apprentice.

Humpherus, Watermen, i. p. 124. Rules, 1626. Ibid., ii. p. 148. Rules, 1733.

Ferguson, Carlisle, p. 215. Glovers' Rules, 1665. Ibid., p. 195. Shoemakers' Rules.

[1] Ibid., p. 225. Glovers' Rules, 1740. Repeats order of 1690. Apprentices taken out of the liberty of the city shall not be admitted or enrolled as brothers.

[2] Ferguson, *op. cit.*, p. 184. Shoemakers' Rules, 1595

[3] Ibid., p. 66, Dormont Bk., 1602. Rule 46.

[4] Surtees, vol. 93, pp. 27–29. Rules, 1554, 1676.

[5] Musicians, p. 61. Rule 12, 1606. *Cf.* Mercers, p. 86. Rules, 1504.

[6] Ferguson, Kendal, p. 164. Rules, 1641.

educated and of good conversation, and any base begotten." [1]
In 1676, the latter company, which had been troubled with
many thefts, ordered that no son of a man who had been
convicted of felony should be accepted as an apprentice.[2]
When the Quaker movement began stipulations as to
religion were added by some companies to their rules,
Quakers being expressly disqualified. Boys suspected of
unorthodoxy might not have their names enrolled. "Thomas
Turner, his indenture having been read in court before and
twice having moved it should be inrolled At present it is
suspended till the Company be satisfied that he repair to
public ordinances, he being suspected to be a Quaker." [3]

The Statute of Artificers had introduced certain rules as
to the social position of apprentices. No householder of a
corporate or market town might take as apprentice the son
of a labourer or of men engaged in husbandry.[4] In the
case of certain of the more important trades the class from
which apprentices might be drawn was restricted to the sons
of freemen of corporate towns who had estates of 40s. yearly
value,[5] and in market towns to those possessed of estates of
£3 yearly.[6] A certificate of the father's property, signed by
three justices of the peace, had to be produced when the boy
was bound to one of the specified trades. There seems,
however, to have been little demand for such certificates.
Possibly the extraordinarily rapid fall in the value of money,
the effect of which was beginning to be felt at the close of
Elizabeth's reign, rendered this property qualification of no
account.[7] In 1741, when the Merchant Adventurers took
advice as to whether the fathers of intending apprentices

---

[1] Surtees, Merch. Adven., p. 28. Rules, 1656. Repealed 1771.

[2] Ibid., p. 29. Rules, 1676.

[3] Ibid., p. 256. May, 30, 1733. Letter from Wm. Mitford complaining of the
hardships and heavy fine of 100 marks for taking a Quaker as apprentice. Asks
for repeal. September 26, 1733. Wm. Leighton asked that a Quaker whom he had
bound might be enrolled. This was deferred as he did not produce the indentures. *Cf.* p. 183. Case of one suspected.

[4] 5 Eliz. c. 4, f. 26.

[5] Ibid., f. 27.

[6] Ibid., f. 29.

[7] Bott's Laws Relating to the Poor, i. p. 516. Property qualification obsolete.

to merchants need have an estate or inheritance of the yearly
value of 40s., the Recorder declared that "Tis quite probable
when 5 Eliz. was made it might be then intended that if the
father had 40s. per annum he might give his son a competent
fortune to set up in trade and the master would be better
secured. But, say the books, such an estate now is scarce
sufficient to make the son a cobbler. So that this day it
seems a matter quite indifferent whether such certificate be
or no."[1] Moreover, the practice of paying premiums, which
was growing up in James I.'s reign, made any statutory
property qualification unnecessary. It is obvious that a
husbandman could apprentice his son only to one of the
poorer trades, where a premium was not demanded. Such
trades would be, as a rule, the rough handicrafts mentioned
in the Act, but no objection would be raised if a labourer's
son were apprenticed to some other poor trade, since the
spirit of the Act would be observed. The letter undoubtedly
was broken, for it is possible to find many instances of
apprenticeship contrary to the Act, especially in later years.
A fair number of the boys apprenticed to Oxford tradesmen
were the sons of labourers and husbandmen.[2]　In Bristol
a certain number of labourers' sons were apprenticed throughout the seventeenth century,[3] and the Bakers of York occa-

---

[1] Surtees, Merch. Adven., p. 258. Mins., July 12, 1741.

[2] MS. Hanaster Bk., Oxford :—

1625.	50 boys apprenticed, of whom 7 were sons of labourers.				
1626.	32	„	„	11	„	„
1627.	100	„	„	14	„	„
1635.	80	„	„	17	„	„
1636.	76	„	„	17	„	„
1637.	87	„	„	21	„	„
1638.	60	„	„	38	„	„

The proportion was, therefore, by no means regular.

[3] MS. Enrolt. Bks., Bristol :—

1630.	c. 321 apprentices ;	24 enrolts. examined ;	3 labourers' sons.
1635.	276	56　　"	13　　"
1640.	286	25　　"	6　　"
1645.	149	49　　"	6　　"

This incomplete examination of enrolts. proves only the point raised here ;
there is not sufficient evidence upon which to base any statements as to proportion
of labourers' sons, &c.

sionally accepted the sons of husbandmen.[1] These are but
a few instances of what was going on throughout the
country : any town where the enrolments are detailed will
afford similar examples. Among the indentures preserved
at Hertford there is one of the son of a husbandman to a
cordwainer of the town.[2] This lad is apprenticed for nine
years, and it is worth while noting here that the sons of
labourers frequently served longer terms than was the
general custom, and perhaps it was thus that they made
themselves acceptable.[3] Such information throws some
light upon the classes from which apprentices were drawn,
and shows that the Statute of Artificers did not succeed
in perpetuating the caste system as much as has been
sometimes suggested. The difficulty of drawing any very
definite conclusions as to the classes which engaged in the
various branches of industry rests, of course, on the fact
that the dignity and prestige of any one trade would vary
in different towns. Certain rough distinctions can, however,
be drawn. The goldsmiths were almost invariably recruited
from the wealthier, the cobblers and pin-makers from the
poor if not pauper families.[4] But there were certain trades
which, it is fair to suppose, flourished in some localities, and
were of less importance in others. Then, too, not every
trade in a town would be organised into a gild or company,

---

[1] At York, the Bakers took 7 apprentices in 1643 ; 1 was a labourer's son.   In
1638, 3 out of the 4 enrolled, and in 1639 the only 2 enrolled were labourers' sons.
MS., 33,853, Brit. Mus.

[2] Hertford MSS., vol. 26.   Indenture of John Cook, Dec. 9, 1636.

[3] At Oxford, those apprentices who were bound for long terms were generally
the sons of labourers.   In 1624, the only lad bound for 12 years was a labourer's
son ; in 1637, a boy of the same rank was bound for 14 years.

Cf. Bristol MSS., Enrolt. Bk., 1640–1658.   May 22, 1654, Husbandman's
son bound for 12 years.

Oxford MSS., Hanaster Bk., vol. 1697–1707.

1699, Labourer's son bound to cordwainer for 9 years.

1707, Labourer's son bound to tailor for 11 years.

[4] 816, m. 13. (88 & 89), Brit. Mus. Petition *v.* Mr. Killigrew's monopolising act.
Pinmakers' Co. consists of poor people who have neither credit nor money to purchase wire or keep stock ; and they are daily increased by reason of the unlimited
number of apprentices, so that they are not able to live one by another when they
come out of their time.   Generally take poor people's children as apprentices.

and there would be little opposition to a labourer's son entering such a trade, even though it were not open to him by the Act. The sons of townsmen flocked into any and every trade. Yeomen's sons are at first on a par with the most well-to-do tradesmen, but in the early eighteenth century it is noticeable that in many parts of the country they were entering the better trades only with the aid of a premium, provided by a charity or by the overseers of the poor. In Bristol, in the seventeenth century, yeomen's sons were apprenticed to good trades; in the early eighteenth century, when premiums were common, yeomen were paying premiums, but only small sums, when they bound out their children, while many yeomen's sons were apprenticed with charity money. In 1739 the change in the fortunes of yeomen is more marked: their sons were bound either without premiums or with charity money.[1] In Bath, yeomen's sons were apprenticed to all sorts of trades, even in the middle of the eighteenth century, but it was seldom that more than a small premium was paid with them, and frequently none at all was given.[2] This was also the case in Oxford: the premiums given with yeomen's sons, who were apprenticed to all sorts of trades, were small, nil, or paid from charitable funds.[3] These records throw a sidelight on the agricultural revolution which was taking place in the early eighteenth century. More scientific methods had been adopted with regard to the rotation of crops, the dressing and draining of land, breeding and food-stuffs, and agriculture was becoming a remunerative occupation. But the new farming required a considerable amount of capital, while it was possible to make it pay only when it was conducted on a large scale. There was thus on the one hand a keen desire on the part of capitalists to throw small farms into large ones; while on the other, the yeoman class, unable to compete with the large farmers, were selling their holdings, and were being reduced to the standing of hired labourers. Farmers and farming prospered, and we are

[1] MSS. Bristol, Enrolt. Bks.
[2] MSS. Bath, Enrolt Bk., vol. 224.
[3] MSS. Oxford, Hanaster Bks.

accustomed to look upon this period as the Golden Age in the history of agriculture. The yeomanry, however, were depressed, and these enrolments are a reminder of the darker side of the picture.

Sons of gentlemen entered industrial callings in comparatively large numbers. Even in Elizabeth's day the gentry did not think it derogatory to bind their sons to a trade; so at least we can gather from a contemporary writer, who states that the reason for the property qualification for the apprentices of goldsmiths and certain better class artificers was to give gentlemen a chance of placing out their younger sons.[1] Aikin, writing of Manchester and the neighbourhood, states that it was unusual for the gentry there to apprentice their sons until quite a late date. He says that it was not until the time of George I. that "many gentry began to send their sons apprentices to the Manchester manufacturers."[2] This may be true of that part of the country, but from the sure evidence of enrolment books we know that in other places at a far earlier date some gentlemen at any rate apprenticed their sons. As would be supposed, apprentices of gentle birth are to be found generally in the mercantile companies or in the wealthier trades. The Hostmen of Newcastle were recruited almost entirely from the gentry and yeomanry,[3] while in the eighteenth century gentlemen's sons were frequently apprenticed to apothecaries, who were now leaving the ranks of the tradespeople for the lower grades of the professional classes.[4] Possibly, when a gentleman had

---

[1] S. P. D., Eliz. 93., , 26.

Cf. Strype's Stow (1720), ii. p. 329. "But because the Apprentices of London were often Children of Gentlemen, and Persons of good Quality, they did affect to go in costly apparel. . . . "

[2] Aikin, Forty Miles Round Manchester, p. 183.

[3] Surtees, Hostmen, p. 285 *seq.* Enrolts., 1603–1800.

Cf. MSS. Bath, vol. 224. 1768, two gentlemen's sons to bakers; premiums £15 15s., £21. Ibid., gentleman's son to mercer.

MSS. Bristol, Enrolts., 1625–1640. 1630, gentleman's son to glover. 1635, gentlemen's sons to white tawer, mercer, tailor, soapmaker.

Bk. 1640–1658. Gentleman's son to mercer in bond of £200. July 31, 1651.

[4] MSS. Bath, vol. 224. In 1754, two gentlemen's sons were apprenticed to apothecaries; again, in 1763.

many sons, he placed them out as best he could.   In Bristol, we find a labourer's son and a gentleman's son apprenticed to the trade of wire-drawing.   Perhaps the trade was a good one, and the latter was apprenticed with the fixed idea of his becoming a free master, while the former aspired to no higher position than that of a journeyman.   Or perhaps the gentleman's fortunes had suffered in the war.   Such fragmentary information can lead to few conclusions, but to many conjectures which may not be unfruitful.

CHAPTER IX

WORKING WOMEN AND THE GIRL EMPLOYEE

IT is not uncommon to find the wide employment of women in non-domestic work regarded as a characteristic of the nineteenth century. As a matter of fact, it is by no means a new development; at all times women of the lower middle class took a large share in the work of the nation, being employed in numbers both in agriculture and in every sort of industrial occupation. But the front rank in both classes of work was, generally speaking, held by men, while it was they who preserved and inscribed its records, the records chiefly of gilds and towns. Consequently, as it lay with them to decide what was worthy of recording, it is not unnatural that what they wrote and preserved should have appertained mainly to men themselves. On this account, and because, as we have said, women were generally debarred from positions of prominence, there is little special mention of their work, and our information concerning them is very much more imperfect and disconnected than is that relating to male labour. It has therefore been necessary in the preceding pages to treat almost entirely of male apprentices and of boys' employments. Still, though it is impossible to speak with as much certainty of women's as of men's work, there are sufficient indications of the part played by women and girls in our economic development to give us a fairly definite idea of their work and its conditions.

The most striking feature of female labour is its volume and extent. No appreciable limitation appears to have been placed upon it on the score that heavy manual toil was unsuitable to wives and mothers. Any objections raised to their employ-

ment on such grounds are so rare as to be almost negligible.
The London Needlemakers, in 1664, demanded that women
should be forbidden to make needles because they were not
strong enough to do the work properly.[1]   Still, at this time
the trade was over-supplied with labour, and the members'
were doing everything in their power to limit the number of
new workmen.   The women, they said, made bad and insufficient needles " by reason of the weakness of their sex," but it
may be doubted whether the women would have been weak if
they had not been competitors with the men for the trade of
the city.   It is interesting to observe in this connection that
women's employment was not restricted by masculine jealousy,
at any rate it was not restricted in volume, though it may
have been the influence of men's ideas as to what was the
rightful position of females which confined the latter almost
unexceptionally to subordinate and subsidiary work.   However that may be, it is noticeable that the attitude of men
towards women workers was one of friendliness.   Of course,
if women infringed the rights of the gilds, opposition was
shown to their employment.   But they then met with hostility,
not because they were women, but because they were unskilled, or because they were illegal workers—that is to say, not
apprenticed, or not free of their trade gild—or because they
were being employed upon unlawful work.   At Salisbury the
Barber Surgeons agitated against unskilful women who
meddled in the trade.   "Whereas," they declared, "there are
divers women and others within this city, altogether unskilful
in the art of chirurgery, who do oftentimes take cures on them,
to the great danger of the patient, it is therefore ordered, that
no such woman, or any other, shall take or meddle with any
cure of chirurgery, wherefore they or any of them shall have or
take any money, benefit, or other reward for the same, upon
pain that every delinquent shall for every cure to be taken in
hand, or meddled with, contrary to this order, unless she or
they shall be first allowed by this company, forfeit and lose to

---

[1] Needlemakers, p. 36.

Cf. Norwich Records, ii. p. 378.   Women and maids forbidden to weave
worsteds because they " be nott of sufficient powre."

the use of this company the sum of ten shillings."[1]   Women's
work might also be forbidden when the workers in question
were skilful enough, but were unqualified at law.   Andrew
Bowyer, a pewterer, was fined in 1590 for employing a
woman to do the engraving upon his pewter.   It is compli-
mentary to the woman's work that he persisted in doing so,
and was fined again.[2]   In the Girdlers' Company the officers
forbade their members to employ foreigners and maids, not
out of any animosity to the women, but because unscrupulous
workmen had been underselling their fellows by employing
cheap labour.[3]   Women who worked illegally could be
punished, just as men could be, at quarter sessions, and we
find in the Hertfordshire records that Dorothy Benniall, of
Stocking Pelham, was indicted for exercising the trade of a
grocer without having been apprenticed.[4]   The employment
of women in illegal forms of work was also prohibited.   The
Carpenters were not allowed, by the company's rules, to buy
timber at the wharfs from men not free of the company, and
when they evaded the law by employing their wives to buy
for them, the work of women was prohibited and their
husbands were fined.[5]   In the Girdlers' records we find
an entry to the effect that two bundles of girdles were
taken from widows Maybury and Bliss, and they were
ordered to pay five shillings each by way of a fine for
making and selling unlawful wares.[6]   Proceedings were
taken against them, however, not because they were
women, but because the goods were bad.   Finally, where
there was a fear that qualified men would be thrown out of
employment by women, the work of the latter was forbidden.
At Hull the weavers would not allow women to work.   The
employment of aliens also was forbidden.[7]   At Bristol the

---

[1] Hatcher, History of Modern Wiltshire, Old and New Sarum, i. p. 34 (1613).
[2] Welch, *op. cit.*, ii. p. 6.   Jan. 14, 1590.
[3] Dumville Smythe, Girdlers, p. 90.
[4] Hardy, Herts Quarter Sessions, p. 254.   1675.
[5] Jupp, *op. cit.*, p. 377.   Entries, March 8 and 10, 1547.
[6] Dumville Smythe, *op. cit.*, p. 87.   1627.
[7] Lambert, Two Thousand Years, p. 206.   Rules, 12, 1490.
   Cf. Fox and Taylor, Bristol Weavers, p. 38. 1562. Women forbidden to work.

weavers complained that men were employing their wives and daughters and maidens to work at their looms, or let others employ them, whereby men likely to serve the king in his wars are vagrant and unoccupied. They therefore passed a rule forbidding the employment of women and aliens.[1] That the craft gilds should have attempted to prevent women from working under these circumstances does not prove hostility to their employment; men who were unskilled or who were working illegally met with at least equal and usually more opposition. Speaking generally, therefore, the employment of girls and women was not limited by any opinion as to what was suitable and wholesome for them, nor by the jealousy of men. The one great limitation upon their work was the heaviness of their household duties. These, it must be remembered, were even more exacting in the old days than they are now. The transformation of domestic work is not yet complete, but it has gone so far that it is hard to realise what must have been the amount of housework when not merely the cooking, mending, and cleaning, but also the greater part of the spinning and weaving, the washing of clothes, the baking, brewing, and preserving were done by women in their homes. It must have fully occupied the time of a large proportion of girls and women.

Yet though domestic work was undoubtedly exacting, it did not constitute woman's sphere. Girls were employed in farmwork so largely that when, towards the close of the fourteenth century, countrymen began to send their children into the towns to learn trades as apprentices, the loss of the girls' labour, even as that of the boys', was regarded as injurious to agricultural prosperity, and an Act was passed forbidding the apprenticeship to trades of either boys or girls who had worked until twelve years old at husbandry.[2] In the sixteenth century women's employment in the fields was so usual and accepted a feature of life, that, in 1562, the Statute of Artificers declared that not only all men, but all women also, who were not otherwise employed, could be compelled to work by

---

[1] Bickley, Little Red Book, ii. p. 127.
[2] 12 Rich. II. c. 5; 7 H. IV. c. 17.

the year at husbandry.[1]   Married women were excused ; they,
of course, had their household duties to attend to, and could not
be taken from their homes for a year.[2]   But in harvest time any
person who was "meet to labour" could be obliged, even
though he or she had regular work, to serve by the day in the
fields under penalty of two nights in the stocks.[3]   One concession to women was made by this Act : men between the ages
of twelve and sixty were "compellable" to serve,[4] but in the
case of women the old age exemption was lowered to forty.[5]
It would be out of place to deal here at any length with the
agricultural employment of women ; it must be sufficient to
say that it was quite usual, and that the Commissioners who
were appointed in 1842 to inquire into the nature of that employment, found that, at the beginning of the century, girls
who were bound to farmers by the poor law officers as agricultural apprentices were sent to the fields with the boys and
did similar work,[6] while free adult women were engaged in
heavy manual toil on farms, not, as might be supposed, merely
in such occupations as dairy and poultry work.[7]   They were
farm labourers, trudging out to their work with the men, even
though many were married and had small children at home.
The conditions of the English peasantry were probably at
their worst in the first half of the nineteenth century, and it
is natural to suppose that not so many women, and certainly
not so many married women, would have taken part in the
heavy work of the fields in the seventeenth and eighteenth
centuries, though there is no doubt that much agricultural
work fell to their share then too.

In industrial work, also, the employment of women was
very general.   According to the Statute of Artificers women

[1] 5 Eliz. c. 4, f. 24.

[2] Ibid., f. 24.   [3] Ibid., f. 22.

[4] Ibid., f. 7.   [5] Ibid., f. 24.

[6] Report of the Special Assistant Poor Law Commissioners on the Employment
of Women and Children in Agriculture, 1843, p. 28.

[7] See Ibid. Also Arch, Joseph Arch, p. 250. He writes of 1850-1860. Very
young children and women worked in gangs in the fields.

Heath, Peasant Life in the West of England, p. 49.

Hasbach, History of the Agricultural Labourer, pp. 69, 227, 230.

Marshall, Rural Economy of the West of England (1805), i. p. 113.

no less than men had to serve a seven years' apprenticeship before they could engage in a trade. The law, however, was by no means invariably enforced against them. It appears that, before the Act was passed, the gilds had customarily allowed their members to employ their own wives and children unapprenticed to help them in their work. Generally speaking, this was an unwritten custom, but occasionally we find indications of its existence in the gild rules. The Leather-sellers had a bye-law requiring that "no one shall set any man, child, or woman to work in the same trade if such person be not first bound apprentice and enrolled in the trade, their wives and children only excepted." [1] An earlier rule is that of the Girdlers, forbidding the employment of women, except in the case of a "wedded wife or daughter." [2] At Northampton, the participation of wives in their husbands' trades was taken for granted : the bye-laws of the Butchers in 1558 show that women were employed even at the public stalls. "None of the occupation, their wives, or servants, shall call any person or persons that are buying at any other stall until they be parted from the said stall." And again, "None of the occupation, their wives, or servants, shall sell any manner of flesh in their stalls or shops on the Sabbath Day." [3] It appears that this privilege was continued after 1562, notwithstanding the fact that the Statute of Artificers made apprenticeship compulsory. It will be remembered that the gilds, with whom lay the administration of the Act, did not enforce it in any way which told against their interests or customs, and that the Crown, having no better adminis-trators, was obliged to tolerate these deviations. Various persons who were not permitted by the Statute to engage in trade were allowed to do so by the gilds. Amongst these technically unqualified workers were, presumably, the wives and daughters of gild members. At any rate, we find that the widows of men who had used trades as free masters for

---

[1] Black, Leathersellers, p. 21. 1398, 1482.

[2] Dumville Smythe, Girdlers, p. 63. Rules, 1344.

[3] Northampton Records, Cox, ii. p. 280.

Cf. Coventry Leet Book, Part III., transcribed M. D. Harris, p. 673. Cappers to teach their wives and apprentices only. 1520.

seven years were allowed to carry on their husbands' occupations. Probably this was allowed just because wives did work
with their husbands, and it was felt that if the women had
been in touch with the trade for seven years, the period necessary for an apprentice, it was only fair that they should be
allowed to support themselves by it. With regard to the
work of unapprenticed daughters, it is most exceptional to
find rules forbidding the practice, though the Merchant
Tailors in 1613 ordered that no children were to be employed
unless apprenticed.[1]

The privilege thus accorded to craftsmen had a very great
influence upon the extent and nature of girls' labour. In the
first place, the services of his daughters and wife were, generally speaking, the only cheap casual labour which a man could
obtain. Apprentice labour was comparatively cheap, but an apprentice could not be taken on for a day or a week when the
pressure of work was great ; journeymen could be hired for
short periods, but they had to be paid a standard wage Girl
labour, therefore, had a peculiar value, and we may suppose
that more girls worked at crafts and manufactures than
would have been the case if they had been obliged to serve an
apprenticeship. In the second place, scope being given for
the employment of girls and women in such time as they had
to spare, there was comparatively little advantage to be gained
by apprenticing them. There was in consequence no systematic training and technical instruction for girls as there
was for boys. Some girls who worked with their fathers were
no doubt as carefully taught as were boys, while others were
apprenticed upon the same terms as their brothers, and served
their seven years. But apprenticeship played no part in the
life of girls as a whole ; they missed the general education which
it afforded, and their training tended to be casual and irregular. Regarded from another point of view, we can say that
their lives were more varied than were those of their brothers ;
the girl's life lay between the house and the shop or the field,
and one of the first things she had to learn was to apply herself promptly to whichever form of employment temporarily

---

[1] Clode, Mems. Merch. Taylors, p. 222.

required her services.   This casualness and irregularity of
girls' labour was not the only result of the tacit permission
accorded to them to work unapprenticed.   It had the further
result of keeping women in an inferior and subordinate position in the working world.   That women's position was one
of inferiority cannot be denied even by their most ardent
supporters to-day.   For though it is true that they worked
hard and that the total amount of their labour has contributed
largely to our industrial development, it was only exceptionally
that they attained to the standing of employers and industrial
leaders.   It is interesting to see how the lack of apprenticeship led inevitably to their taking a second place.   Craftsmen
were allowed to utilise the services of their wives and
daughters unapprenticed, and naturally they took advantage
of this privilege and did not go to the trouble or expense of
apprenticing them ; the consequence was that girls and
women were seldom qualified at law, as their brothers were,
to practise a trade, and they had to confine themselves to
subordinate work, which was tacitly sanctioned by the law. Of
course, those girls who were bound and who served seven
years could attain the position of independent mistresses and
rank with master craftsmen ; but the rest, the majority, who
had not been apprenticed because their fathers found more
profitable methods of employing them, could work only as the
assistants of their male relatives. What Englishwomen
might have done under other circumstances is a profitless
question, but the incidental effects upon women of this
privilege granted to men are of real significance and importance.

Though apprenticeship was not the rule for the daughters
of craftsmen as it was for their sons, it was not unknown
amongst them. As early as 1389 it was practised sufficiently
often for girls to be included with boys in the Act forbidding
labourers to apprentice their children,[1] while in London the
Corporation undertook the supervision of girl apprentices as
well as of boys ; their fees were fixed in 1413,[2] and the names
of girls were entered on the books of the City, without com-

---

[1] See p. 146. 7 H. IV. c. 17.   [2] Riley, Mems., p. 590.

ment as being anything exceptional. In 1479 Ricarte, in his book of the customs of London and Bristol, states that in London women using certain crafts could take girls as apprentices, and their indentures had to be enrolled, just as were those of boys, before the Chamberlain at the Gild Hall.[1] Thus in the City, the customs of which in 1562 were to be held up as a pattern for the country at large, the apprenticeship of girls was an accepted fact. In the days of the Elizabethan system, girls were bound to many of the skilled trades in London. In 1675 a girl claimed admittance to the Carpenters' Company by right of apprenticeship, and complained that her mistress would not bear witness to her true service of seven years.[2] A more fortunate maiden was admitted to the freedom by right of service in 1712, and the records bear evidence to the apprenticeship of many others.[3] In the seventeenth century women were not infrequently admitted to the Wheelwrights' Company by right of apprenticeship, though this seems an unsuitable trade[4]; and in the eighteenth century the records of the Clockmakers' Company show that it was not uncommon for its members to receive girls as apprentices.[5]

It was not only in London that girls were apprenticed; from the indentures which are still preserved, and from the enrolment and minutes books of towns and gilds it is apparent that both in the country and in provincial towns girls were bound to men in all kinds of trades throughout the sixteenth, seventeenth, and eighteenth centuries. Some of these girls, however, were not industrial apprentices, that is to say, apprentices bound for the purpose of learning a trade, and in accordance with the Act of 1562. A poor law of Elizabeth's reign gave to justices of the peace the power to apprentice the children of poor persons who could not maintain their families.[6] Boys and girls were so apprenticed, but such

---

[1] Ricarte, Calendar, p. 102.
[2] Jupp, Carpenters, p. 161.
[3] Ibid., pp. 543-4, 1692, 1695, 1699, 1710.
[4] Scott, Wheelwrights, p. 16.
[5] Overall, Clockmakers, p. 155, 1715, 1725, 1730-1733, 1434, 1747.
[6] 43 Eliz. c. 2.

apprenticeship is more akin to the present-day boarding out of poor children than to industrial apprenticeship as practised by the gilds.   Men were assessed, and instead of paying poor rates they had a child billeted upon them.   The business of the justices was merely to find men of sufficient means to maintain these children, not necessarily men who had a handicraft to teach.   They were often placed out with farmers, and the gentry and clergy had to do their part. Where the master was a craftsman, such children might be taught a trade, but on the other hand they may have been employed in the house.   This makes it difficult to estimate the extent to which girls were taught skilled trades, for although the conditions were entered in the indenture, it is often impossible to tell how the children were employed.   A large number of parish indentures are preserved at Corsham in Wiltshire, and show that poor girls were apprenticed to men in trades of all classes.[1]   One was bound to a clothier, one to a labourer, another to a broad-weaver, another to a joiner, to learn " all his honest and lawfull employ which he now useth."   This, however, appears to have been merely a set phrase, for it is used again of a girl whose mistress seems to have had no other profession than that of a widow.   The probability is that the greater number of girls apprenticed by the poor law authorities were employed in domestic service, and that, even if they helped now and again in the workshop, they would not have been fully taught the trade.   Judging from the indentures available to-day, by far the greater proportion of girl apprentices were parish children, which is the same thing as saying that not so many girls as at first sight appears were actually apprenticed to skilled trades.   When the indentures are lost, the chief sources of information are the enrolments in the town or gild books, from which it is difficult to tell whether the girls were industrial or parish apprentices.   The enrolment only occasionally gives an indication of which was the case, as in the entry of a girl bound in 1628 to " William Blacknall and his wief vj yeares, he

---

[1] MS. Indentures at Corsham Court.

gevinge her 30ˢ· in dubble apparell in th' end of vj yeres."[1]
The assumption is that this was not an industrial apprenticeship, for then the term would have been seven years at least.[2]
For such a girl, and for other parish children, apprenticeship
was a system of maintenance and general training, rather
than of technical instruction. Even girls of well-to-do
families were often bound apprentice, not so much, it
appears, in order to learn a trade as for the sake of the
general education and discipline which apprenticeship
afforded. It is doubtful if any apprenticed girls took up
the freedom of their masters' companies, and worked at the
end of their term as independent craftswomen, which suggests that proficiency in a trade was not the main reason for
their binding. Probably some were bound by parents who
had no intention of paying the necessary fees for admittance,
but who regarded skill in a trade as a good form of dowry ;
others may have been deterred by marriage from taking up
their freedom. Sometimes it is quite clear from the indentures or enrolment, that the girl was not being taught the
trade of the master to whom she was bound, but was being
trained in housework, or at the wife's occupation when she
had one. Of one girl bound at Norwich in 1653, it is said
that she was to be educated in housewifery for seven years.[3]
At Bristol [4] the enrolments are fuller than is often the case,
and from them can be learnt that though the girls, like the
boys, were bound for seven years, and were to be given
" meat, drink, lodging, apparel both linnen and woollen, and
all other things necessary and convenient for an apprentice,"
and at the end of their term double apparel and a small sum
of money, yet in their case it is usually added that they were
to be " brought up in all things belonging to a servant maid."
Occasionally it is stated that the girl is to learn the wife's
trade. A girl was presented and enrolled at the Pewterers'
Hall by a master pewterer " to learn the Art of Childs Coat-

---

[1] Guilding, Reading Records, ii. p. 452. Diary of Corporn., Feb. 11, 1628.
[2] But she might have served some other master one year.
[3] *Cf.* MSS. Gt. Yarmouth Quarter Sessn. Mins., March 29, 1734.
[4] MSS. Bristol, Enrolment Books.

making which his Wife now followeth ";[1] and in 1714 a girl was bound to a carpenter for seven years " to learn ye art of Milliner being his Wife's trade."[2]

It has been said that women workers were usually the assistants and subordinates of craftsmen. There are instances, however, of women working on their own account ; and though this seems never to have been very general, it was not so unusual as to arouse comment or surprise. For the most part women who had their own businesses were widows carrying on the work of their deceased husbands ; while other women who were admitted to the gilds as equals of the men, though it is not clear whether they always had their own workshops, were the daughters of freemen basing their claims to admittance on rights of patrimony.[3]

It was the custom of most gilds to allow widows to take up the freedom of their husbands' companies, and to carry on their work. Their admittance was generally taken as a matter of course, and therefore, though incidental references are to be found, there are few rules on the subject.[4] Free-

---

[1] Welch, Pewterers, ii. p. 174.   Feb. 23, 1704–1705.

[2] Jupp, Carpenters, p. 544.

[3] It must be noticed that since those women, who became members of the gilds and worked on their own account, had by no means always learnt their trade as girls, their independent work has no necessary relation to girl labour.

[4] Welch, Pewterers, i. p. 18.   Rules, c. 1450.   " Sustren " pay quarterage.

MSS. Norwich, Freemen's Book, i.   Women (widows) entered as paying quarterage 1666–67.

Prideaux, Goldsmiths, i. p. 35.   1502.

Dowling, Poulterers, p. 52.   Rules, 42, 1692.

Fox, Merch. Tailors, Bristol, p. 82.   Rules, 1640.

Clode, Mems. Merch. Taylors, p. 32.   Bequests to six poor men or women, ree of the company.

Welch, *op. cit.*, ii. p. 139.   Mins., Nov. 25, 1668–69.   Widow asked to have an extra apprentice allowed her. Ibid., p. 180.   April 13, 1713–14.   Girl bound to a widow.

MSS. Norwich, Grocers' Rules, 7, 1698.   Widows of freemen may sell grocery.

Fox, *op. cit.*, p. 82, Rules.   No person unless free of the city and craft to use the trade (" widdowes whose husbands were free of ye saide Crafte duringe the tyme of their wyddowhedd vsinge ye same with one Jorneyman And one Apprentice only excepted." *Cf.* Overall, *op cit.*, p. 31.   Rules, 1632.

Needlemakers, p. 33.

Shickle, Merch. Tailors, Bath, p. 55.   Rules, 21, 1625.

Cotton, Elizn. Gild, p. 16.   Rules, 1561.

women are mentioned with freemen as paying their dues to
the gilds, or as taking apprentices; sometimes they are included in the wording of the rules, while occasionally the
constitutions of a gild will explicitly sanction their work.
A widow, when admitted to her husband's gild, succeeded to
all his trading privileges; she could own his workshop, and
his apprentices had to serve out their time with her. She
could also take fresh apprentices, bound to herself. In 1701
Katherine Eyre had a girl bound to her for seven years, and
paid her "quarterage," or subscription, to the company. In
1705 she took another girl, and in 1707 another, so that
during these years she had on the average two apprentices in
her employment.[1] Yet other unapprenticed women who had
a place in the gild, and the right to work independently,
were, as we have seen, the daughters of freemen who could
claim admittance by patrimony. This, it will be remembered, was the right of the eldest son born to a man after he
had taken up his freedom to be received into the company
without serving an apprenticeship, and sometimes even upon
the payment of lower fees. This much-cherished privilege
was extended to daughters in London, and possibly elsewhere. In the Carpenters' Company we find Mary Wiltshire and Ann Callcutt taking up their freedom by right of
patrimony. In Anne's enrolment it is especially stated that
she paid to "ye Company ye usual fees." In 1733, 1734,
and 1737 there are other instances of admission to this
company by patrimony.[2] In 1633 a pewterer's daughter was
made free, and paid 9s. 2d., a sum rather above the usual
entrance fee.[3] Yet it may be questioned whether women
would have been granted these privileges or recognised as

---

[1] & [2] Jupp, Carpenters, pp. 543, 545.

Cf. In 1747 Mary Temple was made free of the Girdlers' Company by right
of patrimony. She gave 3s. 4d. for the freedom, 6s. 8d. in lieu of a silver spoon,
2s. 6d. for the poor box, and 2s. for stamps. (Dumville Smythe, p. 128.)

[3] Welch, Pewterers, ii. p. 92; *cf.* ibid., p. 179, 1711; p. 191, 1742.

It is not clear whether a daughter could claim admission only if a
brother had not claimed by patrimony, or if the eldest daughter and the eldest
son could both claim. Or perhaps the girl could claim only if there were no
sons.

men's equals if they had not at one time or other had the honour to belong to a male member of the company.

One word must be said in conclusion. We have seen that though girls did not receive technical training, and though their work and the work of women tended to be irregular, yet work they did : there can be no doubt about that. And the species of work in which they were engaged were the heavier and physically more arduous employments, husbandry, manufactures, and handicrafts; the sedentary and physically less exhausting occupations which employ so many women at the present day, work which lies in the office or in the schoolroom, the easier forms of mechanical work and professions which tend always to be more leisured, were practically non-existent until modern times. There were women teachers in the convents before the Reformation, and in the dames' schools later, while wise women with their lore in herbs and simples shared with the barber surgeons the work of doctoring the multitude. Their number, however, was always small. Manual labour, and often heavy labour, was the portion of the majority. Women began to work when fully as young as their brothers, and they worked after marriage. It is necessary to bear this in mind when any question arises as to the connection between women's work and the national physique. The respective merits of freedom for women to work as they choose and of legislation which restrains their freedom cannot, of course, be discussed here. All that we have to notice in this connection is that the arduous and constant labour of women is no modern phenomenon.

CHAPTER X

THE CHOICE AND OPENING OF AN INDUSTRIAL CAREER

INDUSTRY to-day is frequently haphazard and wasteful in her methods of recruiting her workers. Most boys start their careers in a temporary situation : they are "taken on" at some factory or workshop upon terms which allow of their being flung aside, dismissed at short notice, not for any fault of their own, but owing to slackness in trade or the competition of cheaper labour. Others drift into some odd job, errand work, or a weekly situation, which they may or may not retain. There may be something to be gained from so lax and unstereotyped a system, but a certain amount of wastage is inevitably involved. The start in the industrial world during the days of apprenticeship was a more methodical and serious undertaking ; methodical, because it had to be made by apprenticeship, and serious, because it was, generally speaking, irrevocable, the master and the learner having to pledge themselves to a seven years' agreement. Even though many of the details have been already referred to, it may be useful to summarise in this chapter the considerations which had to be weighed and the formalities which had to be observed by any boy or girl who wished to enter any branch of industrial work. Special considerations which may have affected some young people in certain localities or at certain periods cannot be dealt with here.

The first step, of course, for the boy who wished to enter a trade was, as now, to find a master. The choice lay with the lad and his parents. It was limited in various ways, naturally enough, by the law of supply and demand, which must have been especially rigid in those trades in which the gild rules limiting the number of apprentices were strictly enforced.   Naturally, too, the sphere of choice was narrow, for a father could have little knowledge of the conditions of work and the reputation of workmen outside his own neighbourhood.   Some boys certainly were apprenticed at a distance.   A large proportion of the apprentices taken by the London Stationers in the middle of the sixteenth century were country lads, and came from as far north as Cumberland, Northumberland, and Yorkshire.[1]   The Bath apprentices, in 1754, were drawn from Bath itself and from the villages and country towns within a twenty-mile radius, but a few came from Hampshire and Gloucestershire.[2]   A Hertford boy was bound to a London musician in 1631,[3] while the apprentices of the York bakers were, more often than not, countrymen's sons, though it was not usual for them to come from any but the adjacent counties.[4]   In most companies, probably, there was this outside element, but, as a rule, children were apprenticed to men in the immediate neighbourhood.   Even now, in the days of railways and penny postage, lads are apt, in all but the largest trades, to drift into the employment of the man round the corner.

Besides these natural limitations, there were the restrictions imposed by the Statute of Artificers.   It is impossible to say

[1] Arber, Transcript Stationers' Recs., p. 167.   Receipts for presenting.

[2] MSS. Bath, Enrolts., vol. 224.   In 1765 a Yorkshire clergyman apprenticed his son to an apothecary in Bath.

[3] MSS., Hertford, vol. 26, August 9, 1632.

[4] MS. 33,853, Brit. Mus., 1630–50.

Cf. Dendy, Hostmen, p. liv.   Only 17 per cent. of the boys apprenticed to the Newcastle Hostmen were sons of Newcastle men.   The others came from the surrounding counties.

MSS. Norwich, Bk. 1625–49.   1645, sons of a London tailor and a King's Lynn oatmeal maker apprenticed to Norwich tailors.

Bristol, MS. Enrolts., 1630–45.

MSS. Oxford.   Hanaster Bk., 1697–1777.   In 1708 fifty-eight boys bound, of whom thirty-one are sons of townsmen ; in 1705 fifty-two were bound, eleven being country lads.

how far these conditions were observed. At the close of the eighteenth century the age qualification had undoubtedly become obsolete,[1] but in the preceding century there are indictments of men who took apprentices contrary to these clauses;[2] while the gilds, which were the most powerful of the agents administering the Statute, had rules[3] much on the same lines, so that the probability is that the age and householders' qualifications were fairly well observed in the seventeenth century. The gilds and towns, by their regulations, or by refusing their freedom to apprentices who had not served with gildsmen, made it practically compulsory upon a boy to be bound only to a freeman. Alien birth had in the old days disqualified a man from taking apprentices, but such rules seldom appear later than the sixteenth century.[4] In Carlisle it was only married men who might take apprentices; this had been the tailors' rule before 1562, and we find it in the rules of the shoemakers, and on the books of the merchant gild in the seventeenth century.[5] Another qualification, due, probably, to the growth of a monopolistic spirit, was adopted by some gilds in the seventeenth century. Men were not allowed to take apprentices before they had been freemen a certain number of months or years. The period for the weavers of Kidderminster was one year;[6] in 1656 the Merchants' Gild of Carlisle passed a rule

[1] Chitty, Law of Apprenticeship, p. 24.

Durnford and East, iv. p. 196. Boy bound to a lad of fourteen, resident in his mother's house. Held to be good (1791).

[2] Atkinson, North Riding Quarter Sessions, Part II., p. 94. A tailor sued for employing an apprentice, not being a housekeeper and under twenty-four years old. (1615) Similar cases, ii. p. 231.

[3] *E.g.*, Clothworkers, Rules, 1639, 1.

Surtees, Hostmen, pp. 119, 137, 164, 183, 192.

[4] Ferguson, Carlisle, p. 248. Butchers, 1668, 23. Ibid., p. 139. Smiths' Rules. Order of Town Council, September 21, 1696. No freeman who lives outside the town may take an apprentice.

Surtees, Hostmen, p. 100. April 27, 1655. "Indenture of Nicholas Newbie, Apprentice to John Cole Hoastman was read and desired it might be enrolled (respited) in regards the said John Cole is not an inhabitant of this town."

[5] Ferguson, Carlisle, p. 212. Glovers' Rule, 1665.

Cf. Surtees, Newcastle Adventurers, p. 11. Rules, 1555.

[6] Burton, Kidderminster, p. 175. Borough ordins., 14.

insisting upon six months' free mastership.[1]   In the Needlemakers' Company the period adopted in 1664 was three
years;[2] in 1683 the Wheelwrights passed a rule making
five years necessary.[3]   In the choice of a master, attention
had to be paid to these rules, or a lad might find, when he
had finished his service, that he was disqualified from taking
up the freedom because his master had not been qualified to
employ him.   Their observance, however, appears to have
caused no inconvenience to men who sought masters for
their sons ; there was never any complaint that they were
hampering, and there were seldom any reported breaches of
the law.   It is possible that they were not strictly enforced.

It is difficult to say how far lads were apprenticed to men
in the same trade as their fathers.   Not so much, perhaps, as
might be imagined by those conversant with Trade Union
practices at the present day.   The custom of patrimony,
according to which a man might teach his eldest son
unbound, enabled men who wished to keep their sons in the
trade to do so without apprenticing them.   The enrolments
bear witness to a considerable amount of dissimilarity in the
trades of father and son.

Masters were occasionally allowed by the gild rules to
take boys upon trial, but this would only be for a short
period and with the definite idea of binding them, if they
proved satisfactory, for seven years at least as apprentices.
They had not the option of employing them by the week, or
for odd jobs.   The career of the apprentice, then, opened
with the drafting of his indentures, the written agreement
between the master and the boy, or those responsible for
him.   Children were as a rule bound by their parents, but
the justices of the peace were in some cases empowered to
bind out both boys and girls.   By the Statute of Artificers
children, not otherwise legally employed, could be com-
pulsorarily apprenticed if any qualified person petitioned for

---

[1] Ferguson, *op. cit.*, p. 102.   Rules, 1656, 16.   *Cf.* p. 186, Tailors' rules.
[2] Needlemakers, Rules, 1664, p. 30.
[3] Scott, Wheelwrights, p. 58.   Rules, 1683.
    See p. 125.

their services.[1]   There seems to be no record of any such petition and compulsory binding, and perhaps there were too many boys eager to enter industrial callings for such request to have ever been made.   There is, however, ample evidence of the use of the second power vested in justices.   The poor law of 1601 ordered the justices of the peace to bind out as apprentices the children of poor parents who could not support their entire families.[2]   Such children were bound by indentures in which the justices were one of the parties to the contract.   In ordinary bindings, it is the father's name which appears.   The apprentice was competent, at any rate in later times, to bind himself even when under age, but he could not be sued for breach of contract, and it was therefore usual for the friends or parents to be parties to the agreement.[3]

The main terms of the indentures vary hardly at all, and even in the eighteenth century they resemble not only in spirit, but also in wording, the indentures of the sixteenth century.[4]   In every case the apprentice swears to serve his master truly and to be of good moral conduct, while the master on his side promises to instruct the apprentice in his craft and to provide him with all necessaries.   If not drawn up by the justices, the indentures had to be made by the clerk of the company to which the master belonged.[5]   It was written twice over on a sheet of parchment or paper, and the two copies were then cut apart in such a manner as to leave each with a jagged or indented edge, which gave to the document its name.[6]   Later

---

[1]   5 Eliz. c. 4.   [2]   43 Eliz. c. 2.

[3]   Chitty, *op. cit.*, p. 30.   [4]   See Appendix.

[5]   *E.g.*, Surtees, Hostmen, p. 164.   Indenture drawn up by other that the clerk shall not be enrolled.   Feb. 9, 1704.

Watermen, Constns. of the company.   1708, x.

Lambert, Two Thousand Years, pp. 128, 362.   Rules.

Ferguson, Carlisle, p. 100.   Merch. Gild Bk., 1656.   Ibid., p 128.   Weavers, 1679.

Glass-sellers, p. 124.   Rules, 1664.

Clode, Mems. Merch. Taylors, p. 208.   Rules, 1613.

[6]   5 Eliz. c. 4 required the binding to be by indenture.   3 Wm. and Mary, c. 11, required the binding of parish apprentices to be by indenture.

It was held the deed must be indented until 31 Geo. ii. c. 11, when a deed legally stamped was declared sufficient.   Chitty, *op. cit.*, p. 27.

on, printed forms were used, containing spaces for the
insertion of the names of master and boy and other individual
information.   Until this indenture had been formally made
most companies jealously forbade their members to employ
the boy, though, as we have seen, a period of trial was
allowed in a few companies.[1]   In the Glass-sellers' Company
it seems to have been compulsory.   No one might take an
apprentice until he had been on trial for thirty days ; then, if
he were found fit for the work, he might be bound and
enrolled.[2]

The Statute of Artificers contained no detailed instructions
for the enrolling of apprentices, but it made universal the
order and custom of London.   In London, the name of an
apprentice and the effect of his indenture had to be entered
in the gild book within a certain period after he was bound.[3]
In many places the same formality had to be observed at the
town hall: the apprentice had to be presented to the Mayor
or his deputy, and his name was registered on the city books.[4]
Both the enrolments by the gild and by the town were kept
in order that there should be some record to which reference
could be made when the apprentice asked for his freedom ;
and in order, also, that apprenticeship should be better regu-

Cf. Austin, Law of Apprenticeship, p. 16.

Const, Laws Relating to the Poor, p. 523.

[1] Watermen, Constns. of the Company, 1708.   Rule 15.   Forty days' trial
allowed.

Shickle, Merch. Tailors, Bath, p. 71.   Plasterers' and Tylers' Rules, 1752.
No person to employ a boy for more than a month before binding him.

[2] Glass-sellers, p. 124.

[3] Lambert, op. cit., p. 244.   Tailors, 1680, 5.   To enrol within a year.

Ibid., 262, Barber Surgeons, 1714.   Within one month.

Surtees, Hostmen, p. 87.   1646.   Enrol within a year.

Clode, Mems. Merch. Taylors, p. 210.   Rules, 1613, 9.   Enrol within
a year and a day.

Latimer, Merch. Tailors, Bristol, p 77.   Rules, 1618.   Within six months.

Holmes, Pontefract, p. 373.   Wrights' and Bowers' Rules, 1664.   Within
twenty days.

[4] Chitty, op. cit., p. 59.   It is necessary, according to the custom of some places,
that the indentures should be enrolled ; as in London, if the indenture be not enrolled before the Chamberlain, within a year, upon a petition to the Mayor and
Aldermen a scire facias may be issued to the master to show cause why it was not
enrolled.

lated, and fraudulent employment prevented. This had been the custom before 1562, and in the seventeenth and eighteenth centuries it was the universal rule in all trades which were organised into gilds, and in places where there was a corporation. In all the bye-laws regulations are to be found for the presentation of the apprentice and the enrolment of his name at the court of the Master and Wardens, which was held at fixed intervals for the purpose of transacting the company's business.[1] The meeting would be held in the hall, if there was one; if not, in some convenient place. This public enrolment was of value, since it prevented fraud on the part both of apprentice and master. If friends or parents had bound the lad, all unknowingly, to an unqualified master, here was the opportunity for them to discover their error, for in this public meeting evil would out if ever. If the boy was not qualified to become an apprentice, discovery could hardly be escaped in open court.

After the indenture was read and the apprentice approved by the court, its effect was enrolled by the clerk in the company's books. In different companies and at different periods the enrolments vary in the amount of information they contain; some are but the briefest records of the name of the apprentice and the name and trade of his master. Others contain information as to what clothes and money he was to receive at the end of his term,[2] what premium was paid, and what was the trade of his father. The enrolments begin to be

---

[1] See pp. 76, 110.

[2] *E.g.*, MSS. Bristol, Enrolts., vols. 1626–1699.

April 25, 1654.

" The same day

" Thomas Brittain the sonne of John Brittain of Bitton in the County of Gloucz carpenter bound to Robert Pope of the citty of Bristoll house carpenter and Jane his wife for seaven yeeres. And to serve one yeere as a covenant yeere and to have forty shillings at the end thereof."

Ibid., March 3, 1687.

" Eodm—

" Samuel fil John Evans (   ) de Citate Glouc Woolcomber posuit see Appnticm Thom Bayly Pewterer et Avis ux ejus pr octo annis Maria mater inven appar, the M to pay xx[s] for last yer service in case he serve faithfully."

fuller in some places during the personal government of Charles I.

A fee was invariably charged for enrolment. The maximum charge had been fixed by statute at 2s. 6d. ;[1] in some companies it was less; in others it often amounted to more.   It was usual to pay small fees to the clerk and beadles,[2] and possibly even where these charges are not mentioned in the rules, their payment was customary, for few companies made any other provision for paying these officers.[3]   Apart from this, several companies charged more than the legal 2s. 6d. for enrolling apprentices.   The Merchant Tailors of London were charging 30s. in 1661 ;[4] in the Poulterers' Company the fee was 2s. 6d. if the apprentice was bound in court, and 5s. if bound out of court, in which case the clerk's fee was correspondingly higher.[5]   A fee of 11s. 6d. had been customary with the Sheffield Cutlers ; in 1750 they gave it a more legal appearance by charging 2s. 6d. as apprentice fee, and 9s. as "each master's contribution to the common stock."[6]   The fee was generally paid by the master, but at Hull the Shipwrights' rule was that the friends of the apprentice should pay for the

---

[1] 22 H viii., c. 4.

[2] Ferguson, Carlisle, p. 100.   Clerk's fee, 6d. each enrolment.   Merch. Gld., 1656.

Lambert, *op. cit.*, p. 346.   Shipwrights, 1686.   6d. to clerk for indenture, 6d. for enrolment, and 4d. to beadle.   Ibid., p. 296, Coopers, 1681.   Clerk's fee, 20d. for indenture and 4d. for enrolment.

Dowling, Poulterers, p. 36.   1692.   8d. for enrolment.

Glass-sellers, 124, 1664.   2s. 6d. to clerk for indenture, 1s. for enrolment, 6d. to beadle.

[3] Ferguson, Carlisle, p. 212.   Glovers' Rules, 1665.   Clerk received 3s. for every pair of indentures and 6d. for each enrolment, "and for his allowance every quarter one shilling."

Ibid., p. 150. Tailors, Rules, 1677.   Clerk to have 6d. each enrolment, "noe other salary for ye trade but only ye benefit of making ye indentures."

Dumville Smythe, Girdlers, p. 143.   Clerk had salary of £20 a year at end of eighteenth century, and residence and allowance for coal, ink, &c.

[4] Clode, Mems. Merch. Taylors, p. 54.

[5] Dowling, *op. cit.*, p. 36.   Rules, 1692.

[6] Leader, Sheffield Cutlers, 1750.

Less than 2s. 6d. was charged by small or poor gilds.   Ferguson, Carlisle, p. 244.   Butchers, Rules, 1665.   Fee, 6d.   Ibid., p. 173.   Shoemakers, Rules, 1595. Fee, 6d.

Lambert, *op. cit.*, p. 296.   Coopers, Rules, 1681.   Fee, 6d.

presenting, binding and enrolling, "except the Master be otherwise contented." [1]

Apprentices to seamen had, it seems, been enrolled at Trinity House, the headquarters of the Corporation of Mariners, who had received their charter from Henry VIII. But by the end of the seventeenth century, if not before, the Corporation's supreme control of apprentices to sea service was breaking down, and many or even most of the lads were, according to Strype, bound elsewhere.[2]

In many corporate towns apprentices were ordered by their gilds to enrol themselves, as they had to do in London, at the town hall. Probably this enrolment took place even where not expressly enjoined, but it is not clear. It was at least a general custom, and in the larger cities, such as Bristol and Norwich, it was certainly enforced.

Though enrolment was usual, it is impossible to believe that it was universal. Where a trade was organised into a company the enrolment would be enforced, for it was to the interests of the company that a record of apprentices should be preserved. But every trade was not so organised : at Bath the coopers formed themselves into a gild only in 1752,[3] and in cases such as this, and in the country, the registration of apprentices must have been a difficulty. Possibly, the municipal authority undertook the work, while in the country the apprentice might have been enrolled upon the parish books, as had been ordered by Elizabeth for the weavers, the effect of whose indentures were " to be registered within three months in the parish where such master shall dwell, and to pay for such registering four pence ; upon pain of forfeiture of twenty shillings for every month that any person shall otherwise take any apprentice."[4] But there must sometimes have been insuperable difficulties in making arrangements for the

---

[1] Lambert, *op. cit.*, p. 346. Rules, 1682.

[2] Strype's Stow, ii. p. 287 (1720 edition).

5 Eliz. c. 5, s. 12. Where boys are bound to seamen, their indentures are to be enrolled in the next corporate town.

[3] There may have been an earlier company, which might have collapsed.

[4] 5 Eliz. c. 4, f. 3.

registration of apprentices, and in seeing that they were bound
according to law.

The period of a lad's apprenticeship closed, as it had begun,
with a public act. The intending apprentice had been brought
before the gild court, and had seen his name inscribed upon
the books ; now, at the end of his term, he again appeared in
the assembly court, this time to ask for his freedom. As a
rule, this would be seven years later.[1] Longer terms were
sometimes served : in the early seventeenth century eight
years was very common, but from 1650 it was not usual for
apprentices to be bound for more than the legal and minimum
term of seven years. When a longer period was served we can
generally trace some special reason for it. The boy was an
orphan ; it was natural, therefore, that those responsible for
him should wish him to be kept under control until he reached
manhood ; or he was very young, in which case he would have
to serve for a longer term in order to comply with the rules
forbidding apprentices to come out of their time until twenty-
one, or in some cases twenty-four years old. Sometimes the
boys bound for long periods are the sons of labourers, or they
were taken without a premium ; presumably, such apprentices agreed to serve for a longer time in order to

---

[1] Addit. MSS., 33,853 (Brit. Mus.), p 10.   York Bakers, seven years usual.

MSS. Bath, Enrolt. Bk., 1625–1649.

MSS. Hertford, vol. 26.   Enrolts.

MSS. Norwich, Enrolts., 1625–49.   Seven years usual but 8 years not uncommon.

MSS. Oxford, Enrolts., 1624.   Seven years most usual.   Out of the 50 enrolled, 35 boys were bound for 7 years ; 8 for 8 years ; 4 for 9 years ; 2 for 10
years ; 1 for 12 years.   1645, 7 years almost invariable.

MSS. Bristol, Enrolts., 1630–1848.   In 1630 the term is 7 to 12 years.
1635, 7 or 8 years most usual.   By 1685, 7 years practically universal.   In 1710,
7 years had become the rule.   We find the following entry for April 8, 1710 :—

"Edwrs Buckstone fiil ffranci Buckstone [   ] de Civit Bristoll Gardiner
defunct posuit se apprentic Georgio Blinko Bricklayer et Marie Uxor ejus pro
septem annis

[   ] the agreement was for eight yeares But (being contrary to Custome) this
Indenture is to be delivered up at the end of one yeare and then to be bound for
Seaven Yeares " (p. 256), cf. p. 260.   John Ockford's indenture, he being bound
for eight years, "were delivered up and cancelled and bound for seaven yeares."

Guilding, Reading Records, ii. p. 423.   Names of apprentices taking up
freedoms.   Most have been bound for seven years.

recompense their masters for taking them. Whatever the length of a lad's apprenticeship, he would, when he came to take up his freedom, have reached manhood. According to the Statute of Artificers he must be not less than twenty-four years old at the end of his apprenticeship.[1] Probably this clause had not always been observed, for many companies found it necessary to make bye-laws to enforce it,[2] while others made a new rule of their own, fixing the minimum age at twenty-one.[3] We can at least be sure that no well-regulated company would admit an apprentice under this age.

Sometimes an apprentice did not attempt to take up his freedom immediately upon the expiration of his term. Possibly the expenses of admittance caused him to hesitate, or he may have waited until there was an opportunity for opening his business. In some companies this delay on the part of apprentices was forbidden, and fines were imposed upon those who did not apply for the freedom within a certain period after their service had ended.[4]

Generally, however, the apprentice was ready enough to ask for his freedom. It was his master's duty to make him free.[5] Together they went to the gild hall or other place of meeting, where the master publicly testified to his appren-

---

[1] 5 Eliz. c. 4, f. 26.

43 Eliz. c. 2. Females to be bound to 21 or marriage. Parish apprentices.

18 Geo. III. c. 47. Fixed age of males at 21.

Chitty, *op. cit.*, p. 80. Says it has sometimes been held that ordinary apprentice is free when he comes of age. Lord Kenyon said (34 Geo. III.) : " It is clear that the apprentice must be discharged ; every indenture of an infant is voidable at his election."

[2] *E.g.*, Cotton, Eliz. Gild, p. 172. Apprentice to be 24 when he comes out of his time. 1578, Rules.

Rep. on MSS. Miscel., i., 1901, p. 75. Weavers' Rules, 24 years old.

[3] *E.g.*, Sellers, Eastland Company, York, pp. 4, 5. Age 21 for sons.

Ibid., p. 68. Apprentices may be admitted at 21 instead of 24. 1688.

Surtees, Merch. Adven., p. 238. Mins., 1691.

Holmes, Pontefract, p. 380. Grocers' Rules, 1700. Ibid., p. 379.

[4] Cotton, *op. cit.*, p. 173. Apprentice had to take up his freedom within a year, or fined when he did come. Rules, 1595.

Surtees, Merch. Adven., Newcastle, p. 16. Similar rule, 1780.

[5] The apprentice was made free of the occupation to which his master was bound, and not to the occupation of which he was free by redemption. Surtees, Merch. Adven., p. 15. Rules, 1562.

tice's true service. This could be verified by turning up the entry of the boy's name and term in the books.[1] In some companies, even though his period of service was complete, the freedom would not be granted until he had proved himself a capable workman by performing a given piece of work, called test-work or master-piece.[2] This was exceptional, but in all companies the ex-apprentice had to pay fees for admittance. The legal sum was 3s. 4d., but small fees had invariably to be paid to beadles, clerk, or other gild officers, so that as a rule the total sum was much more. Often, and this was especially the case in the late seventeenth and eighteenth centuries, the company openly raised the fees, and we find that such sums as ten, twenty, or thirty pounds were demanded ; while even where definite rules did not exist, it was quite common for the new freeman to give a breakfast or dinner to the company, or " of his beneficence " to make it some present, such as a silver spoon or a considerable sum of money. [3]

It would be interesting to know what became of those apprentices who were too poor to pay their fees and set up for themselves. Some may have moved into a country district outside the sphere of gild supervision ; others may have left the trade altogether and have found employment in some form of unskilled labour. Or they may have obtained leave to work as journeymen, paying the gild a small quarterly or yearly sum for the privilege. Some companies allowed men who were not free to work on these terms. At Carlisle the Tailors' rule was that no one was to set any foreigner to work without licence of the four Wardens and two undermasters ; [4] and in Hull strangers were allowed to work if they paid a fine and obtained a licence. [5] In Bristol the Merchant

---

[1] Dumville Smythe, Girdlers, p. 135. " The apprentice was made free by the appearance of his Indenture and the testimony of his said master."

[2] See Chapter XIII.

[3] See pp. 91; 124.

Holmes, Pontefract, p. 379. Man, if apprenticed without the town, must bring a certificate and pay £5 to the Mayor and £40 to the company.

[4] Ferguson, Carlisle, p. 146. Rules, 1558.

[5] Lambert, *op. cit.*, p. 191.

Tailors charged "strange sowers" a fee if they worked for more than fifteen days in the city, and, presumably, upon its payment they might work unmolested.[1] The term "stranger" is generally applied to non-townsmen, but probably the privilege extended to them would be granted also to workmen trained in the company. In Bath journeymen tailors had to gain permission of the Master of the Tailors' Company, and pay 3d. for free sewing, and 2d. quarterage.[2] Occasionally, after paying quarterage for some years, they were admitted to the freedom.[3] Possibly, therefore, those apprentices whose masters were not by agreement or custom obliged to pay for them, and who could not themselves pay the admission fee at the end of their term, were allowed to work as journeymen, and save from their wages the necessary sum. But this is not clear. The companies and gilds have no definite rules on the matter. We know that, generally speaking, non-freemen might not work ; and possibly it was only those sons who, in the due course of time, would succeed their fathers in the freedom by right of patrimony, who were allowed to work without paying the admission fees.[4] Upon his admittance to the company the young man could set up as a free master. Whether he did so depended upon his having the necessary capital, and upon whether he could find an opening. Otherwise, he would work for wages as a free journeyman by the day, week, or year, or by piece-work. Occasionally, however, he was not given the choice, but was obliged to serve as a "hireman" for a certain period before he might work as a free master. This rule was a part of the general policy of limiting numbers in the interests of those

[1] Fox, Merch. Tailors, pp. 67, 86. Rules, 1640. "8ᵈ for poor and xiiᵈ to wardens of ye sowers."

Holmes, Pontefract, p. 368. Butchers allowed persons without the town to sell at a stall on paying 8d. a time.

[2] Shickle, Merch. Tailors, Bath, p. 21.

[3] Ibid., p. 22.

[4] The instance Mr. Shickle gives is that of John Blowen, who, after paying quarterage for some years, was admitted to the freedom in 1671. His father died in 1670.

who were already established in the trade. No doubt, also,
this plan was adopted by masters because when more than
seven years' service became unusual, it was the only way in
which they could obtain labour rather more cheaply, and
retain in their service workmen who were used to their ways.
It had, of course, always been to their interests to have
apprentices bound to them for a long term, as the boys' work
was of more value as the years went on. Whether the
apprentice became a journeyman or set up as a free workman it was customary for his master to fit him out, to some
extent, for his start in life. All through the seventeenth
century it is common to find the master providing his
apprentice with a double suit of apparel at the end of his
term ;[1] sometimes he gives him the tools necessary to
his occupation.[2] The eighteenth century indentures contain
similar conditions, but the paternal feeling of masters
towards apprentices was then breaking down, and they were
consequently readier to pay the lad a sum of money and be
quit of all further obligations towards him. Small sums
were given in addition to clothing, even in the seventeenth
century, but it was not until the next century that such
payments became frequent.

The capital necessary to start business was not great in
the sixteenth and seventeenth centuries, when trade was on
a small scale, and the turnover rapid. But in the eighteenth,
when the market was wider and there were many large

---

[1] MSS. Hertford, Norwich, Bristol, Oxford.

Northampton Records, ii., Cox, p. 321. Transcript of enrolts., 1563, 1565,
1575. Double apparel and sometimes small sums of money.

[2] MSS. Bristol, Enrolts., 1645. Son of a gunsmith bound to a joiner, who is
to give him tools at the end of his term.

Williams, Barber Surgeons of Norwich, p. 19. Extracts from enrolts.,
1582 : "Johy Elvye had apprenticed to him one William Haynsworth to
whom he was to deliver 1 bason, 2 shaving cloths, 1 ewer, 1 comb, a pair
of scyssors, 1 rase-knife with a case, and double apparel."

Other similar entries.

Cf. Leader, Sheffield Cutlers, i. p. 43.

Cox, Northampton Records, ii. p. 323. Oct. 6, 35 Eliz. Master to teach
apprentice the mistery or science of a musician, and to give him at end of
term "double apparel, fyve shillings in money, and a treble violene."

businesses, it must have been hard for an unestablished man to make any way at all, unless he had a considerable amount of capital behind him. A few benevolent persons bequeathed money for the purpose of launching young tradesmen,[1] but there still would have been many who had not sufficient means of their own, and who yet were not chosen as the recipients of such charities. For them there was little chance of rising above the rank of journeymen.

[1] Howell, Conflicts of Capital and Labour, p. 73. Young men of good repute would get credit for as much wool as would enable him to start as a small master.

Ravenhill, Case of the Grocers. Apprentices on ending service were lent money to set up.

"To be lent to young men that had served their times to members of this company on security, with little or no Interest, to set up, to be returned again."

CHAPTER XI

THE CONDITIONS OF LIFE AND WORK OF THE INDUSTRIAL CHILD

IN its best days apprenticeship was not merely a system of technical instruction, it was also a method of education, and indeed the only method available for the majority of boys. It is true there was little book learning, but general training and the formation of character were as much the master's business as the teaching of a handicraft. This double nature of apprenticeship was openly and universally recognised by the gilds, which until the last days of their existence made bye-laws regulating the conduct and domestic life of apprentices, and thus gave their support to masters in this side of their work ; it was recognised also, as late as 1814, by the House of Commons, when the chief motive of those who opposed the repeal of the Statute of Artificers was the belief that apprenticeship had a social value apart from any question as to its necessity in the workshop.[1] This educational purpose of apprenticeship clearly influenced the conditions of service. In the first place, until the decadent days of apprenticeship in the eighteenth century, the "indoor system" was strictly enforced ; the apprentice, that is to say, lived in his master's house, and was regarded as a member of the family, for whose moral and physical development the master was responsible all day and every day. Further, the gilds saw to it that the lad was bound to a suitable master. Many of them would not sanction the binding unless the prospective master was capable of supporting and teaching an apprentice, or unless he were a married man or had

---

[1] Hansard, Parl. Debates, xxvii. pp. 573, 879.

a house of his own.   It can be seen at a glance that these rules were largely dictated by the self-interest of towns or gilds, but motives are invariably mixed, and a desire for the apprentice's welfare played its part too.   There was more chance that he would be well taught if his teacher was himself a skilful workman, with a seven years' apprenticeship behind him, and more certainty that he would be cared for if his master had attained to years of discretion, and was a householder, not a casual lodger or " chamber dweller."

The instruction of an apprentice in his trade was, of course, contracted for in the indentures.   It is, as a rule, expressly stated that the child is to be fully and completely taught his master's art, and if the conditions of the agreement were broken, the contract, like any other contract, could be declared null and void.   The Statute of Artificers gave to justices of the peace the power to decide all differences between the contracting parties,[1] and in the last resort the apprentice might complain to the justices, who could either oblige the master to instruct his apprentice, or could free the boy altogether from his agreement.[2]   Probably,

[1] 5 Eliz. c. 4. This Act required four justices for the cancelling of indentures. By later Acts two only were necessary if the indenture was returned at the next sessions with the reason for cancelling.
     Chitty, Law of Apprenticeship, p. 75. Apprentice could sue his master in case of non-observance of the covenants.
[2] Report on MSS., vol. i., Miscellaneous (1901), p. 129, Wilts Quarter Sessions. Robert Hobbes of Malmesbury discharged from his apprenticeship as his master has run away for debt (1654).
     Norwich MSS., Book XI., Quarter Sessions Minutes, 1639–54. May, 1653 : " Upon compleynt of Adam Pye ye older that Adam Pye his sonne apprentice wth Thomas Oliver to ye trade of Calender his master beinge now gone unto New England and his wife having left ye said Trade & not beinge able to maynteyn ye said apprentice." It was decided that Adam was to take his son and employ him. If Oliver did not return before Christmas next, the son to be fully discharged of his apprenticeship unless the wife was able to set up in trade.
     Ibid., May 14, 1653. Complaint against master.
     Ibid., May 17, 1654. Boy discharged from master who had not observed the agreement.
     Ibid., Book XVI. Quarter Sessions Minutes, July 19, 1700. Butcher has failed and is unable to employ and instruct his apprentice. Boy discharged.
     Ibid. (loose leaf), Oct. 11, 1 Wm. and Mary. Thomas Stone, son of a gentleman of Wicklewood, Norfolk, has complained before the justices of

however, the supervision of the gilds over their members, and, to a lesser extent, that of the municipal authorities over freemen, was a far greater protection to the boy against a bad master than was the then weak arm of the law. The periodical inspection of the searchers and other gild officers made it hard for a master to abuse his trust, while the courts of the gilds were much more accessible to the apprentice than were those of petty or quarter sessions, appeals to which involved a certain amount of trouble or expense. It was, in fact, the gilds which made of apprenticeship a sound working system. Prompted by the searchers, or appealed to by the boys, they obliged masters to teach their apprentices, or transferred the latter to new and more trustworthy masters if the old proved incorrigible.[1] The gilds, too, acted as arbitrators between master and apprentice when they could not agree. "It is Ordayned," ran the Merchant Tailors' rule, "that if any controversy fall betwene any Brother of this ffraternity and his Apprentice whereby the same doth growe to such an extremity that they are not to contynue the one with the other, then the Maister of the same apprentice shall bring into the Comõn Hall of the said Ffraternity the same Apprentice with his Indenture and there the cause of the variance to be examined And if the variance betwene them cannot be reconciled but that both be willing to depart the one from the other If it be thought convenient by the Maister and Wardens that they shalbe

---

the peace that his master, a chemist, has not for three and a half years used his trade "nor taken any care of his said apprentice for his maintenance and information in the said trade," as he has been a prisoner in the Common Gaol. The boy is discharged and turned over.

Yarmouth MSS. Quarter Sessions Minutes, March 18, 1745. Peter Frederickson complained of his master, a mariner, since he was not provided with meat, &c., nor instructed. Master says he is out of employment. Boy freed from his agreement.

[1] MS. Court Minutes, Norwich, Jan. 18, 1616. Complaint by father that his son, who had served six years as apprentice, is not employed in his trade. Master complains of misdemeanours. Case postponed.

Guilding, Reading Records, ii. p. 240, Diary of Corporation, June 22, 1625. Complaint against man who had left the town and made no provision for the instruction or maintenance of his apprentice.

severed the one from the other then the same Apprentice with his Indenture shalbe delivered over to the Maister of the Company for the tyme being and then the Maister and Wardens shall endeavour to provide a new Maister for the same Apprentice."[1] It may be noticed that the conditions under which trade and manufactures were carried on until the Industrial Revolution undoubtedly favoured sound apprenticeship. In the first place, the workshops were on a small scale ; probably in the majority of cases there would be only one or two journeymen and two or three apprentices or sons ; and, secondly, the master, though an independent workman, owning his materials, worked side by side with his employees. There was thus an opportunity for thorough instruction which the large workshop of an absentee master would not have afforded.

Hours of work must have been long. The working day for artificers and labourers hired by the day or week was defined by the Statute of Artificers as from 5 a.m. to 7 or 8 p.m. from the middle of March to the middle of September, inclusive of breakfast, dinner or drinking, in all not above two and a half hours—"that is to say, at every drinking one half hour, for his dinner one hour, and for his sleep when he is allowed to sleep, the which is from the midst of May to the midst of August, half an hour at the most, and at every breakfast one half hour."[2] From the middle of September to the middle of March the hours were "from the spring of the day until night." Probably these were the normal hours of work in the sixteenth century, and neither then or at any other time is it likely that the apprentices or young wage-earners who assisted adult workmen would have been given a shorter day. After all, though tailors sometimes worked at the houses of their customers, while workmen such as builders and watermen of course went out to their work, the greater number of trades were carried on in workrooms attached to or a part of the house. In these trades the hours of work would tend to be such

---

[1] Clode, Mems. Merchant Taylors, p. 225.   Rules, 1613, 34.
[2] 5 Eliz. c. 4, f. 12.

as daylight, meal times, and the demand for goods dictated.[1]
Craftsmen could if they chose work shorter hours, for they
were their own masters, but it was not until the nineteenth
century that there was any real reduction in the statutory
working day: in 1721, in an Act dealing with the wages
of London tailors, the working day is taken as from 6 a.m.
to 8 p.m., with one and a half hours for breakfast and one for
dinner.[2]   Sundays, festivals and feast days were kept entirely
or partially free from business,[3] so that the apprentice had
some holidays, while night work was specifically forbidden
by many gilds, and was everywhere uncustomary.[4]

After 1562, as in the old days, all the work which apprentices did was for their masters ; they were not allowed to
trade on their own account except in some of the merchant
companies, where buying and selling was a prominent part
of the business.   In these companies there was almost
always some rule limiting the amount of an apprentice's
trade.   For instance, at Newcastle, the Merchant Adven-

---

[1] *Cf.* Leader, Sheffield Cutlers, i. 64.   Masters worked unreasonable hours,
and some became lame in consequence.   Maximum day fixed : 6 a.m. to 8 p.m.
A fourteen hours' day.

[2] 7 Geo. I. c. 13.

[3] Ferguson, Carlisle, pp. 94, 176, 294.   Rules, p. 147.   No work on holidays.
Ferguson, Kendal, pp. 179, 142, 145, 146.   P. 127, Butchers' rule, limited to
certain hours.

Prideaux, Goldsmiths, i. p. 66.   Rules, 1566.   No Sunday work.

Clothworkers, p. 158.   Rules, 1639.

Humpherus, Watermen, i. p. 214.   Rules, 1626.   Ibid., p. 284.   Rules, 1662.
Holmes, Pontefract, p. 368.   Rules, 1652.

Fox, Merchant Tailors, Bristol, pp. 51, 68.   No work on Sundays and
festivals.

Clode, Mems. Merchant Tailors, p. 216.   Rules, 1613.

Schickle, Merch. Tailors, p. 52.   Rules, 1628.

Musicians, p. 63.   Rules, 1606.

Lambert, Two Thousand Years, p. 320.   Cordwainers' Rules, 1564.   Ibid.,
p. 247.   Tailors, 1680.   No work after 9 o'clock on Saturdays, and not to carry
home garments on Sundays.

[4] The Minstrels, probably for the convenience of the public, were not allowed
to play between the hours of 10 at night and 5 in the morning.   The City waits
were especially exempted from this rule.   See Musicians, p. 111.   Rules, 1555.

Prideaux, Goldsmiths, i. p. 66.   Rules, 1566.   No man to work by candle-
light after sunset.

See Chapter II.

turers' apprentices were not allowed to trade until they had served for seven years, and then not above ten pounds. "Forsomuch as dyvers and sundry brethren of this Felowship, havyng apprentices, do permytt and suffer theym, even in theyr furst yeres, to occupie gret sumes of money to there owne use and commoditie, under the clocke and cover of theyr master's trade, wherby the said apprentices, being at no nedeful chargs nor expenses, do not onely become hawtie mynded, high stomoked and wanton condycyoned, but also become less obedyent, and serviable to theyr maysters, not knowing there dewtie to theyr superyours."[1]

Apprentices received no wages. Chitty, writing in 1812 on the law of apprenticeship, states that the master was

---

[1] Surtees, Merchant Adventurers, Newcastle, p. 6.   Rule, 1554.
Cf. Chapter II.
Strype's Stowe (1720), ii. p. 330.
Add. MSS. (Brit. Mus.), 18,913.   Apprentices might ship 100 cloths a year after they had served seven years out of their nine.
Mercers' Charter, p. 70.   Rules, 1504, p. 82.
Sellers, Eastland Company, p. 69, General Court, Feb. 6, 1688.   Sum not to exceed £300 in any one year.
Cotton, Elizabethan Gild, p. 17.   Exeter Merchant Adventurers allow apprentices to trade upon their receiving permission of Master and Wardens (1561). They paid 6s. 8d. for permission.
Ferguson, Kendal, p. 138, Boke off Recorde, Shearman's rules, 1587.   No apprentice to trade during service.
Holmes, Pontefract, p. 380.   Rules, 1700.   No apprentice to buy or sell to his own use.
Clode, Mems. Merchant Taylors, p. 233.   Rules, 1613.   "Ordynaunce against Maisters that suffer their Apprentyces to buy and sell to theire owne uses."
Fox, Merchant Tailors, Bristol, p. 62.   No servant shall make work for his own profit.   Rules, 21 Eliz.
Surtees, Newcastle Hostmen, p. 159.   Trading forbidden, 1702.   Ibid., p. 165.   Committee to inquire into what apprentices have traded.
Surtees, Merchant Adventurers, pp. 7, 131, 191.   Minutes, Feb. 17, 1658. Apprentice brought before the court for trading.   Ibid., p. 242, Mins.   March 23, 1704.   Complaint against apprentice for "importing into Sunderland Hollands topp tow and other merchants goods."   Ibid., p. 248, Mins., Aug. 30, 1710.   Apprentice is refused his freedom since he had traded contrary to orders. Ibid., p. 263, Mins., May 6, 1771.   Act against apprentices trading repealed.
Welch, Pewterers, i. p. 240.   Rules, 1564.   No covenant servant to buy or sell, and no man of the said craft to buy or sell to a journeyman or apprentice. Ibid., p. 282.   Man fined for disobeying, 1575.

entitled to all the earnings of the apprentice, either in his own service or in the employment of another.[1] In 1744 the Pewterers consulted the Chamberlain as to the legality of paying wages in London, and he declared that "a master by his oath could not give his apprentice wages and the apprentice forfeits thereby his freedom."[2] Where mention is made of wages, it is generally in the building trade[3] or in a craft such as tailoring,[4] where master and apprentice went out to work upon the material or upon the premises of the customer. They each received so much for their day's work, but the master pocketed both wages.[5] To pay wages to an apprentice himself was against the custom of apprenticeship and the rules of his company. At Newcastle complaint was made in 1704 that in the Hostmens' Company "Severall ill-disposed brethren who regarded not the publick good but their own private Interest did give great wages to their apprentices and make private agreements with them to give

---

[1] Chitty, Law of Apprenticeship (1812), p. 67. *Cf.* Austin, Law of Apprenticeship, p. 61. What the apprentice earns if he runs away belongs to his master.

Vezey, i. p. 83. Hill *v.* Allen (1748).

Salkeld, Reports, i. p. 68. Barber *v.* Dennis. Whatever apprentice earns belongs to his master.

[2] Welch, Pewterers, ii. p. 191. Mins., 1744.

Cf. Mercers' Charter, p. 86. No master to give money for his apprentices' services.

[3] Thorold Rogers, Agriculture and Prices, vi. p. 694. Wages assessments for masons', carpenters', and plasterers' apprentices (1684). Ibid., p. 693. Ditto for apprentices of joiners, plumbers, and masons (1651). Ibid., p. 690. Ditto for those of joiners, carpenters, coopers, tilers, joiners and sawyers, &c.

Hamilton, Devon Quarter Sessions, p. 13. Assessments for apprentices of masons, plasterers, &c., 1594.

[4] Ferguson, Kendal, p. 148. Boke off Record, Oct. 17, 1612. "It is ordained and constituted by the Alderman and Burgesses . . . That every tailor now or hereafter dwelling within this borough or the liberties thereof shall upon one weeks warning repair and go to the house of every free inhabitant and there work and shall receive for the wages of their apprentices everyone 2ᵈ for a day's work for the first three years of each apprenticeship and for the fourth and fifth years of their apprenticeship 3ᵈ for a day and not above and for the sixth and seventh years etc. 4ᵈ for a whole days work and not above."

[5] Indentures at Corsham, April 4, 1785. Boy bound to a cooper. "And in case the said Robert Clark shall not have Sufficient Work in the summer season for the said apprentice to work all the harvest such as Haymaking and Reaping and what money he earns to be Paid to the said master."

them part of their time and suffered them to trade or some other clandestine agreemts." What their object was is not quite clear, but possibly such masters extorted higher premiums ; at any rate, the petitioners' annoyance is due to the fact that they cannot get premiums with their apprentices.[1]

The lad received instruction and maintenance, not money, in return for his work. This is always set forth in the chief terms of the indentures ; the master is to supply teaching, meat, drink, and lodging, and the apprentice is to give in return obedient service.[2] The details of the agreements varied ; occasionally clothes and washing were also expressly included, and sometimes it was especially mentioned that the master was to pay for the boy's tailoring and mending, sometimes for his doctor.[3] Such details were really superfluous, for it was an understood thing that the apprentice was to be found in all necessaries. It was a different matter when the conditions were reversed, and the parents or friends of the apprentice were required to supply either clothes or washing or doctoring. Such special arrangements were naturally entered in the indentures. This was a change which began to creep in about 1650, and which must be considered later on. The housing of apprentices was of the simplest and the food of the plainest. Even Manchester merchants at the close of the seventeenth century breakfasted off water potage, made of oatmeal, water, and a little salt, boiled thick, and poured into a dish. Master and apprentice, each with a

---

[1] Surtees, Hostmen, p. 165, March 16, 1704. *Cf.* Reports on MSS. Miscell., vol. i. (1901), p. 71. Wilts Hilary Sessions. Presentments of unqualified persons who employ journeymen and apprentices. One unqualified clothier has two apprentices to whom he did not give "no meate, drinke nether apparell, but geve them money by the yere, xx^s a piece." 1602.

[2] Salkeld, Reports, i. p. 66. Upon death of master executors must provide for apprentices. By master's death, only the covenant for instruction fails (10 Wm. III.).

[3] Chitty, *op. cit.*, p. 75. If unwell and there is probability of his recovery, he can oblige his master to provide for him.

MSS. Norwich, Book of Enrolments, 1625-49. Meat, drink, washing, lodging, and at end of term double apparel, are always given.

MSS. Bristol, Enrolments, 1630-60.

Leader, Sheffield Cutlers, i. pp. 39-42. Various conditions.

wooden spoon, dipped into the same dish, and thence into the milk pan.[1] But rough and ready fare was the order of the day, and unless the master was really a scamp, apprentices were no more hardly treated than the children of the house. As a rule they were of the same class socially as their employers; father and master were equals in the town, and the status of the apprentice was therefore not that of a servant, although his position, it is true, was a subservient one, and the menial work of the house often fell to his share.[2] He carried up the water from the river or acted as his master's errand boy, except in those companies where this had been forbidden as not being in accordance with the dignity of the society.[3] Still, this subserviency was enforced upon him not because of his apprenticeship, but because of his youth. Humility and a backward demeanour were considered becoming in the young, and a master would have failed in his duty if he had not instilled these virtues into those entrusted to his care. Sons taught at home were on the same footing as apprentices, for the boys were treated alike, and would have worked, played, and probably slept together.

Of education other than technical the apprentice had little. A few companies required that an intending apprentice

---

[1] Aikin, Forty Miles round Manchester, p. 183. *Cf.* Leader, *op. cit.*, p. 39. It is said of the shipwrights who went out to work with their apprentices, that their wages "together with the exorbitant Demand they make of Bread and Drink, which they generally receive five Times a Daye, amount in all to about 5l." Surtees, Hostmen, p. 185. Entry, Jan. 17, 1719.

[2] Defoe, Complete English Tradesman (1738), p. 149.

Aikin, *op. cit.*, p. 183. They carried the goods on their shoulders through the streets.

Leader, *op. cit.*, p. 40. Often they did domestic work after their working hours.

Strype's Stow (1720), ii., book v., p. 482. "Anciently it was the general Use and Custom of all Apprentices in London (Mercers only excepted, being commonly Merchants, and of better Rank, as it seems) to carry Water Tankards, to serve their Masters Houses with Water, fetched either from the Thames, or the common Conduits of London."

But see Aikin, *op. cit.*, p. 183. Apprentices in Manchester were considered "rather as servants than pupils."

[3] *E.g.*, Clothworkers' Rules, p. 156. The carrying of merchandise from place to place is forbidden, 1639.

should be able to read or write,[1] but book learning was
at a discount for the workman.   The apprentices of the
Merchant Adventurers were allowed to go abroad to learn
foreign languages necessary to their trade,[2] but it was not
until the late seventeenth century that parents stipulated for
the schooling of their sons, and even then it was exceptional.
Joshua Stork, cobbler, bound his son to a cutler of Sheffield
in 1697, and entered it into the agreement that the lad should
be allowed to go home for a month in the summer in the first
two years in order to learn to write.[3]   Another Sheffield
apprentice was to have one month in the first and last year
"to learn at ye writing school."[4]   Another, bound in 1706,
was to be allowed six weeks in his two first years "to go to
ye writing school (ye apprentice friends to pay ye writing
master)."[5] About 1715 stipulations to attend writing schools
are fairly frequent in Sheffield.   To an indenture of a boy
bound in 1706 at Corsham, a note was added, " Memorandum
it was agreed before sealing hereof by all parties therein concerned that the said William Godwyn shall teach his said
Appntice to write well before he is forth of his tyme."[6]

As a member of the household, the apprentice shared in
whatever moral teaching the family received, at any rate in
the best days of apprenticeship.   Defoe, writing in 1715 an
imaginary conversation between the master and father of an
apprentice, causes the former to ask, " Why, what would you
make of me ? Must I be a father and a master too ? Father.
No question of it ; he is under your family care.   As to his
body, he is your servant ; and as to his soul, I think he is as

[1] See p. 45.
[2] Surtees, Merchant Adventurers, i. p. 258 (1714).
[3] Leader, Sheffield Cutlers, i. p. 46.
[4] Ibid., p. 47.
[5] Ibid., p. 47.
    Cf. ibid., p. 47.   Son of a clothier bound to a Sheffield cutler for $9\frac{1}{4}$ years,
and was allowed three months in first two years, and two weeks in third and
fourth years for schooling.
[6] MS. Indentures at Corsham.   Peter Bush, bound May 20, 1706.
    Cf. Hardy, Beds Quarter Sessions, p. 48.   In 1777 an apprentice to a
Luton surgeon was freed from his indentures as his master had neglected to teach
him Latin, as he had promised in the agreement.

much your son as any child you have ; and I cannot acquit you of the obligation and duty of a parent to your servants, do you discharge your conscience of it how you please." [1]

The most useful work of apprenticeship lay, perhaps, upon its non-technical side, namely, in the formation of character and training for adult life and citizenship, the full value of which can best be appreciated by comparing the age of apprenticeship with the late nineteenth and early twentieth centuries. When the Elizabethan system was in force, boys while still under parental discipline, were bound apprentices ; that is to say, they were until manhood under the control of some responsible master, who had at his back the authority of the gild and the justices of the peace. There was no period of demoralising freedom between the lad's home life and his entry upon his career ; he passed straight from parental control into the hands of his master. Though he was under constant supervision, his sense of responsibility was nevertheless encouraged, for he had started upon his profession and he had a definite object before him, the attainment of his free mastership, which was to be gained not merely by the running out of his years of service, but by his own industry and good conduct. In our present state of rapid change it is impossible to generalise about any but the shortest periods, but if we consider the condition of industrial society in the twenty years previous to 1910, we shall find that the majority of boys became their own masters when, at fourteen years old, they left school. As wage-earners either in casual or regular work they were almost entirely free from parental control, and received little more supervision from their masters than did the adult workmen with whom they were employed. It was only the sons of well-to-do parents who were kept under control in our public schools until a later age. Long before Elizabeth's day it had been customary to bind the apprentice to good conduct and faithful service. " Taverns, inns or alehouses he shall not haunt, at dice and cards he shall not play," ran the old jingling formula

---

[1] Defoe, Family Instructor, part ii. p. 262. *Cf.* Clothworkers, p. 158. Rules, 1639. Members to see that apprentices go to church.

which was passed down through the centuries. He promised
civility to his master and abstention from loose living. The
gilds made rules for the conduct and behaviour of their
apprentices. In some towns the boys were not allowed to
be out after nightfall, while games of chance and the fre-
quenting of taverns were invariably forbidden.[1] Masters
who allowed their apprentices to run wild were summoned
before the court of their town or gild, disobedient apprentices were punished,[2] and penalties were inflicted upon those
who connived at evil conduct. The Sheffield Cutlers had a
rule, according to which any master who did not keep his
apprentice under his rule, government, and correction within
his own house and among his own family, but suffered such
apprentice to be absent from him above fourteen days in one
year, should forfeit 3s. 4d. for every day above the fourteen.[3]
In Reading in 1632 we find retribution falling upon an
apprentice's accomplice. A cobbler complained of a victualler who had received his apprentice and allowed him to
spend 10s. 6d. of his master's money. "And when search
was made for the apprentice he was denyed and shutt up in
a cupbord." The victualler was suppressed and ordered to
take down his sign that afternoon, "or ells it shalbe beaten
downe."[4] In their general conduct apprentices had to con-

---

[1] Court Leet Records, Manchester (Earwaker), i. p. 159. Sept. 30, 1573.
No man's servants or apprentices to be out after 8 in winter and 9 in sunmer.

Report on MSS. Miscell., i. (1901) p. 75.

Ferguson, Carlisle Records, p. 179. Shoemakers' Rules. No master to
allow an apprentice to play cards in his house. *Cf.* pp. 278, 286.

Sellers, Eastland Company, York, p. 27. Rules, 1617.

Brit. Mus., Addit. MSS., 18,913, Merchant Advens. "None apprentice shall
use anie excessive quaffinge or drinking himself . . . or shall play openly or
secretely at Cardes tables dyce or anie other game."

[2] Surtees, Merchant Adven., pp. 26, 27, 185, 192, 199, &c. Rules and
Minutes, 1562–1660.

Glass-sellers, p. 125. Rules, 1664.

[3] Leader, Sheffield Cutlers, ii. p. 10. Rules, 1662.

[4] Guilding, Reading Records, iii. p. 186. Aug. 16, 1663.

Cf. Ferguson, Carlisle, p. 278. Court Leet Records, Oct. 25, 1623. "We
present Edward Durance of Castlegait for keeping of Thomas Pearson being a
prentice and divers other at cards in mer. vi[s] 8[d]." Ibid., p. 287. "We present fine and amercy Andrew Foster for harbouring and entertayning honest mens

form to the standards of their masters, who stood to them *in loco parentis*. The latter had a legal right to correct their apprentices,[1] but the gild and municipal authorities were frequently being called upon to give their support to masters of refractory boys, runaways, and those who were guilty of more serious offences, such as thieving and embezzlement. One man appealed to the town court of Reading against his apprentice, " for his misdemeanour of striking and threatening him," and received permission to be quit of the lad.[2]   A Norwich apprentice was punished " in ye Assembly Chamber for Imbessilinge his maisters mony."[3]   Three Reading apprentices were imprisoned and whipped by order of the Corporation for " abusing Christopher Graye by throwinge turneps at him and hurtinge him therewith, as appeared by prooffe."[4]   One master complained to his gild court of a violent apprentice who " did threaten him in an unusuall manner, and often swore he would be his death, and would crush his head against the table, with many such like provokeing expressions."[5]   Apprentices could be sued in the courts of law for any act unconnected with the contract, but no action could be taken against them for the non-observance of their duty, except in London, where there was a particular custom.   Apprentices could, however, be taken before the

children and apprentises att unlawfull tymes and suffering them to tiple and drinke in his house and to waist their parents and masters goods and therefore we doe amercy him xl[s]."
Musicians' Company, p. 79.   Master punishable if he allows apprentice to play any unlawful game.

[1] Chitty, *op. cit.*, p. 73.   In London freemen could dismiss their apprentices for gaming.   *Cf.* Leader, *op. cit.*, i. p. 40.

[2] Guilding, Reading Records, ii. p. 335, 1626.

[3] MS. Court Book, Norwich, xv., May 3, 1620. Another apprentice was punished on the same day for a similar offence. *Cf.* Atkinson, North Riding Quarter Sessions, v. p. 222.   Apprentice sent to the House of Correction for purloining his master's goods.

[4] Guilding, *op. cit.*, iii. p. 352.

[5] Surtees, Merchant Adventurers, p. 246.   Minutes, Dec. 13, 1704.

Cf. Jupp, Carpenters, p. 249.   " Thomas Harris appntice to Joyse Buckley widdowe punished for pphaning the Lords Sabbaoth, lyeng out of his mrs howse, cominge home late, and breaking her windows with Stones." *Cf.* pp. 141, 381.

Norwich MSS., Court Book, xv., April 18 and May 3, 1620.

justices of the peace and quarter sessions, and be punished
by them.[1] Some Hertford apprentices were presented for
disturbing " ye people in ye church at ye tyme of divine
service." [2] The cases which most frequently came before the
justices were those of runaway apprentices, especially towards
the close of the seventeenth century. Writs had to be issued
for their arrest, and they were often tracked to a considerable
distance.[3] When brought back they were generally whipped
or sent to the Houses of Correction or Bridewells for a time,
but even this was not sufficient to prevent their making fresh
efforts after freedom.

Apprentices in their turn could appeal to the gild and
municipal authorities against their masters in cases of over-

[1] Chitty, *op. cit.*, p. 75. Ibid., p. 93. Two justices of the peace on complaint
of the master may commit the apprentice for the month to the House of Correction or discharge the indentures. 20 Geo. II. c. 19.

Modern Reports (1700), p. 886. It was urged by plaintiff that justices of
the peace had no power to discharge a master of his apprentice in case the fault
be in the apprentice, but only to minister due correction and punishment to him.
Declared this had been over-ruled. 29 Ch. II. in B.R.

[2] MSS. Hertford, vol. 9, p. 118, Oct. 7, 1635.

Cf. S. P. D., Ch. I., ccciv. 96 (1638).

MSS. Norwich, Case XI., Shelf G. Bundle of quarter session papers for
Lynn, &c., Oct. 14, 1669. Ibid., Case XX., Shelf A, Book xvi., Quarter Session
Mins., April 13, 1700.

MSS. Yarmouth, Quarter Session Mins., April 14, 1712. Joiners' apprentice is idle and is discharged.

[3] 5 Eliz. c. 4, f. 47, gave justices, mayors, and bailiff powers to issue writs of
capias.

MSS. Norwich, Court Book, xv., March 25, 1626. Peter Frost, apprentice
with a tailor of Derenham, found a vagrant in the City and punished and sent
back with a pass. Thomas Brown, runaway, is punished and delivered to his
dame. Ibid., Oct. 4, 1620. Two boys punished and sent home. " Thomas ffaire-
man for running away punished and sent home and his master to pay his charges
in Bridewell " (c. Oct. 4, 1615 ; Feb. 27, 1616 ; May 27, 1620). June 28, 1620 :
" Edward Burges Apprentice with John Grene of Yarmouth ys punished and sent
to his maister wth a passe." July 27 : apprentice from London punished and
sent back with a pass.

Hardy, Herts Quarter Sessions, p. 241. Warrant to the keeper of his
Majesty's House of Correction at Hertford, April 1, 1674.

A method of dealing with runaways, adopted by some gilds, was to cross
their names off the books—*e.g.*, Surtees, Hostmen, p. 91 (1649).

Surtees, Merchant Adventurers, p. 189 (Mins., 1657), pp. 205-7 (Mins.,
663).

severity or actual cruelty. There were, of course, bad masters who starved or otherwise ill-treated their apprentices: that was inevitable. Such cases were, however, fairly promptly taken up by the gilds, and the grievance was remedied if possible, or if the case were flagrant the master would be punished or the boy transferred to some other crafts-man.[1] Thomas Palmer, who broke "Henry Bourefelde his apprentice's hedd without any juste cause" was committed to prison by the Merchant Tailors' court, and was made to pay the money "owing to a surgion for healing the apntices heede of the said Henry, broken by the said Thomas."[2] A Reading apprentice whose mistress had mal-treated him, was discharged from his service by the City court, and the woman was obliged to deliver up his inden-tures and clothes, and to pay 2s. 6d. in money.[3] Another apprentice of the same town was not so lucky, for his master, who had "greivously kickt and throwne his said apprentice against the ground," was allowed to keep him upon promise to use him well.[4] A Newcastle apprentice, bound to a Merchant Adventurer, was discharged from his bond and given three months in which to find a new master, because the first "did violently beat him, and endeaverd to thrust him headlong downe staires."[5] In the last resort, four justices

[1] By the custom of London a freeman might turn over his apprentice (see Chitty, Law of Apprenticeship, p. 78). Apparently the London custom was adopted elsewhere. A justice of the peace could not turn over an apprentice, though parish apprentices could be assigned with consent of two justices of the peace by 32 Geo. III. c. 57, s. 7. Justice of the peace could mediate between the parties by 5 Eliz. c. 4, f. 35. If they submitted to his decision it was binding (Chitty, p. 89). Justice of the peace could compel apprentice but not master (ibid., p. 99). If master did not conform, justices might take bond to oblige him to appear at the next sessions. Sessions might be applied to in the first case (ibid., p. 89). 20 Geo. II. c. 19, s. 3, two justices of the Peace could discharge a parish apprentice or one with whom not more than £5 premium was paid.

[2] Clode, Early History Merchant Tailors, p. 209. Court Mins., 1563.

[3] Guilding, Reading Records, ii. p. 351. Mins., 1627.

[4] Ibid., iv. p. 550. Mins., 1654.

[5] Surtees, Merchant Adven., p. 241. Mins., 1699.

See also:—

MSS. Hertford, vol. 18, p. 152, Aug. 13, 1776. Examination of Charl

of the peace in quarter sessions could free an apprentice from his engagement.[1] It is obvious that the apprentice had a far better chance of good treatment and of redress from bad when the companies were flourishing and their system of search was being energetically conducted. When the

Slocomb, taken on oath. His master, a hatter, had ill-used him, "and sayd he would have broke his ribs if he could."

MSS. Norwich, Court Book xv., Jan. xv., 1616. Complaint of father that master has ill-used his son. Surgeon required for his recovery.

Ibid., May 13, 1615. Apprentice discharged from his master by the town court because he has been neglected.

Guilding, Reading Records, ii. p. 259. Mins., 1625. Master fined 10s. and the apprentice discharged because "the boy did lacke meat and drinke, and al other needful thinges. Cf. ibid., June 9, 1624 (ii. p. 188). Mins., p. 260.

North Riding Quarter Sessions, vol. 6., pp. 6, 9. Apprentice proves his master's "great and unhandsome usage" and obtains a discharge. 1658, ibid., vol. 7, p. 46. An apprentice to a mariner proves his master's ill-usage. He is therefore to be assigned over by his master to other mariners for voyages and his master is to receive his wages. When on shore he is to live with his friends (1681).

[1] F. Const, Laws Relating to the Poor, p. 572.

35 Ch. II. Court held that an apprentice could not according to 5 Eliz. c. 4 be discharged except at a General Sessions. Rex v. Gately, 7 Wm. III. Power of the sessions to discharge apprentices extends only to such trades as are specially named in the Statute.

MSS. Norwich, Book xi., Quarter Session Mins., Sept. 16, 1639. Complaint against Norris concerning his apprentice. Boy is discharged and master is to give him a fitting suit of apparel. Another man is to treat his apprentice well. If there is complaint again the court will discharge him.

Ibid., book xvi. Entry Oct. 7, 1692. Worsted weaver's apprentice turned over. Boy complained to the Mayor of ill-usage and other matters, " which Mr Maior declared he could not accommodate between them but left the same to this Court." The case is heard and the boy is to be assigned over to such master dyer as his parents may choose.

Cf. MSS. Yarmouth, Quarter Session Records, 1738.

Hardy, Hertford Quarter Sessions Records, pp. 82 (1743), 118 (1771), 122 (1772), 128 (1774).

MSS. Hertford, vol. 18, p. 120. Petty Sessions Minutes, Nov. 17, 1773. Printed warrant with written insertions. "To the Constables of *the Parish of Allsaints* in the said *Borough*

"Whereas complaint hath been made unto us *John Green Mayor of the said Borough* and *Richard Cutler Gentleman* two of his Majesty's Justices of the Peace in and for the said *Borough* by *Charles Slocomb* apprentice to *Jacob Law* of the *Parish of all Saints* in the said *Borough Hatter* that he the said *Jacob Law* hath misused and illtreated him the said *Charles Slocomb* these are therefore to require you to summon the said *Jacob Law* to appear before us."

gilds became weak and less active apprentices had less protection. Theoretically they could appeal to justices of the peace, but practically they hardly ever did so.

The least well treated of all apprentices were probably the parish apprentices, both those pauper children who were bound by the overseers and also the sons and daughters of poor people who were bound by the justices. A premium was generally given with them, and for the sake of it they would be taken by men who often could not very well support them and who had no particular appreciation of their duties. Parish apprentices were often forced upon unwilling masters, and were not unusually bound to men in the rougher and poorer trades, such as cobbling and pin-making, where the competition was great and the conditions of work miserable. Such apprentices, even when apprenticeship was at its best, would have had many hardships to endure and little hope of betterment at the end of their time. As to the ordinary apprentices, it was only in exceptional cases that they had reason to complain. The cruelty of which we hear in connection with the apprentices of chimney-sweeps and others at the close of the eighteenth century is not typical of apprenticeship as a whole. Then the doctrine of *laissez faire* was in the ascendant and had paralysed the action of the justices of the peace and rendered impossible the minute supervision of the gilds.

Of well-intentioned harshness, however, there was more than enough. Still, this was not meted out to apprentices only, but to the young as a whole. Even the children of the well-to-do were treated with severity by their elders. Youth was regarded as a phase of life which all too easily could become tiresome in the home and unprofitable in the market-place. The rules of the gilds and the entries in their court minutes books show a persevering intolerance towards all the natural inclinations of youth. Sports and games, dancing, music, and the simplest conceits of dress were forbidden to apprentices. This severity was not confined to the age of the Puritans; they may have made a special attack upon unshaven heads, but even in the rollicking days of the Restoration the same strict regulations were observed against the boy.

The sports and pastimes of apprentices were almost universally discountenanced. Dice and cards were, naturally enough, prohibited, but in some localities apprentices were not allowed to attend the play; mumming and dancing were forbidden, and even "the use of musik" was considered unsuitable. The Merchant Adventurers had a rule to this effect.[1] Perhaps they found that music led to rowdiness; certainly their apprentices appear to have been boisterously inclined, for the company passed a rule at this time forbidding them to walk abroad in the night "or knock or ring at men's doors or beat at windows." Nor were they allowed to entertain their friends: "None apprentice shall make anie sett bankett dinner or supper either at his loudging or in anie other place."[2] In 1697 the Newcastle branch of the company forbade their apprentices "to get to fencing or dancing schools, nor to music houses, lotteries, or playhouses, neither to keep any sort of horses, dogs for hounting, or fighting cocks."[3] The playing of football was vigorously opposed in many places. In Manchester the complaint was made that apprentices played "giddye yaddye or catts pallett and ffoote ball,"[4] and in 1618 there is an entry in the Court Leet minutes: "Officers for ye foote ball, John Beswicke, George Richardson, Robarte Boarman,"[5] whose duty, we may suppose, was the prosecution of apprentices athletically inclined. The Shoemakers have an entry about 1595, "Item it is fully condiscended and agreed upon by the fellowship of this gyld that no journeyman or apprentice shall make any foot balle to sell or play withal without consent and knowledge of his or their maisters and that

---

[1] & [2] Addit. MSS. (Brit. Mus.), 18,913 (1608). *Cf.* Surtees, Merchant Adven., Newcastle, p. 22 (1603). No brother or sister to permit their apprentices to "daunce dice carde mum or use any musick eyther by night or daye in the streetes."

[3] Surtees, Newcastle Adventurers, p. 25, Nov. 24, 1697. *Cf.* Strype's Stow, ii. p. 432. Proclamation by the City authorities, 1582.

[4] Earwaker, Court Leet Records, Manchester, ii. p. 432 (1609).

[5] Ibid., iii. p. 4 (1618). *Cf.* ibid. ii., p. 239 (1608).

they shall not play at football within the liberties of this cittie." [1] The fine for playing football at Kendal was 12d. every time every party and 3s. 4d. for every window broken. [2]

Extravagances in dress and personal adornment were usually suppressed with an iron hand. The standard upheld for the clothes of an apprentice was plainness, yet decency, for the honour of the company, while the apprentice had to wear his hair neatly trimmed and not in curls or ruffianly about his ears. Such regulations weighed heavily upon the more spirited apprentices, for handsome clothes were as much desired by them as by the young townsmen who swagger about our streets to-day. The youths of the seventeenth century especially endured a vast amount of bitterness of spirit owing to their masters' predilection for sober garments. Not even the innocent vanity of a gay shoelace was tolerated by the companies. In 1649 the Merchant Adventurers of Newcastle regulated the price of the lads' coats and hats, the cut of their clothes, and the fashion of their shoe strings. [3] Those whose dress was not sufficiently sober were brought into the court, stripped of superfluous ribbons, and sent to prison. In some companies it was expressly ordered that apprentices should wear only such clothes as were allowed them by their masters. In London the Lord Mayor issued an order upon dress, which was followed by an Act of Common Council, forbidding apprentices to wear clothes of their own providing, and stating minutely what articles of dress might not on any account be worn. [4] At Newcastle, even as early as 1554, extravagance in dress had reached such a pitch that an " acte for the apparell of apryntyses " was passed, giving to the Mayor, Aldermen, and Sheriffs the power to make any regulations they chose as to how apprentices should dress. Masters were to be fined if their appren-

---

[1] Ferguson, Carlisle, p. 180. Rules, 1595.
[2] Ferguson, Kendal, p. 170 (1641). *Cf*. Mercers' Charter, p. 75. Rules, 1504.
[3] Surtees, Merchant Adven., p. 23 (1649).
[4] Heath, Grocers, pp. 90–1 (1611).
    Strype's Stow, ii. p. 432. Proclamation issued by the City, 1582.
    Clode, Early History of Merchant Taylors, i. p. 43.

tices appeared clad contrary to the bye-rules, while the lads themselves were to forfeit the time they had served.[1] In 1603 it was ordered that a special gaol should be opened for the reception of disobedient apprentices, and that an officer should be appointed to look after them.[2] Possibly the earlier rule was thought to be too harsh. In many gilds it was general enough to forbid an apprentice to wear velvet, lace, and embroidery, and to limit the price of his coat. Brethren and sisters of the Merchant Adventurers' Gild at Newcastle might not allow their apprentices to "weare anie undecent apparell, but plain, and of cloth under x^s the yarde, or fustian of or under iij^s the yeard, nor to wear any velvate or lace . . . neither anie silke garters."[3] In 1608 the London company passed an order to the effect that if any apprentice wore any apparel which, in the opinion of the governors, was not fit for his estate, " but rather beseeming some courtier serving man or some other lyke psone," such as gold or silver buttons, lace and jewels, he should have them taken from him for the first offence and be punished for the second.[4] It is, of course, in the wealthy companies, such as the Merchant Adventurers and the great London companies, that we find records of strife over dress. Sons of small gildsmen bound to masters in the less wealthy companies would have been unable to supplement the clothes given them by their masters.

The most penniless apprentice, however, could grow a becoming crop of hair, and he clung pathetically to his locks, his one little touch of fashion. Alas, the gildsmen were entirely unsympathetic and sternly suppressed all frivolity of a hirsute nature! At Newcastle there was a long-drawn battle. It opened, apparently, in 1603 with an order that

[1] Surtees, op cit., p. 20. Mins., Nov. 14, 1554.

[2] Ibid., p. 22.

[3] Ibid., p. 22, cf. p. 122 ; Mins., cf. pp. 26, 28. Privileges of trading restricted to those apprentices who conformed to acts as to dress, hair, and behaviour. P. 248, Mins., June 6, 1711. Complaint against John Lawson, apprentice, for wearing gold and silver lace on his hat and ruffles at neck, breast, and hands. Fined 20s.

[4] Addit. MSS. (Brit. Mus.), 18,913.

apprentices should not "weare their haire long nor locks at their eares like ruffians."[1] The matter did not end there. In 1649 the Master and Wardens, who were probably godly and sadly clad Puritans, made a vigorous attempt to "order" the hair of their apprentices. "Every apprentice, belonging to the brethren of the saide Fellowshipp, shall cutt his haire from the crowne of the heade, keepe his foreheade bare, his lockes (if any) shall not reache belowe the lapp of his eare, and the same length to be obsered behynd."[2] This was in October; in November all those bound to officers of the company had to come before the court for inspection;[3] on December 7th nine who had refused to obey were brought into court and there shaved, after which operation they were sent to prison.[4] A few days later all other apprentices were ordered to appear before the Wardens, and three, "being not cutt suitable to the said act, they were all three ordered to go to John Hall the barber to bee better trimmed and to come again to court."[5] Strangely enough, it was the apprentices who emerged triumphant from this conflict. On January 18th the act of October was suddenly annulled, as the court had been overworked ever since it was passed "by correctynge some apprentices superfluityes of hayre and apparell."[6] In London an apprentice coming before the Pewterers' court with unseemly hair had his locks then and there cut off;[7] in 1638 the Ironmongers refused to grant any apprentice his freedom until he had "orderly cutt and barbed his hayre," to the liking of Master and Wardens, since of late young men had worn their hair "unseemly over long, more like to ruffians than to citizens' apprentices."[8] At the close of the

[1] Surtees, Merchant Adven., p. 22.
[2] Ibid., p. 23.
[3] Ibid., p. 153, Court Minutes.
[4] Ibid., p. 154.
[5] Ibid., p. 155, cf. pp, 158, 161.
[6] Ibid., p. 24.
[7] Welch, Pewterers, ii. p. 86. Mins., 1628.
[8] Nicholl, Ironmongers, p. 228. "Because many young men doe take unto themselves a liberty in their apprentishippe, by their m^r his conivence, to wear their hayre unseemly overlong, more like to ruffians then citizens' apprentizes, and after their terme of their service ended, come to demand their freedome of this Company in that disguised manner; for remedy thereof, it is now ordered that hereafter, if any master shall make free any of his servants before he have orderly cutt and barbed his hayre to the liking of the m^r and wardens of the

seventeenth century there was a new difficulty : the attraction of ruffles, ribbons and curls faded before the glory of wigs, and new regulations had to be devised. " Noe apprentice shall weare long wiggs nor any short wiggs, above the price of fifteene shillings." [1]

It is a relief to turn from these rules to the Court Minutes of various towns, there to see the number of lads presented for setting the gild regulations at naught, by playing games, or engaging in sport, as did Puckridge of Reading, who bought a horse with his master's money " and kept it secretly at great charges, to ride at his pleasure." [2]   Of course, these apprentices were punished,[3] but probably then, as now, the sufferers were out-numbered by those who successfully evaded one or other of these numerous bye-rules.

It is noticeable that, from the close of the seventeenth century onwards, apprentices became more and more out of hand.   It was found necessary to include apprentices in the parliamentary Act of 1692 forbidding hunting. "Whereas great mischief doe ensue by inferiour Tradesmen apprentices and other dissolute persons neglecting their Trade and Employment who follow Hunting fishing and other game to the ruin of themselves and damage of their neighbours," [4] they were now forbidden to engage in these pursuits.   In 1757 yet another statute forbade apprentices and journeymen to play cards, dice, shuffle-board, mississipi or billiards, tables, skittles and ninepins in public-houses.[5]

Company for the tyme being, the m^r of the apprentice shall pay to the Comp^y for every suche neglect xx^s for a fine."

[1] Surtees, Merch. Adven., p. 25, Nov. 24, 1697.

[2] Guilding, Reading Records, iii. p. 185. 1633.

[3] Yarmouth MSS., Quarter Sessions Minutes, April 17, 1738; Jan. 13, 1740; Nov. 17, 1741.

MSS. Bath, book 85, Oct. 21 and 24, 1776 ; Jan. 16, 1777.

MSS. Hertford, vol. 18, p. 193. May 31, 1773. Apprentice departed from his master's service and did not return until " last night " and now declares " that he will not do him any more good."

Hardy, Herts Quarter Session Records, ii. pp. 129, 131.

Surtees, Hostmen, p. 167. Complaints of apprentices for their disorderly lives. 1705.

[4] 4 Wm. and Mary, c. 23.

[5] 30 Geo. II. c. 24, f. 14.

All through the eighteenth century there were numerous disputes between masters and apprentices; the latter constantly ran away before their term of service had expired, just when their work was beginning to repay their masters for their earlier trouble.[1] In 1766 cases of such desertion were so frequent that an Act was passed to enable masters to compel their runaway apprentices to serve for so long as they had been absent in addition to the nominal term,[2] and in 1789 an association was formed at Sheffield for the apprehension of absconding apprentices.[3]

Perhaps it was because apprentices were becoming more troublesome to manage that men began to be unwilling to take them on the old conditions; at any rate, it was about this same time that masters demanded larger premiums and began to shirk sometimes one detail, sometimes another of their old duties. Defoe draws attention to the difference in the relations of master and apprentice about the year 1726 and their attitude to each other about 1670. "The case of tradesmen differs extremely in this age from the case of those in the last, with respect to their apprentices and servants; and the difference is all to the disadvantage of the present age. Fifty or sixty years ago, servants were infinitely more under subjection than they are now; they were content to submit to family government and the just regulations,

---

[1] MSS. Yarmouth Quarter Sessions Records. Richard Waller's case, June 24, 1730. Master complains boy is "very undutiful and dishonest and hath oftentimes run away from His Service . . . so that he hath had little or no Good of his Time."

MSS. Hertford, vol. 26, p. 205, May 31, 1779.

MSS. Bristol, book 1684–1699. Oct. 5, 1689, boy bound; October, 1692, crossed off the books for running away.

Leader, op. cit., i. pp. 51, 76.

Vict. Cnty. Hist., Northamptonshire, i. p. 309. Advertisement in the Northampton Mercury for a runaway apprentice.

[2] 6 Geo. II. c. 25, s. 1. "Whereas Persons employed in several Manufacturies of this Kingdom frequently take apprentices who are very young, and for several years of their apprenticeships, are rather a Burthen than otherwise to their Masters: And whereas it frequently happens that such apprentices, when they might be expected to be useful to their Masters, absent themselves from their Service: And whereas the Laws in being are not sufficient to prevent these inconvenience . . ."

[3] Leader, op. cit., i. p. 51.

which masters made in their houses, were not scorned and contemm'd, as they are now ; family religion also had some sway upon them, and if their masters did keep good orders, and preserve the worship of God in their houses, the apprentices thought themselves obliged to attend at the usual hours for such services ; nay, it has been known, that if the master of the family has been sick, or indisposed, or out of the town, the eldest apprentice has read prayers to the family in his place." [1] No doubt some allowance must be made for the tendency, common amongst moralists, of regretfully looking back upon the good old days. It is, however, clear that the relations of master and apprentice were changing. Whereas in Elizabethan times the master had found the apprentice in everything, food, drink, lodging, washing, mending, clothing, and doctoring, it was not uncommon, from about 1680 onwards, for one or other of these items to be omitted from the contract. Sometimes it was especially agreed and entered in the indentures that the parents should keep the apprentice supplied with hose and linen ; elsewhere they paid for his washing, or half his medical expenses when he had small-pox. [2] From other indentures we can conclude that

[1] Defoe, Complete English Tradesman (1738), p. 143.
[2] Cox, Northampton Records, ii. p. 321 seq.

Leader, op. cit., i. p. 40. Sheffield Cutlers used printed forms in the eighteenth century. The terms included good, wholesome, and sufficient meat, drink, washing and lodging and 6d. yearly, but clothes were not always given ; a space was left in the printed form for stipulations as to apparel (pp. 41-3).

Bristol MSS., Enrolment Books 1630-1848. C. 1660, master gives the apprentice double apparel and the freedom of the city at the end of term. C. 1680, friends generally provide clothes during term. C. 1724, friends provide clothes almost always and premiums are often given—e.g., p. 55, Oct. 28, 1686, father finds apparel. Oct. 28 and 29, 1686, mother provides it. Oct. 6 and 13, 1686, friends provide it.

MSS. Oxford, Hanaster Book, 1697-1717. Aug. 6, 1696. Yeoman's son bound to a cordwainer. Master to provide him with clothes and other necessaries half his time and the other half his friends are to do so.

MSS. Norwich, Enrolments, Oct. 2, 1749. Francis Church, a yeoman, bound his son with a premium of £30. His master was to supply him with meat and drink and other necessaries, "except wearing clothes of all sorts and washing and mending them." For this the father was responsible. "And further in case the said Thomas shall at any time during the said term be ill with the Small Pox, that then the said ffrancis Church his Exrs and Admors shall bear and pay

apprentices were occasionally given money. These sums are often so small that it is obvious they were not intended as anything but the lad's pocket-money, but as time went on they assume the character of a definite wage; they were paid regularly and often rose year by year as the lad's work became more valuable.[1] Probably, whenever such wages or allowances were given, the apprentice had agreed to pay for his clothing or some other necessary, for the whole tendency of latter-day apprenticeship was for masters to demand more recompense for taking apprentices, and they would not have paid wages unless their own trouble and responsibility had been decreased.[2] This substitution of allowances for some part of the provision ordinarily made by masters is a sign of the change now taking place in apprenticeship, a change which eventually transformed apprenticeship from a close personal relationship between masters and pupils into commercial arrangements between employers and their hands. The next step was the adoption of the out-door system. Even at the close of the seventeenth century apprentices were beginning to live apart from their masters, partly, perhaps, because they were becoming more independent, but also because their masters wished to rid themselves still further from their responsibilities. In Newcastle and Sheffield, as we shall see, out-door apprentice-

to the said Master one half part of all the charge and Expences attending such Illness and Cure thereof."

MSS. Oxford, Hanaster Book, 1695–1780. Feb. 26, 1736. Berks labourer's son bound to a tailor. If the apprentice shall be visited with the small-pox during the said term that then the charges thereof shall be borne by uncle and brother of the apprentice.

Indenture at Corsham, of Thomas Tanner, July 16, 1750. Master is to pay half the expense of the small-pox. (This not unusual at that time at Corsham.)

[1] Cox, Northampton Records, ii. p. 325 seq. Transcript of enrolts.

Leader, op. cit., pp. 41–3.

Hardy and Page, Bedfordshire County Records, i. p. 24.

MSS. Hertford, vol. 26, July 2, 1796. George Deacon received £2 2s. yearly.

[2] Leader op. cit., p. 42.

MSS. Bristol, Enrolt. Book, p 58. Dec. 31, 1687. Friends find apparel in consideration whereof the master to pay 20s. for six years and 50s. for the last year.

ship was apparently coming into vogue in the early
eighteenth century.[1] In 1714, at Oxford, John Parratt was
enrolled as an apprentice, and to the ordinary entry of his
name and estate it was added, " His master finds him in
nothing." [2] In the West Country we find a Bristol apprentice
living out in 1739,[3] while in the rural districts the change
does not seem to have begun until later : at Corsham it
was about 1760 that boys began to live at home, or at any
rate not with their masters.[4] Apprentices serving on the
out-door system of course received wages. It was not
unusual to enter the amount to be paid in the indentures
in place of the old clauses as to board and lodging, but at
Corsham, in the early days of the change, masters appear
to have felt dubious as to the legality of the new method,
and preferred to use the old indenture forms, promising
maintenance and instruction, adding a note to the effect
that the master was indemnified from all charges for housing
and feeding his apprentice in return for a certain sum of
money to be paid each year.[5] This device appears to
have satisfied conservative minds. The adoption of the
out-door system was no doubt rendered inevitable by
the change in the methods of carrying on business

[1] See p. 232.

[2] MSS. Oxford, Hanaster Book, small vol. F, 4, 9.

[3] MSS. Bristol, Enrolt. Book. June 29, 1739. Son of a yeoman bound to a
scrivener. Friends to find apparel and lodging.

[4] Corsham Indentures. Jan. 6, 1765. Father to keep the boy, and master
pays 3s. a week rising to 6s. 6d. in last year. Not to be paid if absent through
illness. Cf. indenture, March 25, 1766, Richard Norris.

July 10, 1791. Indenture of Stephen Kirton to Richard Wyatt, of Chippenham. Ms note on the back of indenture : " Memorandum it is agreed between
the said Parties hereto that from the Date hereof the said Richard Wyatt shall
allow the said Stephen Kirton the sum of Three shillings and sixpence per week
for the first year ffour shillings the second year and the third year ffour shillings
and the ffith year ffive shillings and sixpence and the Sixth year Six shillings and
the Seventh and last year Seven shillings in lieu of and as an equivalent for his
Meat Drink Washing Lodging and apparell during the said Term."

[5] Indenture of Ch. Sherton to Rich. Hyatt, July 4, 1795. Terms as usual.
Note on the back of the indenture promising a wage in lieu of board and lodging.
July 10, 1791, Kirton's indenture.

June 13, 1791. Provisions as to finding apprentice crossed through and
promise of wage of 3s. 6d. weekly rising by 6d. a year entered by hand.

and manufactures. The small workrooms, with their
four or five workmen were being replaced by larger
establishments, employing sometimes forty hands, and
masters could not be expected to have their houses over-
flowing with apprentices. The boys necessarily had to
live out. But however inevitable the change may have
been, the supersession of the indoor by the out-door system
removed one great argument in favour of apprenticeship.
It could no longer be claimed that apprenticeship was
valuable as a method of general training and supervision.

CHAPTER XII

THE COST OF TECHNICAL TRAINING

IT is a little startling in these days of innumerable general and technical schools to look back to the seventeenth century and to consider that in all probability the Elizabethan system of apprenticeship was the most efficient system of training which has ever been available for the masses of the nation. Certainly it was, in its best days, the cheapest system of training and education we have ever possessed. The nation neither paid for class-rooms nor for teachers and inspectors, since the gildsmen served as inspectors, and master and boy entered into an agreement for their mutual advantage, which required, therefore, no payment on either side. For although the apprentice received not only instruction, but board and lodging, there seems to have been no idea, when, first the system of apprenticeship was developed, that the training and education which it provided should be paid for in money. It was upon the services of the apprentice, especially at the end of his term, that the master had to count for a return for his trouble and the lad's maintenance ; and it was his business to see that the period of servitude was sufficiently long to allow of this as well as of the apprentice's sound training. This was in early times ; later on a change set in, and one of the complaints made against apprenticeship by eighteenth-century writers was the heaviness of premiums charged by masters upon taking apprentices. Still, even then premiums were not always paid, and when they were, the cost of training and education was not immoderate considering how much the master did for the lad. According to Defoe, the premium had originated in a small present occasionally given to the master's wife, and this harmless custom had grown into the premium system, which in his day had set its firm, and, as he considered vicious, grip upon apprenticeship. A present, he says, was given to the mistress "to engage her to be kind to the youth, and take a motherly care of him being supposed to be young when first put out. By length of time this compliment or present became so customary as to be made a debt, and to be conditioned for as a demand"[1] Defoe does not say whether he had any authority for this statement, but when first we hear of premiums they certainly are small and are only occasionally paid. "It was a great matter in former Times," says one writer, speaking of an age previous to 1603, "to give 10l to bind a youth apprentice."[2] There is an entry in the court books of Norwich in 1620 which appears to refer to the payment of a premium : in this case the sum given was only £1.[3] From a rule of the Merchant Adventurers of Newcastle we can gather both that the custom of paying premiums was not established without some opposition, and that in the middle of the sixteenth century it was still unrecognised in this important company as an ordinary feature of apprenticeship. In 1555 this company, in which as a society of capitalists, the premium system would have appeared in its earliest days, passed a rule forbidding the brethren to take money or other goods with their apprentices by any way of covenant.[4] Unfortunately there is very little information as to premiums in the sixteenth century, and even in the seventeenth the obscurity surrounding them is not completely lifted. Few recorded instances of their payment exist, and our information is drawn from eighteenth-century writers whose knowledge generally did

[1] Complete English Tradesman, 1738, p. 147.

[2] Strype's Stow, p. 432

[3] MS. Mins., Norwich, Court Bk. 15, Nov. 18, 1620. "Richard Burman to pay 10s. to Roland Bushell, grandfather of Thomas England, late apprentice with Burman, towards his necessary clothing And that the other Tenn Shillings appointed to be paid by England ye ffather shalbe contynued in his hands untill a fitt maister may be found to whom to assigne ye said England ye sonne for ye reside of ye tearme."

[4] Surtees, Newcastle Merchant Adven., i. II.

not extend beyond London, and from a few scattered notices, bearing indirectly on the subject, in the records of towns and gilds. Scarcity of records is, however, no proof that premiums were not often, and even widely, given. Their payment, until the Stamp Act of 1709,[1] was a purely private transaction between father and master, and there was no occasion to enter it in the enrolments or in the indentures. It was not until after 1709, therefore, when the sum given with an apprentice had to be named in the indentures, that there is any considerable information to be gained from the enrolment books.

So far as London is concerned, the payment of premiums seems to have become established in the seventeenth century. Amongst the State papers is a petition from young Barbary merchants complaining of a patent granted to certain merchants, giving them a monopoly of the trade, although they, the petitioners, had served their apprenticeship, while their parents had given great sums of money to breed them merchants.[2] Strype, writing in the early eighteenth century, bears witness to the payment of premiums in the reign of James I., though such premiums were still comparatively small. Twenty, forty, sixty, and sometimes one hundred pounds were then, he says, given with an apprentice.[3]

The payment of premiums was not merely a London and localised custom. From a pamphlet written in 1681, it appears that throughout the country they were paid to men engaged in retail business. "It will cost a round sum of Money," says one writer, "before a child can be settled in any Shop-keeping Trade. First, to breed him at School and to make him fit for the same. Secondly, to place him forth to the said Trade when he is fit: Which will cost in a Countrey Market-Town not less than fifty or sixty pounds, but in London upwards of an hundred."[4] Probably members of the wealthy merchant companies in the provinces received

[1] 8 Anne, c. 9, i. 35.
[2] S. P. D., Ch. I., ccccix., 1638. Calendar, p. 329.
[3] Strype's Stow (1720), p. 329, vol 2, bk. v.
[4] Trade of England Revived (1681), p. 30.

premiums with their apprentices ; the Newcastle Hostmen
took it as a matter of course at the close of the seventeenth
century that they should have thirty or forty pounds with an
apprentice.   The lesser tradesmen certainly could command
small sums, for we find references to such payments in the
borough court books, the court having been called to
adjudicate between discontented parties. At Norwich one
master is obliged by the court to repay part of the premium
he received with an apprentice ; the latter had complained
against him, and presumably had proved the charge.[1]   At
Nottingham there is a similar case ; an apprentice to a
butcher complained of ill-usage and begged for discharge
from his master and the restoration of his premium.   The
sum given was five pounds and two loads of coal, " being
almost the whole state," complained the youth, " which my
father [was] able to Disburs, but onely for my good."[2]   At
Hertford, too, we learn indirectly that premiums were frequently given at the close of the seventeenth century.   This
information is particularly valuable, since it shows that they
might be given even in a town which was not a great
industrial centre, and where there were no wealthy companies.   About 1587 the corporation was presented with
" The Humble Peticon of ye small tradesmen and ffreemen
of ye said Borrough."   They complained of the admission
and licence of strangers to the trade of the town, on the
grounds that many of the petitioners had served their
apprenticeships to their several trades, " upon encouragement
of enjoying the said privileges of right belonginge to them.
And other persons uppon the said encouragement doe put

[1] MS. Court Book, Norwich, vol. 15, Oct. 7, 1615.   " Ffrancis Pendleton
being compleyned of by Miles Pytcher his apprentice ys required to pay to his
said apprentice xl[s] peell of mli wch he had wth him and so to be dischardged
of his sd sd apprentice the mony to be payd into the hands of Peter Wyttheericke
his father in Lawe [stepfather] xx[s] in hand & xx[s] upon the second of ffebruary
next."

[2] Stevenson, Nottingham Records, v. 156.   Transcr presentment at sessions,
May 6, 1633.

Cf. Guilding, Reading Records, ii. p. 380.   Difference between shoemaker
and apprentice who complained of lack of food.   £3 14s. had been given with
him (1627).

forth their children as apprentices & give greate sumes of money with them to severall of your peticon[er]."[1] According to Aikin, it was about the same time, the close of the seventeenth century, that it became usual to pay premiums at Manchester.[2] At Sheffield the Cutlers were paying premiums in 1632, though the practice was not common until 1644. The earliest instances are those in which the father contributed something towards the clothing or board of his son; he was to provide shoes, linen, or one shirt a year, or "three metts of wheat at Michaelmas next ensuing." Leader points out that where premiums were paid, no better terms seem to have been secured. He states, however, that a large number of the boys bound out with premiums were the sons of gentlemen, well-to-do yeomen, and the wealthier tradesmen.[3] We may conclude that there was some tacit understanding for favourable treatment, or that these better class boys were being placed out with picked masters. The sums given were not yet large; Leader gives 40s. as the most usual amount, though the sums varied from £1 to £40.

By the eighteenth century the practice of paying premiums had become very usual, while the sum given was larger than before. Strype, writing in 1720, said that sums of five to eight hundred pounds were given in London,[4] while Defoe declared that two or three hundred pounds was common enough, and that five hundred and even one thousand were given.[5] Indeed, at the beginning of the century the payment of large premiums was so usual as to be regarded by

[1] MS. Hertford, vol. 25, p. 43, c. 1687.
[2] Aikin, Forty Miles Round Manchester, p. 182.
[3] Leader, Sheffield Cutlers, i. p. 45.

Premiums were given with children bound out by the overseers of the poor and by the justices of the peace or town officers long before they had become general in the population at large, and it would be a mistake to conclude that because premiums were paid by charities or from public monies, on behalf of parish apprentices, they were as commonly paid by private persons. The poor law apprentices were a class apart.

[4] Strype's Stow (1720), ii. p. 329.
[5] Defoe, Complete English Tradesman (1738), p. 147.
Family Instructor (1715), p. 261.

the Government as a profitable source of revenue, and in 1709 a stamp duty of sixpence in the pound was imposed upon sums of fifty pounds or under, and one shilling upon sums of over fifty pounds, which were paid with clerks, apprentices, or servants placed with any master or mistress to learn a profession or trade. The amount given had to be named in the indenture, and if the full sum received was not charged, the indenture was void, the duty being levied not only upon the money, but upon the value of things given with the apprentice. The indentures were to be brought to the head office or to one of the collectors within two months after the date of binding, the master then paid the duty, and the indentures were stamped.[1]

If indentures had been generally preserved we should from this time onwards have possessed the fullest information as to those trades or localities in which premiums were most usual. Unfortunately, it is only the indentures of those children who were bound under the poor law that are to be found in any number. In a few towns, however, a note of the premium was entered, with the other details of the indentures, in the enrolment books. In Bristol it had been customary, when enrolling indentures, to make a really full entry, giving the boy's father and place of birth ; and from about 1720 the premium paid was also entered. From such

[1] 8 Anne, c. 9.

Later Acts raised the tax.

44 Geo. III. c. 98 ; 48 Geo. III. c. 149 : 55 Geo. III. c. 184.

Although the tax was sometimes avoided, a considerable sum was paid yearly into the Exchequer

Year 10 Oct., 1786,	to 10 Oct., 1787,	£7050	15	2.—Corrs.	Jals., vol. 43, p. 102.
,, ,, ,, 1787,	,, ,, ,, 1788,	7149	13	11.—Ibid.,	vol. 44, p. 122.
,, 5 Jan., 1789,	,, 5 Jan., 1790,	7266	8	2.—Ibid.	,, 45, p. 51.
,, 10 Oct., 1789,	,, 10 Oct., 1790,	7425	4	6.—Ibid.	,, 46, p. 82.
,, 5 Jan., 1791,	,, 5 Jan., 1792,	8160	0	8.—Ibid.	,, 47, p. 59.
,, 10 Oct., 1791,	,, 10 Oct., 1792,	8521	5	9.—Ibid.	,, 48, p. 69.
,, 5 Jan., 1793,	,, 5 Jan., 1794,	6900	1	11.—Ibid.	,, 49, p. 114.
,, 10 Oct., 1793,	,, 10 Oct., 1794,	7675	7	11.—Ibid.	,, 50, p. 17.
,, 10 Oct., 1794,	,, 10 Oct., 1795	6140	0	3.—Ibid.	,, 51, p. 42.
,, 5 July, 1795,	,, 5 July, 1796,	5905	0	3.—Ibid.	,, 52, p. 52.
,, 10 Oct., 1796,	,, 10 Oct., 1797,	6785	11	6.—Ibid.	,, 53, p. 162.

expected, and it is borne out by the fact that relatively high premiums are to be found, whatever the trade, if the lad apprenticed was of gentle birth, while higher premiums were very frequently paid with fatherless boys.[1] Gentlemen binding their sons, and guardians binding well-to-do orphans, would presumably choose out masters with the best reputations and houses, and we may fairly conclude that it was on this account that the higher premium was paid, and not because the trade was essentially aristocratic.

Defoe attributes the increase of premiums, both in occurrence and amount, to the master's greed of gain. " Many masters," he says, " seem to have given up all expectation of duty

from about 1690 onwards with the fact that gentlemen then began to apprentice their sons. (Forty Miles, p. 182.)

[1] Premiums paid with fatherless boys and gentlemen's sons.

In Bath :—

FATHERLESS BOYS.			GENTLEMEN'S SONS.		
Master.		Premium.	Master.		Premium.
1767. Cabinetmaker	...	£ 25	1768. Baker	...	£15 15
Linendraper *	...	105	1769. ,,	...	21
1768. Painter	...	Gns. 40	1772. Cabinetmaker		25
1769. Jeweller *	...	£ 15 15	1772. Mercer *	...	50
1770. Linendraper *	...	100			
Cabinetmaker	...	40			
Surgeon *	...	262			
1771. Carpenter †	...	20			
1773. Silversmith	...	20			
Carpenter †	...	14			

These premiums, though small if compared to those given in London, are above the average paid in these years at Bath.

In Bristol :—

FATHERLESS BOYS, 1725.			GENTLEMEN'S SONS, 1725.		
Father.		Premium.	Master.		Premium.
Sailor	...	£40	—	...	£21
Soapmaker	...	30	Grocer	...	30
Clothmaker	...	20			
Mercer	...	100			
Yeoman	...	20			
Clothier	...	30			
Master Salter	...	100			

Out of 133 enrolments examined, 68 contain mention of premiums. Of

---

* High premiums usually given.

† It was very unusual to pay as much to carpenters.

middle classes, and, as a consequence seldom now cost
less than a hundred pounds with his apprentice. Of
other trades, clothiers, glaziers, linendrapers, jewellers, and
members of the merchant companies paid relatively large
sums as premiums for their sons, and in their turn received
relatively large sums when themselves taking apprentices.
In the mass of trades there appears to be little method or
custom, for sometimes quite a considerable sum might be
paid, and at other times, in the same trade, a small one or
none at all. Probably, it would not be far wrong to say
that there was so much competition for entrance to the
wealthy companies that masters were never under the
necessity of taking apprentices who could not pay a substantial premium. In the less wealthy companies the sum
would vary according to the master's reputation and the
consideration and degree of comfort which the father desired
for his son whilst apprenticed.[2] This is what would be

[1] MS. Enrolt. Bks., Bristol. *Cf.* Hardy, Bedfordshire Quarter Sessions,
i. p. 48. 1777. Boy bound to a Luton surgeon with £100 premium.

[2] HIGH PREMIUMS AT BATH.

	Parent.		Master.		Premium.
1766.	Victualler	...	Jeweller	...	£ 40
1767.	Widow	...	Linendraper	...	05
1769.	Yeoman	...	Jeweller	...	42
	Merchant Tailor	...	? Carpenter	...	6
1770.	Widow	...	Linendraper	...	10
	—	...	Plumber	...	70
1772.	Gentleman	...	Mercer	...	50
1774.	—	...	Haberdasher	...	30
1775.	Clerk	...	Linendraper	...	140

The other premiums are all under £40; or, if larger, were paid to apothecaries and surgeons. [MS. Enrolt. Bks., Bath.)

HIGH PREMIUMS AT BRISTOL.

1725. 133 enrolments examined; 2 were relatively large. £70 was paid by
a butcher to a haberdasher, and £105 by a grocer to a linendraper.

1739. 88 enrolments examined.

Parent.		Master.		Premium.
Gentleman	...	Haberdasher	...	£150
Woollendraper (dead)	...	Haberdasher	...	150
Apothecary	...	Haberdasher	...	100
Clerk	...	Linendraper	...	200
Ironmonger of Birmingham	...	Merchant	...	105

Aikin connects the payment of moderately large premiums at Manchester

cutler.[1] In smaller towns, and in less wealthy companies, smaller sums were paid. At Yarmouth, in 1737, a cordwainer received £6 with his apprentice, and was excused from finding him in clothes.[2] An upholsterer of the same town received £30 as premium, and was excused from finding the apprentice in clothes, and the mending and washing of them.[3] In the minutes books of Hertford, there are occasional notices of premiums : leave was given to a butcher to take Richard Studley, son of a Puckeridge innholder, as apprentice, " Consideration mony 20ˡ." [4] A labourer's son was bound to a chimney-sweep " in consideration of the sum of five shillings " paid by the father [5] ; and a Risborough farmer bound his son to a Hertford grocer with a premium of £50.[6]

From these various records some slight information can be gained as to the amount of the sums paid, and the trades in which they were most usually given. High premiums are never to be found in poor trades ; this was natural, for no father who could afford to expend a considerable sum on his son's education would be so foolish as to bind his son to a sweated and over-crowded trade. In the wealthiest trades, in which it may be supposed that premiums were most commonly given, two or three hundred pounds were not unusual sums, and even eight hundred might be given.[7] From the records of Bath and Bristol we find that relatively high premiums were given in those occupations which were beginning to rank rather as honourable professions than as trades ; the apothecary was emerging from his place among barbers and grocers into the non-commercial dignity of the

---

[1] Leader, Sheffield Cutlers, i. p. 49.
[2] MS. Quarter Sessions Records, Yarmouth, Jan. 9, 1737.
[3] MS. Bk. of Enrolments, Norwich. 1749. Th. Church's enrolt.
[4] MSS. Hertford, vol. 21, p. 352. Aug. 20, 1743.
[5] Ibid., vol. 26. March 17, 1796.
[6] Ibid., vol. 21, p. 563. Oct. 19, 1796.
    Cf. ibid., vol. 21, p. 316. July 14, 1736. " Ordered that Thomas Sayes be bound an apprentice to Roland Keep a Shoemaker for 7 Years 5ˡ money." This and other " orders " probably relate to parish apprentices.
[7] See note 4, p. 203.

entries we can discover the extent to which premiums were given. In 1725 they are mentioned r rather over half the number of enrolments, the sums varying from £3 to £108. In 1739 the proportion bound out with premiums is much the same, the sum varying from £5 to £105.² In Bath there is no general mention of premiums until considerably later than in Bristol, possibly because they were not so usually given until later, or perhaps in Bath the town clerk was slower in changing the customary form of entry than was the clerk in Bristol. In 1745 there is no mention of a premium; in 1758 we are told that Dan Smith, mason, received £10 consideration money with his apprentice²; in 1766 premiums were given with six of the thirteen boys enrolled; and in the four following years half the number of enrolments mention premiums; while from 1771 onwards the proportion is higher.³ Indeed, so usual had the payment of a premium become, that in 1769, and again in 1770, we find enrolments of lads, bound to their own fathers, who paid themselves, for form's sake, a premium of sixpence. If we allow, both in Bath and Bristol, for the boys, often a considerable number, who were bound to their fathers and relations, and with whom no premium would be given, the proportion of lads bound out with premiums is sensibly increased.⁴ At Sheffield the payment of premiums was very common in the eighteenth century, and there was a marked increase in the amount A Stourbridge ironmonger paid £90 for his son in 1772; in 1773 a Sheffield ironmonger paid £100. The largest sum paid was £132 in 1775 by a

---

¹ MSS., Town Hall, Bristol. Enrolt. Bks.
² MS. Enrolt. Bk., vol. 224. July 21, 1758.
³ MS. Enrolt. Bk., vol. 224.
⁴ MS. Enrolt. Bks., Bath.

Year.	Total Number of Boys Enrolled.	With Premiums.	With Premiums or to Relatives.
1766	13	6	9
1767	18	9	15
1768	12	6	7
1769	16	7	13
1770	13	5	11
1771	13	11	12

from their apprentices for a sum of money ; what is now taken with apprentices being exorbitant compared with what it was in former times." [1] His editor, however, attributes the change to another cause. " I will venture to say that the rise of this demand is owing more to the unreasonable fondness and partiality of parents for their children, than from any other consideration. For who does not know that many persons have been so weak, as, when they have put out a child, to insist, that he shall be exempted from such and such menial offices, which were wont to be required of younger apprentices, and that frequently, as so many marks of their subjection and humility? Nay, not so satisfy'd, how common a thing has it been, that they have stipulated, that their son shall not eat with the other servants, but be allowed to sit at table with their master and mistress? For this indulgence, a larger praemium has been given as indeed it ought ; and this by degrees became more and more practised, and so enhanced the demand of the masters, who having conditioned, that their apprentices shou'd the first day commence a sort of journeyman, were obliged to take servants of lower degree to do those servile things." [2] Prob-

these 68 premiums, 40 are of £10 or under ; the above sums, therefore, though apparently small, are above the average.

FATHERLESS BOYS, 1739.			GENTLEMEN'S SONS, 1739.		
Master.		Premium.	Master.		Premium.
Apothecary	...	£20	Sailmaker	...	£ 25
Carpenter	...	14	Merchant	...	300
Cordwainer	...	20	Cutler	...	42
Haberdasher	...	150	Hooper	...	50
Barber Surgeon	...	9	Haberdasher	...	150
Joiner ...	...	30	Cutler ...	...	45
Shipwright	...	10	Hooper	...	50
Currier ...	...	28			
Hooper	...	15			
Sadler ...	...	30			
Haberdasher	...	100			
Carpenter	...	20			
Hooper ...	...	36 15			

Of the 88 enrolments examined, 54 mention premiums ; 26 out of the 54 premiums are under £20 ; the above sums are, therefore, relatively large.

[1] Complete English Tradesman (1738), p. 12.
[2] Ibid., p. 148.

14

ably neither explanation is sufficient in itself, though both
together may go far in supplying the reason for the extensive
use of premiums. There can be no doubt that the expenses
of maintaining an apprentice in the eighteenth century were
very much greater than they had been in the old days. In
the sixteenth century master and servant lived and fared
much alike, and the simplest accommodation was deemed
sufficient. Apprentices were, of course, no better boarded
and housed, while the public opinion of the day was all in
favour of the subserviency of the young, and it was not
thought derogatory to an apprentice to perform menial
offices, however wealthy his parents might be. In the
eighteenth century the standard of comfort had risen
enormously ; and this affected apprenticeship in two ways :
in the houses of the wealthier merchants and tradesmen
there was a sharp dividing line between servant and master,
and the apprentice, who ranked with his master's sons, could
no longer be expected to perform servant's duties. In the
second place, he had to be provided with better food, accommodation, and clothing than in the old days. It was only
apprentices who were of a lower social order than their
masters—for instance, children bound out by the overseers
of the poor—who could be subjected to the full rigours
of their servitude. An apprentice was thus more expensive
and less useful than he had been formerly, and there was
always a chance that his work would not cover the cost of
his training. It was just, therefore, that his master should
receive a premium, though no doubt the custom was open
to abuse, and masters may have taken lads for the sake of
their money.

It has been observed that premiums were most commonly
given in the wealthiest companies, and the question naturally
arises as to whether there is any connection between the
growing spirit of monopoly in the companies and the increase
in the value and occurrence of premiums. No doubt it was
harder for poor lads to enter good trades when premiums
became so customary that a master who wanted an apprentice had no difficulty in getting a handsome sum into the

bargain. But it would be a mistake to say that the payment of premiums was part of the monopolistic policy of the companies. They countenanced premiums, but they never used them directly as an instrument of monopoly. The poor lad would have been barred quite as effectually from the better trades had premiums never come into vogue, for the gilds and companies had other means of preserving their privileges. To the last the payment of premiums was a matter of private arrangement between the master and those responsible for the apprentice; none of the companies have rules enforcing it; they charged no fee upon premiums, and, though the sum given had to be mentioned in the indentures, this was solely for revenue purposes.

We have lastly to consider what was the effect of the payment of premiums upon apprenticeship generally. Where the premium was large the position of the lad was changed from that of a humble apprentice to that of a lucrative pupil, who was to be persuaded rather than commanded to his work. Defoe greatly regrets these excessive payments, regarding them as the cause of the unruliness and lack of subjection in the apprentices of his day. He illustrates his point in an imaginary conversation between a master and a father who had complained that his son had not received the supervision and correction which a master owed his apprentice. The master replied, " Pray do you think I'll trouble myself with my apprentices at that rate? No, no, not I. I never struck an apprentice in my life; and if I should, who do you think would stay with me? Apprentices nowadays are not like what they were when you and I were apprentices. Now we get a hundred pounds, or two or three hundred pounds apiece with them; they are too high for reproof or correction." [1] In a note it is added that the payment of large premiums is " a wicked and abominable custom, which, as no religious parent can be easy in, so no religious master ought to be subjected to." [2] But it may well be doubted whether this wicked custom was as responsible for the altered manners of appren-

---

[1] Family Instructor (1715), ii. p. 261.
[2] Ibid., p. 261.

tices as our authority would have us believe. The general increase of wealth and the growth of the spirit of individualism in the eighteenth and late seventeenth centuries inevitably altered the position of apprentices and the attitude or the times toward the young.

CHAPTER XIII

THE MASTERPIECE

ONE of the most interesting customs connected with apprenticeship is that of Testwork, better known, perhaps, as Masterpiece, because of the use of that term in connection with apprentices in Germany, where the practice of exacting a masterpiece from the aspirant to the freedom of a gild was one of the distinctive features of the apprenticeship system. In England the custom is found under the name of testwork, masterpiece, artpiece, or proofpiece, but it seems never to have been very generally adopted, nor to have been so fully developed as in Germany. There the young man was required to make a definite piece of work from start to finish, and so present it in its completed form for the inspection of his judges. Testwork appears sometimes in the same form in England, but more often it was a less formal inspection of a man's work.

There is not at present much information as to English testwork before the seventeenth century ; then it is connected with the monopolistic side of gild life, and is seldom to be found in companies which were not in other ways exclusive in their policy. In Germany, also, it was employed as a means of limiting numbers, and was an effective instrument for preserving the monopoly in a trade. Nevertheless it does not seem that in England, at any rate, it was the invention of jealous craftsmen. Rather it appears to have originated in those examinations of intending brethren which were a usual method of recruiting new members before the days when the gilds had become monopolistic. It will be remembered that at the close of the thirteenth century apprenticeship was only one of the methods of entering a gild, and, judging by the small number of crafts which made rules for apprentices, it was not the most important method.[1]   New members were recruited from sons who had worked with their fathers, by patrimony, namely, and from those workmen who came into the town with a good reputation for craftsmanship, or who proved their skill in some way.   Rules were often made by the gilds forbidding the admittance of men who had not been "abled" and proved sufficient workmen.   Thus, at Northampton, no tailor was allowed to set up shop until he had been approved by the master of the craft aforesaid learned and skilful in it, and by his character fit for the utility of the said town.[2]   No glover was to set up in Hull until abled by the Alderman and Searchers.[3]   Complaint was made in 1445, at Bristol, that the work of the dyers was bad owing to the admittance of ignorant persons, and a rule was made that no one was to dye until presented to the Master to see if he was able and sufficient.[4]   It is not always clear whether any definite examination or test-work had to be undergone ; abling may have been nothing more than the testimony of a friendly member that the aspirant to the freedom was a suitable man for the honour. But in some gilds, although the word "testwork" is not used, it is apparent that a definite masterpiece had to be performed.   This was certainly so at Bristol among the Merchant Tailors, whose rule in 1401 was that no one was to be made free of the craft until he was tried by four lawful workmen, appointed by the Master, to see if he was skilful, and also if he were of good conversation and living.[5]   If testwork had been of independent growth, and due to the monopolistic movement in the gilds, we should not expect to find traces of it earlier than the middle of the fifteenth century, and not, as at Bristol, in 1401.   It seems most probable that testwork

---

[1] See p. 36.
[2] Northampton Records, i. p. 281   Liber Cus., 1444.
[3] Lambert, Two Thousand Years, p. 217.   Rule ix., 1449.
[4] Bickley, Little Red Book, ii. p. 172.
[5] Fox, Merch. Tailors, p. 17.   Rules 2 H. IV.

originated in those old examinations, formal or informal, which were not uncommon in the earliest days of the gilds. It is true that this method of admitting workmen dropped out of use as the gilds increased in membership and prestige, and became more unwilling to share their privileges with any but those who had undergone apprenticeship. The rules as to abling gave way to others enforcing apprenticeship. But in some companies the old qualification of sufficient skill was retained, and the qualification of apprenticeship was demanded in addition. This was the case at Bristol in the Tailors' Company ; a man who wished to be admitted had both to be apprenticed and tried by four workmen to see if he was able ; and at Northampton, in the Fullers' Gild, he had to be both apprenticed and proved able.[1] Vaguer is the rule of the Worcester Cordwainers in 1504, that no apprentice was to be admitted unless he was of " good name and fame and sufficient in cunninge and knowledge." [2] Such references to the old abling may have been merely verbal survivals ; but whether this were the case or no, these bye-laws kept alive the tradition of some sort of examination or trial, and perhaps made it easier for the companies later on to reintroduce testwork and require it from their apprentices.[3]

This they appear to have done late in the sixteenth century. Of the London companies, the Pewterers, in 1588, and the Goldsmiths, in 1574, refer to it in their rules, without explanations, which suggests that it had been in use for some time. In the provinces it was in working order at Carlisle about 1595, and in Bristol in 1611. There is a difference, of course, between the testwork as now practised by these companies and the old examinations, tests, or ablings which had been in vogue in the fourteenth and early fifteenth centuries. Then the use of testwork by a gild enabled adult workmen who had not been apprenticed, or who were strangers, to become freemen, and to practise their trades; it opened the door, in fact, to skilled men, even though they had not been

[1] Fox, *op. cit.*, p. 17.
[2] Markham, Northampton Records, i. p. 292. Liber Cus., 1452.
[3] Noake, Worcestershire, p. 28.

connected previously with the gild or town. It is unusual at this early date to find a rule requiring an apprentice to perform a masterpiece at the end of his service. But the test-work of the sixteenth century and after was imposed upon the apprentice at the end of his term, and in addition to his apprenticeship. Adult workmen who had not been apprenticed could not now take the test and be admitted by virtue of their skill. In short, testwork was not, as formerly, a direct means of admittance, but was another obstacle placed in the path of those who wished to set up in trade. Not all the gilds which adopted testwork employed it in the same form. Some insisted upon a definite masterpiece ; thus, the Needlemakers of London obliged a man to make five hundred needles of various sizes,[1] while the Carlisle Shoemakers ordered that no one was to be admitted until he had been given four pairs of " dobble soled shoes " to make, and his work had been approved.[2] In the Framework Knitters' Company, which was of late date, the proofpiece was a pair of silk stockings.[3] In other gilds in which a proofpiece was demanded, the workman appears often to have been left free to decide what form it should take. The Pewterers and Clockmakers, for instance, required masterpieces, but the rules do not lay down what object was to be made.[4] One clockmaker is mentioned as having made a watch with his own name engraved upon it,[5] and this probably was his own choice. The assumption is that no masterpiece would have been accepted if below a traditional standard of value and difficulty.

Then, again, some companies had not masterpieces, but testwork in the strict sense of the word. Men wishing for admittance into the Clothworkers' Company had to work

[1] Needlemakers, p 31. Charter, 1664.
Rep. Livery Companies, iii. p. 603. Rules, 1670.
[2] Ferguson, Carlisle, p. 179. Rules, c. 595.
[3] Coms. Jals., xxv., 1753, p. 789.
[4] Welch, Pewterers, i. p. 201. Rough Mins., 1558.
Overall, Clockmakers, p. 30. Rules, 1632.
Cf. Rep. Livery Cos., iii. p. 483 ; Glass-sellers p. 505 ; Gunsmiths, 1670.
Ibid., p. 202. Broiderers' Rules, 1562.
[5] Overall, op. cit., p. 151. 1656.

with some honest and good workman " to be assayed for the space of three days at least whether he be a good workman."[1] In the Weavers' Company at Hull the applicant does not seem to have been obliged to make a definite masterpiece, but the Wardens and Searchers were sent to examine his work and tools.[2] This may have been the practice in the Painters' Company, to which no one might be admitted until approved and allowed, by the Master and Wardens and six assistants, to be an expert, skilful, and able workman.[3]

Mention may be made here of the examinations of barber-surgeons, apothecaries, and musicians, though they are slightly different in character from testwork. The Master and Wardens of the Musicians' Company were empowered to summon periodically all their members, and even masters might be tested, to see if they were competent musicians.[4] The London Apothecaries would admit no apprentice until he had been examined, proved, and tried concerning his knowledge and election of simples before the Master and Wardens.[5] The Barber Surgeons had to qualify by examination from the year 1511, when an Act was passed forbidding any one to practise the art without a licence, which could be obtained only upon gaining the approval of a board composed of the bishop of the diocese and four expert persons.[6]

Though the records are all too brief and few, we can gain some slight information as to how testwork was regulated, by whom it was judged, what was the standard required, and what were the fees.

The judges in some companies were the members of the Court of Assistants, presided over by the Master and Wardens. This was so in the Pewterers' Company; the apprentice who desired the freedom had to " bringe in a sample of his work to be sene vewed and adjudged by the master and wardens

[1] Clothworkers, p. 137. Rules, 1639.
[2] Lambert, *op. cit.*, p. 211. Weavers' Rules, 1673.
[3] Rep. Livery Cos., iii. p. 617. Rules, 1581.
[4] Musicians' Company, p. 58. Rules, 1606.
Rep. Livery Cos., iii. p. 593. Charter, 1604. Rules, 1706, p. 596.
[5] Barrett, Apothecaries, p. xxxii.
[6] Williams, Barber Surgeons, Norwich, p. 20.

and assistants and they to give their verdeyt whether the ptaye be a mete man to set up or not."[1] The Glass-sellers and Gunmakers had to present their procfpieces to the Master and Wardens,[2] while in the Clockmakers' Company each person had to " show to the court assembled a masterpiece of his own making."[3] The Broiderers had a similar rule.[4] In other companies the court appointed the judges. The Carlisle Shoemakers chose six of the ancient of the gild to view and try the masterpieces.[5] The Watermen could, of course, make no masterpiece, but they had to be "abled" before admittance, the judges being the overseers and six assistants.[6] The Needlemakers had to make their five hundred needles before the Wardens or those appointed by them.[7] At Norwich it seems to have been customary to swear in men to act as judges for the time being. Three men were sworn in to try John Grumble's work;[8] three others to see a felt-maker make his felts.[9] This method of appointing temporary judges appears to have been in use in the Merchant Tailors' Company at Bristol, for we find sets of four brethren judging the work of candidates.[10] It is not clear whether the masterpieces were always executed in public ; in some companies the workman may have been allowed to make his piece at home, and bring it when finished before the appointed judges.

There is little record of any fee for the examination of masterpieces, but in all probability it was charged. We know at any rate that the companies were not inclined to do anything for love, and that they always had a weather-eye upon a possible fee. In the reports on framework knitting, in which the company's fees are given in detail, we find a charge of

[1] Welch, Pewterers, p. 201. Mins., 1558.
[2] Rep. Livery Companies, iii. p. 483 (1637 ; p. 504 (1664).
[3] Overall, Clockmakers, p. 151. Rules, 1581.
[4] Rep. Liv. Co., iii. p. 202 (1562).
[5] Ferguson, Carlisle, p. 179, c. 1595.
[6] Humpherus, Watermen, i. p. 214.
[7] Rep. Liv. Co., iii. p. 603.
[8] MSS. Norwich, Court Book 15. May 3, 1615.
[9] Ibid., ibid., Nov. 15 1620.
[10] Fox, Merch. Tailors, p. 98. Mins., 1725.

13s. for the proofpiece, in addition to 15s. for admittance.[1] Possibly there is so little separate reference to the masterpiece fee because it was entered with the admission fee, under one heading. Thus, in the Needlemakers' Company, the fee for admittance, which had to be paid after the proofpiece had been accepted, was 10s.,[2] and in the Gunmakers' Company it was 13s. 4d.[3] Still, it must be admitted that other companies than those which used tests were at this time demanding more than the legal 3s. 4d.

When a man, in other respects qualified for the freedom, had presented his masterpiece, or performed his testwork, and had been acknowledged to be able, he was forthwith admitted to the company. If, on the other hand, his work was not altogether satisfactory, it appears that he was allowed to work as an underling in the trade, though he might not set up as a free master. At Carlisle the Shoemakers refused to allow him to work as a journeyman, but he might be engaged as a hireman, the difference being that the former had constant employment and pay, being taken by the year, while a hireman was engaged and paid by the job.[4] Possibly he might appeal for admission later, when he had become proficient, as was the custom of the London Clothworkers. Apprentices in this company were, at the end of their term, "appointed by the Master or Wardens or some of them to some honest and good workeman and can his occupacon sufficiently wel and perfectly or noe and if he be found a sufficient workman then to be admitted to work by Journeyworke or to take wages according to the custome and manner of the said Art or Mistery But if he shall not be found a sufficient workman Then the Master and Wardens shall appoint him to worke with some other sufficient workeman of the said Company and fellowshipp by yeare or by weeke until he can sufficiently and perfectly his occupacon and shall also assign him what wages he shall take."[5] In the tailoring trade at

---

[1] Commons Journals, xxvi. p. 790. 1753.
[2] Rep. Liv. Co., iii. p. 603 (1664).
[3] Ibid., p. 505 (1670).
[4] Ferguson, Carlisle, p. 179. c. 1595.
[5] Clothworkers, p. 137. Rules, 1639.

Bristol men were allowed to make those garments in which they had proved themselves expert even when they could not qualify as all-round workmen. While Rolande Frye was made free and allowed a perfect workmen for men's and women's clothing, Anthony Basset was passed as perfect only in whalebone bodices.[1]

It may seem at first sight as though testwork was a beneficial institution, insuring to the public the services of really skilled workmen. But there can be little doubt that it was employed more as an instrument of monopoly than for keeping up a high standard of work. It was of use as a protection of gild privileges, because even when no high fee were charged, materials and tools had to be bought while the work itself was no day's job, and the young man would have to be prepared to forgo remunerated work for a considerable length of time. Apprentices had no wages which they could save against the hour of need, and it was, therefore, only the sons of the comparatively well-to-do who would be able to enter those companies where testwork existed. It is worth noticing that some of the earliest traces of testwork are to be found in the tailors' craft, one of the first trades to be conducted upon capitalistic lines.[2] At Bristol it was undoubtedly in use in 1401, while the most probable of the dubious examples of testwork in early times is that of the Northampton Tailors. In its later history the monopolistic character of testwork is unmistakeable. It is commonest among the London gilds, which were the wealthiest companies, and were ever trying to limit their membership. It is also to be found in Bristol and Norwich, cities which were industrially only second in importance to London, and in which we may expect to find wealthy companies. When testwork was practised in cities of lesser importance it was generally in capitalised trades ; for instance, in Carlisle it is the Shoemakers who use the custom, while in Hull the Weavers had some more or less definite test, and both

---

[1] Fox, op. cit. p. 21 (1629), p. 19 (61). Cf. p. 21, Dec. 8, 1661 ; April 16, 1633. Thomas Adye admitted as hosier only.

[2] Cf. Unwin, Industrial Organisation, p. 27. Paris tailors capitalistic in sixteenth century.

weaving and shoemaking were capitalised trades. Further, in those companies which adopted testwork, there are often to be found clear indications of a monopolistic spirit. The Pewterers possibly had some property qualification : there is an entry in their Rough Minutes to the effect that a certain Gabriel Spencer was allowed to set up upon his master making " report of his substance xx marks." [1] The Clockmakers, another company which practised testwork, granted their freedom only when a man, qualified in other respects, had served two years as a journeyman.[2] This was the rule in the Gunmakers' Company,[3] while in the Painters there was a compulsory period of one year,[4] and so too in the Broiderers' Company, though in 1609 the period was raised to three years.[5] In the Needlemakers' Company there was a narrow rule of a different description : a man had to be three years out of his apprenticeship before he might employ an apprentice.[6]

It seems to have been early recognised that the masterpiece could be used as an instrument of monopoly and extortion. In a complaint laid against the gilds, about 1576, a special attack appears to have been made upon testwork, for in " Thanswere to the suite agaynst wardens for exactinge of prentises," the writer makes a point of defending the custom.[7] On the whole, there is remarkably little complaint of masterpieces until we come to the great struggle in 1733 between the Framework Knitters of the provinces and the London company. One of the charges against the company was that it obliged a man to make a proofpiece before he might take an apprentice. The fee on presenting the masterpiece was 13s., a comparatively large sum, for framework knitting was a poor trade.[8] Witnesses from different parts of the country declared that the company's officers took the fees, but that no request was ever made for the production of

[1] Welch, Pewterers, i. p. 258. Feb. 12, 1567.
[2] Overall, Clockmakers, pp. 30, 151. Rules, 1632, 17.
[3] Rep. Liv. Co., iii. p. 505.   [4] Ibid., p. 618.
[5] Ibid., p. 202.   [6] Ibid., p. 603.
[7] Lansd. MS., 22, No. 56.
[8] Commons Journals, xxvi. p. 789. (1753). Rules, 1745.

the proofpiece,[1] which showed it was not the standard of work with which the company was concerned, but that their motives in maintaining this rule were merely mercenary. That there should have been so little complaint of testwork in other companies is, perhaps, to be accounted for by the fact that, in the sixteenth and early seventeenth centuries, grumblers would have met with scant sympathy while later on testwork was confined to wealthy companies, with the exception of the Framework Knitters'. It mattered little to a lad whose father could pay the premium required by a wealthy gildsman, and the fees demanded by his gild, that he should be forced to perform an expensive artpiece at the end of his term. Testwork was undoubtedly an instrument of monopoly, but it was one amongst other methods of barring out the poor man, and therefore escaped much individual abuse.

[1] Commons Journals, xxv. p. 790.
Ibid., pp. 781, 790.

CHAPTER XIV

THE DECLINE OF APPRENTICESHIP

IT will be remembered that when order was restored at the close of the Civil War, the companies once again attempted to enforce apprenticeship. The dissatisfaction and criticism which it was beginning to arouse must not be allowed to obscure the value which it still could claim, nor the part which it still played in national life. In spite of opposition, it was holding its own, and at the beginning of the eighteenth century the country stood possessed of a great system of general training and technical instruction ; great, because whatever were its shortcomings, apprenticeship contributed annually to the wealth of the nation a large number of skilled workmen, and moulded the character of a vast number of English boys, whom it then sent out into the world with the ability to keep themselves from want and unemployment.

Yet though the same old round of binding, enrolment, service, and instruction went on as before, there were warnings that a change, adverse to apprenticeship, was setting in. The opposition of free traders to the Statute, the frequent weakness of the gilds, the alienation of legal opinion, and the indifference of the towns to the principles of the Act, forbode ill to the apprenticeship system. In the next century these warnings were fulfilled.

Its dissolution was so gradual that it is impossible to give any one year as definitely marking the period at which apprenticeship ceased to be a flourishing institution and entered upon its decline. At a date when, perhaps, it had clearly broken down in two or three trades, it is to be found elsewhere possessed of full vitality. Even in the last years of

the national system contradictions are rife. On the one
hand there are unmistakable signs of dissolution, widespread
criticism of the system, and complete disregard of the Act ;
on the other are petitions for its enforcement, a stolid conviction that it cannot be bettered, and the persistent efforts
of the gilds to maintain the old order ; indeed, as late as
1752 there is the formation of a new company at Bath,
sanctioned by the Mayor, and bent upon enforcing the
system.[1] But, in spite of some contradictory evidence,
apprenticeship had really entered upon its last phase in the
early decades of the eighteenth century. From this time
forward its history is the account of the non-observance of
the Act, first in one locality or trade, and then in another. The
year 1720 perhaps best dates the time at which the definite
collapse began. About this time trades were becoming
more capitalistic. It is true that capitalism had existed
long before this ; indeed, in some places it had appeared in
the woollen trade as early as the sixteenth century. But
about 1720 there was a speeding-up in the process of
reorganising trades on a capitalistic basis. Various statutes
were passed at this time—the first in 1720, which prohibited
combinations of workmen for raising wages, and laid heavy
penalties upon those who stole the materials upon which
they were working ; while others forbade masters to pay
their workmen in truck.[2] These Acts bear witness to the
growth of capitalism, for there was no question of embezzling
materials, nor of raising wages, when men were their own
masters ; while the Acts against combinations indicate that
capitalism was now strong enough to oblige workmen to
combine if they wished to fight upon equal terms with their

[1] Shickle, Gild of Merchant Tailors p. 60.   Several trades attempted to form
gilds. The Plasterers' and Tylers' was formed in 1752.

[2] 7 G. I. c. 13.   Act to prevent combinations of journeymen tailors in London.
   12 G. I. c. 34.   Act to prevent combinations amongst woollen workers.
   12 G. I. c. 35.   Act to prevent combinations amongst brickmakers and tilers.
   9 G. II. c. 27.   Act to prevent journeymen shoemakers selling, exchanging
or pawning boots, shoes, slippers cutle—ther or other materials for making boots,
shoes, or slippers.
   13 G. I. c. 23 ; 4 G. II. c. 16.

employers. This capitalistic organisation of industry was inimical to apprenticeship, and the speeding-up in the growth of the one meant the speeding-up in the dissolution of the other. The enterprising man with capital behind him was not going to observe the regulations of any company as to the number of workmen he might employ or the amount of goods he might sell. He meant to get a return for the money he invested, even if in so doing he ousted some poorer workman from the trade. Capitalism told against the gild regulation of industry and the domestic system, and what told against the gilds told against apprenticeship. It is therefore natural enough that the signs of collapse should have become marked about 1720. It is true that, even before this date, apprenticeship had almost disappeared in the Devonshire worsted trade. Now, from 1720 until the repeal of the Act in 1814, it was breaking down first in one locality and then in another; while in those trades and places where it was still the rule, it was maintained only with increasing difficulty, and often in an altered form : in the better-class trades heavy premiums were paid, and the boys did not give, nor were they expected to give, the service and obedience rendered by apprentices in former times ; and in some of the poorer trades apprenticeship was little more than a name used to cloak sweated labour.

The definite dissolution of apprenticeship showed itself nowhere earlier than in the woollen industry, in various branches of which its observance was irregular at the very beginning of the eighteenth century. In 1701 a committee of the House of Commons was appointed to consider the petition of the worsted and serge makers of Somerset and Devon, whose chief grievance was the competition of illegal workmen. There is nothing new in such a complaint, for even in the palmiest days of apprenticeship gildsmen were apt to grumble. But it is significant that, according to the witnesses, not one-half of the 3,500 woollen weavers in Taunton and the surrounding five miles had served apprenticeship.[1] The unapprenticed workmen declared that serge

---

[1] Commons Journals, vol. 14, p. 67. *Cf.* ibid., vol. 13, p. 376.

weaving did not come under the Act, and that there was no
obligation upon them to serve.[1] This may have been true,
but no such plea could be urged for wool-combing, which
clearly came within the Statute. As early as 1700 complaint
was made to Parliament that at Peterborough there were
numbers of workmen who had not been apprenticed for the
legal term of seven years. These men further transgressed
the law by taking as many as fourteen so-called apprentices
binding them for one or two years only. As soon as their
short period of service was over these "apprentices" of
course set up for themselves, and worked upon similar lines.[2]
In other branches of the woollen trade apprenticeship seems
to have fallen equally into abeyance. The Leicester wool-
combers petitioned Parliament in 1700[3]; in 1740 the clothiers
of Stroudwater, Witney, and various parts of Gloucestershire
begged for the suppression of illegal workmen.[4] No information is given as to what proportion of the workers were
apprenticed; but the frequency of the petitions, and the wide
area from which they were made, suggest that disregard of
the Act was very general, even at this early date. Later in
the century Arthur Young gives an account of the trade in
Essex, which points to neglect of apprenticeship. There the
industry was spread throughout the country-side, and was so
poorly paid that the workers forsook it in summer for
husbandry.[5] The employment of women and girls, not
merely for spinning but for weaving, he takes as a matter of
course, for he gives their wages without any comment.[6]
Judging from other trades, women and girls were not
employed to any extent where there was strict company
control and a careful system of apprenticeship; and it was in
such industries as this, loosely organised and not very highly

[1] Commons Journals, vol. 14, p. 338.
[2] Ibid., ibid., p. 383.
[3] Ibid., ibid., p. 404.
[4] Ibid., vol. 13, pp. 664, 665, 686. Cf. vol. 13, p. 404. Petition from
Cirencester and Gloucestershire; p. 657, petition from Taunton; vol. 16, p. 352,
petition from Oxford linen and woollen drapers [1709].
[5] Six Weeks' Tour (1768), p. 65.
[6] Ibid., p. 99.

paid, that it was hardest to enforce apprenticeship. But no fuller evidence is needed than that given by the two reports on the woollen trade made in 1803 and 1806. The witnesses for the earlier report declared that for many years there had been no prosecutions of illegal workmen,[1] and that by far the greater number of those engaged in the trade had never been apprenticed.[2] One witness affirmed that eight-ninths of the persons employed in his factory were not qualified according to the law [3]; another, that only five out of the seventy-five men in his factory were so qualified.[4] That this disregard of the law was not of purely recent date is borne out by the answer of one witness. He declared that he gave no preference to apprenticed persons who applied for work, but was on the whole disinclined in their favour, since they were generally old men.[5] The Commission which made the report of 1806 states that apprenticeship was more congenial to the domestic than to the factory system, and was therefore maintained more in the North than in the West; [6] but as a matter of fact, the evidence of this better known and wider report testifies to a very general decline of apprenticeship in the North. Though the report was not made until 1806, it gives information as to the conditions of the trade twenty years earlier. Many of the witnesses had been engaged in this industry from an early age, but had not been apprenticed, nor had they ever inquired as to whether their journeymen had so served.[7] The majority declared that the Act had been ignored, and it seems that boys were apprenticed or not according to the idiosyncrasies of particular masters.[8] This combined evidence shows that there was a breakdown of the Elizabethan system in certain branches of the woollen industry at the beginning of the century, and that by 1780 it had spread into all departments of the trade.

[1] Report on Woollen Manufacture in Wilts, &c. (1803), pp. 4, 5. H. C., 1802–3 (30), v. 243.

[2] Ibid., pp. 5, 6, 7, 8.   [3] Ibid., p. 6.

[4] Ibid., p. 3.   [5] Ibid., p. 4.

[6] Report on Woollen Trade (1806), p. 13. H. C., iii. 569, 595.

[7] Ibid., Mins. of Evidence, pp. 176, 185, 378.

[8] Ibid., ibid., pp. 71, 139, 176, 197, 247, 400.

Apprenticeship was dispensed with in framework knitting almost as early as in the woollen trade. The Knitters had been incorporated into a company for England and Wales in the early years of Charles II.'s reign. Its headquarters lay in London, but it had the right to appoint deputies to control the trade at a distance.[1] Its bye-laws amongst which were the old rules that no one should teach or employ any one but his apprentices or apprenticed workmen[2] duly admitted to the company were confirmed in 1745;[3] but they must have been already out of date, for only eight years later petitions were sent from Nottingham, and various towns in Surrey, complaining that these rules were oppressive,[4] and a parliamentary committee was appointed to inquire into the matter. Not only from the evidence of the petitioners, but of the deputies who were called on behalf of the company, it is clear that apprenticeship had fallen into desuetude. The Nottingham deputies as early as 1731 had written to the company declaring that they had little business to transact: they had bound two boys at the two last courts, and none the court before.[5] The rules of the company were openly disregarded. "We sent our beadle in the country," wrote the deputies, "and summoned several offenders, that are admitted members, to come at last court and bind their boys; and four of them came, but instead of complying, barely defied our court." The evidence of master workmen conclusively showed that apprenticeship had broken down. They stated that no inquiry was made as to whether journeymen had served an apprenticeship;[6] and that every one employed persons not free of the company. The deputies themselves did so.[7] What was more, the company itself had disregarded the law until the dispute arose, and without demur had admitted men who had never served a legal term.[8]

---

[1] Felkin, Account of the Machine Wrought Hosiery Trade (1845). In 1669 there were 200 frames in London and 2 in Nottingham. In 1753 there were 1,000 in London, 1,000 in Leicester, and 1,500 in Nottingham.

[2] Coms. als. xxvi. p. 789. Rules 16, 18, 20

[3] Ibid., p. 789.

[5] Ibid., p. 782.

[7] Ibid., p. 781.

[4] Ibid., p. 780.

[6] Ibid., p. 790.

[8] Ibid., p. 785.

The story of the collapse of apprenticeship in these two trades is most illuminating. It shows that long before 1814 the marked decline began, and it illustrates the class of trade in which the Elizabethan system first broke down. Unlike as they were in many respects, the woollen and the knitting industries had three characteristics in common. Both were carried on more or less upon capitalistic lines; this had always been the tendency in woollen weaving, and the Act, passed in 1726,[1] to prevent the filching of materials by workmen, shows that those engaged in the trade were now divided into employers and employed, with their divorced interests. In short, the trade was capitalised; and so too was framework knitting, in which trade the greater number of workers hired their frames from big masters, and were not the owners of their own tools and materials, as the independent craftsman had been. Secondly, both trades were spread over a wide area; it was impossible for the Framework Knitters' Company, with its clumsy system of deputies, or for the various weavers' gilds to exercise any effective control over trades which were not centred in some town or city, but were practised throughout the country. We have seen that in the late seventeenth century the enforcement of the Statute was being left more and more to the gilds and companies, and it is therefore natural that apprenticeship should first disappear from industries which were for any reason out of gild control. There is a third characteristic common to framework knitting and the woollen trade. Both were poor industries; framework knitting had been a favourite occupation upon which to employ parish children, and the condition of those engaged in it had never been good. Woollen weavers who complained to Parliament of various imported goods pressed it as a claim to the goodwill of the House that the weaving trade was the support of the poor.[2] It was in such trades that apprenticeship invariably broke down; in the highly skilled trades the companies were stronger, and could more easily enforce their ordinances. Moreover, training for them was really necessary,

[1] 13 Geo. I. c. 23.
[2] Coms. Jals., vol. xi. p. 475 (1695), p. 633 (1696).

but in an ill-paid and low-skilled trade it was not worth while to serve an apprenticeship.   One of the witnesses before the committee on framework knitting put the case convincingly. Hose, he said, were made at three-halfpence the pair, "in which branch of trade no person will work who has served an apprenticeship of seven years."[1]

In other trades the continuance of the Elizabethan system was less general than at first sight appears, because often it was preserved in name when it had broken down in all essential respects.

The so-called apprentice was merely a junior employee, a wage-earner, living at home, and seldom bound to his master by a legal agreement. In the report on the calico trade, made in 1804 but retrospective over fifteen years, it is stated that masters declined to enter into indentures, but took their boys upon a verbal agreement to serve seven years.   To enforce it the master exacted a bond from the boy's parents for £50, and also withheld a certain proportion of his earnings.[2] Thus the youth was under compulsion to keep his contract, but not so the master, who could, and did, dismiss the boy at pleasure ; and if at any time business was slack, he visited his misfortunes upon the lad and forced him to serve the time over again, so that he was often not quit of his engagement until a year or more after he should have been free.[3] The boy entered upon this pseudo apprenticeship not because he was by its means thoroughly taught his trade, but because he could get the work and its wage in no other way.   And masters took apprentices merely in order to obtain cheap labour.   If the supply were deficient, they refused to take any journeymen but those who had sons to apprentice, and threatened to dismiss workmen who refused to bind their children.[4]

From other trades comes similar evidence that the interests of apprentices were not considered, and that they were not properly taught.   In the wool-combing industry in Devon apprentices were very generally taken, but were dismissed at sixteen or eighteen years old.[5] Bad, too, were the conditions

[1] Coms. Jals., xxvi. p. 781.   [2] Reports, 1803–4, v. p. 12.
[3] Ibid., p. 4.   [4] Ibid., ibid.
[5] Coms. Jals., xlix. p. 1794. Petition against combing machines.

of boy labour at Coventry. From about 1780[1] the Watch-makers, " in order to get their work done at a cheaper rate, take a number of boys, to whom they pay comparatively nothing ; these apprentices earn their masters various sums ; from eighteen shillings to twenty-four shillings per week are the prevailing tasks ; by these means they are enabled to undersell the London and all other manufacturers who do not act upon the same principle."[2] The apprentices were often outdoor, and the industry was carried on in factories, and was very highly specialised, there being about a hundred different branches. Few apprentices learnt more than one, and were turned off as soon as their terms had expired in order to make way for cheaper labour. Very few could obtain employment as journeymen, they knew too little, and there was no opening for them. The majority turned to weaving and to unskilled labour.[3] This so-called apprenticeship had little in common with the Elizabethan system. It was simply a cloak used by masters for the employment of cheap, and even sweated, labour.

In the better-class skilled trades, for which, as has been said, a long training was still necessary, and in the wealthy trades where the gilds were strong enough to enforce it, apprentice-ship was still the rule. But it was often an apprenticeship of an inferior order, and even so its enforcement sometimes taxed the strength of the gilds to breaking-point. The change in the character of apprenticeship had set in at the close of the seventeenth century, with the increase of wealth and luxury. The apprentice in the better trades now would be used to comfort, and accustomed to having servants under him ; upon such a boy it was impossible to impose the old servitude, with its hard and often menial work, its lack of all amusements, and its demand for obedience and a humble spirit. His training, therefore, tended to give his master more trouble than his services were worth, and the custom grew up of taking

---

[1] H. C., vi. 285. Report on petition of Watchmakers, 1817 ; pp. 75, 82.
[2] Ibid., p. 82–84.
    Cf. Coms. Jals., xlv. 264. Petition of Coventry Silk Weavers.
[3] H. C., vi. 285., pp. 73-75.

apprentices only with heavy premiums, which paid the master
for the lad's board and lodging.   This was especially the case
in London, the home of the wealthy companies and wealthy
merchants.   Such large premiums were given with apprentices
in the eighteenth century that it was said an apprentice was
" looked upon rather as a boarder than a servant : He takes
little care of his Master's Business, and the Master as little to
instruct him in the Mystery of his Profession." [1]   Of lawyers'
apprentices, in particular, the complaint was made that "they
are under no Manner of Government; before their Times are
half out, they set up for Gentlemen, they dress, they drink,
they game, frequent the Playhouses, and intrigue with the
Women ; and it is a common thing with Clerks to bully their
Masters and desert their Service for whole Days and Nights
whenever they see fit." [2]

Apparently in some companies this desire to set up for
gentlemen led the lads to live apart from their masters ; or
perhaps the latter refused to trouble themselves by having
such fine young men in the house.   At any rate, there are
indications of the rise of this practice of outdoor apprenticeship at the close of the seventeenth century.   The Hallamshire Cutlers passed a rule in 1652 by which any apprentice
who resided out of his master's house was disabled for ever
from taking up the freedom.[3]   At Carlisle, the Butchers in
1680 ordered that unless special leave was obtained from the
Company, all apprentices were to live with their masters.[4]
In the eighteenth century non-resident apprenticeships were
quite common in Sheffield.[5]   At Newcastle the Merchant
Adventurers' and the Hostmen's Companies were obliged to
take active steps to enforce the indoor system.   Merchant
Adventurers had been " giving liberty to their apprentices to
goe beyond sea, and there remaine for a long time, and not
in their masters' actuall service." [6]   This was forbidden upon

[1] Strype's Stow, vol. ii. (1754), p. 559
[2] Ibid., ibid.
[3] Leader, Cutlers of Sheffield, ii. p. 10.   Rules 23.3, 22.2.
[4] Ferguson, p. 296, Miscel. Entries, Feb., 1680.
[5] Leader, op. cit., i. p. 56.
[6] Surtees, Newcastle Merch. Adven., p. 19.   July 24, 1701.

pain of a fine of £100. About the same time the Hostmen
were perturbed in their minds as to the disorderly lives of
their apprentices, who used unlawful games and absented
themselves at night from their masters' houses.[1] In 1707
they found it necessary to pass a rule to the effect that any
apprentice who was absent "for the Space of six months at
any time duringe the terme of his Indentures" should be debarred from his freedom.[2] A few years later a committee was
appointed for the special purpose of inquiring into what apprentices "do not cohabit with their Ma^{rs} nor make them
faithful service."[3] But though the gilds still made bye-laws,
they were often not strong enough to put them into execu-
tion, and were obliged to tolerate irregular apprenticeship, and
even its complete omission. Already, at the close of the
seventeenth century, the task of enforcing apprenticeship had
sometimes been beyond their powers, owing to the determined
opposition of free traders, the lack of support from municipal
authorities, and the unwillingness of magistrates to execute
the Statute. In the eighteenth century this opposition and
indifference had not decreased, and every year saw the gilds
becoming less capable of coping with the law-breakers. Their
very efforts to enforce the Act exhausted them even to the
point of collapse. This was the case with so important a
company as the Merchant Tailors of Bath. For a long time
they carried on a vigorous struggle against interlopers, and
legal proceedings were frequently taken against unapprenticed
persons.[4] The expenses of the fight must have been heavy,
for the income of the company seems to have been insufficient to meet them. Various methods were devised for raising
the necessary money. Men were admitted sometimes only
upon condition that they contributed to lawyers' charges ;[5]
illegal workmen were allowed to compound ; heavier redemption fees were imposed—one man, in 1735, paid £20 for

[1] Surtees, Hostmen, p. 167. Feb. 13, 1705–6.
[2] Ibid., p. 177. Oct. 8, 1707.
[3] Ibid., p. 181. May 13, 1713.
[4] Shickle, Merch. Tailors of Bath, pp. 25–30.
[5] Ibid., p. 24. Mins., Jan. 9, 1735.

his admission;[1] while a common fund was started in 1732, to which each member had to contribute one shilling a quarter, probably to carry on the disputes at law.[2]   These legal proceedings injured the company in prestige and authority, as well as financially, for, in the course of the trials, their right to make bye-laws was questioned.   Finally, in 1765, the company entered upon two long disputes with Glazeby and a man of the sinister name of Evill.[3]   Glazeby won, and the Merchant Tailors appear to have felt that if they could not enforce apprenticeship it was of no use their attempting to inspect the trade, nor even to administer those of their bye-laws which were uncontroversial.   When any one at all might use the trade or teach it, the position of the company became untenable.   The members therefore met together, and one by one they made a declaration of secession.[4]   The company was thus dissolved.   Equally significant is the fact that the powerful company of Hallamshire Cutlers was unable to punish those who broke the ordinances.   The court of the company met to hear complaints and conduct business, just as it had done in the best days of apprenticeship ; offenders were summoned and careful inquiries were made into their ill-deeds.   Heavy fines were inflicted upon those who were proved to have broken the gild rules.   But in almost all cases the fines were remitted, so that the bye-laws could really be broken with impunity.   One man, who was fined 20s. for employing another's apprentice had 19s. returned to him ;[5] a similar fine was imposed upon a member for allowing his sons and apprentices to work for hire, and he also had to pay only 1s. of it.[6]   It was sometimes given as a reason for returning the fine that the culprit was ignorant of the law, but such excuses were probably made by the company for the sake of appearances, and there is nothing of deeper moment in this interesting outburst of ignorance.   In 1735 it was agreed that

---

[1] Shickle, Merch. Tailors of Bath, p. 26   Mins., Jan. 29, 1735.
[2] Ibid., p. 26.   Nov. 4, 1732.
[3] Ibid., p. 30.   [4] Ibid., p. 32.
[5] Leader, *op. cit.*, ii. p. 17.
[6] Ibid., p. 18.
    Cf. many similar cases.   1710 to 1740, pp. 17, 18.

a fee of £5 should be charged for the turn-over of an apprentice, but as a matter of fact it could not be collected, and the custom sprang up of remitting it as soon as imposed. In 1740 the fee was raised to £10, but the entries show that £9 19s. was usually remitted.[1]   In 1745 the bye-law was withdrawn as it had become a farce. The records of Hull have a similar tale to tell of the inability of the companies to enforce their rules.   There, too, the gildsmen, in the effort to maintain the old privileges, made stricter rules which they could not enforce, and imposed fines which remained unpaid.[2] Even the London companies could not always hold their own. As early as 1752 the Hatters did not attempt prosecutions against workmen who encroached upon their privileges; indeed, it was said that they " winked " at them.[3]

Often their well-established rules were even more than the gilds could enforce at the close of the century, since if the case were taken before a higher court, the judges showed themselves biased in favour of no restraints.   We have seen that in the seventeenth century legal opinion was opposed to the Elizabethan system, and the decisions now given tended still further to limit the scope of the Act.

It was decided that manufactures which were not in existence in 1562 were exempt,[4] and that compulsory apprenticeship extended only to those trades in which it could be expedient—that is to say, to trades which required skill and experience. This was a somewhat arbitrary decision, and from the first was considered open to question.[5] Yet another decision, given in 1756, must have weakened the position of those who were fighting for apprenticeship and desired the support of the courts.   An action for debt was brought against a man for using the trade of a brewer unapprenticed.   The verdict was given for the defendant on the grounds that every man had a right naturally and legally to

---

[1] Leader, *op. cit.*, ii. pp. 18, 19.
[2] Lambert, Two Thousand Years, p. 192.
[3] Reports and Other Matters (Reprints), ii. pp. 372–6.
[4] Chitty, Law of Apprenticeship, p. 115.
    Cf. 2 Salkeld, 64. Lord Raymond, 511, 1188, 1410.
[5] Chitty, *op. cit.*, p. 116.

exercise what trade he pleased.[1]   In 1798 it was decided, in a
case brought against the Coopers' Company at Newcastle, that
the limitation of the number of apprentices by a corporation
or company was void, as in restraint of trade.   In connection
with this case Lord Kenyon said that bye-laws were
brought to him for his consent, and that not long before
he had refused to allow some, because they restrained
masters in the number of their apprentices, and he thought
it illegal.[2]

The gilds continued their efforts until 1814, but the fight
was really over before this. So far as any definite date can
be given for the collapse of apprenticeship, the year 1780
perhaps best marks the complete breakdown of the Elizabethan system.   By that time it had broken down in the
woollen and knitting trades and in watchmaking ; it was
practically non-existent in the calico trade ; and in the skilled
trades, which were still organised into companies, the authority
of those companies was so disputed that as often as not they
were unable to enforce their rules.   It was, apparently, not the
concentration of labour in large factories, due to the introduction of expensive machinery, which led to the collapse of
apprenticeship.   Neither the woollen nor the knitting trade
was conducted upon the factory system at the time when
apprenticeship was fast disappearing from them.   The
woollen trade in the North was still pursued upon the
domestic system, while the framework knitters carried on
their industry in their homes, either as small masters or
journeymen.   Rather, the chief cause of its collapse was the
growth of capitalism.   It has been pointed out that wealthy
masters were unwilling to endure the restraints which
apprenticeship involved, while they were too powerful to be
intimidated into obedience by the gilds.   Further, the
expansion of foreign trade led to a change in commercial
and industrial ethics, and threw into discredit the old beliefs
in stints, non-competition, and the minute regulation of the
individual.   Overseas trade could not be carried on by the

---

[1] Burrows, Reps., vol. i. p. 3.
[2] Durnford and East, Term Reports, vol. 7, p. 543.

petty master working on domestic lines; foreign trade required a knowledge of the tastes, seasons, and markets in distant countries which the small man had no opportunity of studying; moreover, it required men who were able to wait a considerable length of time for a return on their capital. Thus the capitalist not only had an opening, but was actually necessary to the commercial prosperity of the nation, and public opinion was alienated from the old methods and ideas and from the gildsmen who supported them. The collective opinion of lawyers was, as we have seen, opposed to the principles of the Statute of Artificers. The House of Commons was equally averse to its strict enforcement. Numerous petitions were presented to Parliament by lawful workmen throughout the eighteenth century; but, though there was no doubt as to the truth of their complaints that the Act was disregarded, the Commons made little effort to provide a remedy. As early as 1701 a committee, appointed to inquire into the grievances of the serge and worsted weavers, reported that the petitioners' allegations were true, but that nevertheless "the said trade ought to be free and not restrained."[1] In 1724, it is true, the Commons gave their support to apprenticeship in an Act passed for the manufacture of cloth in the West Riding; no one was to make cloth but those who had served apprenticeship.[2] In 1726 a second Act was passed providing that inspectors should be chosen yearly in each county. They were to supervise the trade, and had power of entry into all mills, shops, and houses.[3] Thus there was some attempt to put the Acts in force. All the same, the chief interest of the Commons was centred in the prevention of "deceitful" work, such as the straining and damping of cloth;[4] they did not really concern themselves with the training of workmen and the enforcement of apprenticeship. Municipal corporations, where existed a body of opinion which might have been of service to the gilds, were as little disposed to support them as were the courts or Parliament. They had become indifferent to

[1] Coms. Jals., vol. 13, p. 783.
[2] 11 Geo. I. c. 24. f. xvii.
[3] 13 Geo. I. c. 23.
[4] 11 Geo. I. c. 24; 11 Geo. II. c. 28.

the Act at the close of the seventeenth century, and Eden, writing of apprenticeship in 1790, states that corporations seldom entered into litigations at that time "except upon occasions when their elective franchises are concerned."[1] He disputes Adam Smith's assertion that the corporations, by enforcing their bye-laws, were injurious to trade;[2] and there seems every reason to believe that he was right, and that the corporations never forbade persons to work at their trade merely because they were not freemen and had not been apprenticed. There was still some scattered opinion in favour of apprenticeship. Defoe, in 1726, wrote at considerable length upon the subject in his "Complete English Tradesman," and evidently did not regard it as an out-of-date method of training.[3] But the individual adherents of the system had no power to enforce the law, and the only organised supporters—the gilds—were every year becoming weaker, not only because public opinion was forming against them, but also because each year of laxness in the administration of the Act, and each failure on the part of the gilds to enforce it, meant a loss of their power and administrative authority. In the good old days admission to a company had conferred the right to work and to teach others, which was a coveted privilege since it enabled a man to obtain cheap labour, and even a premium. But now that these old advantages were shared with unlawful workmen and non-members there was little to be gained by membership, and the companies dwindled for lack of members and funds.

The irremediable collapse of the apprenticeship system was, however, not so apparent to contemporaries as it is to us, with all the facts before us; and those who still believed in it thought that just a slight effort on the part of the Crown would put the system in working order. But public opinion was too strongly in favour of freedom from all industrial restraints, and apprenticeship was too closely connected with

---

[1] Eden, State of the Poor, i. p. 456.
[2] Ibid., i. p. 435.
[3] Defoe, Complete English Tradesman, chap. i. pars. 2, 3.

the gilds and monopoly for the Government to make any such effort. Thus it was that as the eighteenth century advanced apprenticeship was limited to those trades where the gilds were powerful, or where it was felt to be really necessary as a means of training.

CHAPTER XV

THE END OF THE NATIONAL SYSTEM

IN 1814 two and a half centuries after it had come into being, the Statute of Artificers was repealed.[1] By the irony of fate the repeal was brought about by the pleas of the supporters of the Act for its stricter enforcement. If such petitions had not been made to Parliament, it is very possible that the question would never have arisen. The Elizabethan system was no doubt out of date, but it was some way advanced in a process of quiet disintegration, and those who wished to do so could, as a rule, ignore the Act with impunity, so that there was no need to agitate for its repeal. It was dying a natural death, and there would probably have been little objection to allowing it to remain on the statute books had not discontented workmen suddenly realised that the clauses as to wages and a seven years' apprenticeship might still be enforced, and attempted to enforce them in order to remedy their grievances. They prosecuted men who, technically, were " unlawful," but who were as skilled as any of the agitators, and against whom the only real cause of complaint was that they were in work, which some of the qualified workmen were not. Further, they petitioned Parliament for a strict administration of the Act, and thus the whole vexed question was brought to public notice.

The course of the repeal is worth following, not only because it forms the last chapter in the history of compulsory apprenticeship, but because it serves as a study in parliamentary psychology. The Elizabethan Act was unsuited to the new methods, new markets, and new trades of the nineteenth century, and it would have been impossible to force

[1] 54 Geo. III. c. 96.

upon the country a system which the great trades had discarded. Nevertheless, almost all the representations and petitions made to Parliament were in support of the Act, and the evidence which the Select Committees actually laid before the House was unfavourable to its withdrawal; a state of affairs which suggests that there was probably a real need for some general form of training and public control, even though the old apprenticeship system, with all the anomalies and inequalities which it had accumulated through the centuries, could not be allowed to stand unchanged. But this was the time when the doctrine of *laissez faire* was at its height, and the House of Commons, imbued with the teaching of the fashionable political economists, was impatient of any restriction upon industrial freedom. Indeed, Onslow, who brought in the Bill for repeal, might have dispensed with his arguments. The House was with him, and from the first there was no doubt that the Commons would pass his measure. A substitute for the Elizabethan system was never even mooted. The repeal was, in fact, a striking example of the influence of doctrinaire opinion upon practical politics.

The whole question of the policy of the Act came under consideration, as we have noticed, owing to the agitation of distressed workmen for its enforcement. This distress arose from various causes. In the last quarter of the eighteenth century, heavy machinery, which had hitherto been used only in the important but unorganised industry of mining, began to be employed in the chief industries of the country. In the building trade to-day, and in trades concerned with horse traction, we have an example on a small scale of the suffering and the dislocation of labour which the introduction of machinery and improved implements involves. At the close of the eighteenth century the textile trade was passing through this period of transition from hand labour to machinery. At any time this revolution in one of the greatest industries of the country must have caused widespread distress. But the introduction of machinery coincided with the Napoleonic wars, which in themselves would have been sufficient alone to have caused acute economic disturb-

16

ance. This was not all. Men in the building trade to-day
have poor relief between themselves and starvation, while
their Trade Unions ameliorate the lot of members. The
Industrial Revolution took place not only at the period of the
great wars, but at a time when the Poor Law was most in-
efficiently administered, and before the days of Trade Unions.
Moreover, the use of more expensive machinery involved the
concentration of the industrial classes around factories, in
cities or villages which alike had not sufficient accommodation and no sanitation. This increased the misery, and was,
indeed, an aggregation of evils ; and though the conditions of
work had at no time been good, men in these days of acute
distress, looked back upon the past as a Golden Age, and
demanded an enforcement of the old laws, in the belief that
their strict observance would restore the old conditions.

It was the agitation of the woollen weavers that first
brought the Act before the notice of Parliament. A large
number of weavers were thrown out of work by the invention
of the flying shuttle, and sought relief by demanding the
administration of existing laws, especially the Statute of
Artificers, which, if fully observed, would protect apprenticed
weavers from the competition of workmen technically unqualified.[1]   Prosecutions were instituted against the law-
breakers throughout the country, but many of the Acts concerning the woollen trade, such as those regulations for the
length and breadth of cloth, were so antiquated that it
would have been absurd to enforce them. The judges were
placed in an awkward predicament, and in 1803 Parliament
suspended the laws for the woollen trade, and a Select Committee was appointed to hear evidence. The report was
made in 1806, and was chiefly concerned with the Statute of
Artificers.   The most vital question was whether seven
years' apprenticeship could fairly be enforced upon the
weavers. This was, naturally enough, demanded by those
who had served the legal term, and now saw their chances of
employment endangered by the competition of workmen unqualified at law.   On the other hand, a short training of two

[1] See Cunningham, Growth of English Industry (1903), iii. p. 657.

or three years had been in vogue since about 1790,[1] and it was obvious that if the Act were enforced a very large number of workmen would be deprived of their means of livelihood. It was said that three-fourths of the Saddleworth merchants would be thrown out of work if the Act were enforced,[2] while a manufacturer of Bradford stated his belief that nineteen-twentieths had not served regular apprenticeships.[3] There was a certain amount of conflicting evidence as to the value of seven years' service : some witnesses declared that no weaver could be fully trained in less than seven years, others urged that a five years' apprenticeship was long enough, while some said that a man could learn the trade in two or three years. More conclusive was the evidence of employers, who almost unanimously declared that so little did they think a seven years' apprenticeship necessary that they never inquired of their workmen whether they were legally qualified or not. If a weaver proved himself a bad workman he could be dismissed : it was ludicrous to think that good work could only be safeguarded by apprenticeship.[4] It was finally the inconsistency of the weavers themselves that decided the Committee to set aside the Act. The Yorkshire weavers had been loudest in the demand for the observance of the Act and a seven years' apprenticeship, but they had for some time past openly countenanced a five years' term. The Cloth Hall of Leeds was the recognised market for the cloth of the northern manufacturers, and was under the control and regulation of the men in the trade. It had been a rule that only those who had been apprenticed seven years might show their cloth at the Hall, but in 1796 the regulation was altered to five years instead of seven.[5] Further, it became apparent in the course of the inquiry that the demand for the strict administration of the law was largely due to the jealousy of weavers working on the domestic system towards those who carried on their work in

[1] Report on Woollen Trade, 1806. Mins. of Evidence, pp. 10, 71, 171, 184.
[2] Ibid., Mins. of Evidence, p. 139.
[3] Ibid., ibid., p. 184. [4] See p. 227.
[5] Ibid., ibid., p. 10.

factories; these men would be seriously hampered in their
business if the law were enforced, and if all their employees
had to be apprentices or journeymen.[1] It also transpired
that the complaints against illegal workmen were prompted
by a desire to prevent competition in times of trade depres-
sion, for until comparatively lately there had been no prosecutions of unqualified workmen, and so little attention had
been paid to the Statute that even educated and substantial
men had barely heard of its existence.[2] In their report the
Committee stated that it was "notorious that our woollen
manufactures have been for some time gradually improving
in quality and increasing in amount on the one hand, while
on the other the system of apprenticeship had been in many
parts of the country greatly disused, until the general attention was called to the subject by the discussions which commenced less than four years ago."[3] They declared that it was
"the right of every man to employ the Capital he inherits or
has acquired according to his own discretion, without molesta-
tion or obstruction, so long as he does not infringe on the
rights or the property of others."[4] The Commons therefore suspended the apprenticeship clauses of the Act, so far
as the woollen trade was concerned, for another three years,
and in 1809 set them permanently aside. This was a step
of great importance. The clothing trade was one of the
oldest and largest industries of the country, and the fact that
apprenticeship had been dispensed with for weaving must
inevitably have influenced opinion in favour of a general
repeal. The struggle was fought out in cotton weaving,
which had been over-developed by speculators before and
during the Revolutionary War The wages had been so good
that any number of new men flocked into the trade. But the
boom did not last long. First the difficulty of obtaining raw
material during the war, and, secondly, the resumption by the
Continent of its own manufacturing as the war came to a
close, led to a decrease in demand, and a terrible fall in
wages in the over-crowded market.[5] An Arbitration Act was

---

[1] Report on Woollen Trade 1806. Mins. of Evidence, p. 447.
[2] Ibid., pp. 13-14.   [3] Ibid., p. 14.
[4] Ibid., p. 12.   [5] Cunningham, *op. cit.*, p. 634.

passed for the settlement of disputes and wages, but apparently it gave no relief. The weavers petitioned for a statutory minimum wage, but this was refused. It was then that they discovered that the Statute of Artificers provided for their needs, and in 1812 they petitioned quarter sessions for an assessment of wages.[1] The only result was that the question of assessment was brought up in Parliament. Petitions in support of the Act were presented from various parts of Lancashire, and it appeared that not only the weavers, but the magistrates and employers, were in favour of the Act or some substitute.[2] Indeed, there seems to have been no demand for repeal. Nevertheless, the assessment clauses were abolished.

The repeal of the apprenticeship clauses for the woollen trade, and of the wages clauses generally, caused the Act as a whole to come under discussion, and a committee on the apprenticeship laws was appointed in 1812. The petitions presented to the House were almost all in favour of the Act, and were sent from every quarter.[3] Signatures perhaps mean little, yet there were 300,000 in favour and only 2,000 against the Act. Of more real significance is the fact that the chairman of the Select Committee was converted by the evidence from an opponent to a firm supporter of apprenticeship. This evidence was gathered from a large number of the more skilled trades in London and the provinces. The general trend of it was that if apprenticeship were not enforced the quality of goods and the standard of skill would decline, and we would lose our foreign trade. This was said to have occurred already in coach-building ; the intrusion of unqualified masters into the business had led, it was averred, to bad work, and the trade with the East Indies and America had been lost.[4] The organ industry was also said to have suffered. A London organ-builder declared

[1] Cunningham, *op. cit.*, p. 635.

[2] Coms. Jals., lxviii. 229. Quoted by Cunningham, p. 637.

[3] Parliamentary Debates, Hansard, vol. 25, cols. 1093, 1094, 1129 ; vol. 27, pp. 224, 423, 545.

[4] Report from Committee on several petitions respecting the apprenticeship laws, 1813, p. 8. Reports, 1812–13, iv. p. 659.

that the exportation of barrel-organs had declined owing
to bad work.[1] Lack of skill certainly seems to have led to
some inconveniences ; in one instance a workman repaired an
organ so badly that its owner did not know whether it was
playing "God save the King" or "Chevy Chase." The
evidence generally—evidence which was of a more weighty
character than the organ-builder's—showed that those who
supported compulsory training had no bad case. It is clear
that the demand for the enforcement of the Act was largely
due to a desire to limit competition. But it was even clearer
that in the majority of the industries of the country, which
were still, it must be remembered, highly skilled handicrafts,
a regular training was really required. After all, it did not
follow that because apprenticeship was unnecessary in a
comparatively unskilled trade such as weaving, it could be
safely dispensed with in the mass of skilled trades ; and, in
default of any better method of training, it was not altogether
unreasonable to cling to the Elizabethan system. This was,
apparently, the view of the chairman of the Committee.
Further, the evidence showed that where unqualified men
had been employed, it was often because they were willing
to take less wages. In none of the trades concerned was
there a shortage of qualified workmen. Unqualified men
were engaged by masters who hoped to undersell their
neighbours, and to win the market through the employment
of cheap labour and by shoddy work. Such employers, who
were the spiritual ancestors of the sweating masters in the
East End to-day, naturally found that the Elizabethan
system hampered their business, for that system was based
upon economic ideas which were opposed to cut-throat
competition and the conduct of business by these methods.
In 1814 it was largely because cut-throat competition meant
to have its way that all the restraints imposed by the Act
were set aside.

Yet though there was much to be said for some sort of
control, there were any number of objections to continuing

[1] Report from Committee on several petitions respecting the apprenticeship
laws, 1813. p. 27.

the compulsory apprenticeship system as it stood.   The law was unequal, for it did not apply to Scotland and Ireland, nor to any trade which had arisen since 1562, the decisions of the courts having limited it to those industries which had been in existence when the Act was passed.[1]   It was full of anomalies ;   one absurdity which was pointed out was that a gardener did not come within the scope of the Act, because he was unskilled, yet a pippin monger did.   Onslow, who introduced the Bill for repeal, urged that it was a most burdensome restriction which prevented a man from changing from one occupation to another according to the fluctuations of a trade, or as his health required ;   and that the time necessary to acquire skill was different in different trades.[2] He pointed out that various classes of persons and several trades had been exempted from the Act :   sailors, soldiers, and militiamen, persons who convicted two offenders of coining, hawkers and pedlars, hatters, wool-combers, dyers, and woollen workers,[3] might work unmolested, even though not apprenticed.   It was, of course, an advantage to those who supported the repeal that a precedent should already have been created for setting the Act aside.   Its irregular dispensation weakened the case of those who stood for apprenticeship, and the few who did so based their opposition to the proposed Bill chiefly on the grounds that the training was of moral advantage to the young.[4]   But this consideration was not sufficiently weighty to reconcile the House to a statute which was based upon ideas contrary to the economic beliefs of the day, and the repeal of the penal clauses of the Act was carried by a large majority.   An agreement of apprenticeship, as one form of contract, was of course still enforceable at law, but henceforth no one could be prosecuted for practising a trade without having served as an apprentice to it for seven years.   Compulsory technical training no longer existed.

[1] Chitty, Law of Apprenticeship, p. 115.
  2 Salkeld, 611 ; Lord Raymond, 514, 1188, 1410.
[2] Parliamentary Debates, Hansard, vol. 27, p. 566.
[3] Ibid., vol. 27, p. 566.
[4] Ibid., ibid., p. 879.

CHAPTER XVI

APPRENTICESHIP AS A DEVICE OF POOR RELIEF

FROM the time of Henry VIII. apprenticeship has been used as a method of poor relief. The support and training which it supplied were utilised by the public authorities on the one hand to relieve the rates, and on the other to launch out into the world the children for whom they were responsible. Numbers of orphans and the children of widows, or of persons in destitute or very poor circumstances, were for these reasons bound apprentice. There were other means of assisting poor parents and of providing for pauper children ; sometimes out-door relief was given ; sometimes there were special departments for children in the bridewells or work-houses,[1] while there were a certain number of charity schools or orphanages. Still, until comparatively recent times, it was by apprenticeship that the majority of parish children were maintained. Such apprenticeship is quite distinct from the industrial apprenticeship with which we have hitherto dealt ; indeed, it is so distinct that an account of it would have no place in the history of child labour, if it were not for the fact that, at the close of the eighteenth century, the fortunes of the pauper apprentice had a very considerable influence upon apprenticeship in general ; the terrible way in which pauper apprentices had been and were being abused became a matter of common knowledge, and the revelations which were then made discredited apprenticeship generally, and undoubtedly tended to reduce the number of those who were opposed to the abolition of Elizabeth's compulsory system.

The policy of dealing with pauper children by apprenticeship was initiated in Henry VIII.'s reign by an Act requiring

---

[1] Leonard, Early History of English Poor Relief, p. 217.

that vagrant children between the ages of five and fourteen should be arrested and bound apprentice.[1] This device for preventing pauperism was further developed a few years later by an Act of Edward VI.; sons of vagrants might be apprenticed until 24, daughters until 20 ; punishment for rebellion against their masters was slavery.[2] There can be little doubt that later on Burleigh and his fellow-statesmen were, when drawing up the Statute of Artificers, keenly alive to the value of apprenticeship as a preventive of pauperism ; [3] and at the close of Elizabeth's reign, when the whole Poor Law policy of the country was being overhauled, apprenticeship was definitely established as part of the Elizabethan system of poor relief. The churchwardens and overseers of the poor were empowered to bind any children whose parents were not able to support them. Male apprentices were to remain bound until 24 years old ; female, until 21, or marriage. The binding was invalid unless made by indenture, and sanctioned by two justices of the peace.[4] Henceforward, until the Poor Law reform in 1834, apprenticeship was a most important feature of English poor relief.

The agreements under which parish children served were similar to those of industrial apprentices ; there is one slight difference in the wording of the indentures in the case of the former, namely, that the overseers are parties to the bond and are mentioned in the indenture by name. Further, from 1601, it was not unusual to give a small premium with parish apprentices, a custom which did not come into vogue in connection with industrial apprenticeship until somewhat later, and was then less uniformly practised. The sum given was not large, two to five pounds was the usual fee in the earlier days.[5] The money was found by the poor rates, or was drawn from charitable funds, of which there appear to have been a considerable number even in the first decades of

---

[1] 27 H. VIII. c. 25. [2] 3 Edw. VI. c. 3.
[3] See p. 70. [4] 43 Eliz. c. 2 (1601).
[5] *Cf.* Leader, Sheffield Cutlers, i. p. 49. £5 or £6 given in the eighteenth century.

the system, for little more than ten years after it was established an Act was passed with the object of securing the proper use of funds which had been left to bind poor children as apprentices.[1] Still, though premiums had generally to be given, apprenticeship was the cheapest method of dealing with pauper children, for the charity schools and houses of industry, which existed in some places, could never have been sufficient to meet the needs of the country generally. We may take it, therefore, that the Act was at once enforced so far as it concerned children actually on the rates, simply because apprenticeship was cheap and easy. It does not appear, however, that the further injunctions of the Act were observed, or that the justices of the peace "sought out" and apprenticed the children of poor persons who were unable to rear and train their families in a suitable manner. There was, of course, no special inducement upon the overseers and justices to undertake this piece of their work, since the children were not actually on the rates, and it was not until Charles I.'s reign, when, as we know, the activity of the Privy Council led to better administration of the laws generally, that this clause of the Act was observed. Then, however, the justices of the peace were required to make reports upon their work,[2] and from these returns we can see that a certain number of children was, each year, apprenticed in almost every parish.[3] The total number who acquired their training and start in life by this means must have been very large.

It has been said that Poor Law apprenticeship is distinct from industrial apprenticeship. Its primary object was not so much to teach the child bound a trade as to remove him from injurious surroundings and provide him with maintenance. His position was, in fact, rather that of the

---

[1] 7 James I. c. 3.

[2] Cf., Leonard, Early History of English Poor Relief, pp. 215–217.

Guilding, Reading Records, iii. 234, June 18, 1634. Churchwardens and overseers to search their parishes for poor children whose parents are not able to keep them. They were to take their names that they be bound apprentice.

[3] State Papers (Domestic), cccxiv., Charles I., Nos. 43, 62, 71, 76, 77, 78, 102, 103, 114, 115, 116, 131, &c.

"boarded-out" child to-day. He might be taught a trade if the master to whom he was bound happened to be a craftsman, but his apprenticeship in the usual sense of the term was not an essential part of his contract. What the overseers and justices had to do was to provide him with board, lodging, and a guardian, not with technical instruction. Dalton, who in 1619 drew up for the guidance of country justices a summary of their duties, states this frankly, and declares that the majority of parish apprentices were bound not to trades, but to husbandry and housewifry.[1] We frequently find, both in the returns of the justices in Charles's reign and in the indentures preserved at a later date, that children were bound to craftsmen and tradesmen who, of course, had trades to teach. Yet it does not necessarily follow that they were taught their masters' trades. The boys were probably employed in the workshop because there they would be most useful, but the girls we may suppose more often helped the wife in her household duties.

Parish apprentices were by no means popular amongst better-class people; often they were placed out when so young that their labour could be turned to little account, while it was immaterial to the officers if they could find the children a home whether the master had work upon which he could employ them or not, and thus a craftsman might find himself billeted with a destitute child when his shop was already fully staffed with journeymen and apprentices. The gentry and clergy were also obliged to become the unwilling masters of young paupers. The Poor Law authorities not infrequently had difficulties in finding masters; men who would have been the best guardians declared they were not obliged to receive apprentices, and country magistrates were not always clear themselves as to how the law stood. Indeed, in 1633 some of them appealed to the justices of assize as to what description of persons could be obliged to take apprentices.[2] Occasionally the support of the quarter session judges had to be invoked

---

[1] Dalton, Country Justice, 1619, p. 85.
[2] S. P. D., Charles I., cclv. 46.

against recalcitrant masters. The Minutes of the Worcester-shire Sessions bear witness to the unwillingness of many men to accept their burdens ; [1] one obstinately refused ; [2] another allowed the boy bound to him to "wander up and down," and declined to keep him in his service. [3] How heavy the burden might be is revealed by the complaint of one man who managed to establish his case against the overseers. He was a farmer with a wife and six children, and declared with some show of right that he was unable to maintain the boys allotted to him by the parish. It was decided that this was a "heavy charge" upon him, and the overseers were ordered to make him an allowance of eighteen pence a week "for the time past and henceforth." [4] Such an allowance, however, was quite exceptional. Better-class tradesmen and the gentry sometimes paid a poorer neigh-bour to take the children off their hands ; a Sheffield mercer paid 40s. to a cutler to take the boy assigned to him ; 50s. was paid by a gentleman to another cutler to take over the son of a deceased husbandman. [5] The gentry of Sheffield and its neighbourhood appear to have attempted to establish their immunity from the system of billeting on the plea that they had no trade to teach, but it was ruled against them, "That ye meaning of ye statute was not for the education of boys in arts but for charity to keep ym and relieve ym from turning to roguery and idleness, so a man's house was, as it were, a Hospital in yt case, rather than a shop of trade, for they might be brought up to husbandry, cookery, dayery, and the like services in an house." [5] Sometimes when there were difficulties in finding masters a lottery was held, and men were obliged to take the children who fell to them by lot. [7] Still, parish apprentices were not always unwelcome.

<hr />

[1] Willis Bund, Worcestershire Quarter Sessions, Mins, 1634–1639, i. pp. 538, 618, 662, 664.

[2] Ibid., i. 609 (1636). [3] Ibid., i. 638.

[4] Ibid., Mins., Sept. 9, 1620.

[5 & 6] Leader, Sheffield Cutlers, i. p. 76, note, p. 57.

[7] Hardy, Quarter Sessions, Hertfordshire, ii. p. 125. Jan. 27, 1773. Order in vestry that the children of poor people who receive alms of the parish and are above seven years of age be bound apprentice to such masters as by lot fell out this day by drawing tickets in vestry by the consent of two justices of the peace.

They were bound until twenty-one or twenty-four years old, and in the last years of their terms their services must have been of real value to those who were not fully staffed, whatever their rank in life. Parish apprentices were the cheapest form of labour. On this account, and because even a small premium was coveted by them, men who were in a poor way of business were ready and indeed eager to receive parish children.

The reluctance of the one type of master and the readiness of the other to accept Poor Law apprentices affords us an indication of what must have been the fortunes of the children who were bound. The better class of master often had no trade to teach, nor when they had is it likely that they would regard and treat pauper apprentices as they did industrial apprentices, as members of their families ; yet the latter, as we know, had no easy lot. The children bound to poor masters must have had an even harder time. The industrial apprentices of such men were supervised by the gild officers and could appeal to the gild court in case of ill-usage. But parish apprentices did not come within gild control ; and though they might appeal to the magistrates, the ordinary machinery of the law was always far less readily set in motion than that of the gilds. There are instances of parish apprentices being discharged from masters who ill-treated them, and of masters being reprimanded or fined in cases of less flagrant abuse.[1] But action was taken only after complaints were lodged ; it was no one's business to see that apprentices bound by the public money were not over-worked and ill-used. Even if a master were well intentioned it must have been a temptation to struggling men to overwork assistants who were so absolutely at their command, while in several trades to which parish apprentices were commonly bound the general conditions of life and work were so bad that, even if the master gave of his best,

---

[1] *E.g.*, Atkinson, North Riding Quarter Sessions, vii. p. 176 ; ibid., viii. p. 175.

Guilding, *op. cit.*, iii. p. 233. Complaint against a master who has received a premium of £7.

the circumstances of his apprentices could not have been otherwise than miserable. Children were frequently bound to cobblers, who were generally men in a poor way ; while the pin trade, in which the conditions of work were wretched, was carried on largely by pauper labour.

Nevertheless, the apprenticeship of poor children stood high in the favour of the philanthropic public. Numerous bequests were made in the seventeenth and eighteenth centuries for the purpose of binding poor boys and girls as apprentices.[1] The recipients of these charities were by no means necessarily pauper apprentices, though the money was often used for the benefit of the latter. But the number of these bequests in every part of England is interesting from the point of view of the pauper apprentice ; it shows how fully contemporaries approved of this method of helping the poor.

The dislocation in civil government caused by the Great War no doubt reduced for a time the number of children bound out by the parishes ; we know that the whole administration of the Poor Law was disorganised. But upon the restoration of peace the apprenticeship of children whose parents were actually on the rates was certainly continued with as much regularity as ever, though it seems that less effort was made to "seek out" children who might become chargeable or who were not well cared for by their parents. At the close of the seventeenth century and in the eighteenth the endowment of charity schools was as favourite a form of philanthropy as were apprenticeship bequests, which suggests that amongst the charitably-minded the apprenticeship of poor and pauper children was not regarded with that

[1] Hutchins and Harrison, History of Factory Legislation, p. 3.
Kirkman Gray, History of English Philanthropy, p. 41.
Burton, Kidderminster, p. 147. Bequest of £200, 1665.
Monk, Burford, p. 158. 1660, £20 bequeathed. 1739, house bequeathed, the rent to go to apprenticing boys.
MSS. Norwich, Court Book 34. June 19, 1776. Reference to Bloomfield's charity.
Leonard, Early History of English Poor Relief, pp. 215, 216.
Reports of Charity Commission, vi. pp. 522, 457, 381, 155.
Guilding, Reading Records, iii. p. 512.

complete approbation which it had formerly commanded.[1]
At the close of the eighteenth century, however, there was
a new and a strong inducement to parish officers to apprentice as many children as they could. This new inducement
was that settlement policy which was adopted in 1691 after
various experiments since 1662. Previous to this latter year
it had been quite common for impoverished people to transport themselves into those parishes which provided the best
relief for their poor. Such a practice laid an unfairly heavy
burden on certain districts, and created considerable dissatisfaction with the law as it stood. In 1662 an attempt was
made to remedy this state of things by enacting that a parish
was to be responsible only for those poor who had acquired
a settlement within it, a settlement being held to be acquired
by those who lived for forty days at least within a parish
as natives, householders, sojourners, or servants.[2] This Act
failed to meet the needs of the case, since the poor were
bribed to hide themselves within a parish for forty days.
In 1685, therefore, a remedying Act was passed.[3] Notice
now had to be published in church, and a settlement could
be gained only by notice, given in writing.

Owing to the dishonesty of parish officers, this Act did not
check all abuses, and in 1691 a new law was passed, by which
a settlement could be gained only by paying parish rates,
serving as a parish officer for a year, hiring for a year, and
apprenticeship within the parish.[4] Poor Law officers could
now no longer rid themselves of their poor with a bribe to
remain hidden in a neighbouring parish. But they could
induce petty craftsmen and other poorer inhabitants, by the

---

[1] Kirkman Gray, *op. cit.*, p. 110.

Beatrice and Sidney Webb, MS., Policy of the Poor Law. Eighteenth century and early nineteenth only children actually chargeable to the rates were, as
a rule, apprenticed. 1772, Leeds Vestry restricted apprenticeship to those whose
parents were actually in the workhouse.

[2] 13 & 14 Ch. II. c. 12.

[3] 1 Jas. II. c. 17.

Cf. Adam Smith, Wealth of Nations (ed. Cannan, 1904), pp. 137, 138.

[4] 3 & 4 Wm. and Mary c. 11.

At Corsley, in Wilts, men were paid a few shillings for "wearing" or
"warning" out the "outcomers" lest they should gain a settlement. Maud
Davies, Life in an English Village, p. 37.

payment of a premium, to receive their pauper children as apprentices, and so free themselves for ever not only from the maintenance of the child, but also from the possibility of supporting his wife and children in the future. Henceforth there was a regular traffic in apprentices. Any man who wanted two or three pounds could, whatever his character and circumstances, obtain the sum by taking an apprentice. The sole concern of parish officers was to be quit of the children, and they took no trouble to find good masters. Dr. Burn, in his history of the Poor Law, described it as the chief duty of parish officers "to bind out poor children apprentice, no matter to whom or to what trade, but to take special care that the master live in another parish."[1] The dumping system did not, of course, entirely supersede the older method of allocating pauper children amongst the householders of their native parish; indeed, the obligation to receive them was more strictly defined by an Act passed in 1696, making it compulsory upon any person to whom an apprentice was assigned to receive that child, on pain of a fine of £10, which could be levied by distress or sale of goods.[2] Men sometimes preferred to incur the penalty of the law rather than take apprentices,[3] but there was no question now as to their liability, whatever their station in life, to receive them. Dumping, however, was the more popular method with the overseers, because it relieved the parish of future as well as of present responsibilities. Yet it is unlikely that any parish really gained by this policy, for dumping was systematically practised, and though the officers in any place might conscientiously carry out the duty of depositing the burdens of their own parishioners upon the shoulders of unknown and distant ratepayers, they could not protect themselves from similar treatment by their neighbours. As for the unfortunate children of whom every one was so eager to be quit,

---

[1] In 1764. Quoted by B. and S. Webb. See above.

[2] 8 & 9 Wm. III. c. 30, repeated 20 Geo. III. c. 36, 1 (1780). The obligation to receive apprentices continued until 1834.

[3] Leader, Sheffield Cutlers, i. p. 76 n. Men paid £10 in lieu of accepting apprentices.

they undoubtedly suffered through the Act. They were now, whenever possible, bound at a distance from their native place, to a master over whom the officers who apprenticed them had no control, while they were far from the reach of any friends or relatives they might possess in their old homes. Further, the class of man who would receive them was not likely to make a good master. Gentlemen and well-to-do people who had been obliged to take their share of paupers under the old system never, of course, accepted a "dumped" child. Men who took them for the sake of the premium sometimes ill-treated them with the direct intention of driving the children from them, so that they obtained the money without having to perform the duties for which it was paid. William Bailey, who wrote upon the Poor Law in 1758, said that " Few of these poor children now serve out their time, and many of them are driven by neglect or cruelty into such immoralities as too frequently render them the objects of public justice. Many of those who take parish apprentices are so inhuman as to regard only the pecuniary conditions; and having once received that, they, by ill usage and undue severity, often drive the poor creatures from them, and so leave them in a more destitute condition at a riper age for mischief than they were when first they became the care of the parish officers." [1] The conditions were so bad that as early as 1697 the Board of Trade was authorised to inquire into the matter.[2] Though a Bill was drafted no action was as yet taken. The dumping system continued, and even though feeling against it was growing, the conditions of parish apprentices became worse rather than better as the eighteenth century advanced. This was due to the advent of the capitalist and the organisation of industry upon the factory system. The invention of heavy machinery which had to be worked by power aggravated the evil. It was the use of water power rather than of steam from which pauper

[1] Bailey, Treatise on the Better Employment and more Comfortable Support of the Poor in Workhouses, 1758, p. 5. Quoted by B. and S. Webb. See above.
[2] Alfred, History of the Factory Movement, i. p. 3.

17

children suffered most.   Water mills were frequently situated in country districts, because they had to be built where water could be obtained, regardless of whether or no the population of the neighbourhood could supply sufficient labour.   This in many country places was quite insufficient, and children were brought by the cart-load from distant workhouses.   The Lancashire and Yorkshire mills were worked largely by young paupers from London.[1]   They were housed and fed terribly badly, and were overworked to a degree which it is now difficult to imagine.   Feeling against the general abuse of pauper apprentices and the absolute freedom of their masters to treat them as they chose was, however, slowly forming.   We have seen how, in 1697, an inquiry had been set on foot, but it was not until nearly a century later, when sympathy had been more strongly aroused by the wholesale deportations of pauper children to large businesses and mills, that there was any effective movement for reform.   Investigations were made into the state of parish apprentices by a committee of the House of Commons, and, in 1767, it recommended that a higher premium should be given with apprentices, since the sum generally given was from 20s. to 40s. only, which the Committee considered inadequate to the procuring of good masters.   The Committee also held that the binding of boys to the age of twenty-four, as was required by Elizabeth's Act, "resulted in many inconveniences, checked marriage and discouraged industry"; the Committee therefore recommended that children should be bound for a shorter time than was prescribed by the law.[2]   An Act was passed for the children of London and the neighbourhood on the strength of these recommendations.   It required that not less than £4 2s. should be given as premium; 40s. was to be

---

[1] Alfred, *op. cit.*, i. chap. ii. p. 15.   *Cf.* chap. iv.

[2] Journals H. C., vol. 31, p. 249.

7 Geo. III. c. 39.   "Whereas sums of 20s. to 40s. now usually given with a Child placed out by the parishes, are no longer adequate to procure such Masters and Mistresses as are in general fit and proper, And whereas there is a general neglect in the moral and religious instruction of apprentices; and some pecuniary encouragement may excite Masters and Mistresses to discharge their duties in this respect," &c.

paid after seven weeks from the executing of the indentures, and 42s. after three years' service. This postponed payment of the fee was a happy idea, in that it offered an inducement to masters to treat their apprentices well. A register of all apprentices placed out by the parishes named in the Act was to be kept by the vestry clerk or other proper officer, and a return was to be made annually to the Company of Parish Clerks. Lastly, the children of these parishes were to be apprenticed for seven years only, or until they had reached the age of twenty-one years. In 1778 a general Act declared that no apprentice should be held bound after twenty-one years old ;[1] and in 1792 the transfer of parish apprentices without the consent of public officers was forbidden.[2] In 1801 the benefits of registration were extended to apprentices generally.[3] But these Acts were palliatives only, and did not satisfy the reformers, who, though few in numbers as yet, were fully alive to the evils of the Poor Law apprenticeship system. The prevalence of fevers in cotton mills at the close of the century brought the matter home to a larger section of the public ; the question of parish apprenticeship and the employment of children in the mills was seriously taken up ; and the subsequent revelations of the ghastly conditions of life and work made it impossible for the matter to be shelved, even though the doctrines of *laissez faire* were paramount, and legislative interference was considered undesirable. The deplorable conditions of pauper apprenticeship which forced the House of Commons to take action are too well known to need repetition here, while the story of the reform movement will be found in a later chapter. We shall have to see how impossible it was to reform the conditions of pauper apprentices without taking into consideration and reforming the conditions of ordinary apprenticeship and of unindentured child labour as well, and how the inquiries instituted into the former revealed the existence of conditions not quite so bad, but yet requiring immediate attention, amongst unapprenticed

[1] 18 Geo. III. c. 47.
[2] Journals H. C., pp. 382, 824, 1071.
[3] 42 Geo. III. c. 46.

and nominally free children. Thus the story of the pauper apprentice, which has hitherto followed a course distinct from that of the industrial apprentice, now converges with it, and the fortunes of pauper children, who had been a class apart, had a very striking influence upon the conditions of apprenticeship and child labour generally. In the first place, the ill odour surrounding pauper apprenticeship threw industrial apprenticeship into disrepute, and rendered the House of Commons and the public disinclined to sympathise with those who opposed the repeal of the Statute of Artificers ; and secondly, it was the miseries of the pauper apprentice which brought into being that reform movement which ultimately achieved the regulation of child labour generally.

CHAPTER XVII

CHILD LABOUR UNDER THE SEARCHLIGHT OF THE NINE-TEENTH-CENTURY REPORTS

THE early nineteenth century has acquired an unpleasing notoriety as the period when the conditions of labour were at their worst. At this time the changes attendant upon the Industrial Revolution were making themselves acutely felt; the reorganisation of trade upon modern lines, involving as it did a dislocation of the customary methods of life and labour, inevitably brought much discomfort and even misery in its train. The small independent workman found himself crushed by the capitalist, whose predominance was assured by the general use of machinery. He now ceased to be independent and became a wage-earner, a " hand." The application of steam power to machinery necessitated the concentration of the industrial population in districts within the reach of coal, and the workman and his family were huddled together with other workmen and other families in cities which made no provision for their comfort or health, the art of sanitation being still ignored.[1] Work was carried on amidst noisy and impersonal surroundings, in machine sheds and factories instead of in the workers' own homes and shops. This absorption of the small business by the large, and the transfer of labour from the domestic workshop to the factory, were not in themselves necessarily changes for the worse. But they were undoubtedly changes which required a readjustment of society and a readjustment of the political ideas directing the social and industrial machine, and until

[1] The Report of 1843 gives, incidentally, information as to the extraordinary lack of decent conditions and care for health—*e.g.*, H. C., 1843, xiv. p. C 25; H. C., 1843, xv. p. Q 40.

these adjustments had been achieved disorganisation and needless suffering were unavoidable. The mediæval regulation of labour, which had lingered on into the eighteenth century, had now disappeared, and the governing classes had not yet gained the knowledge required for a new system of control. Nor did they yet see the need for such regulation ; it was a common belief that the amazing advance recently made in commerce and industry depended for its continuance upon the freedom of the manufacturer to develop his business in his own way. England could keep her place ahead of her Continental rivals only, it was thought, under the rule of *laissez faire*, and the nation, engaged at this time in the Napoleonic wars, actually could not afford to cripple the manufacturers, who, it must be remembered, largely supplied her war funds. Thus there was no real attempt on the part of our statesmen to grapple with the difficulties nor to hasten their solution.

It must not be supposed that the conditions of work which darken the pages of nineteenth-century history were of sudden birth. Many of the disadvantages under which the working classes laboured in the last century, many of the evils they had to face, had existed long before ; they did not spring into being with steam power and the factory. Capitalisation had been creeping in for a century or more, and the independent workman had been disappearing from certain trades, the woollen trade, for example, since 1700 ; and as the capitalist gathered business into his hands the factory supplanted the domestic workshop. As for insanitary surroundings and long hours of labour, they had existed at all times. It is sometimes thought that child labour did not become widespread until the introduction of machinery in the nineteenth century. We, who have followed the history of juvenile labour, know that there was nothing new in the universal employment of children, nor in the long hours of their work, nor in the early age at which that work began. But in the early years of the nineteenth century the evils and difficulties which had been in existence long before made themselves more acutely felt. The fact of the matter is that they were now given greater scope by the more general employment of machinery and the capitalisation of first one trade and then another. Moreover, it was just at this time that the belief in *laissez faire* was at its height, and the freest rein was given to the employer to use labour as he chose. The child, as the employee least able to protect himself, suffered the most from the absence of any industrial regulation.

The new industrial conditions gave juvenile labour a commercial value which it had not possessed in the old days, before the extensive use of machinery had created new fields of work for children, and when the insistence upon apprenticeship had prevented parents and employers from exploiting child labour. Apprenticeship, of course, had not yet disappeared ; the Act was not repealed until 1814, and though the Elizabethan system had already broken down, apprentices were still taken in trades conducted upon a small scale. But numbers of children worked unapprenticed as wage-earners ; they were driven to the mills and factories or to the sweating shops by their parents' need or greed for their wages, or by the pressure brought to bear upon the latter by the manufacturers.

Speaking generally, the position of juvenile workers now was vastly inferior to what it had been under the compulsory apprenticeship system, when children were ensured both a fair return for their labour and protection from the misuse or abuse of their masters or parents. But in estimating the changes in their fortunes at the beginning of the nineteenth century, it is necessary to take into account a fact of considerable importance. Now, for the first time, we have really full and direct information as to conditions of juvenile labour. With the nineteenth century the age of parliamentary inquiries and commissions begins, and thus child labour is to be seen under the searchlight of the reports. Casual observers of nineteenth-century conditions, reading the information given by the reports—information which is so detailed and so easily obtainable—tend sometimes to forget that because there are no similar revelations as to the abuses of child labour at an earlier date, there was nothing to reveal.

As a matter of fact, though full information as to the conditions of work was new, the conditions themselves were not new. The truth of this is brought out by the reports themselves. Some of the worst conditions existed in industries which were being carried on upon methods exactly similar to those of the seventeenth and eighteenth centuries. The most appalling report is that of 1842 upon mines and collieries, but labour in mines had never been regulated by the gilds, and apprenticeship had never afforded its protection to the young people employed in the trade. We may fairly take it that what children suffered in the nineteenth century they suffered in the eighteenth and earlier. In a quite dissimilar branch of work which was dealt with by the reports, the abuses of child labour were acute, but here, too, the methods were those employed prior to the Industrial Revolution, and the evils revealed in the nineteenth century must have existed long before. This was in the small metal trades at Willenhall, amongst the locksmiths, keysmiths, and currycombers. The workmen were all small men ; most of them had no shops,[1] and were therefore unrestrained by public opinion in their methods of work and their treatment of the children. They generally took several so-called apprentices, and if they had work employed them from dawn until nightfall ; when they had no orders the boys either had to starve with their masters or were hired out by them to some other workmen. Even when employment was to be had the existence of these small men was precarious, and they made bad masters, feeding and clothing their apprentices very poorly, and often treating them with great brutality.[2] There must, in fact, have been fully as much misery in such trades as in any of those conducted upon modern methods, by machinery and in factories. This is true at a later date. The report upon various employments in 1862 showed that the conditions of work in the hosiery trade were far worse in small workrooms than in the factories. Children were also

[1] H. C., 1843, xiii. 307. App. ii. p. Q 38. (Second Report of Commissioners Trades and Manufactures).

[2] Ibid., ibid., pp. Q 38, Q 45.

largely employed in the domestic manufacture of stockings,[1] and, owing to the irregular habits of the men, they would be idle the early part of the week and then overworked. It was said that " an excessive pressure of work is thrown periodically upon very young children, and some are employed almost as infants." The rooms were very crowded and ill lit, and there was often only one room for workshop and dwelling-place, in which owners and workers of the frames lived and slept and worked and ate.[2] Bad conditions of this nature were not checked by the gilds nor by the apprenticeship system, with the exception of night-work, which the gilds in their best days did not allow. It is, in short, impossible to over emphasise the fact that the Industrial Revolution and the introduction of machinery did not create juvenile labour nor the abuses connected with it.

Still, the Industrial Revolution did alter the conditions of child labour for the worse in more ways than one. It has been said that juvenile labour acquired in the nineteenth century a higher commercial value. Whereas, therefore, children had hitherto been employed often because their parents had nothing else to do with them or because they were on the spot, there was now an actual demand for them. This was due partly to the introduction of machine work, for which, especially in its early days, child labour was peculiarly suited. For instance, some of the first machines used in the woollen trade stood very near the ground, and children were preferable as pieceners not only because they were cheap, but because they were of a height to work easily and rapidly at the billy-boards.[3] And in part this increased demand was due to the speeding up in competition which led employers to snatch at cheap labour whenever possible. In the factories children could often find employment more easily than their parents, just because they were cheap, and they were therefore sometimes compelled to help to support

[1] In which the best goods were made, though the cheapest were in factories.
[2] *Cf.* Hutchins and Harrison, History of Factory Legislation, p. 157.
  H. C., 1864, xxii. p. xxxv.
[3] Ure, Philosophy of Manufactures, 1835, p. 180.
  H. C., 1831–32, xv. p. 120.   Children nimbler and quicker than adults.

the family ; even when this was not the case, they could always command a wage, and were consequently sent to work by their parents when very young. There was a second change in the conditions of juvenile employment which rendered children's work more burdensome. The introduction of machinery into a trade generally led to the transformation of the juvenile worker from an assistant and odd jobs' man into an independent workman, whose absence from his post or whose slight carelessness meant an economic loss to his employer. There was thus far more responsibility upon the child than there had hitherto been, and no likelihood of his faults being overlooked or of his hours of labour being shortened. Indeed, his new industrial character was a strong inducement to his master to overdrive him.[1] In the third place, the work upon which children were now so largely employed was both physically dangerous and stunting and mentally exhausting. The machinery was unguarded, and accidents were frequent, while the constant alertness which had to be exerted throughout the long hours of the working day in order to attend the machines and escape injury was a terribly heavy strain on the young worker. Fourthly, the transference of manufactures from home-workshops to unregulated factories was in some ways a change for the worse. Parents no doubt overworked their children, or corrected them harshly, and the workshops were anything but sanitary ; but parents and skilled craftsmen were seldom such bad masters as factory foremen and the coarsened factory workers, while the noise of the machinery, the dirt and dust of the mills, and the herding together of hundreds of workpeople in unventilated factories involved a greater degree of discomfort, injury, and risk of infection than was ever known to the old workshop. Then, again, a master manufacturer who had in his service a large number of employees whom he probably seldom saw felt little, if any, of that personal responsibility for his young workers which had been so marked a characteristic of his relationship with them in the old days. The disappearance

[1] Cf. H. C., 1831–32, xv. pp. 169, 210, 236, 270.

of the personal tie, however inevitable, was a real loss to juvenile labour. Lastly, the employment of children, whether in factories or in the garrets of Willenhall, suffered from the acuteness of competition. Small men were struggling against machinery, water mills were striving to compete with steam mills, and in this bitter struggle for existence principles went to the wall. The general belief in *laissez faire* and the importance of leaving the manufacturer unhampered left the combatants free to use what methods they chose in the fight, and the one which came easily to hand was the exploitation of the health and strength of children and young people.

The reports show that certain general features were common to child labour, in whatever branch of industry it was employed, but that in many respects the conditions of work varied enormously with the trade and even with the locality. Long hours and an early age of employment were universal ; but physical injury was confined almost entirely to mills and factories, though it was common enough in them, whether large or small. The worst conditions were to be found not in the largest factories, where there was the greatest amount of machinery and the biggest number of hands, but in small businesses of all kinds, in the small mills which were struggling to hold their own, and in the garrets and sheds of men who were in too poor a way to own workshops.[1] Such men were not a high class of workmen, and the young people employed by them were very possibly coarsened by contact with their masters. But as a rule the moral atmosphere was worse in factories than in workshops, and worst of all in coal mines. The chances of a permanent career varied also in different trades, but the reports revealed that in many branches of work in which children were engaged there was little or no opportunity for their employment as adults, while the work gave them no training which could be of any service in another branch of the business. In fact, they were employed not because the trade was expanding and would require them later, but because their labour

[1] *Cf.* Hutchins and Harrison, *op. cit.*, pp. 20, 27.

was cheap. Adult workmen were available, but they were passed over and children taken in their place. For though the latter did not do the work as well, they were paid only about half the wages which adults would have received, and thus it was to the advantage of the manufacturer to employ them. Sometimes parents were forced to send their children to the factories or they would have been themselves refused employment.[1] But after the first few years of the existence of factories, during which no respectable working man would have allowed his children to work at a mill,[2] it was eagerness for their wages, small as they were, which as a rule led even well-to-do parents to permit their children's employment, and this though it was known that the work would teach them nothing of value for later life, and might render them stunted or crippled. Employers and parents were, in fact, combined in the exploitation of children for the sake of a little present profit. This is a feature of child labour in the early nineteenth century which has been handed down to the present day, and since it will later on be given full consideration, it is not necessary to do more than mention it here.

The parliamentary reports, to which reference has already been made, give a very fair idea of juvenile labour in the early nineteenth century. One of the earliest is that upon the calico trade, and was published in 1804. It deals with the trade as a whole, but the conditions of child labour received considerable attention. Here, as was almost universally the case, young people were employed in large numbers and when very young. But the real evil in connection with their employment was that their work led to no after career ; they were taken in place of adults at a lower wage and turned off as soon as they were not content with it.[3] Other evils, judged by our standards of what the conditions of labour should be, no doubt existed, but no

---

[1] Reports, 1803–4, v. p. 4. Report on Calico Trade.
    Cf. Reports, 1831–2 (H. C., xv)., p. 126.
[2] Alfred, History of the Factory Movement, i. p. 16.
[3] H. C. Reps., 1803–4, v. pp. 4, 6, 19.

complaint is made of them : the commissioners were not appointed for the purpose of inquiring into them ; moreover their ideas as to what must be tolerated were very different from ours. How greatly the conditions of juvenile labour varied in different trades is revealed by contrasting its use in the calico trade and in the woollen industry, into which inquiries were made in 1803 and 1806. Children and young persons were employed in large numbers in the woollen trade, though few were bound apprentice.[1] There was, however, no complaint of their employment from the journeymen, for there was work for all ; [2] one witness stated that in his neighbourhood all the inhabitants from seven to seventy years old were engaged in weaving.[3] It is clear that children were not employed, as in the calico trade, merely as cheap labour, to the detriment of adult workers and of their own future ; and that, though unapprenticed, they learnt their business and continued it in after life. The immediate conditions of work were not, however, all that could be desired. Children began to work at a very early age,[4] and owing to the use of machinery much of the work was conducted in factories, many of which we know were utterly insanitary even at a later date. In 1806 a report was made upon the woollen trade in the North. In Yorkshire, as in the South, there were few but pauper apprentices,[5] but the employment of children was universal. They lived in their own homes,[6] and from the age of five or six, they either went to work at the factories[7] or were employed at home upon similar work,[8] earning in both cases about sixpence a day.[9] The majority of those employed appear to have had little difficulty in finding occupation in the trade in later life, though in bad times woollen weavers had to seek other work.[10]

[1] H. C. Reps., 1802–3, v. 305, pp. 4, 6, 7.
[2] Ibid., p. 7.   [3] Ibid., p. 8.
[4] Ibid., p. 7.
[5] & [6] Report on the State of the Woollen Manufacture in England, 1806 (H. C., 1806, iii. 569), p. 14.
[7] Ibid., pp. 175, 400.   [8] Ibid., p. 175.
    bid., p. 400.   [10] Ibid., p. 14.

In 1816 the first report was made upon the employment
of children in manufactures, the inquiry having been
instituted with a view to finding out whether legislation
would be advisable.   It is apparent from this report that the
cotton trade employed a great number of pauper apprentices,
partly because the earliest mills were worked by water
power, and were situated in country places, where, as Sir
Robert Peel pointed out, "there was no opportunity of
getting young labour but from large towns abounding with
population,"[1] and it was generally only pauper children who
were sent as apprentices to mills at a distance from their
homes.   The treatment of these unfortunate apprentices is
notorious ; Poor Law officers paid manufacturers about £5
a head for each child taken off their hands, and as soon as
they were carted off by their masters it was nobody's concern
what became of them.   They were often ill-treated, and their
position was to all intents and purposes that of slavery.
The hours of work were very long, a fourteen hours' day
being by no means unusual.   But as fresh labour could
easily be obtained, masters were not willing to shorten the
working day, however exhausted their workers became.   As
one witness to a fourteen hours' day pointed out, if children
stopped earlier, so must the machinery.[2]   And that, of
course, meant loss of profits.   Even in other trades, in which
pauper apprentices were not employed, and in which the
conditions were not so bad, the working day was seldom
shorter,[3] and children under ten years old were regularly
employed.[4]   In the Stockport hat trade children worked
from the age of five ;[5] in the silk trade they did not begin
until a year or two older, and the hours were shorter.[6]   Few
but pauper children were apprenticed.   In this same year a
report was made upon the chimney-sweeping trade.   The
little climbing boy, weeping through a week's soot as a
brutal master drove him up a chimney with blows, pin

[1] H. C., 1816, iii. 235, p. 140.   Mins. of Evidence.
[2] & [3] Ibid., Mins. of Evidence, p. 53.
[4] Ibid., pp. 5, 6.   [5] Ibid., p. 41.
[6] Ibid., p. 74.

proddings, and even with the lighting of a fire beneath his feet, is an appealing figure which looms largely in the popular imagination.   There is no doubt that the boys were treated with intentional cruelty, and that in addition they had many hardships to suffer owing to the poverty of their masters.[1] The number employed, however, was not, comparatively speaking, large, nor were their fortunes really so much worse than those of many other juvenile workers.   In short, though their case is undoubtedly deserving of pity, it is no more so than that of thousands of other children in quite dissimilar occupations.   The next report is that of 1818, upon the Coventry ribbon trade.   This industry employed a large amount of juvenile labour.   Children of eight or ten were engaged in the simpler branches, such as winding. They went to the loom generally at eleven years old, and were bound apprentice by irregular indentures.   The majority of these so-called apprentices were girls.   They maintained themselves, receiving half the money which they earned at the loom, the undertaker, or employer, receiving the other half.[2]   We may suppose that the younger girls lived at home and were partially supported by their parents, since the wages they received did not constitute a living wage.   But the statement in the report that the wages were so low that the workers often supplemented them by poor relief or prostitution,[3] shows that the conditions of the older apprentices were often hopelessly bad, and that there must have been no chance of an after career for many of those bound as children.

By 1830 an influential section of the public was alive to the fact that many of the conditions of juvenile labour were deplorable, and as a consequence of their agitation for reform reports made with a view to ascertaining the success of the remedial Acts which had been passed, or the need of yet more

---

[1] Report from the Select Committee on the Employment of Boys in Sweeping Chimneys, 1817, pp. 3, 4, 5, 15.

[2] H. C., 1818, ix. 1.
   Report on the Ribbon Trade, 1818.   Minutes, pp. 5, 17.

[3] Ibid., pp. 5, 130.   Declaration of the Mayor and Corporation of Coventry, condemning the system.

legislation, followed each other in rapid succession. Those who were opposed to legislative interference declared that the evidence was one-sided. It is possible that the reform party, in its desire to carry the legislation it had at heart, presented the blackest side of the case. The opponents of reform certainly had this to complain of, that the bad conditions, the existence of which might be revealed in one trade or in one employer's workrooms, were often attributed by the public to children's labour in general, the fact being overlooked that inquiries had been made, and could only be made, into certain trades and into certain localities. Undoubtedly, there was sufficient evidence of injurious employment to justify legislative action, but it was not fair to attribute to masters and workshops in general abuses such, for example, as were revealed by the Committee of 1831, witnesses before which bore evidence to cases of brutal beatings of boys and girls, which resulted occasionally in death,[1] and to many more cases of stunted growth, illness, and deformity due to over-work.[2] Such extreme abuses were not a necessary accompaniment o juvenile labour, while the conditions of work were too various for any sweeping generalisations to be made.[3] How true this is, and yet how far from satisfactory, according to modern ideas, were the circumstances of juvenile wage-earners, and how little real improvement had been made upon the conditions existing at the opening of the century, can be gathered from a description of their work in the middle of the nineteenth century.

By that time the terms upon which children and young persons were engaged were, as a rule, similar to those of their adult fellows ; they were wage-earners, employed by the time or by the piece, according to the custom of their occupation. But in some trades a bad system of so-called apprenticeship was in vogue, its chief feature being that

---

[1] H. C., 1831-2, xv. Report upon the Employment of Children in Manufactures, pp. 19, 39, 193.

[2] Ibid., pp. 12, 19 39, 143, 110, 132. 169, 196, 237.

[3] Cf. H. C., 1833, xxi. Second Report. Medical Commissioners declare they found few cases of stunted growth, ill-health, or deformity amongst the children examined by them. See pp. 2, 3, 4, 14.

children received lower wages than their work was worth. It was nothing more than a device of the sweating master to obtain cheap labour, and afforded neither a sound training nor protection to the child. There was, however, a certain amount of actual apprenticeship. It will be remembered that the Act of 1813, repealing the Statute of Artificers, had abolished not apprenticeship but its legal necessity. The Commons recognised that it was an excellent form of training, and believed that it would hold its own without the support of legal compulsion.[1]   In this view they were only partially justified. Apprenticeship was still practised, but throughout the century less and less is heard of it; there are fewer entries in the borough records, and it became from the most the least usual method of entry into industrial callings.[2] Early in the century it appears to have been practised to a considerable extent, not with the direct object of attaining proficiency in a trade, but for quite other reasons. This non-industrial apprenticeship was primarily due to the fact that in ancient boroughs service as an apprentice was one method of acquiring the parliamentary franchise,[3] which, until 1832, the year of the Reform Bill, was in boroughs practically the monopoly of free burgesses. In all old corporations the municipal franchise and burgess-ship were obtained by birth, servitude, gift, or purchase, servitude being the only door open to those who were not fortunate enough to be wealthy, distinguished, or the eldest sons of freemen, and undoubtedly apprenticeship was served by many who, after the repeal of the Act, would have dispensed with it if it had not possessed incidental advantages. At Coventry men bound themselves for seven years to ribbon weaving, a sweated and over-crowded trade, almost entirely in the hands of girls, in order to obtain the franchise.[4]   Apparently in those cities and towns in which the electoral franchise was reserved to free-men, lads were bound apprentice irrespective of the degree

---

[1] Hansard, Parliamentary Reports, xxvii. 564.
[2] *Cf.* Report of Labour Commission, 1893, p. 16.
[3] *Cf.* Chitty, Law of Apprenticeship, p. 110.
[4] Report on Ribbon Weaving, 1818.   Mins., p. 5.

of skill required by their several trades: at Bristol, in 1831, there were 105 enrolments of apprentices; the boys were bound not only to masters in those wealthy companies which we might suppose would have been strong enough to enforce apprenticeship, and not necessarily with workmen in trades which required a high standard of skill, but with men in all classes of occupations.[1]   Possibly a second reason for the occurrence of apprenticeship not strictly industrial in motive, was the reservation of commerce and trade within ancient boroughs to their own freemen In such places a man might find himself forbidden to engage in any form of manufacture or trade if he had not acquired the freedom.   There was thus a special reason for apprenticing boys, even though the occupations which they intended to follow required no long training, because any one who served seven years in a corporate town was entitled to claim the freedom. This right of corporations to restrict trade had been disputed, and in the case of Winton *versus* Wilks Lord Holt decided that a custom to exclude a person not a freeman from trading in a town was bad except in London.   His decision had, however, to be over-ruled by the courts, much against their will, as there was too much case-made law in its favour.   Nevertheless, opinion was against the custom, and it is very doubtful whether at this time it had any influence at all. Certainly the small corporations could not enforce it. Eden, who wrote at the close of the eighteenth century, considered it was almost obsolete,[2] and at any rate the Municipal Corporations Act of 1835 [3] abolished the exclusive rights of freemen. This Act and the Reform Act of 1832,[4] removed practically all inducements to serve for non-industrial reasons, though in London and the larger boroughs lads may have bound themselves apprentice in order to acquire the municipal franchise, which still conferred a certain degree of local distinction. Apprenticeship for strictly industrial reasons was, of course, unaffected by the Acts of 1832 and 1835, and

[1] MSS. in Town Hall, Bristol. Enrolment Books, 1830–49.
[2] See p. 238.   [3] 5 & 6 Wm. IV. c. 76.
[4] 2 & 3 Wm. IV. c. 45.

was still in use in the middle of the century. In those trades which required a high standard of skill, and in those which were conducted upon a small scale, it was natural that it should be preserved, for it was still the soundest method of keeping up the supply of skilled workmen, and was a convenient system of instruction in country trades which were carried on upon the old leisurely lines. Leisureliness has never been a characteristic of factory work, and wherever machinery has been introduced apprenticeship has tended to disappear. This was the case in woollen weaving, which had been a skilled handicraft in early days, but from which improved appliances and machinery had driven apprenticeship even before the repeal of the Act.[1] But in the two first decades of the nineteenth century the application of machinery to trades other than textile was not great, and for a long time to come apprenticeship was in accordance with the needs of a large number of industries. It is interesting to notice that even where machinery was used, and subdivision had taken place, so that the trade as a whole did not demand more than mechanical labour, apprenticeship was preserved in those branches which required skill. Paper-making could be carried on to a large extent by comparatively unskilled and child labour, but apprentices were employed in the drying-lofts [2] ; and in the Warrington pin trade, which was a notoriously unskilled and low order of occupation, they were taken in certain branches in which skilled and adult labour was employed.[3] Apprenticeship, then, was still useful as a means of training. Regarded as a means of protection for juvenile workers, which it had been in the old days, it was no longer of any general value. Sound apprenticeship after the old order existed only in the better class trades in which, even without it, lads would have been fairly sure of consideration ; elsewhere, the apprentice, so called, was more at the

---

[1] H. C. Reports, 1802–3, v. 243, p. 3 *seq.*
    Ibid., 1806, iii. 569. Minutes of Evidence, pp. 171, 447, &c.
[2] H. C., 1843, xiv. xv. 1. Report ii., on Employment of Children in Manufactures, 1843. Appendix i. p. A 1.
[3] Ibid., App. ii. p. M 5.

mercy of his employer, over whom there was now no supervision, than was the weekly wage-earner. In the report on
children's employments in 1842, the Commissioners state
that in the majority of trades into which inquiry had been
made, it was usual to employ apprentices.[1]   But these
apprentices were generally either young paupers, whom the
Poor Law authorities sent in cart-loads to the mills and
factories, and who, their training and welfare being matters
of interest to no one, were hopelessly at the mercy of their
employers and their foremen.   Or they were children who
were bound, it is true, by their parents, and even living at
home with them but were seldom indentured legally, since
their master would take them only upon his own agreements,
which were made entirely in his favour, while their parents'
poverty prevented them from standing out for fair conditions
of training and service against the omnipotent, who had at
their disposal work and wages.

The conditions of these children about the middle of the
nineteenth century, and of their fellow-workers as to whom
there was no pretence of apprenticeship, are revealed by the
reports of 1842 and 1843.   The latter deals with the employment of children and young persons in a large number of
trades and manufactures.   Two points stand out clearly :
now, as at the beginning of the century, conditions were
worse in small factories than in large, and still worse in
workshops in which trades were carried on necessarily upon
a small scale.   In all trades and factories, however, children
were still employed when very young.   London was almost
the only exception,[2] since the supply of children was greater
than the demand.   In the provinces infants of four years
old were employed in the calico trade [3] and in lace-making.[4]
In paper-making children under nine years old were
occasionally taken, but on the whole the use of machinery
in this trade checked their early employment.[5]   In the pin

[1] H. C., 1843, xviii. p. 26.
[2] Second Report, 1843, Appendix i. p. F 26.   (H. C., 1843, xiv.)
[3] H. C., 1843, xviii. p. 12.
[4] Ibid., p. 10.   [5] Ibid., p. 13.

industry a large number of children were employed; often they began to work at five years old, and as the trade was a poor one they received only a sweating wage.[1] In the hosiery trade Nottingham children sometimes began to work when five years old, and both there and at Leicester they were regularly employed at seven years old.[2] In machine lace-making here and at Derby children of two years old went out to work, and it was quite usual to find employees of four, five, and six years old.[3] In other parts of the country they were often equally young. The report, in fact, showed that children were employed as soon as they could be of any service, regardless of whether the hours of labour or the nature of their employment were injurious. In many occupations children were not engaged by the owner of the factory or workshop, but by individual workmen.[4] It was the prevalence of this custom which was the chief cause of the employment of very young children; on the one hand employers could not prevent their work unless they were prepared to set the customs of the trade at defiance. On the other, the workmen, who had to pay their assistants out of their earnings, chose out the youngest children who could possibly do the work, because the youngest were the cheapest. The hours of work were still often very long. In calico print works, in which numbers of children under nine years old were employed,[5] the machines seldom ran less than ten and a half hours,[6] and night work was common;[7] while no particular care was taken to secure to the workers suitable time for rest and meals during the working day. Similar

---

[1] H. C., 1843., Appendix ii. pp. M 6, 10, 12; and Report (H. C., 1843, xiii.), p. 7.

[2] Ibid., p. 11.   [3] Ibid., p. 10.

[4] Ibid., p. 23.

Amongst those trades into which inquiry was made, this was the custom in all except paper-making and calico printing, elsewhere than in Lancashire, Derby, and Cheshire. In lace and hosiery children worked as a rule with their parents.

[5] H. C., 1843, vol. xiii. p. 12.

[6] Ibid., p. 59. In some districts, children of five and six commonly worked fourteen or sixteen hours.

[7] Ibid., p. 68.

hours of labour prevailed in other trades. And in none
could the sanitary conditions be designated as anything but
disgraceful. Intentional ill-treatment seems to have disappeared from the mills and factories by this time.
Unfortunately no such favourable report could be made of
the employment of children in manufactures which were
carried on not in factories but in shops and out-of-the-way
places. In such trades the general conditions also tended
to be bad, and in reading of them we cannot but realise the
value of those gild rules which had prohibited work "in
chambers or uppon staires," out of the range of public opinion.
These small men carried on a precarious existence, working
often for middlemen from whom they received a sweating
wage, and the young people they employed had to endure
many hardships apart from any actual cruelty. In the
Kidderminster carpet trade it was the custom for big
masters to give out the yarn weekly to their weavers, who
frequently worked long hours and on Sundays in order to
finish the work. Each weaver engaged some child or young
person to assist him, but as those who had children of their
own employed them,[1] and for no shorter hours, we may
suppose that it was the needs of the trade and the poverty
of the weavers, and not indifference to the young people's
welfare, which led to the over-working of the latter. Of the
Sheffield trades it was said that unduly long hours were
worked in those places and those processes where there was
no steam power, because there the manufacturer had no
control over the working master [2] that ill-usage was almost
solely to be found amongst the small cutlers; [3] and that
over-working and insufficient food were as a rule the result
of the master's poverty.[4] The lock and key trade at
Willenhall, was also carried on by small men, and the conditions of employment were noticeably bad; [5] and at
Wolverhampton, where, again, the various trades were in the

---

[1] H. C., 1843, xiv., Appendix i. pp. C 22–E 24.
[2] Ibid., ibid., p. E 4, and H. C., 1843, xiii. pp. 52–3.
[3] & [4] Ibid., ibid., p. E 10.
[5] Ibid., Appendix ii. p. Q 45, C 39.

hands of small masters, who took their trade to some factor, the hours were long and other conditions were not good, rather because of poverty amongst the masters than because they were purposely unkind.[1]   Still, there is no doubt that actual cruelty existed, especially when work was done by the piece, for the men then tended to work erratically, spending the first days of the week in drinking, and working abnormally long hours at the end of the week, in order to finish their job.   Drink and weariness made them no easy masters during these long spells of work, which in themselves were so heavy a strain on the child.[2]   Even in factories ill-usage was not unknown.   Ure, who was a staunch supporter of the factory system, and wrote in its defence in 1835, admits that there was a good deal of cruelty in factories or in departments in which the treatment of the children depended upon the temper of individual masters.   He acknowledged that cruelty existed in the slubbing departments in weaving mills, in which branch of the work the men engaged their own assistants,[3] though he held that ill-treatment was, generally speaking, of rare occurrence, and that in this respect factories were infinitely in advance of workshops.[4]   His opinion as to conditions as a whole is well worth reading in connection with the evidence given by the report.   He based his account upon personal visits to mills at all times of day.   The information thus acquired led him to the conclusion that the outcry as to the abuses of child labour had been very greatly exaggerated, and had been a device on the part of the men to obtain shorter hours for themselves.   "In London and the agricultural counties," he writes, "the Spinners' Union succeeded perfectly in mystifying their dupes by romantic representations of white slavery, and of the hecatombs of infants sacrificed annually on the calico-crowned altars of Mammon ; but they durst not utter such barefaced falsehoods in Lancashire."[5]   It is

---

[1] H. C., 1843, xiv., Appendix ii. p. Q 9–11.
[2] *Cf.* Ibid., Appendix i. p. C 24.   *Cf.* Hutchins and Harrison, *op. cit.*, p. 153.
[3] Ure, History of the Philosophy of Manufactures, pp. 179, 180.
[4] Ibid., p. 301.   [5] Ibid., p. 302.

quite likely that the denunciations were exaggerated, and
that the witnesses before the Commissioners were biased,
but the following passage from Ure's book suggests that he
was not free from bias himself. Writing of young employees
he had seen at the mills, he says, " The work of these lively
elves seemed to resemble a sport, in which habit gave them
a pleasing dexterity. Conscious of their skill, they were
delighted to show it off to any stranger. As to exhaustion
by the day's work, they evinced no trace of it on emerging
from the mill in the evening ; for they immediately began to
skip about any neighbouring play-ground and to commence
their little amusements with the same alacrity as boys issuing
from a school." [1] What he apparently failed to see, in his
anxiety to defend the factory system, was that though conditions of work in shops might be worse than in factories,
the conditions in the latter could still be bad.

It was in the coal mines, however, that the conditions
were worst of all. The hours of employment varied in
different localities from eight to eighteen hours a day. Less
than twelve hours was exceptional[2] The ordinary age at
which children entered the mines was between eight and
nine years old, but they were employed even at four and
six years old.[3] A great deal of suffering was entailed by
the difficult conditions under which the work was conducted,
the narrowness and lowness of the cuttings, and the primitive
methods of transporting the coal.[4] The latter was often the
work of boys and girls, who were harnessed into little trucks
and set to draw the coal from the miners to the wider
openings ; sometimes they had to drag this weight in a
crouching position because the passages were so low. There
was in addition much intentional cruelty, and the whole
atmosphere was degrading and brutalising.[5] The account
is barely readable, while the report upon children's employ-

[1] Ure, History of the Philosophy of Manufactures, p. 301.

[2] H. C., 1842, xvi. Appendix to First Report of Commissioners on Mines,
Part I. pp. 9, 34, 126, 167.

[3] Ibid., pp. 8, 33, 91, 98, 123, 166, 535.

[4] Ibid., pp. 11, 35, 178, &c.   [5] Ibid., p. 25, 196, &c.

ment in manufactures, with which we have just dealt, though less ghastly it is true, contains more than sufficient evidence of the youth of the workers and the circumstances of their employment to show how great must have been the misery they had to endure. To dwell on it now may appear purposeless, since the evils have been happily remedied. It is, however, no page from the Dark Ages which can be overlooked. The conditions of work which have been described here were the conditions under which were employed men who are to-day but little more than middle-aged, and it was under conditions such as these that the fathers and mothers of the present generation were obliged to work. For the greater number of trades into which inquiry was made in 1843 were carried on upon the same lines until 1860 and after; industries other than the textile and the allied trades not being regulated until 1864 and 1867. The reports of the Commission appointed in 1861 showed that the children employed in numerous industries at this date began work as young and worked for as long hours and under as unhealthy conditions as those whose labour was reported upon in 1843.[1] In the straw plait schools children of three years old were employed and worked all day.[2] Many were as young in the hosiery trade, and they often worked at night; while the workrooms were dirty and ill-ventilated, and no precautions on behalf of health or sanitation were taken.[3] To deal with the conditions of labour in 1860 would, however, be mere repetition; if the dates were not given, it would be almost impossible to tell that the reports of 1863 were not a part of the report of 1843;[4] in fact, the abuses of industrial labour are of such recent date, that they must be taken into account in any

---

[1] H. C., 1863, xviii. *Cf.* Hutchins and Harrison, *op. cit.*, p. 150.

[2] H. C., 1864, xxii., pp. xxvi, xl. See Hutchins, &c., p. 155. *Cf.* Report, 1863, p. lxxxi, for conditions in lace-making.

[3] H. C., 1863, xviii. p. 264; *cf.* Hutchins, p. 157 *seq.*

[4] The report has also been dealt with briefly, because it is treated fully by Miss Hutchins and Miss Harrison, *op. cit.*, chap. viii.

It is worth noticing that in spite of the Act, 3 & 4 Vict. c. 85, regulating juvenile labour in chimney-sweeping, boys were still employed as young as six or

criticism or estimate of the standard of national physique, intelligence, or refinement to-day.

The recognition of the evils connected with juvenile labour dates from the close of the eighteenth century, though it cannot be claimed that the interest of the public was as yet aroused. It was the misery of parish apprentices which at first attracted attention. The Government, of course, since it sanctioned and encouraged their apprenticeship, was peculiarly responsible for them ; this could not be denied even by the staunchest adherents of *laissez faire*, while in their case there was a long tradition of legislative interference and control. This made it very much easier to demand that inquiries should be made with a view to discovering if legislation were required. In this way pauper apprenticeship had a great influence upon juvenile labour in general, for when once the movement for reform had begun, the conditions under which the ordinary child worked became known too, and though inquiries and reforms were confined at first to the work of pauper apprentices, they could not end there. The recognition of the public's responsibility for juvenile workers, and eventually for the working classes, was the outcome of the eighteenth-century movement for the welfare of the parish child.

The reform movement was forced into existence by the outbreak of an infectious and devastating fever in some Lancaster cotton works, in consequence of which Dr. Percival and other medical men were appointed by the

eight years old, and there had been an increase in the total number. (H. C., 1863, xviii. p. lxxxiv.)

In the metal trades the conditions of work in 1864 showed no improvement upon those of 1842. Boys of eight years old were employed in blast furnaces, mills, and forges ; and children of eight were employed in the miscellaneous trades. In the former trades, night work was common ; in the latter, children worked the same hours as men, from 5 or 7 a.m. to 9, 10 or 11 p.m. (H. C., 1864, xxii. p. vi.) In the Birmingham metal trades the conditions were those of 1841 (ibid., p. x). The men often kept " Saint Monday," and then worked overtime the rest of the week (ibid., p. xi). The children, of course, had to attend them.

See H. C., 1863, xviii. p. lxxvi for conditions of fustian cutters, and ibid., p. lix for paper-staining.

justices of the peace to report upon the causes. They did not, however, confine their investigations to the fever, and in their report they brought to the notice of the justices and the public the long hours during which children worked and the lack of all recreation and instruction.[1] This was in 1784, and in the same year, on the strength of this report, the Manchester magistrates agreed to forbid the apprenticeship of children, under their control, to owners of " cotton mills and other works in which children are obliged to work in the night or during more than ten hours in the day." [2] But there was not as yet any general desire to put the industrial house in order. The band of those who attempted improvement was small, and they based their case upon matter-of-fact arguments as to the effect of juvenile labour upon the national health—arguments not calculated to arouse public sympathy as did the sentimental appeals of the later reformers, and their pictures of the horrors of child slavery. It has been aptly said that this early factory reform move- ment was eminently " a ' common-sense ' one, in contrast to the excited speeches and overcharged style which charac- terised the ten hours' agitation later on." [3]

The more sentimental movement, which, owing to the nature of the House of Commons, was the more useful movement, was aroused by various dismal revelations as to the employment of pauper children, the most notorious of which was that concerning Jourvaux, an impoverished work- man, who was convicted, in 1801, for ill-treating his apprentices, and whose trial created considerable stir.[4]   In 1802 the first Factory Act was passed.[5] Its object was to effect certain simple sanitary improvements for workers in general in the cotton mills, and to provide for apprentices in particular some education and regulated hours of labour. It has been said of it that " it was in reality not a Factory Act properly speaking, but merely an extension of the

[1] Hutchins and Harrison, *op. cit.*, p. 8.
[2] Quoted by the above, p. 9.   H. C., 1816, iii. p. 377.
[3] Ibid., p. 10.   [4] Ibid., pp. 14, 15.
[5] 42 Geo. III. c. 73.

Elizabethan Poor Law relating to parish apprentices."[1]
Even in this respect it was useless, chiefly because its
enforcement depended on the magistrates, no inspectors
being appointed. It is in its failure, however, that its
greatest value lies. The conditions of apprentices in the
textile trades were no doubt the worst, and had the Act
succeeded, it might have been felt that sufficient had been
done for the time, and that the Government could rest
satisfied; while the reform party would certainly have
been handicapped by being deprived of some of their most
useful, because the most ghastly, facts with which to excite
the compassion of the public. As it was, they continued
their exertions, and widened the scope of their inquiries.
In so doing they acquired information which convinced
themselves, and ultimately the public, that the abuses of
children's employment were not confined to apprenticed
labour nor to mills and factories. Thus the failure of the
Act of 1802 led directly to the inclusion of wage-earning
children in the schemes for reform.

The progress of this reform was, however, very slow.
This was largely due to the opposition of manufacturers
towards any restriction upon their freedom to carry on their
business as best suited their interests. They had a fairly
strong case based on the pleas that an improvement was
taking place without any legislative interference and that the
children needed the wages. There was also an argument
which we may call the Jingo argument, namely, that a
continuance of our remarkable prosperity depended upon
the freedom of the manufacturer, and that if he were
injured by the proposed legislation, as, according to this
argument, he would be, the trade of the country as a
whole, with which our position as a great nation was so
inextricably woven, would decline. In the "History of
Factory Legislation" there is an interesting analysis of
the opposition to the Act of 1819, which can be applied to
the opposition of the whole of the early reform movement.
"Again and again we find the fixed idea that it was cruel

[1] Hutchins, *op. cit.*, p. 16.

to prevent or restrict children's labour, because they 'must starve' without it. The promoters of Factory Bills would be told that they were legislating on the choice between too much work and too little to eat.[1] . . . The arguments used to weaken the Act of 1819 are those that belong to the mercantilist order of ideas, and are based on the two-fold assumption that (*a*) the protection and preservation of industry on its commercial side should be the object of the State, and (*b*) that the proposed regulation would injure trade, and drive it out of the country, eventually reducing not only the capitalists, but also the workers, to beggary. This appears to have been the most general line of attack. It is a view still widely held, though perhaps no longer with regard to restrictions on child labour." [2]   " We may note also the singular assumption that—not idleness but— leisure is the root of all evil, and that the people were entirely incapable of employing sensibly even an hour for themselves. This idea recurs over and over again, with reference not only to adults but even to children, who, it was urged, would take to bad courses if allowed any interval between work and sleep. Thus the curious pamphlet already cited says, ' All experience proves that in the lower orders deterioration of morals increases with the quantity of unemployed time of which they have command. Thus the Bill actually encourages vice—it establishes idleness by Act of Parliament ; it creates and encourages those practices which it pretends to discourage.' [3]   This line of argument evidently springs from a conception of the manual working or so-called lower classes as being an order apart, almost an inferior race, without any claim on the humane or liberal side of life, who should be kept carefully to their one proper sphere, namely, hard manual work.   A third argument we may distinguish in the year 1819, of a somewhat different and more respectable nature.   It might be called the

[1] Hutchins and Harrison, *op. cit.*, p. 25.
[2] Ibid., p. 27.
[3] An Enquiry into the Principle and Tendency of the Bill for Imposing Certain Restrictions on Cotton Factories, 1818.

optimistic argument, and was practically based on Adam Smith's doctrine, and destined to develop into what has been called 'Manchesterianism.' Its contention was that things were not so bad as represented, that their inherent tendency was to right themselves if left alone, and that conditions were better on the whole in cotton factories than in other industries. In this last statement lay the strength of the position, for there seems good reason to think that in the larger and more developed steam factories things were already improving, that a man like Arkwright's son was giving better conditions than the Act required, and infinitely better than those prevailing in the hand industries."[1] Such were the arguments which the reform party had to meet, and until it could educate a substantial body of the public up to the pitch of criticising these views, the progress of reform was bound to be slow. In the first two or three decades of the nineteenth century it was unusual to find any one holding the opinion of Mr. Price, a magistrate who was examined before Peel's Committee, that "if parents were thrown more upon themselves and did not draw a profit from children in their very early years, they might not waste so much of their time, they would work harder, and probably obtain better wages for better work."[2]

It is of course necessary, when criticising their dilatory acceptance of reform, to remember that nineteenth-century legislators had no experience upon which to draw when contriving their remedies ; industrial and social legislation was then quite new, and necessarily proceeded slowly when its promoters were not themselves sure what abuses it was wise, economically speaking, to attack[3] Nevertheless, when all is said for the wisdom and inevitableness of a gradual reformation, these industrial and social laws of the nineteenth century, upon which we sometimes plume ourselves, afford a striking example of the patchwork methods which not invariably, but yet too frequently, characterise English reform, its hesitation, and its extravagance occasioned by

---

[1] Hutchins and Harrison, *ob. cit.*, pp. 28, 29.
[2] Ibid., ibid., p. 26.   [3] *Cf.* ibid., p. 120.

the fear of spending. The titles and number of the Acts upon the statute books are imposing ; if we look at their details, we find that, lacking in courage and foresight, they failed in varying degrees to achieve their objects. The Bill drafted by Robert Owen in 1819, and based on experiments in his own mills at New Lanark, would have prohibited the employment of children under 10 ; the Act passed, compromised with a nine years' limit.[1] Owen asked for a 10½ hours' day for all children and young persons under 18 ; the Act reduced the age of prohibition and lengthened the hours ; a 12 hours' day was allowed for children, while the law excluded workers over 16. Later on, of course, the mistake had to be acknowledged, and new laws had to be passed. Another instance of the Government's lack of courage to adopt radical remedies is its dilatoriness in accepting the suggested method of administering the Act by inspectors. The Act of 1802 had been ineffective because its enforcement lay with the magistrates, who, either intentionally or through laxness, neglected this piece of their work. Owen pressed for the appointment of inspectors in 1819, but the Act of that year and the Acts immediately following left the work in the hands of common informers and the justices.[2] To use the machinery already in existence was a policy which appealed to the parliamentary mind. It was only after thirty years' experience of the futility of trusting to the magistrates for the administration of the Acts that the Government ventured to appoint inspectors. The result of this hesitating policy was that, as Spencer Walpole has it, it took twenty-five years of legislation to restrict a child of nine to sixty-nine hours' work a week, and that only in cotton mills.[3] Eventually the reforms were achieved, but it was not before there had been years of acute misery and suffering, the effects of which are part of our heritage to-day.

The history of the reform movement has been so fully

[1] Hutchins and Harrison, *op. cit.*, p. 21.
[2] See ibid., p. 21.
[3] Walpole, History of England, iii. p. 203. Quoted by Hutchins and Harrison.

dealt with already, that it would be useless repetition to give here more than a summary of its course. Though the Act of 1802 was ineffective, the reform party was not dispirited. Robert Owen, himself a manufacturer, adopted in his own cotton mills various reforms which he desired to see made generally compulsory. His practical work and his writings, based on his experiments and published in 1815, created real interest, and proved how unfounded were the fears that better conditions were economically unsound.[1] Though the Government vacillated, the matter was taken up by private members, and an Act was passed in 1819.[2] It fell far short of Owen's demands, and it applied to cotton mills only. Further, it depended for enforcement upon justices of the peace and informers, and was in consequence ineffective. Its chief merit was that it instituted a maximum working day and a minimum age at which work might be begun, establishing thereby a useful precedent. The next year a Bill was passed relaxing the regulations of the former Act with regard to meal times, and allowing water mills to make up for time lost by working overtime or at night.[3] This meant a set-back to reform, but in 1825 Hobhouse's Bill was passed, fixing a twelve hours' day, exclusive of meal times, for all children and young persons under sixteen, while on Saturdays not more than nine hours were to be worked between 5 a.m. and 4.30 p.m.[4] Considerable light is thrown upon the difficulties which reformers had to face by the fact that it was considered necessary to insert a clause to the effect that owners of mills, or their fathers and sons, were incompetent to hear cases under this Act.[5] The year 1833, however, is the year which really forms the landmark

[1] Hutchins and Harrison, *op. cit.*, iii. p. 21.

Cunningham, Growth of English Industry, ii. p. 776.

Owen, Observations on the effect of the manufacturing system, with hints for the improvement of those parts in it which are most injurious to health and morals.

[2] 59 Geo. III. c. 66.

[3] 60 Geo. III. c. 5. See Hutchins and Harrison *op. cit.*, p. 30.

[4] 6 Geo. IV. c. 63. *Cf.* Hutchins, *op. cit.*, p. 31.

[5] 1831; amended, 1 & 2 Wm. IV. c. 39. See Hutchins, *op. cit.*, p. 32.

in the history of factory legislation. A Bill was passed in this year for textile mills, forbidding the employment of children under nine years of age, except in silk mills.[1] The work of children under thirteen was limited to nine hours a day or forty-eight a week, and that of young persons between thirteen and eighteen to twelve hours a day or sixty-nine a week. Their employment between 8.30 p.m. and 5.30 a.m. was prohibited altogether. But the crowning point of the Act was that it provided for the appointment of inspectors, thus laying the foundation of our system of factory and labour regulation. Inspectors, as yet only four in number, were to be appointed by the central Government ; they had full powers of entry into factories, and could make such rules and bye-laws as they considered necessary. Henceforth there was a chance that the Acts would be enforced. " The introduction of an external authority, free from local bias and partiality, greatly improved the administration of the law, lessened the friction between manufacturers and operatives, and provided a medium of communication between the Government and the people at a time when knowledge of industrial matters was scanty in the extreme."[2] The provisions of this Act were sound enough, but the inspectors found it well-nigh impossible to enforce them, because machinery could be kept running, and adult labour could be employed for longer hours than were allowed to children, and it was therefore very easy for the manufacturer to keep boys and girls at work after they should have been sent home. It was largely in order to overcome this difficulty, as well as because it was felt that protection was needed for them, that in 1844 an Act was passed to extend the protection of the law to women ; henceforth they were to be treated as young persons.[3]   In 1847 a Ten Hours Bill was passed for them and for young persons ;[4] children were not included, though their work

[1] 3 & 4 Wm. IV. c. 103.   [2] Hutchins and Harrison, *op. cit.*, p. 40.
[3] Hutchins and Harrison, *op. cit.*, p. 85.
7 & 8 Vict. c. 15.
[4] 10 & 11 Vict. c. 29.
Hutchins, *op. cit.*, p. 95.

by the week was limited by the Act of 1833. The Act
of 1847 was often evaded because manufacturers employed
their workpeople upon the relay system, a device which
gave them scope for shifting their employees from room
to room, so that it was almost impossible for the inspectors
to detect overtime work. This was prevented in 1850 by
an Act fixing hours of work for women and young persons
between 6 a.m. and 6 p.m., one and a half hours being
reserved for meals.[1] Children were not included because
it was said that any restriction upon their employment on
the relay system would seriously hamper adult male labour.
But the inspectors showed that their exclusion allowed of
evasions, and that they were ofter employed more than the
legal number of hours, and in 1853 an amending Act
included them also.[2] A normal working day was now
established. Meanwhile the miserable conditions of labour
in mines had already been reformed. The report of 1842
was so ghastly that in the same year a Bill was carried with
little difficulty. Boys under ten and women and girls were
forbidden to work in the pits, and inspectors were appointed
to enforce the law.[3]

Mines and textile trades were therefore regulated by 1845.
But outside these industries were any number of important
occupations in which children were employed for long hours,
at an early age, and under injurious conditions. We have
noticed, when dealing with the report of 1843, how various
were the occupations in which children were employed, and
we have seen that in 1863 juvenile employment in many
trades was barely, if at all, improved by the change which
was taking place in public opinion or by the example
of better conditions in the textile trades. The reformers
now turned their attention to this field of work. The years
1845 to 1861 saw the inclusion under the factory law of
the industries allied to the textiles.[4] Acts were passed

---

[1] Hutchins, *op. cit.*, p. 108.
  13 & 14 Vict c. 54.
[2] 16 & 17 Vict c. 104.   [3] 5 & 6 Vict. c. 99.
[4] Hutchins and Harrison, *op. cit.*, chap. vii. p 120.
  Print work Acts 1845 (ibid., p. 131), half-hearted measure. Children under

placing print, bleach and dye works, and lace factories [1] under regulations similar to those which had already been made for the textiles.   Much of the lace trade was carried on as home-work or in the houses of the lace " mistresses," who employed women and girls and children in terribly over-crowded rooms, all the workers, and the children especially, suffering from the strain due to the rapidity of the work.[2] It was only the lace factories which were affected by the Act of 1861, but the revelations of even worse conditions in the domestic manufacture brought up the question of regulating workshops.   This was a difficult matter, but it was clear that it had to be faced, and the years 1864 to 1867 saw the movement for the inclusion of non-textile factories and workshops.[3]   A Commission had been appointed, and had issued its first report in 1863.   It dealt with pottery, hosiery, lace, lucifer match and cartridge making, all of which employed large numbers of children. In the pottery trade the conditions of child labour were aggravated by the men's habit of wasting the first days of the week in drinking, and then working abnormally long hours, during which their youthful assistants were obliged to attend them.[4]   The pottery trade and the general conditions in 1860 were probably fully as injurious to the workers as the conditions in the textile factories in 1820. In the fustian-cutting trade children were regularly employed fourteen hours a day, and often more at the end of

---

8 forbidden to work.   Those under 13 and women forbidden to work between 10 p.m. and 6 a.m.   Children under 13 to attend school 30 days in each year.

Bleach and dye works placed under Factory Acts, 1860.

23 & 24 Vict. c. 78 ; 25 and 26 Vict. c. 8.

Acts for calendaring and finishing, 1863 and 1864.

Consolidating Act, 1870, 33 & 34 Vict. c. 62.

[1] 1861, lace-making in factories placed under the Factory Acts, 24 & 25 Vict. c. 117.

[2] H. C., 1863, xviii. p. lxxxi, and H. C., 1864, xxii. p. vi.

Cf. Hutchins and Harrison, *op. cit.*, p. 146.

[3] Ibid., chap. viii.

[4] Ibid., p. 153.

Arnold Bennett, in his novel, Clayhanger, gives a vivid picture of the work of the potter's boy.

the week.[1]   This and the pottery trade were no exceptional occupations, and the conditions were recognised as being so bad that a Bill was passed in 1864, with practically no opposition, although it contained an innovation, dealing as it did with a home industry, that of fustian cutting.   It is interesting to notice that the attitude of manufacturers and of the public towards legislative control had undergone a profound change since 1819.   We have seen how acute then was the hostility towards State interference.   But as first one trade and then another was dealt with by specially appointed committees and commissions, and information as to the prevailing conditions of work was forthcoming, and when the regulation of the textile trades was accomplished without ruining the nation, the attitude of the public changed from that of distrust of factory legislation to one of acceptance of industrial supervision, even for domestic workrooms. " It was the study and observation of the actual facts that brought home to the Commissioners that while regulation was imperatively necessary in factories, it was still more needed in the smallest workplace.   Thus we see public opinion driven forward, reluctantly perhaps, and slowly, but with irresistible force, towards the principle of collective control of all workers." [2]   And as a rule manufacturers now welcomed legislation.   Individuals often could not themselves afford to adopt reforms which would place them at a disadvantage to less scrupulous rivals, but they accepted restrictions willingly when they were made compulsory upon all employers.   In 1867 a large number of new industries were brought under control.[3]   In 1878 the Acts of 1864 and 1867 were repealed, and the Consolidation Act took their place.   No child under eight was now to be employed in any handicraft; children between eight and thirteen might be employed only upon the half-time system as then used in factories; and young persons[4] might work only for twelve hours, inclusive of meal times

[1] Hutchins and Harrison, *op. cit.*, p. 154.
[2] Ibid., pp. 165, 167.   [3] Ibid., p. 168 *seq.*
[4] And women.

of one and a half hours. No work was to be done by children and young persons[1] after two o'clock on Saturdays;[2] the child's working day was to be between 6 a.m. and 8 p.m., the young person's[3] between 5 a.m. and 9 p.m. This difference of hours was established by the Bill, although differentiations of this sort had been proved to be the best of loopholes for the evasion of the law. Children were to attend school for at least ten hours a week. In 1891 the age of employment for children in factories and workshops was raised to eleven years. In 1886 an Act was passed limiting the hours of work for young people in shops to sixty-six hours a week, and in 1892 their hours were reduced to a level with those of young persons in factories and workshops.[4]

It is necessary to consider the movement for education in connection with that for industrial legislation, because they are closely inter-related, the success of the latter depending largely upon the adoption of general education. When there were no other means of keeping working-class children under supervision and giving them some sort of training, their parents not unnaturally set them to work at an early age. But when, finally, elementary education became compulsory, and there were definite claims upon the children's time, it became very much easier to prevent the employment of those below the legal age, and to enlist parents upon the side of the law. Apart from any other benefit which education conferred, it did check the extensive employment of children at an age when long and constant labour must, according to present opinion, be deleterious. Until 1876 initiative in education had rested with private bodies;[5] for though various of the Factory Acts, from 1802 onwards, required employers to provide education for their juvenile employees, the clauses imposing this obligation were fre-

---

[1] And women.
[2] Except in establishments employing five or fewer persons.
[3] And women's.
   Cf. Hutchins, *op. cit.*, p. 171.
[4] Hutchins and Harrison, *op. cit.*, p. 222.
[5] Royal Lancastrian Institution, founded 1809 ; National Society, 1812.

quently not enforced, or, where they were nominally complied with, the education supplied was often a mere farce.[1] But in 1876 elementary education until ten years of age was made compulsory. This Act and that of 1899, which raised the age to twelve or fourteen, not only improved the discipline and morals of the working-class child but also prevented the regular employment of young children in domestic manufactures which were not under the factory and workshop Acts, though it is obvious that it could not prevent their work out of school hours. Thus by the close of the century the most tangible abuses of child labour—early employment, brutal treatment, and over-long hours, and the other injurious conditions against which the nineteenth-century reformers had declaimed—had either disappeared or were greatly modified.

So brief an account can give no idea of the human interest attached to the story of the reform movement, and the dramatic struggle of its champions against the greed and hostility of employers, the indifference of so many members of the Government and the House of Commons, and the universal ignorance and inexperience as to industrial and social needs. The passionless attitude of the early reformers towards the worst conditions of child labour ; the experiments of Owen at New Lanark ; the declamations of the later reformers, amongst whom stand out the historic figures of Sadler, Lord Ashley, Cobbett, and many others, not the least of whom was Oastler, who in 1830 initiated the newspaper controversy on the subject, with his letters on Yorkshire Slavery to the *Leeds Mercury* ; the rise, about 1830, of the Ten Hours' Agitation, which, by gaining a hold of the working classes, gave a democratic character to a movement which had hitherto come from above ; the manner in which working men and their supporters manipulated public sentiment on behalf of the children for their own ends, and then, when they found that the laws regulating child labour did not, as they had hoped, effect any improvement in their own conditions, the manner in which they backed the movement

---

[1] Hutchins and Harrison, *op. cit.*, pp. 77, 78.

on behalf of female workers, and fought their own battle "behind the women's petticoats"; these are all aspects of the history of reform which are well worth longer study. It is, however, impossible to deal with them here, though it may be useful to point out two less noticed features of the movement. In the first place, the reforms of the nineteenth century were carried only after continuous pressure and agitation. Full evidence as to the conditions of labour were accessible to the Commons, but evidence and reason were not sufficient to stir them into activity. Effective laws were not passed until the outcry of the extremists as to the horrors of child slavery had awakened the emotions of our legislators. To a considerable extent, in fact, reform was sentimental. In the second place, the reforms, great as they were, affected only certain classes of employment. Outside the sphere of factories, workshops, and handicrafts, in which the conditions of labour were defined, there were wide areas of work in which adults and children were employed, for which no legislation had been passed, and in which, therefore, evils were still free to exist. In yet another way these reforms were limited. It will be seen, if they are analysed, that they dealt only with the obvious and intolerable physical and moral evils. Apart from these obvious evils, there were other problems connected with child labour which were far from being solved. In the next chapter we shall have to see to what an extent the legislation of the nineteenth century fell short of the needs of the case.

CHAPTER XVIII

THE DEVELOPMENT OF THE TWENTIETH-CENTURY PROBLEMS OF CHILD LABOUR

THE abuses of child labour as revealed by the reports was exactly the subject to attract attention, the sympathy of the general public being readily stirred by the account of the miserable conditions of the thousands of children in our factories. Their employment became a prominent question of the time, and the interest then attached to it causes it still to stand out as one of the most striking features in the industrial history of the nineteenth century. But whilst the energy of reformers was concentrated in altering the conditions of factory employment, and feeling on the subject was spreading through the country, quietly and in the background various changes were taking place in the nature, methods, and motives of juvenile employment.

These changes, though they were as yet overshadowed by the prominent evils of child labour, were to pave the way to new difficulties, and the reform party emerged triumphant from its struggle for factory legislation only to find itself face to face with fresh problems, far more complex and more difficult to solve.

The most important, because within it lies the germ of one of the pressing questions of to-day, was the exploitation of children as cheap labour. It appeared in various forms: sometimes the young people were employed at work which they were fully able to do, but at low wages and on disadvantageous terms, on the plea of their youth, though it was in effect no disqualification. Or they were engaged in place of men at men's work, because the employer thought that, though they were less efficient, he could make higher profits by economising on wages.

Sometimes, on the other hand, the work was especially suited to children, and was of too unskilled and simple a nature to be worth the labour and wages of adults. For that very reason, namely, because it did not offer employment in later life, it tended to be a peculiarly harmful class of occupation, since it cast the young people adrift at an age when it was most important that they should be started on their careers. Amongst such occupations are to be numbered various forms of machine-minding, and errand and message work, a large demand for which was being created by the development of city life, and by modern requirements. Of course the readiness to take apprentices in the old days was largely due to the fact that, even when the boys' board and lodging and early unskilfulness were taken into account, they were still cheaper than journeymen. But though their work was undoubtedly of economic value to their employers, whether that employer were parent or master, neither the law nor public opinion permitted a workman to exploit their labour for his own profit. The master's obligation to instruct his apprentice was enforced by the Statute of Artificers and by the gilds. Moreover, the opinion of the day was hostile to competition, and master craftsmen were jealously on the alert to prevent any one of their number from underselling his fellows by employing an excessive amount of cheap child labour. It was always a temptation to individual workmen to take more than their share of apprentices, and to run their businesses by juvenile labour while journeymen were left unemployed. But the gilds made strict rules limiting the number of apprentices and turnovers, and thus prevented the practice from being openly or generally adopted. It is impossible to read the parliamentary reports of the nineteenth century without realising the change which had taken place in opinion and industrial ethics. In trade after trade children were employed, and public opinion tolerated their employment, simply as cheap labour, and their after career was a matter of indifference ; the work upon which they were engaged was not a preliminary to more highly paid adult work ; they gained little by it which could be of use to them in later life ; in fact, it injured rather tnan helped them in their careers by exhausting them physically and mentally, and often by degrading them morally.

The calico manufacturers, who obliged their workmen upon threat of dismissal to apprentice their sons, were the first who as a body of men utilised child labour in this way.   This was in 1785.   Journeymen had the utmost difficulty in finding work, and were discharged in every period of slackness,[1] but boys could always find a job.   They were taken nominally as apprentices, but so little attention was paid to their training that they were admittedly unskilful and masters protected themselves from loss by making charges for spoilt work upon the boys' earnings.   At the end of his term the lad was discharged, since his master would not pay journeyman's wages.[2] A younger boy took his place, and the dismissed apprentice drifted out into the world, with little chance of obtaining employment in his own trade.   The evidence given only too clearly proved that boys were taken not in order that they might learn a trade which would require them later, for as soon as they reached manhood they were dismissed ; nor yet because the industry was expanding : this could not be pleaded when numbers of journeymen were standing unemployed.   They were taken solely because they were cheaper than adults : the lad was paid 3s. 6d. a week in the first year, and about 7s. weekly in the last, and did work for which a journeyman would have received 25s.[3]   Similar evidence was given by the witnesses before the Committee of 1831.   In numerous mills and factories children were employed at a very early age.[4]   It was said that they did not do the work as well as adults,[5] yet it was so distinctly to the manufacturer's advantage to employ them, that he was apt to refuse

[1] Reports, 1803–4, v. pp. 4, 19.
[2] Ibid., p. 5.   [3] Ibid., pp. 4, 7.
[4] Reports, H. C., 1831–2, xv. p. 32.
     Ibid., p. 313.
[5] Ibid., p. 66. Cf. p. 120.

workmen who had no young children to put to the trade.[1]
The older boys were employed at men's work, and received
half the wages.[2] Their chances of after employment were
very uncertain ; they might remain on until middle life, but
they were flung on the rubbish heap whenever it was no longer
to the advantage of their masters to employ them. It was said
that nine-tenths of the lowest class in Manchester were the
refuse of the cotton mills.[3] In fact, manufacturers were
making profits, and parents of employable children were
pocketing wages at the expense of the nation as a whole,
which they were burdening with a mass of unskilled and low-
skilled workmen, together with a considerable number of unemployables. The earlier report on the ribbon trade had
thrown light on this aspect of juvenile labour. The trade was
carried on almost entirely by girls, who were bound by irregular indentures as apprentices, and received such small wages
that they had to resort to poor relief to eke them out, unless
they could be partially supported at home.[4] In such cases
the public paid the manufacturer's expenses through the poor
rates, while the girls were too often ruined for later life.

The report of 1843 upon the employment of children in
trades and manufactures shows that a considerable amount of
" blind alley " employment was then prevalent in various
trades carried on not only in factories but in small shops.
The essential evils involved in such work were not compre-
hended either at this time or when the earlier reports were
made ; indeed, the recognition of " blind alley " occupations,
and of the problem they constitute, dates only from the last
years of the nineteenth century. It is true that the Sub-
Commissioners of 1842 were required to make special inquiries
as to how far the early employment of children was of service
to them in obtaining work as adults ;[5] but this was in order
to discover what truth there was in the assertions of those
who opposed legislative interference on the grounds that it was
mistaken kindness to forbid children of six or ten to work,

---

[1] Reports, H. C., 1831–2, xv. p. 126. *Cf.* p. 270.
[2] Ibid., p. 66.
[3] Ibid., p. 320.
[4] H. C., 1818. ix. p. 5.
[5] Second Report, 1842, p. 208.

since they would then be handicapped by lack of skill in later
life. Yet, though it was not collected with that object, the
evidence of the Sub-Commissioners throws considerable light
upon the "blind alley" nature of such child labour in 1842.
It was said that at Birmingham children employed in the
metal trade were taught only one particular branch, "so
that when grown up they find a difficulty in procuring profitable work."[1] At Wolverhampton boys of seven to ten or
twelve were employed in foundries. Some remained in the
trade as adults, but most were dismissed as soon as their
parents asked for better wages for them.[2] Almost all the girls
and boys who worked at nails, tips, and washers left their
employment when fifteen or seventeen years of age, at which
time the wages were no longer sufficient for them ; it was unknown what then became of them set adrift as they were in
the labour market, after four or five years of rough work, and
with no skill to command a living.[3] The young people's
chances varied, of course, with their occupations, as is evident
from the fortunes of the Wolverhampton children. There,
children in mines, in the lock and key trade, and in forges,
remained on in later life, and a great number of the boys and
girls in the japanning trade stayed on But girl polishers
and packers could not obtain work when adults ; they went
into service or married.[4] Straw plaiting was an occupation
which employed large numbers of children, and offered no
assured livelihood. Parents, in fact, bartered away their
children's future for a miserable wage of, at best, about 1s 6d. a
week : such was the pay of children from eight to thirteen years
old. The girls were said to be unfitted for domestic service,
yet, if they remained in the trade, they could earn only 3s. to
4s. a week, working twelve to fourteen hours a day.[5] The
best that could be said of the pin trade condemns it from our
point of view. There was little demand for adult labour.
The Sub-Commissioners reported that "It does not appear

[1] H. C., 1843, xiv. Appendix to Second Report Part I. p. F 18.
[2] Ibid., Appendix, Part II. p. Q 22. Horne's Report.
[3] Ibid., ibid., p. Q 3.   [4] Ibid., ibid., p. Q 22–23.
[5] Ibid., Appendix, Part I. p. A 10.

that this work disqualifies them for other employment, or is of
any advantage to them as regards these employments ; it is a
resource to them if they chance to get maimed at any occupation they may have taken up after leaving it ; they can return
to it, under such circumstances, and earn just enough to keep
them from the workhouse, with prudence and frugality. . . ."[1]
" As domestic servants, the girls who have worked in pin factories or cotton factories would find it difficult to get places ;
those from the rural districts are preferred. The pin-girls,
however, who work at Newton, and are children of agricultural
labourers, are frequently taken as servants at a farm house."[2]
In the locksmiths' trade at Willenhall numbers of boys were
taken by the small workmen as apprentices, though they were
often not bound by legal indentures. There was little opening
in the trade for adult labour, and when the lads' time was out
they were turned adrift.[3] In all these trades the personal
relationship between master and workman had broken down,
and the former had lost his old sense of responsibility for
starting his young employee in life. The disappearance of
this sense of responsibility was undoubtedly connected with,
even if it was not due to, the dissolution of the apprenticeship
system. So long as the Statute of Artificers could be enforced the ideals of duty to the younger generation and to the
nation were held up before all classes, and though it is true
they were not always attained, and were sometimes even
openly flouted, they did serve as a check upon the wholesale
exploitation of child labour. Their influence can best be
realised by comparing the conditions of the juvenile worker
under *laissez faire* and free competition with that of the
apprentice under the Elizabethan system.

There is an interesting report on the watchmaking trade
in 1817, interesting, because it illustrates the difference in
the attitude towards the younger generation of workmen in
London, where the Elizabethan traditions held good, and in
Coventry, where they had been swept away by the breakdown

[1] H. C., 1843, xiv. Appendix, Part II. pp. M 22–23.
[2] Ibid., ibid., p. M 23.
[3] Ibid., ibid., p. Q 45.

of the old system. The act of repeal had preserved to London its customary rights, and, according to the bye-laws of the City, none but freemen might engage in trade, and only those who had served seven years, or who were entitled to the freedom by patrimony, might be admitted as freemen. Consequently apprenticeship survived in London when it had disappeared elsewhere, and, under the influence of its ideals, the London manufacturers declared to the Committee "that it is the paramount duty of every person who has the care of youth, to provide a master to teach him some art or trade, whereby, at the expiration of his apprenticeship, he may gain his own maintenance."[1] Further, it was their opinion "that the pretensions to the allowance of universal uncontrolled freedom of action to every individual, founded upon the same delusive theoretical principles which fostered the French Revolution, are wholly inapplicable to the insular situation of this kingdom, and if allowed to prevail, will hasten the destruction of the social system."[2] In Coventry industrial life rested upon the belief in this uncontrolled freedom of action to every individual. Watchmaking was the chief industry ; for the last forty years it had been the custom to pay apprentices wages, and to take them on the outdoor system. One master would take thirty or forty boys, and set them to learn one minute branch of the trade. The tendency to work on these lines had increased since 1810 ; apprentice labour had been more and more employed, and adults had found themselves ousted by boys, who in their turn were thrown out of work as soon as their time was up. Under this system the boys were utterly ill-taught ; they knew only one branch of their business, and their unskilfulness, as well as the over-stocked conditions of the trade, prevented them from finding employment in it at men's wages. Some turned to weaving : a great number became porters, scavengers, and unskilled labourers.[3]

[1] Reports, H. C., 1817, vi. p. 46.
[2] Ibid., p. 48.
[3] Ibid., pp. 73, 75.
  Ibid., p. 83.

Here, as in other occupations in which the conditions were similar, the employment of children was economically unsound, and apart, therefore, from any sentimental or humanitarian feelings, it must stand condemned. It was a minor point only that child labour meant an economy for the individual employer, or even that it allowed of the rapid expansion of the individual trade. This, of course, was its justification with the economists of the *laissez faire* period. They could argue that the employment of children was best for the nation if best for the employer. Manufactured goods could be more cheaply produced, and the lower price automatically enlarged the market. As to the children, presumably they would find employment as adults in the industry in which they had been brought up, or in some other branch of manufacture or useful employment. But it was just here that their theories clashed with facts. Children engaged in those trades which were carried on chiefly by juvenile labour did not find suitable after-employment. Ure, who wrote in 1835 a defence of the factory system, failed to take account of this ultimate lack of economy, and looked only at the decreased cost of production which child labour meant to the manufacturer. He urged that one of the chief merits of machinery lay in the fact that it tended to diminish the cost of labour " by substituting the industry of women and children for that of men ; or that of ordinary labourers for that of trained artisans."[1] It is, perhaps, hardly necessary to point out what he overlooked, that the wages immediately paid did not form the true cost of labour ; account had also to be taken of the wastage of the nation's future powers of production.

It may be worth while to notice that, though the change in public opinion with regard to child labour coincides with the general adoption of machinery and the predominance of factories, it is independent both of the one and of the other. It was the breakdown of the old ideas and the growth of the spirit of individualism which allowed of the exploitation of juvenile labour. Machine work and factories did not create

[1] Ure, Philosophy of Manufactures (1835), p. 23.

the evil; all they did was to throw it into publicity. As a consequence of its independent growth, this problem of the exploitation of child labour was barely affected by the legislation which dealt with factory employment. Within the factories it assumed a milder form, thanks to the new laws which dealt with the length of the working day and the conditions of employment. But outside the factories it went on much as before. The only real remedy was to alter public opinion to the extent of arousing the old sense of responsibility of the public and the employer towards the juvenile workman. This it was peculiarly difficult to do, partly because there was a strong feeling in favour of leaving the manufacturer as unhampered as possible, in order that he might not drop behind his Continental rivals, and partly because so much of the work was eminently suited to children, and was required in the interests of the public. Machine-minding, for much of which child labour was fully adequate, had become an integral part of modern industry; and to this was added, as the century advanced, a new form of child labour—errand and message work. The development of the latter is noticed by the Commissioners of 1842 who stated that in London the great majority of boys was employed as errand and shop boys.[1] This is the first reference to a class of work which has grown enormously with the growth of city life and the modern demand for messenger work, but in 1842 the evils attendant upon it were not recognised, and it is mentioned almost with relief as a substitute for work in manufactures. Both this and factory work were forms of "blind alley" employment which appeared to be really necessary, and it was hard to see how the ensuing evils could be overcome. The nineteenth century, at any rate, had no solution to offer.

There was another problem which arose immediately upon the dissolution of the Elizabethan system. Unlike that of "blind alley" work which, as we have said, was not appreciated until much later, this problem received early recognition. The difficulty was how to supply some sort of general

[1] H. C., 1843, xiv., Appendix, Part I. p. F 26

training and discipline for the juvenile worker now that he was no longer a pupil, but was practically, from the moment of starting work, a wage-earner and independent member of the labour market. Education in the wide sense of the word and training for life generally, as well as skill in a trade, had been supplied to the working-class boy by the Elizabethan system of indoor apprenticeship, and now that the system had broken down the need for some substitute made itself felt. It was a tribute to the old apprenticeship system that even those who were opposed to any form of industrial restraint appreciated the wider side of its work, and were conscious of the void created by its dissolution. The juvenile worker now was neither under the control of his master nor of his parents ; at home he was a wage-earner, and his independence had to be respected, or he might be driven to betake himself and his wages elsewhere. In the workshop or factory he was a " hand," and all that was demanded of him was satisfactory work and satisfactory conduct during work hours. As a rule he did not fear dismissal, since there was a large demand for juvenile labour, and he could easily find a new job. This absence of any control encouraged instability and even lawlessness. It was said of the Birmingham boys that many of them "will not become regular apprentices, because they like to go from place to place, preferring those establishments where no notice is taken of the irregularity of time. . . . When trade is bad these boys are turned off, and left to themselves, and become thieves." [1] Even those lads who were apprenticed were almost invariably bound on the outdoor system, which, unlike the old, did not supply a general training ; for though a boy might have a good master and be properly taught, he was practically uncontrolled out of work hours. Outdoor apprentices lived with their parents, but, like their unindentured fellows, they were wage-earners, and they soon became independent of parental control. It was said of the watchmakers' apprentices at Coventry that, after two or three years in a factory, they did

[1] Reports, H. C., 1842, xiv. p. 27.

20

as they pleased and refused restraint.[1] The witnesses before
the Commission agreed that the system caused a deterioration in morals.[2] An inquiry was made in 1828 into the
increase of criminal convictions. The chairman of the Court
of Quarter Sessions in Warwickshire attributed the increase
to the outdoor system. He pointed out that the great
majority of cases were from the manufactory towns, and
stated that the boys were brought up with neglect, and were
allowed to go about the town and have their time entirely to
themselves. "Formerly the apprentice was taken into the
house of the master, he was considered one of the family, and
he was boarded, lodged, and educated by the master, who
was answerable for his conduct ; now the master has ten or a
dozen apprentices, and perhaps never sees them ; they work
till the evening, and then all allowed to go where they please
. . . the consequence is that they are all thieves."[3] The
High Constable of the Birmingham division also attributed
the increase of crime to the outdoor system. Witnesses gave
evidence to the effect that there was great difficulty in con-
trolling apprentices, many of whom were idle and dissolute.[4]
This was in 1843, so that both this difficulty and that of the
exploitation of child labour and the entry of children into
"blind alley" employments were definitely developed before
the middle of the century.

In fact, whilst reformers were dealing with the hours of
work and the age of the workers, these far more difficult
problems were gradually being evolved. Steadily they grew
in complexity, on the one hand as apprenticeship was more
generally abandoned and intolerance of restraint took a hold
of the younger generation ; and, on the other, as the practice
of using children as cheap labour spread from one industry
to another, according as the processes were subdivided and
machinery began to be applied. Thus the problems of child
labour were changed, not removed.

[1] Report on Watchmaking, 1817, p. 80.
[2] Ibid., pp. 84-6.
[3] Report on Increase of Criminal Commitments, 1828.
[4] Report on Employment of Children in Manufactures (1843), p. 27.

THE MODERN PROBLEMS OF JUVENILE
LABOUR

THE MODERN PROBLEMS OF JUVENILE LABOUR

In an age sensitive to its social diseases it is natural that questions relating to juvenile labour should arouse general public interest, and be the subject of blue-books, numerous volumes, and controversies in the Press and on the platform. Within the limits of a chapter, however, only a few aspects of so varied a problem of contemporary life can be viewed. It is proposed, therefore, merely to state briefly the general conditions of juvenile labour in the opening years of this century, to show the general awakening to the gravity of the evils involved in it, and to indicate and discuss the remedies which are now being tried or advocated.

In juvenile labour as in other matters the nineteenth century left to the twentieth an unenviable legacy—the legacy of an industrial system which had grown up without forethought, and whose maladies had been treated with spasmodic doses of medicine, administered in a spirit of hopeful experiment rather than with any profound study or understanding of the needs of the system. To most generations it has been obvious that juvenile labour is merely a prelude to adult labour. The nineteenth century forgot this elementary fact. It raised juvenile labour to a fresh dignity, and regarded it as an independent factor in the labour market. As such, no doubt, it stood in need of special regulations, and accordingly an impressive array of regulations were duly formed. An employer must not employ a child for unlimited hours, nor imperil his life and limbs. But the nineteenth century, content with its superficial diagnosis, made no attempt to prevent a child from spending years in work that made no call upon its intelligence, and from undertaking occupations that fitted it only for unemployment.

This failure of insight into the nature of the problem marred all the efforts of the nineteenth century to deal with the fundamental evils of boy and girl employment. But even from its own limited point of view that century was lamentably lacking in thoroughness. The reformers could, of course, claim a number of notable achievements. Successive Acts had put an end to the employment of gangs of pauper apprentices and wage-earning children in textile factories for unduly long hours and under markedly injurious conditions, and had fixed a minimum age and a maximum working day. These regulations, it will be remembered, were extended to non-textile factories and to workshops. In addition, certain special forms of employment received special attention, the most important being the employment of children in chimney-sweeping[1], in agriculture,[2] and in places of entertainment,[3] and in 1889 the hours of children employed in street-selling were regulated.[4]

Nevertheless, valuable though these reforms were, it must be pointed out that they were confined to the employment of children in only a limited number of industries. Outside this area there was a mass of miscellaneous occupations employing thousands of children, in which masters were practically free to treat and employ them as they chose, save only during the school day a period of five and a half hours in the twenty-four. Thus at the opening of the twentieth century there was still ample opportunity for the use of juvenile labour upon lines which even the nineteenth century recognised as injurious. The evidence of various special inquiries made during the opening years of the twentieth century shows the degree to which child labour was used and abused at that time.

The best organised system of juvenile labour was, perhaps,

---

[1] 3 & 4 Vict. c. 85.   [2] 27-8 Vict. c. 37.
[3] 30-1 Vict. c. 130.
[4] 52-3 Vict. c. 44.   Re-enacted 57-8 Vict. c. 41.

that known as the "half-time" system. Devised before the days of universal education [1] it still flourished in the early years of the twentieth century, its existence being recognised in various recent Acts. The Education Act [2] of 1899 gave Local Education Authorities the power to make bye-laws for the purpose of allowing or regulating partial exemption from school.[3] At the age of 12 [4] a child might claim partial exemption under the Factory Acts,[5] or if he had reached the standard of proficiency or previous attendance prescribed in the bye-laws of the Local Education Authority.[6] The Committee appointed to inquire into the working of the system reported [7] in 1909 that it was almost entirely confined to certain processes in the textile industries, and was localised chiefly in Yorkshire, Lancashire, and Cheshire.[8]

[1] It was a device adopted by the Factory Acts of 1833 and 1844, and the Mines Act of 1861, to prevent the over-working and moral deterioration of young children, while yet not denying them the opportunity of working. Before 1870 the half-time system actually meant facilities for education, and " was generally applauded by educationists who were bent upon making education general." When, however, education became universal the conditions were changed, and the practice was condemned by all those primarily interested in education.

[2] Elementary Education Act, 1899 (Robson's Act). 62 & 63 Vict. c. 13.

[3] Authorities could also make bye-laws for total exemption, and were not obliged to make both ; bye-laws for partial exemption do not, therefore, exist in all localities.

[4] The Education Act of 1893 had allowed exemption at eleven years old.

[5] Report on Partial Exemption, 1909, p. 2.

The special position of agriculture is not referred to in this summary. Children between 11 and 13 may obtain exemption if working at agriculture, provided they make 250 attendances during another part of the year (Elementary Education Act, 1899).

[6] There was no regulation as to how such child should spend his free time. He could be employed at home or in odd job work.

[7] Report of the Inter-Departmental Committee on Partial Exemption from School Attendance, 1909 (Cd. 4791).

[8] Ibid., p. 3.

In 1901 the number of half-timers was declining, and the system was not seriously considered by the Committee of that year. (Ibid., pp. 3, 4.) But from 1901 onwards there was a slight annual increase, and on this account the special inquiry of 1909 was instituted. " We believe that this rise is due mainly to the provision in Robson's Act which enables a child to obtain partial exemption by the attendance qualification " (p. 4). " Three hundred meetings are only about 71 per cent. of the normal number of school meetings in the year, and as the average attendance of children throughout the country is almost 90 per cent., it is quite

The cotton mills of Lancashire and the woollen industry in Yorkshire employed the greatest number of children. Out of an average number of 47,360 partial exemption scholars given in the returns for 1906–7, 34,306 were employed in factories; 20,302 of these were Lancashire children, the majority of whom probably were working in the cotton mills; 10,517 were returned for Yorkshire, and they, it may be assumed, were for the most part engaged in the worsted manufacture. Of the remainder, 3,800 were employed in agriculture, and 9,254 in various occupations, chiefly as tradesmen's errand boys and domestic helps.[1]

It appeared that the use by parents of the concessions allowed by partial exemption depended more on fashion than necessity, for the Committee discovered that in those places where children were not required in the principal industries it was not the general custom for them to leave school, and they were therefore not employed in subsidiary industries or for domestic work.[2] Moreover, in a good many cases half-time had been abandoned by the management of mills, and the Committee found there was no desire to go back to it.[3]

The part-time system was condemned by the Committee on the grounds that it was injurious to the education and morals not only of the half-timers themselves but of the children with whom they mixed in school,[4] while it was not of value as a substitute for apprenticeship. The general opinion was that in the textile trade young people who began later were as good workers in a few months as the half-timer with his two or three years' start, and that the partial exemption provisions in rural districts did not have

exceptional for a child who has reached the age of 12 to be unable to qualify for partial exemption in this way ' (Rep., p. 2).

[1] Report of the Inter-Departmental Committee on Partial Exemption from School Attendance, 1909 (Cd. 4791), p. 3.

[2] Ibid., p. 3. Cf. p. 2. "It is not by any means the case that in all areas where partial exemption regulations exist the population care to avail themselves of them."

[3] Ibid., p. 10.

[4] Ibid., p. 5. "The whole class tends to have the pace reduced to that of the slowest children."

the effect of giving the children any useful agricultural training.[1]

The half-time system had, however, the advantage of being a deliberate plan, a carefully devised method by which education and industry co-operated in organising the entry of a child into industrial life. Its failure was due merely to the fact that the plan proved to be a bad one. In other directions the entry of children into industry was, generally speaking, a haphazard and unorganised process, beginning too frequently in casual jobs performed out of school hours. In 1901 a committee was appointed to inquire into the employment of school children out of school hours. As is stated in the report, the investigation was instituted because it was realised that while the employment of children was in most large industries carefully regulated, and in some dangerous cases prohibited, and while children were forbidden to do any work during school hours, their employment in other occupations and at other times of the day was wholly unregulated.[2] It was said that, " Provided they make eight or ten school attendances every week they may be employed (with few exceptions, and these little enforced) in the streets, in the fields, in shops, or at home, for the longest possible hours and on the hardest possible work, without any limit or regulation."[3] This opinion was fully borne out by the evidence collected. A return of wage-earning children made in 1899 had shown that at least 144,000 children who were making a full-time attendance at school were employed for wages out of school hours ; about 40,000 were employed for over twenty hours a week,[4] and fully three thousand for over forty hours.[5] A few worked for over fifty or sixty hours weekly. It is patent that

[1] Report of the Inter-Departmental Committee on Partial Exemption from School Attendance, 1909 (Cd. 4791), p. 9.

[2] Report of the Inter-Departmental Committee on the Employment of School Children, 1901 (Cd. 849), p. 5.

[3] Ibid., p. 5.

[4] Elementary Education (children working for wages), H. C. Paper, 1899, number 205, p. 26.

[5] Ibid., p. 27.

such a high total could be reached by children who were in school during the best hours of the morning and the early hours of the afternoon only by their rising very early, by working until late at night, in the mid-day dinner hour and rest time, and on Sundays. The report of 1901 confirmed this evidence,[1] and further pointed out that in many cases in which the hours of employment were less than twenty a week the entire week's work fell upon Saturday, the children being engaged for thirteen to seventeen hours on that day, so that even a low total for the week might represent very injurious conditions.[2] On the other hand, it is only fair to say that cases in which the hours were longest were not necessarily the worst. A boy who was returned as working $62\frac{1}{2}$ hours a week was found upon inquiry to be employed in a fish and vegetable shop for even longer hours than reported, but under thoroughly good conditions, so that he was fond of his work, and did not suffer in health nor in attention and intelligence at school.[3]

By far the greatest number of children mentioned in the official returns were employed in or in connection with shops.[4] The Shop Hours Act of 1892[5] had limited the work of assistants under 18 to 74 hours a week, but otherwise this form of employment was unrestricted, except indirectly, by the Education Acts. The report states that "children employed in connection with shops are hardly ever salesmen behind the counter. Their chief use is to deliver milk, coals, groceries, newspapers, and other goods to customers at their own homes, and sometimes to watch goods outside the shops." It was admitted that when the work began early, as was the case with the delivery of milk, the children were sleepy in school, and that even if their health did not suffer, their education was retarded.[6] But on the whole the Committee held that it was not an injurious form of occupation, except

[1] Report, 1901, p. 8.
[2] Ibid., p. 9.   [2] Ibid., p. 10.
[4] Ibid., p. 13.   76,173 children out of 144,026. The Commissioners suggest that if half-timers were included, the total number would be over 100,000.
[5] 55 & 56 Vict. c. 62.
[6] Report on Employment of School Children, 1901, p. 13.

where the hours were long or where heavy weights had to be carried ; or when, as in the case of barbers' boys, the sanitary conditions and moral surroundings were bad.[1] Had the Committee sat ten years later, when the twentieth-century point of view had developed, they would not have neglected the question whether such work is not injurious to a child's training for an ultimate occupation.

Domestic work ranked second to shop work in the number of children engaged in it. The Committee estimated those employed for wages at about 50,000.[2] The boys as a rule worked for a few hours only in cleaning boots and knives in respectable private houses, but the girls too often were domestic helps and baby-minders in very inferior places in which they were over-driven. One of the difficulties of protecting children from over-work became apparent in connection with this class of occupation. It was discovered that the severest work, the longest hours, and the hardest conditions were often to be found in the case of children who were employed without wages in doing house-work in the homes of their parents. " Many witnesses spoke strongly of the injury done to girls in this way, but all admitted that they could suggest no remedy." [3]

With regard to the numbers employed in other work, the Committee estimated those engaged in street trading at not less than 25,000,[4] while the miscellaneous occupations of taking dinners, knocking-up, and services in connection with sports, such as shooting and golf, were said to employ about 15,000.[5] A very large number of children attending full time at school during the greater part of the year, were occupied in agriculture during certain months, in harvest and at the fruit-picking season, though not many children under 14 were employed in regular work while still full time scholars, since " the nature of the work and the distances to be travelled make a boy of little use on a farm if he has to be in school from 9 to 12 and from 2 to 4." [6]

[1] Report on Employment of School Children, 1901, p. 14.
[2] & [3] Ibid., p. 14.   [4] Ibid., p. 16.
[5] Ibid., p. 17.   [6] Ibid., p. 14.

Street trading was another form of juvenile labour of an injurious nature. The Inter-Departmental Committee of 1901 and a Departmental Committee, which was appointed in 1909 and reported in 1910,[1] showed that numbers of boys and girls, children as well as young people, were engaged in it.[2] For though the Prevention of Cruelty to Children Act [3] had forbidden street trading and performing to children under 12, those between that age and 14 in the case of boys and 16 in the case of girls might engage in this class of work between the hours of 6 a.m. and 9 p.m. The reports are of interest not only because they give an account of the condition of work in the first decade of this century, but also because they show how those reforms which were generally considered advisable were retarded not by lack of legislation but by weakness in administration of the law. A Local Government Act of 1898 [4] had given localities the power to make bye-laws for the regulation of trading, but the 1901 report observed that in spite of the restrictions imposed by this Act and that for the Prevention of Cruelty to Children, many evils still existed. Street trading was said to be carried on by a worse class of child and under worse moral influences than any other occupation, and to be especially detrimental to young girls, so that at any rate in large centres of population it required special treatment.[5] The Employment of Children Act, 1903,[6] gave Local Authorities power to make byelaws for the trading of persons under 16, and confirmed the old regulations as to age and hours. According to the 1910 report, these powers had been employed by that date in nearly all the largest centres of population ; fifty out of the seventy-four county boroughs in England and Wales had made bye-laws.[7] But comparatively few of the smaller

---

[1] Report of the Departmental Committee on the Employment of Children Act, 1903 (Cd. 5229), 1910.

[2] The parliamentary return of 1899 gave the number of boys employed in street trading as newspaper sellers and hawkers at 17,617.

[3] 52–3 Vict. c. 44.   [4] 61–2 Vict. c. 251.

[5] Report on Employment of School Children, 1901, p. 16.

[6] 3 Edward VII. c. 45.

[7] Report of the Departmental Committee on the Employment of Children Act, 1903, 1909, p. 6.

41 out of 191 smaller boroughs and smaller urban districts ;   1 out of 61

boroughs and smaller urban districts had used their powers. The significant fact revealed by this report was that though the law was in accordance with public opinion, and many localities had made bye-laws of greater stringency than the minimum required by the law, still the administrative machinery was inadequate, and in many places neither the law nor the bye-laws were enforced. The Committee declared that a considerable amount of street trading was, in 1909, still carried on by children under 11.[1] They held that in towns in which bye-laws had been made, " though in exceptional cases much good has resulted from their adoption, on the whole this method of dealing with what we have to consider an unquestionable evil has not proved adequate or satisfactory."[2] " In crowded centres of population street trading tends to produce a dislike or disability for more regular employment ; the child finds that for a few years money is easily earned without discipline or special skill ; and the occupation is one which sharpens the wits without developing the intelligence. It leads to nothing permanent, and in no way helps him to a future career. There can be no doubt that large numbers of those who were once street traders drift into vagrancy and crime. Chief constables testified that street trading is the most fruitful apprenticeship to evil courses.[3] . . . In the case of both boys and girls the effect of this occupation on future prospects cannot be anything but thoroughly bad, except, possibly, in casual and exceptional cases."[4]

This report is dominated by the novel point of view that differentiates the attitude of the twentieth century towards

administrative counties with the exception of London and Middlesex. Almost all the bye-laws made by local authorities contained a prohibition of the trading of girls under 16, unless in company of a parent or guardian, a concession of which full use was made and which was criticised by many witnesses (p. 8). Another common feature of the bye-laws was the regulation of trading by means of badges in London and licences elsewhere. These the Statute required should be given irrespective of character, and their use, since they could be so easily obtained, rendered them an encouragement to trading.

[1] Report of the Departmental Committee on the Employment of Children Act, 1903, 1909, p. 7.

[2] Ibid., p. 8. [3] Ibid., p. 11.

[4] Ibid., p. 12.

juvenile labour from that of the nineteenth. It was at length realised that the early years of an industrial life must not merely be safeguarded against physical injury but must also be made industrially educative. So novel is it, and so recent the appreciation of the evils of " blind alley " work, that even in 1901 the Committee appointed to inquire into the employment of children during school age failed to call attention to the worst feature of such employment, namely, that so much of it offered neither training nor prospects for the future. It is from this point of view that the problem of young people's employment has now to be regarded. Juvenile labour of certain classes has become as definitely a watertight compartment as women's labour. It provides such skill as is necessary at a wage far lower than that paid to men, and on the other hand it can command in the market far higher wages than can economically be paid to young people engaged in learning a trade. Parents faced with the alternative of wages amounting in one case to 7s. a week and in another to, say, 5s. a week cannot always be expected to give due weight to possible contingencies four years hence ; or to remember that while in the latter case, a youth trained for a definite occupation might pass naturally into the ranks of the established workmen in his trade, in the former he might find himself in need of adult wages which the nature of his work would not justify. He would have to make a fresh start in life deprived of the one asset which had hitherto constituted his irresistible weapon in the competition of the labour market, his quality of cheapness.

A variety of causes, however, brought this aspect of the question prominently before the public. Recurring fits of dejection as to the maintenance of British supremacy in commerce left behind them a wholesome sense that the British workman was in some trades inferior in industrial training to his German rival. Attention was therefore inevitably called to the vast output of unskilled and low-skilled labour which was annually being produced in this country. The British method of producing adult labour seemed to be crippling the country in the international struggle for commercial and industrial supremacy. A second cause of the national awakening is to be found in the prominence given to the question of unemployment. This evil, which had long been a blot on our industrial system, received a sudden and belated recognition from party politicians.[1] By 1905 the topic of unemployment had become one of the most cherished properties of every political platform. In the autumn of that year the Unemployed Workmen Act was passed, which only added fuel to the fire of the controversies on the subject. The expedients of this measure were frankly temporary palliatives to be followed by some thorough preventive legislation. At subsequent elections arguments as to the nature of that preventive legislation were always a prominent feature of the campaign, more especially on Tariff Reform platforms. In the discussions aroused by this widespread advertisement of unemployment, all manner of causes and remedies, including the unrestrained use of juvenile labour and its regulation, came under review. Accordingly, the Poor Law Commission, appointed in 1905, obtained from Mr. Cyril Jackson a special report on Boy Labour. This report, published in 1909,[2] showed that a large number of children each year entered occupations which offered practically no prospects of permanence and possessed hardly any educative value either for citizenship or for adult labour. Amongst these occupations must be numbered, first, certain branches of industrial work, such as the worsted manufacture, which employed large numbers of children in special processes and offered little ultimate opening in any branch of the work ; secondly, those forms of irregular juvenile work such as that of telegraph messengers, errand and van boys, pages in hotels and clubs, newspaper sellers, boys in warehouses whose duty it was to fasten labels and fill and fold packets of goods. Some of them might stay on in other branches of their employers' business, but the majority did not.

[1] The year of the highest unemployed percentage, since records begin, in 1860, is 1879. See Beveridge, Unemployment, pp. 11, 38, 39.

[2] Report on Boy Labour, 1909 (Cd. 4632), Appendix, vol. xx., to Report of the Royal Commission on the Poor Laws and Relief of Distress, 1909.

Mr. Jackson admitted that final accuracy could not be obtained from the statistical evidence as yet available. "Trades are so subdivided, the conditions differ so much in different localities and even in different workshops, that there may be no apparent excess in the total figures for the country, and yet in many places scores of boys are being turned adrift because there is no room for them in the place where they have been working."[1] On the other hand, it must be remembered that an excess may be "apparent and not real. In a rapidly rising industry all the boys may be absorbed." There was, however, sufficient evidence that a great deal of wastage was taking place in many branches of labour. The work of pages and coorboys in shops and restaurants was " purely useless and wholly without training, besides being, owing to the length of time the boys are required to stand at that post, sometimes also cruel and injurious to health."[2] Office boys also were said to have very slight prospects, and in addition the work was held to be demoralising, especially in small offices, since the boy spent hours with nothing to do, and the work called for "little intelligence and less initiative."[3] Errand and shop boys had little chance of continuing in the same line of business. In large shops a few boys might find employment in other departments,[4] but in the small shops of a poor neighbourhood the boys' prospects, it was affirmed, "are absolutely nil."[5] Of the boys into whose careers inquiry was made, by far the greater number entered low-skilled trades or became general and casual labourers.[6] "From the forms returned it seems clear," says Mr. Jackson, "that the theory that boys can become errand boys for a year or two and then enter skilled trades cannot be maintained. Very few boys can pick up skill after a year or two of merely errand-boy work." Much of the mechanical and

---

[1] Report on Boy Labour, Appendix, vol. xx., 1909.   Cd. 4632, p. 7.
[2] Ibid., p. 22.
[3] Ibid., p. 19.   *Cf.* Gibb, Problem of Boy Work, p. 32.
[4] Ibid., p. 19.
[5] Ibid., pp. 20, 21.
[6] Ibid., pp. 45, 46.   *Cf.* Gibb, *op. cit.*, p. 23.

low-skilled work in factories and workshops offered no better prospects. In the biscuit trade, for example, as in the worsted and other trades, a boy had but scanty opportunities of entering other branches of his occupation, and large numbers joined the ranks of the unemployed.[1] The returns of Distress Committees corroborated the opinion universally held by investigators and by workers amongst boys, that a noticeable number of the unemployed had started life in some form or other of unskilled labour. They were, in fact, manufactured into unemployables. This view received official confirmation in the Poor Law Report of 1909. It has been so frequently quoted that it is unnecessary to give more than the shortest extract here. The Majority Commissioners state that " the results of the large employment of boys in occupations which offer no opportunity of promotion to employment as men are disastrous. The boy, thrown out at 16, 17, 18, or 20 years of age, drifts into the low-skilled labour market or the army of unemployables."[2] The Commissioners who signed the Minority Report were even more emphatic as to the evils of much juvenile labour. " There is no subject," they declare, " as to which we have received so much and such conclusive evidence as upon the extent to which thousands of boys, from lack of any sort of training for industrial occupations, grow up, almost inevitably, so as to become chronically unemployed or under employed, and presently to recruit the ranks of the unemployable. In Glasgow nearly 20 per cent. of the labourers in distress are under twenty-five, and half of them are under thirty-five. The registers of Distress Committees all over the country not only reveal the startling fact that something like 15 per cent. of the men in distress are under twenty-five, and that nearly one-third of the whole are under thirty, but also that an alarmingly large proportion of those young men are already ' chronic cases '—in fact, are unemployables. ' Most of us,' formally reports the York Distress Committee, ' are inclined to regard the existence of a large class of irregular

[1] Jackson's Report, p. 12.
[2] Poor Law Commission Report, 1909, vol. i. p. 407.

and casual workmen and the presence of a number of unemployables as a necessary condition of modern life. Our registers, however, show one avenue by which men come into these classes, and suggest how it might be closed. There are youths under twenty-one classified as "irregular" and as "been regular." The "irregular" ones must always infallibly spend their whole lives as irregular workers. Many of them are the sons of the poorest class of workmen, but a few are youths whose parents have done their best for them, but who have not stuck to work. Those who have "been regular" have generally started life as errand boys or in some position where a boy can earn good money, but which does not offer the means of learning any trade that will serve him through life.' "[1]

The typical example of the awakening of public opinion is to be found in connection with the employment of boy messengers in the Post Office, work which was frequently of the "blind alley" and parasitic species of labour, since in the case of a large number of boys it led to no permanent employment. In 1891 the closing of sorterships to London messengers prevented their absorption into the adult ranks of the Post Office, and by way of a palliative it was decided that boys over sixteen should be retained in the service only if there was a likelihood amounting almost to a certainty of their being sufficient vacancies for them as adults.[2] It was thought that at sixteen a boy was still young enough to take up skilled or other high-grade work which required a training. In 1897 the Government decided that half the vacancies for postmen and porters should be reserved for ex-soldiers and ex-sailors.[3] Any such reservation, of course,

[1] Poor Law Commission, Minority Report, p. 617 (Reprints of Cd. 4499 (1909), vol. iii).

[2] First Report of Standing Committee, 1911, p. 5.

[3] Report of Royal Commission on the Poor Laws, Appendix, vol xx. Jackson's Report on Boy Labour, 1909 (Cd. 4632), p. 70. *Cf.* p. 219.

First Report of Standing Committee on Boy Labour in Post Office, 1911 (Cd. 5504), p. 3.

Jackson's Report, Mem. from the General Post Office: "No doubt the decision was come to by the Government of 1897—on national grounds, and Mr. Buxton is not prepared to dispute it. But in justice to the Post Office he is bound to point out that the decision was not his nor that of any of his predecessors."

increased the difficulty of providing for the boys, but the Boer War postponed the reduction in the number of posts available for them, and it was not until about 1902 that the effect of this decision upon their fortunes became apparent.[1] Then, for no fault of their own, but because there was no opportunity for promoting them, a large proportion [2] of the boys who entered the service were dismissed from the Post Office, just as their contemporaries were from bottle-washing or tea-packing businesses, without having acquired any skill by which they could earn their living as adults, and frequently at an age above that at which it was customary to receive boys in the skilled trades. Mr. Jackson's inquiries led to the conclusion that boys who left the Post Office at sixteen had a difficulty in finding employment, and that they were often handicapped by their age in learning a trade ; and the information more recently obtained from the officers of the Labour Exchanges bears out this view.[3] From about 1905 the Government began to show a more serious appreciation of its responsibilities as a large employer of boy labour. Attempts were made to recommend the boys who could not be retained in the service to likely employers, and in 1907 employment registers were established at the head post-office in every district for the purpose of assisting boys of good character to obtain work.[4] In 1909 it was said by the Postmaster-General that the results were very satisfactory.[5] For all the boys, whether they would later be

[1] Report of the Standing Committee, 1911, p. 3.

[2] The total number of boys taken into the service of the Post Office in London, in the capacity of messengers, from 1901 to 1906 (inclusive) was 9,840. The total number discharged in London in the same period was 3,775, of whom 1,957 were unsatisfactory, and 1,818 were quite satisfactory but there was no chance of promoting them. Jackson's Report, p. 65. *Cf.* Report Standing Committee, p. 3.

[3] See Jackson's Report, pp. 71, *seq.*

Report Standing Committee, 1911, p. 13. Fifty-six of the officers of Labour Exchanges consulted state that, in their opinion, service as messenger hinders, and sixteen that it helps the boys in an industrial career. The general opinion is that sixteen is too late an age for apprenticeship.

[4] Report Standing Committee, 1911, p. 3.

Jackson's Report, 1909, pp. 66, 70.

[5] Ibid., p. 70. Memorandum supplied by the Postmaster-General.

absorbed into adult departments or not, classes for drill were arranged at nearly every office at which twenty messengers were employed, and institutes were established at which classes were given suited to preparing the lads for examination for the superior posts and for generally improving their education, while facilities were provided for games and sports, as in boys' clubs.[1]   Nevertheless, telegraph messenger work was mainly " blind alley " work.   The Post Office openly took steps to impress this fact on applicants and their parents ; every boy before his engagement was given a form which he and his parent or guardian were required to sign, in which it was stated that the employment was temporary and that work as a messenger until sixteen did not entitle a boy to promotion.[2]   However much credit, therefore, might be given to the Post Office for the excellent organisation of its juvenile labour and for the consideration shown to the boys, the Post Office remained one of the prominent industries carried on by means of an excess of cheap boy labour.   It was not until 1911 that the system was so reorganised as to enable the Post Office to hold out hopes of absorbing into the adult classes of its service the great majority of the boys employed.[3]   The discharge of telegraph messengers in most towns in the country had one advantageous result, that it advertised very widely the evils of ' blind alley " work.   Cases of boys whose services had been utilised by the State for a year or two and who had then drifted helplessly into casual work formed a striking object-lesson.   It was evident that the point of view which allowed the use of boys as mere cheap labour did not ensure the production of satisfactory adult citizens.

We have seen the extent and the nature of the evils of juvenile labour with which the reformers of the twentieth

---

[1] Jackson's Report, 1909, p. 66.

Ibid., pp. 70, 221.

Supported by a Government grant of £2,000 per annum and by the subscriptions of the boys and the efforts of members of the Post Office.

[2] Ibid., p. 70.

[3] First Report of the Standing Committee on Boy Labour in the Post Office, 1911 (Cd. 5504).

century had to deal, and how it was that these evils came so prominently before the public. We have also seen how the old idea, well understood in the Middle Ages, that a boy's work should be a fitting prelude to his work as an adult, gained new strength. The public began to understand that a boy must not be permitted to play at being a cheap man. His years of adolescence must be made educative.

We have seen, too, from the evidence collected by various Committees and the Poor Law Commission that young people entering the labour market have two main difficulties to face. In the first place, much of the work offered to them is almost wholly uneducative and some of it actually demoralising. Secondly, owing to the lack of information as to industrial conditions and to the lack of opportunities for choice of employment, there is an unnecessary number of industrial " misfits " with their accompanying injury to character and waste of potentialities.

We have now to consider the various attempts which have been and are being made to obviate these difficulties and to provide remedies for the evils of juvenile labour. It is clear that these remedies must provide, first, for the general training and development of character and intelligence; secondly, for the better organisation of the juvenile labour market; and, thirdly, for the total withdrawal of some young persons from certain kinds of labour and the further regulation of employment out of school hours. In accordance with their effectiveness in providing these results, the value of different reforms must be judged.

In the forefront of the ranks of the reformers must be placed those numerous private workers amongst wage-earning boys and girls who laid the foundations upon which all current work is being built. During the last years of the nineteenth century and the first decade of the twentieth various movements were promoted, a common object of all being to assist young people through the difficult years of adolescence. Boys' and girls' clubs, boys' brigades,[1]

[1] See Keeling, The Labour Exchange in Relation to Boy and Girl Labour, p. 20. Continuation Schools in England and Elsewhere, ed. Sadler, p. 467.

the Apprenticeship and Skilled Employment Committees, and similar societies, classes for continued education, Children's Care Committees, and societies of the nature of registry offices,[1] were started or developed in London and some of the larger provincial towns.   Their promoters were not attempting to provide panaceas for the ills of juvenile labour, but with their efforts to help individual cases and to win the support of the public for their special remedies, the twentieth century reform movement may fairly be said to have begun. It must be regarded not as an isolated development, but rather as a second phase in that movement for reform which, began in a small way at the close of the eighteenth century and, gaining in strength in the nineteenth, was directed against the glaring abuses of factory employment.   It was their removal which cleared the field for the attack upon the more intricate evil, uneducative juvenile work, and thus the attempt to organise adolescent labour upon sound lines and the development of public opinion on the subject evolved naturally and in due course from the earlier agitation for reasonable hours of work and humane treatment.

The value of the philanthropic efforts of this second stage lay not only in the benefits conferred upon individual boys or girls, but even more in providing a mass of information relating to juvenile labour of which Committees took full advantage, and which has prepared the ground for State action.

One of the most noteworthy of the movements promoted by Social workers was the revival of apprenticeship.   Young people who learnt their trades as apprentices received a comparatively good training and were under control and direction until manhood.   To many the revival of this system seemed to provide the most direct method of securing for a child a complete industrial training and for preserving it from the

---

[1]   *E.g.*, Metropolitan Association for Befriending Young Servants (started in 1874, and in 1910 had 29 branches) ; Post Office Employment Registers (Jackson, Report on Boy Labour, p. 70 ; Sheffield Education Committee Labour Bureau (Keeling, p. 24) ; Finchley Employment Register (ibid., p. 28), &c. See Keeling, *op. cit.*, pp. 17, 30.

M. Frere, Children's Care Committees, pp. 37, 39.

"blind alley." The chief practical result of this opinion was the establishment of societies such as the Apprenticeship and Skilled Employment Committees, one of the aims of which was to encourage apprenticeship.[1] Though the number of children placed out by the Committees and similar societies is exceedingly small compared to the number who each year leave school, the work has been of real value, because the information collected has thrown light on the position of juvenile workers and their chances of after-employment in various trades, while it has helped to dispel the ignorance and indifference of parents as to the true interests of their children, and has called the attention of the public to the need of reviving if not apprenticeship, at any rate that sense of responsibility for the juvenile "hand" which in earlier days characterised the attitude of the public, parent, and employer towards the child. The Committees have shown a wise restraint in not attempting to stimulate apprenticeship in trades to which it was no longer suited. Still, the more general revival of apprenticeship has its supporters amongst those who are not as closely acquainted with the practical facts, and not a little has appeared in its favour in the daily Press.

The systematic enforcement of apprenticeship would, how-ever, be impossible under modern industrial conditions. It is true that the Elizabethan apprenticeship system was of the greatest value both to individual children and to the nation. It is true, also, that apprenticeship exists to-day in various trades in many places, and serves a useful purpose. This is

---

[1] The objects of the Committees are to promote the entry of young people into good trades and occupations which promise after-employment, and to give advice, when desired, to parents. They "collect industrial information, find suitable openings for boys and girls who apply to them for help, and make terms between the employer and the apprentice or 'learner,' with a view to securing fair con-ditions to the employee, and satisfactory workers to the employer." (Report of the Association, 1909, p. 3.)

The Jewish Board of Guardians had worked upon these lines some time before the first Committee was formed, the West Southwark, in 1897. Since that date, other Committees have been formed in London and in Liverpool, Cam-bridge, and a few other provincial cities. In 1905, most of the local societies were united into the Apprenticeship and Skilled Employment Association with a Central Office in London.

chiefly so in those skilled trades which require considerable training, as in trades carried on in good class shops in which bespoke work is undertaken, or in which high-class goods are manufactured. In such trades apprenticeship exists naturally, being in accordance both with the conditions of the work and with its needs. The workrooms are not so large as to make it impossible to teach apprentices; the success of the business depends more on the quality of the goods than on the speed with which they can be produced; and since there is no need for racing with machinery or against other manufacturers working upon other lines, it is possible for foremen to spare time to teach their juniors; while they must be so taught since the trade cannot prosper unless it ensures its supply of good workmen. Boys are sometimes apprenticed in the country, where, of course, there is neither that pressure of competition nor the heaviness of working expenses which drive the town employer to the specialisation of processes and the apprentice out of the workshop. Moreover, apprenticeship also exists either generally or locally in a limited number of large trades, organised upon modern lines.[1]   Yet whatever

[1] Often trades in which apprenticeship is upheld by the Trade Unions. It is difficult to say whether in such trades apprenticeship is on the increase or decrease; for though some trades in many parts of the country are staunch to it, in others it is employed in a few localities only and is not enforced by the Unions in the same trade in another district. One point, however, is clear : there is a general tendency for apprenticeship to be dispensed with as the processes are subdivided. In the Masons' Union in Lancashire and Cheshire apprenticeship was compulsory until quite recent years, when the introduction of new and rival processes changed the conditions of the trade, and in 1908 the rule, it was said, was no longer enforced. (Letter 6. Information as to apprenticeship among Trade Unions is to be gathered from the Report of the Labour Commission, 1893, and from the rules of individual Unions. The statements here as to the condition of apprenticeship in the trades referred to are based upon letters kindly written to O. J. Dunlop by Union secretaries in reply to definite questions in 1908.) Similarly, in the butchers' trade the need for apprenticeship has latterly almost disappeared. With the increasing facilities for transport, the skill required for the trade has greatly decreased; a large quantity of meat is brought over frozen, or live cattle are imported and killed at the port of debarkation. Butchers' work throughout the country is, therefore, very largely distributory only, and many men enter it who have no training and who as a rule do not require it, though it was stated that they are incompetent if they are required to do any slaughtering. (Letter 47.) In the French Polishers' Union apprenticeship has almost completely died

its value may be in these particular cases, its universal revival would be neither possible nor desirable. The subdivision of trades and the specialisation of processes, which are two of the main characteristics of modern industrial development, have rendered employers unwilling to take apprentices and have made apprenticeship less valuable to the boy. Masters do not care to bind themselves to keep a lad who may be unsuited to the work, or to pledge themselves to give an all-round training when their business does not require all-round men and can be more cheaply conducted by allotting different processes to the different "hands." In a vast number of trades to carry on work by apprentices is an expensive method of production.[1] This objection to apprenticeship has been especially felt in recent years in London and other large cities in which land is too valuable and rents too high to have in the shop boys who cannot contribute to the profit-making. As to the boys, even though they may be nominally apprenticed, it is extremely difficult for them to acquire that complete knowledge of their trade which apprenticeship implies. Different processes are frequently carried on in different workshops, and it is not merely because it pays the employer to keep the boy at one job that the latter becomes specialised at an early age, with the result that if for any reason he is thrown out of his job during manhood, he finds it very difficult to obtain another. He is skilled in the use of a few tools or

out, good all-round workmen not being really required, owing to the great specialisation in the trade. (Letter 44.) In the portmanteau trade the change was in 1908 said to be taking place. The Portmanteau Makers' Union had a rule making apprenticeship compulsory, but the trade had begun to be subdivided, and whereas one man had been used to make the whole trunk, the work was beginning to be done in a number of different workshops, and apprenticeship was therefore becoming less and less a convenient method of training. (Letter 39.) Nor is it likely that apprenticeship can for long exist in trades such as the Britannia Metal trade, where, though apprenticeship rules go so far as to require the boy to be bound by indenture, there is, it is said, no real training, and he picks up his knowledge as best he can. On the other hand, new industries may develop which require a long training, and in which, therefore, apprenticeship will be employed. Apprentices are very frequently taken in the comparatively new trade of motor carriage building. (Letter 48.)

For apprenticeship law to-day see E. A. Meyer, Apprenticeship Law (1910).

[1] Cf. Adler and Tawney, Boy and Girl Labour, p. 5.

in one process but unskilled in all else. Modern apprenticeship is also inferior to the old in that it altogether lacks that
important feature of the Elizabethan, the general training and
supervision given by the master to the lad who dwelt under
his own roof. Indoor apprenticeship is now rare, and the
modern apprentice whose life is spent between the large
workshop of an often absentee master and his home, where
he demands the independence of a wage-earner, is generally
under the control of neither.[1]

There is yet a further reason, fully as important as any of
these already dealt with, why apprenticeship cannot be

---

[1] The unsuitability of apprenticeship to trades generally and the infeasibility of
reviving it is well summarised in the report of a committee of the London
County Council, appointed in 1906 for the purpose of ascertaining whether the
old-fashioned method of learning a trade could be revived. The Committee declared that "in London the old system of indentured apprenticeship has for many
years been falling into decay. In the majority of industries it has almost entirely
disappeared; in others it is occasionally found existing in a haphazard and highly
unsatisfactory manner; while in only a few trades can it be said to be the
commonly recognised way of entering the profession. Many causes have contributed to this result. The subdivision of labour, the introduction of machinery,
the development of mammoth factories, and the high rates and consequent limited
workshop space in London, have all tended to render the old practice either
undesirable or impracticable. The large employer does not care to be troubled
with boys if he is compelled to teach them the whole trade. He prefers to divide
his processes into men's work and boys' work, and to keep each grade to its
allotted routine. The boy has no desire to bind himself for a long period of years
to serve for low wages when he can easily earn more money in other ways; while
his father is unwilling to pay a premium when he can obtain no guarantee that his
son will be properly taught the trade. All these are forces inseparably connected
with the conditions of modern industry and the aggregation of workshops in a
large town; it would, therefore, seem time and money wasted to attempt to
revive an obsolescent system. The various apprenticeship charities have found it
no easy task to expend their income. Many of them have applied for new
schemes which allow money, originally bequeathed for the encouragement of
apprenticeship, to be applied to educational and other purposes."[*]

---

[*] The Apprenticeship Question, Bray [L.C.C.], 1906, p. 1. *Cf.* Keeling, The
Labour Exchange in relation to Boy and Girl Labour, p. 5.

Various Trade Union secretaries express it as their opinion that apprenticeship has dropped out of use through the dislike of the boys to be bound. But it is
probably more often the unwillingness of employers to incur the trouble of training
apprentices, apart from any question of whether apprenticeship is still useful, which
leads to its disappearance. *Cf.* Urwick, Studies of Boy Life, p. 115.

accepted as a solution of the problem of juvenile labour. During the last half-century there has been an ever-increasing demand for labour of a low-skilled order, a demand created by the application of machinery to trades which in former days were skilled handicrafts, and by the development of industries which are practically new, namely, all those occupations connected with the transport of persons, goods, and messages, which have sprung up with the enormous growth of city life and the development of railways, and are now so interwoven with the comfort and convenience of the public that the demand for services of this description is not likely to decline. It is possible, of course, that better organisation of labour in industries of this nature and in factory work will be forced upon employers, as has been the case in the Post Office. But even though a certain amount of low-skilled labour might be dispensed with, there would still be an enormous demand for it. This is an industrial requirement which must be met, and it would be worse than useless to attempt to detract young people from the low-grade labour for which there is a demand into the skilled trades which can support only a limited number of workmen. A large number of youths therefore before or upon leaving school will enter low-skilled work. What they require is not technique nor special skill, but in the first place protection from an evil to which the apprentice in a skilled trade is not exposed, but which is inherent in their work, namely, its lack of educative qualities ; secondly, a training which will render them competent for the work they have to do. The aim should be to make them skilled low-skilled workmen. This can be achieved only by developing their powers of adaptability and initiative, and by promoting their physical well-being. While the capital of the high-skilled workman lies in his special skill, the low-skilled workman has nothing but general qualities of this kind to secure for him a permanent economic value, and it is therefore an arguable paradox that the State should take even more pains to secure the developed intelligence of its low-skilled workers

than of its high-skilled. The cultivation of such qualities is
not the function of apprenticeship, nor yet of Polytechnics,
Technical Classes[1] and Trades Schools.[2] These classes and
schools are performing an increasingly valuable work, and it
is to be hoped that as the advantages of education become
more generally recognised their activity will grow. But
regarded as a remedy for the general evil of uneducative
work, they are open to the same criticism as apprenticeship.
Their work is to promote special skill not the adaptability
and general intelligence required by the low-skilled worker.
The Trade Schools, it is true, not only provide practical and
theoretical teaching, but also continue the general education
of their pupils, who at the end of their course, generally two
years, can command really good situations as skilled workers.
But those who most believe in the advantages of such
Schools realise that their value lies in keeping up the
number of high-grade workmen rather than in being a
means of dealing with the mass of working-class children.[3]
The Trades Schools, in fact, no less than apprenticeship and
technical classes, can touch only the comparatively few, and
however excellent their work, it cannot be extended in-
definitely, since they would be turning out a product for
which there is only a limited demand.

The general training which is necessary must be attained
by other methods. The first essential is the raising of the
school age. From an educational standpoint this has long
been recognised as necessary. From a purely financial point

[1] Which since the Technical Instruction Act of 1889 have been established in
all the important centres of industry. For their history and account of their work,
see Report of The Consultative Committee on Continuation Schools, 1909,
pp. 77, 82, 561.
   Continuation Schools, ed. Sadler, p. 706 *seq.*
[2] Started in London in 1905.
   For account of, see Continuation Schools, Sadler, p. 441 *seq.*
   Report of the Consultative Committee, p. 105.
[3] A certain number of scholarships are given both in Trades Schools and in
Technical Schools and Polytechnics; those who do not win them have to pay
small but to that class not insignificant fees. The nation already is bearing a
large part of the cost. Trade Schools in London cost at least £7 per head for
maintenance (Report of Consultative Committee 1909, p. 108).

of view the present practice of cutting the child adrift from
school influences at the age of 13 or 14 is grossly wasteful,
for if education ceases at that age, the previous years of
training are largely thrown away. From the industrial
standpoint to cast a child of 14 on to the labour market is to
invite his employment in temporary and uneducative work.
Lads are not usually taken as apprentices until 15 or 16
years old, while in a large number of trades in which the
work demands physical strength, no boy under 16 can be
employed. Thus so long as there are over half a million
children between the ages of 14 and 15 attending no Day
School[1] and available, therefore, as cheap labour, it is
inevitable that numbers of them will be so used. It is on
this account that the raising of the school age is the most
fundamental of the methods of dealing with the evils of
adolescent labour.

It is not, however, a sufficient remedy in itself. Even were
it enacted that elementary education should continue to the
age of 15, there still would remain a period during which the
State should maintain an educational control over its youth.
After 15, the boy or girl is still in the stage of active development both of body and of character, and is still liable to the
injury resulting from an excessive amount of industrial
labour which gives insufficient opportunites for development.

The system which would perhaps be found best to meet
the requirements of this period is an adolescent part-time
system. By this means a bridge would be provided to
lessen the dangers of the crossing from school to workshop. The defects of the half-time system already referred
to lay not so much in the principle of the scheme as in the
fact that it was applied while the child was too young, and
that the educative value both of the factory life and of the
school teaching was largely lost. It must be remembered
that no form of industrial activity, however low skilled it
may be, is wholly lacking in educative qualities. Its danger
to a youth lies chiefly in the fact that its value for development is soon exhausted and that he or she is kept at it too

[1] Report of the Consultative Committee, 1909, p. 29.

long. There is abundant evidence to show, what common
sense would tell us, that provided a youth spends part of
the day in continuing his general education, a part can be
spent with profit in any form of industry that is not definitely
injurious.   From the nature of the case, no definite proportion can be laid down as to the amount of time to be
spent respectively in the school and in the industry.
Theoretically, no doubt, it should be adjusted differently in
each particular case. The best practical system, however,
by which the principle can be at present applied is that of
compulsory Continuation Classes.

There is at the present day a fairly well-developed system
of evening Continuation Classes supported by Government
grants,[1] and it is noteworthy that of late years this method
of education has become increasingly popular and that the
number of pupils has risen.   This is due in part to the
systematic efforts made by various Local Education
Authorities to interest parents, children, and employers in
these schools.[2] At Halifax there is close co-operation
between the Day School authorities and the Technical
College. Every Saturday a list of the scholars who have
left the Day Schools during the current week is forwarded
by the chief attendance officer to the principal of the College,
and on the following Monday a clerk from the College visits
each boy and persuades him and his parents to continue his
education. If the first visit fails, others are made ; in the
last resort, the boy is visited half an hour before the classes
begin, and is if possible persuaded to accompany the clerk
to the College.[3]   Halifax, perhaps, affords the best example of
organised attempts to encourage continued education, but in
many localities efforts of a similar nature have been made.[4]
Their number, however, must not be over-estimated ; many
Local Authorities, handicapped perhaps by the hostility of
their ratepayers, have shown themselves apathetic to the
foundation of Continuation Classes.[5]

[1] Report of the Consultative Committee (Cd. 4757), pp. 74–79.
[2] Ibid., p. 85.   [3] Ibid., p. 87.
[4] Ibid., pp. 88–95.   [5] Ibid., pp. 126–7.

Attendance at Continuation Schools has also been encouraged by some employers. It is said that their number has increased during the last few years, but on the whole interest in the matter is confined to those in the higher and more scientific trades, such as engineering, and the great majority of employers "are still indifferent to the educational needs of young persons in their employment." [1] Amongst the rank and file of industry, feeling in favour of education generally has for some years been on the increase. [2] Yet it has to be admitted that, in spite of the efforts of various Education Authorities and the growing interest of the working class and of employers, the number of young people who take advantage of this form of education is not yet large. The Consultative Committee reporting in 1909 upon the question of attendance at Continuation Classes referred to them in 1907, estimated the number attending Evening Schools and classes under Government inspection in England and Wales in the years 1906–1907 at only 21·3 per thousand of the total estimated population. [3] "Exact figures," they state, "are not procurable, and in any case it should be remembered that an undefined number of evening and other classes are not enumerated in official records ; but the Committee have made a calculation which they believe to be approximately correct. They estimate that there are rather over 2,000,000 boys and girls in England and Wales between 14 and 17, and that 75 per cent. of them are receiving, on week-days at any rate, no school education." [4] Comparatively speaking, therefore, the number attending Continuation Classes is small. And even of this small number the majority are not those who most require continued education. We have noticed that the greater number of employers who encourage attendance belong to the scientific trades, a fact which suggests that it is the young people employed by them who form a large proportion of the scholars at Continuation Schools. The teach-

---

[1] Report of the Consultative Committee (Cd. 4757), p. 96.
[2] Ibid., p. 139.   [3] Ibid., p. 108.
[4] Ibid., p. 218.

ing there supplied may be of the greatest value to them in
their careers, and it is natural that they should take
advantage of it. But it is, nationally, far less important
that attendance should be made by apprentices and learners
in good trades than that boys and girls in the worst trades
should continue their education. Unfortunately, work of
the latter type offers so little chance of promotion that there
is no special inducement to the young people engaged in it
to seek further schooling while the hours of work preclude
many from the possibility of attendance. Railway van
boys, boys on lorries and vans attached to big warehouses ;
boys in shipping offices and in counting-houses where
accounts have to be made up after the shops are
closed ; boys in the provision trade, errand boys in small
shops, girls in dressmaking shops during seasonal pressure,
are but a few of those who are so situated. All, " though not
necessarily overworked, are employed at times which clash
with the hours of Continuation Classes." [1]   To their number
must be added a class as important as that of any of these
young wage-earners—the girls who are drudges and helps at
home. It would seem a small matter for parents to allow
the girls employed in unremunerated work at home to
attend classes for a few hours a week ; it would be more
to expect them to sacrifice entirely or in part the wages of
their children employed on vans or in other occupations,
even though (as has been shown by investigators) these
young workers are not by any means all drawn from the
poorest homes. Unfortunately, however, it is still the
exception to find parents or children ready to make even
a small sacrifice for the sake of education, while those who
might be ready to accept less wages for shorter hours dare
not ask employers for the time off since the latter can so
easily obtain the services of other children who would not

[1] Report of the Consultative Committee (Cd. 4757), p. 132.

We are informed that all members of the clubs connected with the Oxford
and Bermondsey Settlement were recently required to attend Continuation
Classes. This requirement was willingly complied with, but the system endured
for a short time only, as frequent or occasional overtime work rendered attendance at the classes useless.

trouble them with any such request. The system of voluntary Continuation Classes is therefore no solution for the problem of uneducative work. The fact that prolonged education is one of the very few possible methods of mitigating the evil makes the failure of our present system the more serious, and justifies the conclusion that attendance should be made compulsory. Such continued education for all children, or for all who are not engaged as apprentices or under some definite agreement in educative work, would constitute a radical remedy. All young people alike would be assisted, not merely the fortunate few. Those parents who believe in better education, but who under the voluntary system dare not allow their neighbours' boys and girls to get a start in the labour market, would no longer be penalised by losing opportunities of employment for their own children.

The financing of such classes and the provision of accommodation and teachers would be difficulties in the way of securing general continued education, but the chief difficulty is the industrial. If the young employee receives his education at hours when he is most receptive and when, therefore, the State will get the best return for its expenditure, some degree of industrial disorganisation and inconvenience to the employer can hardly be avoided. Continuation Classes have hitherto been arranged to suit trade interests, and have been held after work hours; but there is a general, though not unanimous, opinion amongst teachers and educationists that many of those who voluntarily attend are too tired to profit by their teaching, and the proportion would of course be higher still under a compulsory system.[1] There can be no doubt that late evening work would never now be advocated. The hours of schooling must therefore, to some extent, encroach on the hours of labour. The Consultative Committee would apparently consent to classes between the hours of 7 and 9 p.m.[2] Even these hours will be held by many to be too

[1] Report of the Consultative Committee (Cd. 4757), pp. 170–3.
[2] Ibid., p. 174.

late. Leaving out of account the question of whether or no
it is wise to compel a youth to attend school at those hours
in the evening after a long day's work, there still remains the
indisputable fact that it would be to a large extent a waste of
the nation's money to provide education at these hours and
under this condition. It is interesting to notice that German
opinion is increasingly unfavourable to the plan of holding
Continuation Classes in the later hours of the evening. In
Bavaria, the State law forbids any Continuation Classes to be
held after 7 p.m.,[1] and this is now about to become the law in
Würtemburg also.[2] In this country evening classes have
unfortunately a traditional authority. Our Continuation
Schools trace a direct descent from the Night Schools founded
by private philanthropists in the early eighteenth century,
when the foundation even of a Night School was a great step
forward.[3] From 1851, when grants were first made to these
still private schools,[4] the system has been developed and the
State has more and more taken control; but though the
curriculum has been frequently altered, the system of late
evening classes, adopted of necessity in the eighteenth
century, has been accepted and handed down unchanged.
The hour at which Continuation Classes now are held depends
perhaps as much upon tradition uncritically accepted by the
public and clung to by conservative employers as upon any
well-grounded conviction that an earlier hour would be
industrially injurious.

That the need for raising the school age and for extend-
ing the system of Continuation Classes is urgent is shown by
the fact that a British Government has this year introduced
a Bill dealing with these subjects. Mr. Runciman's Education (School and Continuation Class Attendance) Bill of
1911 is an important measure which would do much to
lessen the evils of juvenile employment. In this Bill it

[1] Report of the Consultative Committee (Cd. 4757), p. 148.
[2] Ibid. The law comes into full force in 1912.
[3] The first organised effort to establish Evening Schools was in 1711,
Ibid., p. 69.
[4] Ibid., p. 74.

is proposed to raise the school leaving age to 14. This age is to be the normal statutory minimum, and there is only one set of conditions upon which a child may leave at a lesser age. If the Local Education Authority has adopted bye-laws compelling attendance at Continuation Classes up to the age of 16, and if a child is over 13 and is entering an employment likely to lead to permanent employment and to afford useful training, the child may be granted exemption from attendance at an elementary school. Further, Local Education Authorities are to be empowered to make bye-laws raising the school age from 14 to 15.

Even if this measure falls short of what many persons desire, it is impossible not to recognise the reality and magnitude of the advance foreshadowed by this Bill. About 47,000 part-time scholars and 211,000 children wholly exempted from school attendance[1] would either be withdrawn from day industry or compelled to attend Continuation Classes. Moreover (assuming in a given area an equality in the number of persons of the ages of 13, 14, and 15 respectively), for every one of the above children not withdrawn from day industry, there would be two others compelled to attend Continuation Classes.

While it would be a mistake to underrate its value, the Bill presumably would not be regarded as a final measure even by its promoters. Those who desire to see the school age raised to 15, and the system of Continuation Classes compulsory, will have reasonable doubts of the value of the permissive clauses that leave these points to the discretion of the Local Education Authority.

In proportion as the State seeks to exercise control over the later years of youth, so it becomes increasingly necessary that the conditions of control should be laid down by a national rather than by a local authority. All Acts regulating attendance at school have industrial effects. As the age of the scholar with whom such Acts deal is raised, the industrial effects become more important. As a form of

[1] (Taking the figures of 1907.) Report on Partial Exemption, 1909, p. 3. Report of Consultative Committee, 1909, p. 22.

cheap labour the youth of 14 is of far greater value than the child of 12, and if Local Authorities have shown a reluctance to prevent the employment of the latter, it is not to be expected that they will readily deprive local industries of the former.   To say this does not necessarily imply a criticism of the public spirit of Local Authorities.   It is a mere recognition of the inherent difficulties that face Local Authorities when they are called upon to decide questions involving the organisation of juvenile labour within their area.   The fundamental difficulty lies in the fact that an Education Area has no industrial significance.   Where, as is commonly the case, an industry is conducted in a number of different Education Areas, a Local Authority will naturally hesitate to impose within its own area restrictions upon the use of cheap labour which its commercial rivals may continue to utilise.   Even if a number of neighbouring Authorities agreed upon a common policy, they might still have to fear the competition of a distant district comprising a wholly separate group.   Moreover, a progressive Authority may suffer a very real injustice in the matter of rates.   It is possible, for example, that firms living just outside a progressive area may enjoy all the benefits resulting from the employment of workmen endowed with a more expensive education, without contributing a penny to the cost.

A significant example of the reluctance of Local Authorities to take full advantage of permissive powers where industrial questions are concerned may be found in the case of the Employment of Children Act, 1903. By that Act Local Authorities were enabled to make bye-laws setting limits to the hours of child labour and even prohibiting the employment of children in any specified occupation.   Only a very small minority of local Authorities had made such bye-laws by 1907, as the Consultative Committee noticed with regret.   They added[1] that they " earnestly trust that in the interests of school children the provisions of the Act of 1903 may become more generally adopted.   In a great many cases such children are still

[1] Report, p. 50.

grievously overworked out of school hours, and in consequence many of them are too tired to profit by their
instruction in the Day School, and so rendered unfit for
further education later on." Apparently only some eleven
Local Authorities in England and Wales have made such
bye-laws since the above was written, in spite of the fact
that considerable improvement in the conditions of child
labour has resulted in many localities where bye-laws have
been adopted.[1]

A further reason why Local Education Authorities are
unlikely to show enthusiasm in availing themselves of powers
to educate elder children and withdraw them from the labour
market is the financial difficulty. There is undoubtedly a
growing and widespread dissatisfaction at the weight of
education rates. It is unnecessary to elaborate this point.
But taken in conjunction with other causes of reluctance of
Local Education Authorities to adopt permissive powers, it
shows the natural lines upon which reform should progress.
If effective action is desired the State will increasingly have
to lay down definite obligations and at the same time bear
a larger proportion of the financial burden these obligations
impose.

The proposals of Mr. Runciman's Bill are subject to a
different line of criticism, which, however, is also based upon
the fact that the Bill deals with children at more distinctively
industrial ages. It is important to recognise that at such
ages a new policy of exemptions will be required. The
moment when a child should leave school is not a matter to
be decided in accordance with the number of years he or she
has spent in the world, still less in accordance with the area
in which he or she lives. When once a suitable minimum
age, applicable practically to all children, has been reached,
the question how much longer a given child should be
retained at school depends upon the child itself. The
higher, therefore, the leaving age is fixed, and the longer
the period of compulsory Continuation Classes endures, the
more essential becomes the granting of exemptions to indi-

[1] Hansard, Parliamentary Debates, H. C., vol. xxvii., 1911, p. 7.

vidual children. There is only one ground for keeping a
youth from the labour market and compelling him to remain
at school, namely, that his employment is a worse form of
education. In practice it is impossible to lay down a
universal rule by which the relative educative values of
school and industry may be accurately measured. The
factors in the sum are of infinite variety, varying indeed
with different trades, with different firms within a given
trade, and with different youths within a given firm. Not
only are the educative values of individual jobs wholly dissimilar in themselves, but they also are relative to the
youths engaged upon them. An occupation which will
develop the character and intelligence of one youth will
ruin another. Probably there are even men who have been
better educated as children in the perilous activity of street
trading than they would have been in the secure routine of
the school.

If, therefore, we are to avoid a cast-iron system which
will force all youths into the same ill-fitting mould, some
authority combining industrial and educational knowledge
will be required, able freely to grant to individuals about to
enter beneficial employment exemption from further attendance at school.

An organisation which gives promise of fulfilling that
particular function, amongst many others, and which is,
perhaps, the most hopeful feature of contemporary reform
relating to juvenile labour, is the organisation of Juvenile
Advisory Committees. One of the chief practical difficulties
in the way of reformers had been the entire lack of organisation in the juvenile labour market. The entry of boys and
girls into industrial life was a haphazard process depending
upon the caprice of parents, and even of fashions among
school companions, or upon such chances as the observation
of a notice of a vacancy displayed in a shop window. Many
individual workers among boys and girls, more especially
teachers and those in charge of clubs, had taken great pains
to advise and assist young people who came within their
influence. Such advice no doubt helped many children into

useful employment. But even those who were most successful in placing out children in this way were conscious of the
necessary limitations to their activity. Their clientèle of
employers was inevitably small and special, and, while they
were able to do well by the better class and more competent
of their youths, they were least able to assist those most in
need of assistance, the duller children whose ultimate destina-
tion would be the adult low-skilled labour market.

The institution of the National System of Labour
Exchanges in 1910 provided a new machinery for organising
juvenile labour. The dangers of the Labour Exchanges
were at once realised. It was rightly feared that unregulated use of Exchanges might make it all the easier for
employers to obtain youths as mere cheap labour. But it
was also recognised that machinery which centralised the
supply of such labour might so be controlled as to widen
enormously the influence of education authorities and those
interested in the welfare of the young throughout the entire
juvenile labour market. If the Exchanges fulfilled their
functions, those who had hitherto laboriously formed a connection with a few employers might find available to them a
large centralised market, where there would daily be stored
up fresh knowledge of industrial conditions, and from which
the whole field of industry could be surveyed. The size of
the market would enable a better adjustment of children to
jobs to be made. " Misfits " would be reduced in number.
The gaps between one job and the next would be lessened,
and the early habit of unemployment checked. Moreover,
the boy or girl could more easily be kept within touch,
continued education could be encouraged, and the foolish
throwing up of good employment minimised.

It is to secure such advantages as these that Juvenile
Advisory Committees are now in the process of formation
in connection with Labour Exchanges.[1] The Committees

---

[1] We refrain from entering into the controversy as to whether these Committees should be appointed by the Local Education Authority or by the Board
of Trade because we think the question is of minor importance. The essential
point is that the co-operation between the two should be thorough and complete.
On the whole we prefer the Board of Trade Committees which have been adopted

are composed of representatives of educational and industrial interests so as to bring the schools and the Exchanges into the closest co-operation. The exact method of action of these Committees varies in detail. The normal procedure is to obtain the child straight from school with whatever information as to character and qualifications, physical and mental, teachers can supply; to consider vacancies offered by employers; and to advise the child and its parents accordingly. When the child is placed, the Committee endeavour to keep in touch with it, either directly or through its employer, or through some organisation such as a Care Committee, Boys' or Girls' Club, Boys' Brigade, or like institution.

While it is too early to judge of the value of the work of such Committees, there is already evidence that the influence of a strong local body, carrying on a constant propaganda among parents, youths, and employers as to the necessity of educative employment, is producing a desirable effect.

We feel strongly that Juvenile Advisory Committees should be appointed without delay in connection with every Board of Trade Labour Exchange in the kingdom : not only for the sake of the work which they can perform at present, but also as providing machinery of which future legislation can take advantage, and which will enable such legislation to be administered with greater benefit to boys and girls as well as to industry.

The advocates of legislation which, whether by raising the school age, by compulsory Continuation Classes, or by direct prohibition of certain work out of school hours, will have the effect of withholding boys and girls from the labour market,

by a number of the more important towns, e.g., London, Bristol, Exeter, Nottingham, Leeds, Halifax, &c., partly on the ground that the Local Education Authority by obtaining a dominant position within the Exchange is in reality able to exercise a fuller measure of control. But we appreciate the excellent work done in Edinburgh, and the merits of the scheme recently adopted in Birmingham.

For discussion on the subject see Papers and Proceedings of the National Conference on the Prevention of Destitution, 1911 pp 238, 219, 253. Papers by R. D. Denman J. W. Peck, and Mrs. Ogilvie Gordon. Also Juvenile Labour Exchanges and After Care, by A. Greenwood.

cannot shut their eyes to the strength of the opposition they have to face. The interests both of employers and of parents will again be thought to be menaced as on similar occasions in the past. It is necessary, therefore, briefly to examine the nature of the objections that are raised from each of these points of view.

The objections raised by employers come under two heads. First, "the business won't stand" the payment of wages higher than those of a child. Secondly, the school child constitutes the only large source of supply of part-time labour, the labour that can be utilised daily for two or three hours only ; therefore it is essential to certain businesses, such as milk-selling.[1]

The extent to which the first objection is valid no doubt varies with particular trades and with particular firms. As a general argument, however, it carries but little weight nowadays, for the simple reason that it has been consistently and vehemently urged on every occasion when, by Factory Acts or otherwise, the State has found it necessary to inter-vene between capital and labour in the interest of the worker. The regular failure of the events to justify the dismal forebodings of the employers who oppose such reforms has brought their power of foresight into some discredit. Though it would not be justifiable to lay undue stress upon this answer to the objection, there is nevertheless a pre-sumption that, generally speaking, trades would be able to readjust themselves to new conditions as they have been able to do in the past. In so far as a business has only to fear the competition of similar businesses in the same country, a law which equally affects all these businesses will be equally harmless to all of them. In two classes of cases alone can hardship arise, namely, in those trades dependent for their sales on cheap production, and in those subject to the competition of cheaper labour abroad. There are abundant instances to show that here too the introduction of

---

[1] *Cf.* Report on the Bye-laws made by the London County Council under the Employment of Children Act, 1903, by Chester Jones (Cd. 2809), 1906, pp. 9, 24–28 ; and Report by S. O. Buckmaster (Cd. 5497), 1911, pp. 12–14.

machinery and improvement of organisation and processes of manufacture have enabled trades successfully to meet new conditions imposed by legislation. But even were this not so, even if in fact a trade, dependent upon cheap and injurious child labour, were threatened with extinction by the withdrawal of that labour, the State should have the courage to withdraw it. It is unnecessary to repeat the recognised economic arguments as to the injury to the nation of parasitic trades which exist only at the constant expense of the general well-being. Where such trades have been allowed to grow up the State is faced with a choice of evils. If there are no means of making the trade healthy and non-parasitic, it is the lesser of the two evils that it should die.

The use of child labour for part-time work, as, for instance, in the delivery of newspapers and milk, is no doubt convenient for such industries, and would be difficult to replace. The problem of part-time labour, in a community in which services performed in the work of distribution and locomotion are requiring an increasing proportion of the total supply of labour, is becoming increasingly difficult. The best method of dealing with it would provide a fruitful subject for a separate inquiry. It is possible, however, that with the development of Labour Exchanges it may become practicable for a single workman to serve several masters during the day, not only in similar work, as is now done, but even in wholly different kinds of low-skilled labour. It is useless to attempt to generalise on a question of organisation of labour which must differ so widely in different trades. But the difficulties caused by pressure of work at particular hours of the day are well known to many industries, and have been overcome without the use of child labour. There is no reason to suppose that milk-sellers and newsvendors and hairdressers will be less successful in this direction than other employers have been.

The most serious opposition to the curtailment of child labour is undoubtedly that which arises from reluctance to deprive working-class families of the income brought them by the wage-earning child. The position was exemplified very clearly by the Chairman of the Glasgow School Board in his evidence before the Street Trading Committee which reported in 1910. The Board had reason to believe "that something like 75 per cent. of the young children of school age—that is to say, between 12 and 14—are living in quite respectable houses and bringing their wages to their parents, and that they are not misspending the money. You will be told that the sole object of these children is to gain money so as to go to music-halls, and to buy cigarettes and sweets, and so on; and that there is no good end accomplished. As representing the School Board we cannot approve that statement. We believe that, particularly at a time like this, of want of employment, a great deal of suffering is being modified by the earnings of these children selling in the streets." [1] Mr. Cloete gives a special example of the beneficial use of such earnings: "By the time there are two or three of the elder boys at work the family can afford to accept lower wages for the younger ones, and put them to a better trade." [2]

A proper examination of this question would necessarily involve an excursion into the entire field of adult wages and family budgets. But whatever be the conclusions at which one arrives on this wide subject, the general answer to the "parentalists" is that the misuse of child labour is the most extravagant of the means of supplementing adult wages. There can be no more certain way to industrial ruin than to sacrifice the coming generation of industrial workers to the present and passing generation. A vicious circle is created from which it is hard to escape. The mis-development, or under-development, of a child's powers means that he or she in turn becomes an inefficient worker, and so perhaps economically incapable of earning a proper wage

[1] Report (Cd. 5229), 1910, p. 19.
[2] Ed. Urwick, Studies of Boy Life, p. 106; The Boy and his Work, J. G. Cloete.

Cf., too, Chester Jones's Report referred to above, pp. 8 and 9, in which he gives the hardship to parents as one of the reasons for recommending that a London County Council bye-law should not be confirmed.

as an adult, and therefore the more liable to dependence upon the subsidiary wages of children.

The "parentalist" may gain greater sympathy when urging the value of child labour to help a family to meet temporary and accidental misfortune. Here, too, however, the answer is similar. As the Street Trading (Majority) Report puts it [1]: "The cases of widows and others who are now too often economically dependent on child labour should be met, no longer by the sacrifice of the future to the present, but rather by more scientific and possibly more generous methods of public assistance." It may be observed, moreover, that, under modern legislation, the State is increasingly intervening to supply income to those incapacitated from earning it, and that the "parental" argument is, therefore, losing weight. Workmen's Compensation, Old Age Pensions, Sickness and Unemployment Insurance, all combine to lessen the practical need for the immature earnings of children. Further, should it be advisable to allow special licences in special cases, the Juvenile Advisory Committees set up in connection with Labour Exchanges should provide an authority competent to judge of the merits of individual cases, from both an educational and an industrial point of view.

While the advocates of reforms dealing with juvenile labour have less and less to fear the direct opposition of employers and parents, they render their campaign unnecessarily arduous by a lack of generalship and of unity of purpose.

In concluding this chapter we desire to urge strongly the creation of a harmonious policy which brings into a proportioned whole the many aspects under which this question of juvenile labour is viewed and treated. To this end much good may be done by the Juvenile Advisory Committees to which we have referred. One of the functions of the Committees in London is "to focus the existing scattered efforts of different organisations dealing with Juvenile Employment in the locality."

[1] Report (Cd. 5229), 1910. p. 5.

When diverse societies, organisations, and individuals interest themselves in a many-sided problem there is always a danger that some sides will receive undue attention to the detriment of others. It should be an aim of the Juvenile Advisory Committees to bring into proper relationship the industrial work of Teachers, of Trade Schools, of Apprenticeship Committees, and of Boys' Clubs, and to form themselves into centres around which such beneficial activity would be grouped. Only thus can waste of effort and overlapping be avoided.

But it is even more essential that Government Departments responsible for different aspects of the problem should work in far closer co-operation than at present. So long as different Departments legislate without the fullest collaboration and without a common policy, problems of juvenile labour cannot be properly treated. An Act meritorious from the point of view of the Board of Education may be injurious from the point of view of the Home Office. There is a significant sentence in the report of the 1901 Committee which illustrates this. " As the door," they say, " has been closed to the employment of children . . . during school hours, there has been a tendency towards their employment in other occupations before morning school, between school hours, in the evening, and on Saturdays and Sundays." [1] It is no doubt convenient that in certain aspects juvenile labour should be the concern of the Home Office, in others of the Board of Education, in others of the Board of Trade, or even of the Board of Agriculture. No doubt also the co-operation of Departments and of Ministers is sufficient to secure that the activity of one will not be seriously detrimental to the activity of another. But for a vigorous policy of reform more is needed than that.

We suggest that for the supervision of questions of juvenile labour a Standing Inter-Departmental Committee, consisting of representatives of the chief Departments interested therein, should be set up. The principle of setting up such

[1] Report of the Inter-Departmental Committee on Employment of School Children, 1901, p. 5.

Committees to deal with subjects common to several Departments is by now well established. It is only necessary to refer to such Committees as those for Imperial Defence, and for questions relating to Cables, and to Fair Wages, to show that excellent precedents exist. If such a Committee were formed, it might be easier to put an end to the somewhat ridiculous position occupied by a Government which through some Departments does its best to discourage " blind alley " employment, while in others it is itself an active employer of boys for whom it knows no adult situations are available in Government service.[1]

The four main reforms we have advocated—the raising of the school age, the creation of compulsory Continuation Classes, the further regulation of employment out of school hours, and the appointment of Juvenile Advisory Committees —are all at the present time being actively considered by various Government Departments. If all the forces, public and private, which are engaged in the campaign were united in a comprehensive policy the prospects of speedy success would indeed be favourable.

[1] Had such a Committee been at hand to advise those who framed the National Insurance Act, it is hardly conceivable that the provisions relating to juveniles would not have been much improved.

APPENDIX

TRANSCRIPT OF INDENTURE PRESERVED AT NORWICH AND DATED JUNE 10, 1291

" MEM. quod hec est conuencio facta inter Johannem filium
Gerardi le Specer de Norwyco ex parte una et Hubertum filium
Willelmi di Tibenham de Gernemutha ex parte altera videlicet
quod predictus Hubertus stabit in seruicio predicti Johannis contiue
a festo Pentecoste anno regni regis Edwardi filii Henrici regis
decimo nono usque ad terminum sex annorum proxime sub-
sequentium plenarie completorum, eidem Johanni in omnibus prout
decet humiliter fideliter competenter pro posse suo interim deserui-
endo. Et predictus Hubertus erit apprenticius dicti Johannis per
totum dictum tempus. Et precepta eius diligenter faciet per totum
et secreta sua que fuerint concelanda firmiter concelabit et a
seruicio dicti Johannis in terminum nullo modo recedet nisi ab ipso
Johanne prius jure et racione fuerit licenciatus. Et non licebit
dicto Johanni infra dictum terminum dictum Hubertum amouere
de seruicio suo nisi ex racionabili et probabili causa. Et predictus
Hubertus per totum dictum tempus fideliter et honorifice custodiet
et approbabit bona et catalla Johannis in cunctis locis quando
ipsi Huberto fuerint commendata et inde fideliter dicto Johanni
respondebit. Et illa bona nullis dabit nec accomodabit sim licencia
et speciali mandatu domini sui. Et predictus Hubertus infra dictum
tempus nullo modo dampnum dicto Johanni faciet falso et maliciose
ad valenciam vj denariorum vel amplius neque dampnum aut
pudorem dicto Johanni in terminum in aliquo videbit imminere
quin allud impediat pro posse suo vel ipsum Johannem inde pre-
muniat nec aliquam contencionem infra dictum terminum facere
aut mouere inter vicinos et mercatores ex quo dictus Johannes
aliquo modo poterit agrauari. Et si dictus Hubertus in aliquo
contra premisse euenerit ipse Hubertus et eius fideiussores subscripti
secundum consideracionem mercatorum et aliorum virorum fide
dignorum inde dicto Johanni respondebunt et satisfacient competenter. Et si dictus Jahannes decesserit infra dictum tempus

dictus Hubertus seruiet assignato idoneo dicti Johannis cuicunque
ipsum legauerit qui sit eiusdem officii usque in finem dicti termini
plenarie in omnibus sicuti dicto Jahanni fecerit si superstes fuisset.
Et dictus Jahannes per totum dictum tempus docebit dictum
Hubertum officium suum quo utitur emendi vendendi et omnia alia
faciendi que ad illud cfficium suum pertineat diligenter competente
pro posse suo secundum ipsius Huberti ingenii capacitatem. Et
idem Johannes vel eius assignatus per totum dictum tempus inueniet
dicto Huberto cibos et potum vestimenta linea et calciamenta et
unam supertunicam vel tunicam singulis annis infra iiij ultimos
annos dicti termini prout decet talem eruilientem habere. Et si
predictus Hubertus quocunque anno dicti termini moriatur vel si
predictus Hubertus cum dicto Johanne nullo modo stare poterit
propter duritiam vel asperitatem ipsus Johannis vel eius assignati
tunc dictus Johannes vel eius assignatus resituet dicto Huberto vel
eius fideiussoribus quolibet anno qui retro fuerit dicti termini
dimidiam maream argenti. Pro qua quicem erudicione et pro
predicta sustentacione dicto Huberto per predictum tempus
inuenienda dictus Hubertus dedit dicto Jahanni xl solidos sterling-
orum pre manibus ad omnia premissa ex utraque parte obser-
uanda. Predictus Johannes et Hubertus inuenerunt alternatim
fideiussores. [Fideiussores] dicti Huberti sunt Adam de Saham,
Rogerus de Morle. Et fideiussores dicti Johannis sunt Willelmus
frater eius, Radulphus Boleman. In cuius rei testimonium huic
scripto in modum Cyrographi confecto sigilla partium et fideiussorum
alternatim sunt appensa. Testibus Willelmo de Scothowe, Willelmo
de Kyrkeby, Gilberto de Erlham, Rogero de Apeton et aliis."
(" Records of the City of Norwich," Tingey, L. C., i. p. 245.)

TRANSCRIPT OF MANUSCRIPT INDENTURE PRE-SERVED AT CORSHAM, WILTS, DATED JAN. 16, 1708.

" This Indenture made the sixteenth day of January in the
Seaventh yeare of the Reigne of our Soveraigne Lady Anne of
Greate Brittaine ffrance and Ireland Queene Defender of the
ffaith ex Anno q° Dom 1708 Betweene William Selman of the pish
of Corsham in the Courty of Wiltes Husbandman And Richard
Selman son of the sd William Selman of the one pte And Thomas
Stokes holder of the pish of Corsham aforesaid Broadweaver of the

other pte Witnesseth that the said Richard Selman of his owne voluntarie will and with the consent of his sd ffather William Selman Hath put himselfe an Apprntice unto the said Thomas Stokes and with him hath covenanted to dwell as his Appntice from the day of the date hereof untill the full end and terme of Seaven Yeares fully to be compleate and ended during all which tyme the said Richard Selman shall well and faithfully serve him the said Thomas Stokes his master his secrets lawfully to be kept shall keep his Commandm^{ts} lawfull and honest shall doe and execute hurt unto his said Master hee shall not doe nor consent to be done Tavernes or Alehouses hee shall not haunt Dice Cardes or any other unlawfull games hee shall not use ffornication with any woman hee shall not committ during such tyme as he shall stay in his Masters service Matrymony with any woman hee shall not Contract or espouse himselfe during the said Terme of Seaven yeares The goods of his said Masters inordinately hee shall not wast nor to any man lend without his Masters Lycence from his Masters house or business hee shall not absent himselfe or plong himselfe by Night or by day without his Masters leave, but as a true and faithfull servant shall honestly behave himselfe towards his sd Master and all his both in words and deedes And the said Thomas Stokes doth for himselfe his Executors and Administrators promise and Covenant to and with the sd William Selman and Richard Selman his Appntice to teach or cause the said Richard Selman to be taught and instructed in the trade Art science or occupacon of a Broadweaver after the best manner that he can or may with moderate Correction finding and allowing unto his sd Servant meate drinke Apparrell Washing Lodging and all other things whatsoev fitting for an appntice of that trade during the said term of Seaven yeares And to give unto his sd Appntice at the end of the sd terme double Apparell (to witt) one suite for holy dayes and one for worken dayes, In witness whereof the said pties to these psent Indentures interchangeably have sett their hands and seales the day and yeare first above written Sealed and Delived in the psence of

his

Thomas   Stokes

marke

Indenture of 1627 given by Leader, History . . . of Cutlers in Hallamshire [Sheffield], i. p. 39; cf. Cox, J. C., "Three Centuries of Derbyshire Annals," ii. p. 178. Transcript of indenture dated 1710.

BIBLIOGRAPHY

PART I. HISTORICAL.

(This bibliography has been drawn up with a view to the needs of students of the history of apprenticeship. It is not a complete list of the works referred to in this volume.)

A. General Economic History and some Special Questions.

ALFRED, S. K. The History of the Factory Movement from the year 1802 to the Enactment of the Ten Hours Bill, 1857.

ASHLEY, W. G. Introduction to English Economic History and Theory.

BISCHOFF, I. A Comprehensive History of the Woollen and Worsted Manufactures (1842).

CUNNINGHAM, WM. Growth of English Industry and Commerce (3 vols.).

FELKIN. Account of the Machine Wrought Hosiery Trade (1845).

GROSS, C. The Gild Merchant, a Contribution to British Municipal History.

HIBBERT, F. A. Influence and Development of English Gilds, as illustrated by the Craft Gilds of Shrewsbury.

HOWELL, G. Conflicts of Capital and Labour.

HUTCHINS, B. L., and HARRISON, A. History of Factory Legislation.

KIRKMAN, GRAY. History of English Philanthropy.

LEONARD, E. M. Early History of English Poor Relief.

MCARTHUR, E. A. Regulation of Wages in the Sixteenth Century, in *English Historical Review*, vol. v., 1900.

MCARTHUR, E. A. The Boke longing to a Justice of the Peace and the Assessment of Wages, in *English Historical Review*, ix., 1894.

MEREWETHER, H. A., and STEPHENS, A. J.   The History of the
    Boroughs and Municipal Corporations of the United Kingdom
    (1835).

ROGERS, THOROLD.   Agriculture and Prices in England.

UNWIN, G.   Gilds and Companies of London.

UNWIN, G.   Industrial Organisation in the Sixteenth and Seven-
    eenth Centuries.

WEBB, SIDNEY and BEATRICE.   English Local Government.

B. Histories and Printed Records of Gilds and Com-
panies (for customs and rules of apprenticeship, conditions
of life and labour, and administration of statutes and
bye-laws)

ARBER, E., edited by.   Transcript of the Registers of the Company
    of Stationers of London, 1554–1640.

BARRETT, C. R.   History of the Society of Apothecaries.

BLACK, W. H.   History of the Company of Leathersellers.

BOYLE, J. R., and DENDY, F. W.   Extracts from the Records of
    the Merchant Adventurers of Newcastle-upon-Tyne.   Surtees
    Society, vols. xciii., ci.

BURKITT.   Short Account of the Worshipful Company of Curriers
    (1906).

CLODE, C. M.   Early History of the Merchant Tailors.

CLODE, C. M, compiled by.   Memorials of The Guild of Merchant
    Taylors . . . in the City of London.

HEATH, J. B.   Some Account of the Worshipful Company of
    Grocers of the City of London.

Historical Manuscripts Commission Report on Manuscripts
    in various Collections, vol. i., 1901.

HUMPHERUS, H.   History of the Origin and Progress of the
    Company of Watermen and Lightermen of the River Thames.

JUPP, E. B.   Historical Account of the Worshipful Company of
    Carpenters (London).

LAMBERT, J. M.   Two Thousand Years of Gild Life.   [Hull.]

LATIMER, J.   History of the Society of Merchant Venturers of the
    City of Bristol.

LEADER, R. E.   History of the Company of Cutlers in Hallamshire
    in the County of York.   (Referred to as Sheffield Cutlers.)

Charters, Ordinances, and Bye-Laws of the Mercers' Company (London, 1881).

The Worshipful Company of Musicians (2nd edition, 1905).

The Worshipful Company of Needlemakers of the City of London (1876).

NICHOLL, J. Some Account of the Worshipful Company of Iron-mongers (London).

OVERALL, W. H., and ATKENS, S. E. Some Account of the Worshipful Company of Clockmakers of the City of London.

PRIDEAUX, W. S. Memorials of the Goldsmiths' Company.

RAMSEY, WM., compiled by. The Worshipful Company of Glass Sellers of London.

SCOTT, J. B. Account of the Wheelwrights' Company.

SELLERS, MAUD. Acts and Ordinances of the Eastland Company, York.

SHARPE, R. S. Short Account of the Worshipful Company of Shipwrights (London).

SHERWELL. A Description and Historical Account of the Guild of Saddlers.

SHICKLE, C. W. Guild of the Merchant Taylors in Bath.

SMITH, J. TOULMIN (editor). Ricart, "The Maire of Bristowe is Kalendar," Camden Society.

SMYTHE, W. DUMVILLE. An Historical Account of the Worshipful Company of Girdlers (London).

TOWSE, W. B., compiled by. Selections from the Rules and Orders of the Court of the Clothworkers' Company (London).

WADMORE, J. F. Some Account of The Worshipful Company of Skinners of London.

WELCH, C. History of the Worshipful Company of Pewterers of the City of London.

C.—Histories and Printed Records of Towns and Cities

(containing information as to local gilds, their customs and rules, and the custom and law of apprenticeship as upheld by municipalities, and the proceedings of borough sessions).

BENHAM, W. G. Red Paper Book, Colchester.

BICKLEY, F. B., edited by. Little Red Book of Bristol.

BURTON, J. R. History of Kidderminster.

COTTON, WM. An Elizabethan Guild of the City of Exeter during the latter half of the Sixteenth Century. [Merchant Adventurers.]

DAVIES, J. S. History of Southampton.

DENDY, F. W., edited by. Hostmen of Newcastle Surtees Society, vol. cv.

DOWLING, edited by. Charter of the Worshipful Company of Poulters, London.

FERGUSON, R. S., and NANSON, W. S. Municipal Records of the City of Carlisle.

FERGUSON, R. S., edited by. Boke off Recorde (of Kendal).

FOX, F. F. Some account of the Ancient Fraternity of Merchant Taylors of Bristol.

FOX, F., and TAYLOR. Weavers of Bristol.

FRETTON, G. Memorials of the Fullers' or Walkers' Guild, Coventry.

GUILDING, J. M., edited by. Records of the Borough of Reading.

HARRIS, D. M. Life in an old English Town. [Coventry.]

HARRIS, M. D., transcribed by. Coventry Leet Book.

HATCHER. History of Modern Wiltshire, Old and New Sarum.

HOLMES, R., edited by. Collections towards the History of Pontefract.

KEMP, TH., edited by. Book of John Fisher, Town Clerk and Deputy Recorder of Warwick.

MARKHAM, C. A., and COX, J. C., edited by. Records of the Borough of Northampton.

NOAKE, JOHN. Worcester in Olden Times.

RILEY, H. T. Memorials of London.

RILEY, H. T., translated by. Liber Albus.

Charter, Byelaws and Customal of Rochester (1809).

SHARPE, R. G., edited by. Calendar of the Letter Books, London. Corp. of City.

SMITH, J. and L. TOULMIN. English Guilds. Early English Text Society.

STEVENSON and BAKER, W. T., edited by. Records of the Borough of Nottingham.

Survey of the Cities of London and Westminster, written at first in the year 1598, by John Stow; corrected, improved, and enlarged and the survey and history brought down from the year 1633 to the present time, 1720.

TINGEY, J. C., and HUDSON, W., edited by. Records of the City of
Norwich.
TURNER. Selections from the Records of Oxford.

D. Quarter Sessions Records (for administration of statutes and conditions of life and labour).

ATKINSON, J. C., edited by. Quarter Session Records of Yorkshire.
North Riding Record Society.
BOND, J. WILLIS, compiled by. Worcestershire County Records.
(Division I. Documents relating to Quarter Sessions.)
COX, J. C. Three Centuries of Derbyshire Annals, as illustrated by
the Records of the Quarter Sessions of the County of Derby.
EARWAKER, J. P. Court Leet Records of the Manor of Man-
chester, 1552, 1686, 1731–1846.
HAMILTON, A. H. Quarter Sessions from Queen Elizabeth to
Queen Anne (Devon).
HARDY. Hertford Quarter Sessions Records.
HARDY and PAGE. Bedfordshire County Quarter Sessions.

E. Contemporary Books and Pamphlets. (See also Official Publications.)

AIKIN. Description of the Country from Thirty to Forty Miles
round Manchester (1795).
Britannia Languens, or a discourse of trade, 1680.
CHITTY, J. Treatise on the Law of apprenticeship (1812).
DALTON. Country Justice.
DEFOE. Family Instructor (1715).
DEFOE. Complete English Tradesman (1738).
Discourse consisting of motives for Enlargement and Freedom
of Trade engrossed by a company of private men who stile
themselves Merchant Adventurers (1645).
EDEN, F. M. State of the Poor (1797).
Propositions for Improving Manufactures, Agriculture and Com-
merce (1763).
A Remonstrance proving that Confinement of Trade to particular
Companies is of general losse to His Majesty and his people,
c. 1660.
SMITH, ADAM, edited Cannan. Wealth of Nations.

SMITH, A. M. Essay for Recovery of Trade (1661).
Trade of England Revived (1681).
URE. Philosophy of Manufactures (1835).
W. S., gent. The Golden Fleece (1656).

F. Agricultural Labour and Village Life (relating chiefly to later times).

ARCH, J. Joseph Arch.
DAVIES, MAUD. Life in an English Village [Corsley, Wilts.] (A modern study, but valuable as affording analogies).
✓ HASBACH, W. History of the Agricultural Labourer.
HEATH, F. G. Peasant Life in the West of England.
MARSHALL. Rural Economy of the West of England (1805).
NASH, T. B. History of Worcestershire (1799).
PLOT. Natural History of Oxfordshire (1677).
Report of the Assistant Poor Law Commissioners on the Employment of Women and Children in Agriculture, 1843.
YOUNG, ARTHUR. Six Weeks' Tour in the Southern Counties (1768).

G. Official Publications and Reports of Royal Commissions and Select Committees published by the authority of Parliament.

(Chronologically arranged.)

Statutes at Large.
Statutes of the Realm, 1810.
Journals of the House of Lords.
Journals of the House of Commons.
Hansard. Parliamentary Debates.
Report from the Select Committee on the Petition of persons concerned in the Woollen Trade and Manufactures of Somerset, Wilts, and Gloucestershire, 1802–3, v. 243.
Report from the Select Committee on the Petition of Merchants and Manufacturers concerned in the Woollen Manufacture in the County of York and Town of Halifax, 1802–3, v. 305.
Minutes of the Evidence taken before the Committee to whom the Petition of several Journeymen Calico Printers and others working in that trade . . . was referred July, 1804. Reports 1803–4, v.

Report from the Committee on the Minutes of Evidence respecting the Calico Printers, 1806, iii.

Report from the Select Committee appointed to consider the State of the Woollen Manufacture in England, 1806, iii. 569-595.

Report from Committee on several Petitions respecting the Apprenticeship Laws, 1812-13, iv.

Report of the Minutes of Evidence taken before the Select Committee on the State of Children employed in the Manufactories of the United Kingdom, 1816, iii. 235.

Second Report from the same, 1818, ix. 53.

Report from the Select Committee on the Employment of Boys in Sweeping Chimneys, 1817, vi. 171.

Report from the Select Committee to whom the Petitions of the Watchmakers of Coventry, &c., were referred, 1817, vi. 285.

Report from the Select Committee to whom the several Petitions of Ribbon Weavers of Coventry and Leek, of Silk Weavers of Macclesfield and Reading, and of Manufactures of Macclesfield were referred, 1818, ix.

Report from the Select Committee appointed to consider the Laws relating to Watchmakers, 1818, ix. 203.

Report from the Select Committee to whom the Bill to regulate the Labour of Children in Mills and Factories of the United Kingdom was referred, 1831-32, xv.

Report from the Select Committee appointed to examine into the present state of the Silk Trade, 1831-32, xix.

First Report from Commissioners appointed to collect information in the Manufacturing Districts, relative to Employment of Children in Factories, and as to the propriety and means of curtailing the hours of their Labour; with minutes of Evidence, 1833, xx.

Second Report, 1833, xxi.

Supplementary Reports, 1834, xix. 253 and xx.

First Report from the Select Committee appointed to inquire into the operation of the Factories Act, 1840, xi.

First Report of Commissioners for inquiring into the Employment of Children in Mines and Manufactures, 1842, xv.

Reports and Evidence of Sub-Commissioners, 1842, xvi.

Second Report of Commissioners (Trades and Manufactures), 1843, xiii. 307.

Appendix to Second Report, 1843, xiv., xv.

Report of the Commissioners on Children's Employment, 1863,
xviii.
Second Report of the Commissioners on Children's Employment,
1864, xxii.

PART II. MODERN.

A. Reports and Papers of Royal Commissions and Select Committees, published by the authority of Parliament, and Publications of Local Authorities.

(Chronologically arranged)

Elementary Education (children working for wages), H. C. Paper,
1899, No. 205.
Report of the Inter-Departmental Committee on the Employment of
School Children, 1901 (Cd. 849).
London County Council. The Apprenticeship Question, 1906.
Publication No. 925 (drawn up by Mr. R. A. Bray).
Report of the Byelaws made by the London County Council under
the Employment of Children Act, 1903, by Chester Jones.
1906 (Cd. 2809).
Report of Inter-Departmental Committee on Partial Exemption
from School Attendance, 1909 (Cd. 4791).
Report of the Royal Commission on the Poor Laws and Relief of
Distress, 1909 (Cd. 4499).
Report on Boy Labour, 1909 (Cd. 4632). Appendix, vol. xx. to
Report of the Royal Commission on the Poor Laws and Relief
of Distress, 1909.
Report of the Consultative Committee on Attendance Compulsory
or otherwise at Continuation Schools, 1909 (Cd. 4757).
Report of the Departmental Committee on the Employment of
Children Act, 1903 (Cd. 5229), 1910.
Report on the Byelaws made on the 29th of January, 1910, by the
London County Council under the Employment of Children
Act, 1903, by Stanley Owen Buckmaster, 1911 (Cd. 5497).
Papers and Proceedings of the National Conference on the Preven-
tion of Destitution, 1911.
First Report of Standing Committee on Boy Labour in Post Office
1911 (Cd. 5504)

B. Books, Pamphlets, &c.

ADLER, N., and TAWNEY, R. H. Boy and Girl Labour.
AUSTIN, H. E. Law of Apprenticeship, 1890.
BEVERIDGE, W. H. Unemployment : A Problem of Industry.
BRAY, R. A. Boy Labour and Apprenticeship.
GIBB, S. J. The Problem of Boy Work.
GREENWOOD, A. Juvenile Labour Exchanges and After Care.
HUTCHINS, B. L. Gaps in our Factory Legislation.
KEELING, F. The Labour Exchange in Relation to Boy and Girl Labour.
MEYER, E. A. Apprenticeship Law (1910).
PATTESSON. Across the Bridges.
RUSSELL, C. E. B. Manchester Boys.
RUSSELL, C. E. B., and DIGBY, L. Working Lads' Clubs.
SADLER, edited by. Continuation Schools in England and Elsewhere.
URWICK, E. Studies of Boy Life in our Cities (1904).

ERRATA

Page 133, line 28, *for* "army," *read* "majority."
  „ 134, „ 2, *for* "almost entirely," *read* "chiefly."
  „ 134, „ 8, *read* "number though large was surpassed by that of the male."
Throughout, in notes, *for* "Surtees," *read* "Surtees Society"; *for* "Coms. Jals.," *read* "C. J."
From page 72 onwards, "gild" is used as an equivalent for "company."

INDEX

24

The Gresham Press,
UNWIN BROTHERS, LIMITED,
WOKING AND LONDON.